The Rise and Fall of
NADER SHAH

Dutch East India Company Reports,
1730–1747

Willem Floor

MAGE
PUBLISHERS

Cover image and back cover border, courtesy of the Freer & Sackler Galleries, from "Portrait of Nadir Shah," mid-18th century, Mughal dynasty, Ink on paper, H: 19.9 W: 10.5 cm, India, F1907.256

Library of Congress Cataloging-in-Publication Data

Floor, Willem M.
The rise and fall of Nader Shah : Dutch East India Company reports, 1730-1747 / Willem Floor.
p. cm.
Includes bibliographical references and index.
ISBN 1-933823-32-1 (pbk. : alk. paper)
1. Nadir Shah, Shah of Iran, 1688-1747. 2. Nadir Shah, Shah of Iran, 1688-1747--Military leadership. 3. Iran--Kings and rulers--Biography. 4. Generals--Iran--Biography. 5. Iran--History--16th-18th centuries--Sources. 6. Iran--History, Military--Sources. 7. Nederlandsche Oost-Indische Compagnie--Archives. I. Title.
DS294.F55 2009
955'.03092--dc22
[B]
2009016897

ISBN 13:   978-1933823-32-4
ISBN 10:   1-933823-32-1

Printed and Manufactured in the United States

Mage books are available at bookstores,
through the internet, or directly from the publisher:
Mage Publishers, 1032 29th Street, NW, Washington, DC 20007
202-342-1642 • as@mage.com • 800-962-0922
visit Mage Publishers online at
www.mage.com

I am not a human being,
I am God's Wrath and Punishment

CONTENTS

TABLES

INTRODUCTION

This publication is based on letters and reports written by staff of the *Vereenigde Oostindische Compagnie* (VOC) or the Dutch United East Indies Company.[1] It continues the story of what had happened in Persia where the previous publication *The Afghan Occupation of Safavid Persia 1721-1729* ends. I do not repeat what I wrote in the introduction to that publication as to the importance of the Dutch archives for the history of Safavid Persia, or the manner in which I have selected the material, because that also applies here. Although *stricto sensu* this is not a source publication, those who are not able to read the original documents can use this as a substitute. I have tried to stick as close as possible to the original text, in particular by presenting as faithfully as possible the turns of phrase, arguments, sentiments and prejudices of the original authors. However, I strongly recommend reading the original documents.

In this publication, of which a shorter version, without the extensive footnotes, already appeared in Persian in 1988,[2] the emphasis is on the career of Tahmasp Qoli Khan (after 1726), Tahmasp Khan (after 1732), or Nader Shah as he called himself after the usurpation of the Safavid throne in 1736. This publication, like its predecessor, offers practically all the information that is available in the Dutch National Archives on the political events in Persia between 1730 and 1747. It does not offer all data available in VOC documents, because elsewhere and earlier I already have published an important part of that information. First, there is the information that deals with the creation of a Persian navy by Nader Shah. Second, there is the information that deals with Nader Shah's intentions with regards to India and Makran. Fortunately, this information is readily available in the articles that I have devoted to these

---

1. These records are kept at the National Archief (National Archives) in The Hague (the Netherlands). For more information on these documents see Willem Floor, "Dutch Archives," Encyclopedia Iranica as well as the following websites [http://www.en.nationaalarchief.nl/] and [http://www.tanap.net/content/voc/organization/organization_intro.htm].

2. Willem Floor, *Hukumat-e Nader Shah,* translated by Abu'l-Qasem Serri (Tehran: Tus, 1367/1988).

matters.[3] However, I have included the article that I have written concerning the rebellion of Sheikh Ahmad Madani and Mohammad Khan Baluch.[4]

In addition to political information, I also have published a comprehensive discussion on Dutch trade with Persia during the 1730-1747 period, which is included in this publication, and an analysis of the *kork* or goat-hair trade in Kerman after 1730, which is not included here.[5] This publication also does not deal in detail with issues such as the monetary policy of Nader Shah, which I will deal with in a separate publication. What also is missing is a discussion of the history of the short-lived Dutch factory in Bushehr (1737-53), which I have published elsewhere, as well as the discussion whether to restart trade in raw silk, which is an issue that I intend to deal with in a separate study. Where this publication stops (1747) the reader is referred to other publications, which offer the remainder of information on Dutch presence in eighteenth century Persia and the Persian Gulf. In a number of studies I have dealt with the last years of the Dutch factory in Gamron (Bandar `Abbas), the Dutch factory on Khark Island, the Dutch attempt at pearling, and the proposal to conquer Bahrain.[6]

I have limited the footnotes and their length to a minimum, because I want to refer those readers interested in the political and socio-economic background to this era to the studies listed in the bibliography, which shed more light on these issues than can be done in footnotes.

The reporters of the enfolding story are various and from three different geographical points: Isfahan, Gamron (and environs) and Kerman. In some cases there are reports from Mashhad and Tabriz, but these are the exception. All the reporters are personnel employed by the VOC, i.e., the director and his council in Gamron, the chief of the Isfahan factory, and the (usually Armenian) wool factor in Kerman. Of particular importance is the report entitled *Description of the Rise of the Persian Usurper of Vali Ne`mat or Nader Shah* (Beschrijvinge Wegens d'Opkomst des Persischen Opwerpeling Welie Mahamed off Sjah Nadir) that was written in 1740 at the instruction of Karel Koenad, the VOC director at Gamron, which contains much information that is not found elsewhere in the regular remaining VOC correspondence.

---

3. Willem Floor, "The Iranian Navy during the Eighteenth Century," *Iranian Studies* 20 (1987), pp. 31-53; Ibid., "New Facts on Nader Shah's Indian Campaign," in: Kambiz Eslami ed. Iran and Iranian Studies. Essays in Honor of Iraj Afshar (Princeton, 1998), pp. 198-219.

4. Willem Floor, "Shaikh Ahmad Madani in Laristan and the Garmsirat (1730-1733)," *Studia Iranica,* vol. 8 (1983), p. 63-93.

5. Willem Floor, "Dutch Trade in Afsharid Iran (1730-1753)," *Studia Iranica* 34 (2005), pp. 43-93 Ibid., *The Persian Textile Industry in historical perspective,* 1500-1925 (Paris, 1999), chapter five deals with the kork or goat-hair trade in Kerman after 1730.

6. Willem Floor, "A Description of the Persian Gulf and its inhabitants in 1756," *Persica,* vol. 8 (1979), pp. 163-86; Ibid., "Pearl fishing in the Persian Gulf in the 18th century," Persica, vol. 10 (1982), pp. 209-222; Ibid., "Dutch trade with Masqat in the second half of the 18th century," *African and Asian Studies,* vol. 16 (1982), pp. 197-213; Ibid., "The Bahrein Project of 1754" *Persica,* vol. 11 (1984), pp. 129-148; Ibid., "The Decline of the Dutch East Indies Company in Gamron, 1747-1759," *Moyen-Orient & Ocean Indien,* vol. 6 (1990), pp. 45-80; Ibid., "The Dutch and Khark Island, 1753-1770, A Commercial Mishap," 24 (1992) *IJMES,* pp. 441-460; Ibid., "The Dutch and Khark Island, The adventures of the Baron von Kniphausen", in: Européens en Orient aux XVIIIe siècle." Moyen Orient & Ocean Indien (1994), pp. 157-202. All these studies have been reprinted or have been considerably enlarged with additional data in Willem Floor, *The Persian Gulf: The Rise of the Gulf Arabs, The Politics of Trade on the Northern Persian Littoral 1730-1792* (Washington DC: Mage Publishers, 2007), which also includes an analysis of the VOC factory in Bushehr (chapter seven).

Finally, orders or *raqam*s from the shah and letters from Persian officials to VOC staff have also been used.

The letters were not from the director at Gamron or the agent at Isfahan, but from the entire council. For each VOC factory had a policy and trade council that decided on all matters by majority vote. The director or agent was the chief executive, but the council could overrule him. Nevertheless, he was the main player and usually the dominant person in the council, and therefore I refer to the head of the council rather than to the council as a whole as the reporter. There are, of course, also individual VOC reporters such as the dragoman of the Isfahan factory or the Armenian wool buyer in Kerman, who wrote letters to Isfahan and Gamron.

During the period that is covered here (1730-47) the following VOC directors served at Gamron. In addition to being responsible for the factory at Bandar`Abbas, they also were responsible for operations at Isfahan, Basra, Bushehr, and Kerman.

1. Leendert de Cleen (or de Kleene) was from Middelburg and arrived in Persia in September 1722 as a junior merchant. He returned to Batavia in 1723, but was sent back and arrived again in Gamron in September 1724 with the rank of merchant and became head of the Basra factory. He was promoted to chief merchant in 1728 and appointed director of the Persian operations. De Cleen assumed his new responsibility in September 1729. He died in 1735.[7]

2. Dames Hey replaced de Cleen in 1734. He had come to Persia in 1715, and Batavia had explicitly been given instructions that had to go to Isfahan to learn good Persian. After having served in Isfahan and Gamron, he was transferred to Basra, whence he was recalled to take over the management of the Persia directorate.[8] Hey died on December 20, 1734.

3. Carel Koenad (or Coenad), who was born in Hamburg, came to Gamron as a soldier in 1712 at Dfl. 9 per month. Because he could write well, a skill that was in short supply, he was transferred to administrative duties. Coenad became an assistant in 1719 (fl. 20), a bookkeeper in 1722 (fl. 30), a junior merchant in 1726 (fl. 40), a merchant in 1731 (fl. 60), when he was serving in Basra as the deputy chief. In 1731 he was transferred to Gamron, where he became deputy director in 1734. He became acting director after de Cleen's death in December 1734, and was promoted to chief merchant and director in 1736 (fl. 80).[9]

4. George Gutchi came from Bergen op Zoom in 1719 as midshipman (fl. 10). He became assistant in 1722 (fl. 20), bookkeeper in 1722 (fl. 30), junior merchant in 1728 (fl. 40), merchant in 1733 (fl. 60), and chief merchant in 1740 (fl. 80). On October 8, 1740 Batavia relieved Koenad and Gutchi replaced him on October 23, 1740. Gutchi had been chief of the Basra factory prior to that. However, because of his mismanagement of the Basra factory, Gutchi was arrested shortly after his appointment as director (in December 1740), but before

---

7. W. Wijnaendts van Resandt, *De Gesaghebbers der Oost-Indische Compagnie op hare Buiiten-Comptoiren in Azië* (Amsterdam, 1944), p. 254.

8. KA 864, Batavia to Gamron (27/07/1714), f. 703; KA 1740 (13/04/1715), f. 2339 vs.

9. KA 1805, van Biesum to Batavia (17/02/1718), f. 73; VOC 2517, f. 2224; Wijnaendts van Resandt, *De Gesaghebbers*, p. 255.

he was sent to Batavia Gutchi died on June 28, 1741 in the Dutch garden at Nayband; his wife Johanna Magteld van der Grande died on August 3, 1741 in Gamron.[10]

5. Simon Clement had arrived in Gamron in 1727 as a boy (fl. 5), became assistant in 1730, bookkeeper in 1733, junior merchant in 1737, and merchant in 1740. Because Gutchi had been arrested in December 1740 the VOC council at Gamron had to appoint a replacement, until Batavia appointed a new director. On July 9, 1741 the council decided to elect Clement as chief pro-tem. He died on September 15, 1743.[11]

6. Emmanuel de Poorter was from Gent and came as a soldier (fl. 9) in the 1720s; he became a bookkeeper in 1736 (fl. 30). After Clement's death, the VOC council at Gamron decided not to appoint a successor as yet, because three new council members were to arrive on the next ship. Because deputy fiscal Emmanuel de Poorter was the oldest council member and the best linguist among them the full council appointed him as temporary director (*gesaghebber*) on October 2, 1743.[12]

7. Abraham van der Welle replaced de Poorter in July 1744. He had arrived in Batavia in 1732, and was sent to Cochin (Malabar) to serve as fiscal and later as salesman. He returned to Batavia in 1737 where he was promoted to merchant in 1738. In April 1744 he was promoted to chief-merchant and appointed as director of Persia. Because of his indecisive, cowardly and licentious behavior the council at Gamron, in 1748, took an unheard of and unique decision in VOC history. It stripped van der Welle of his authority and sent him back to Batavia to be judged there.[13]

8. Jacob Schoonderwoerd replaced van der Welle in 1748 and remained in function until 1755. He was from Amsterdam and had started in Gamron as an assistant in 1733 (fl. 24) and became junior merchant in 1737 (fl. 40), when he became chief of the newly opened factory in Bushehr. In July 1744, he had been appointed deputy-director.[14]

Other reporters from Isfahan, Bushehr and Kerman include the following persons:

9. Nicolaus van Leijpsigh replaced Nicolaus Schorer in October 1730 as head of the Isfahan factory. He had arrived at Gamron in 1715 and Batavia had given explicit instructions that he had to go to Isfahan to learn to read, write and speak Persian. By that time he already knew the basics of Persian. Van Leijpsigh was buried in Isfahan in the evening of November 12, 1739. Aalmis, who had arrived in Isfahan in July 1739, replaced him. Aalmis was recalled to Gamron, where he died on June 16, 1746.[15]

---

10. VOC 2584, f. 1764-5; VOC 2517, f. 2224; VOC 2510 Secret resolution (05/12/1739), f. 1516-20; see also f. 1521-31; VOC 2583 (31/12/1741), f. 110; VOC 2584, f. 1764-65; VOC 2584, Koenad to Schoonderwoerd (11/07/1741), f. 1451-53.

11. VOC 2584, f. 1764-5; VOC 2517, f. 2224; VOC 2680, Resolution Gamron (16/09/1743), unfoliated; VOC 2584, Koenad to Schoonderwoerd (11/07/1741), f. 1453.

12. VOC 2680, Resolution Gamron (01/10/1743), unfoliated; VOC 2680, Resolution Gamron (02/10/1743), unfoliated; VOC 2517, f. 2224; VOC 2680, van der Welle to Batavia (10/08/1745), f. 170. De Poorter died on August 19, 1746 at Gamron. VOC 2705, f. 123.

13. Wijnaendts van Resandt, De Gesaghebbers, p. 255.; VOC 2784, Schoonderwoerd to Batavia (10/10/1748), f. 2-4; Ibid., Resolution Gamron, f. 310ff

14. VOC 2517, f. 2224; Wijnaendts van Resandt, De Gesaghebbers, p. 255.

15. KA 865, Batavia to Gamron (31/07/1715), f. 883; VOC 2511, Aalmis to Koenad (12/12/1739), f.

10. As in the previous period the main reporters from the Kerman wool buying office were the Armenian factors Auwannees and Gojatoer (1731-1735 and 1737-1740). From 1735, the Kerman office was managed by Clement, and as of mid-1736 by Frans van Loon and then by Emmanuel Martijn until end-1736.[16]

The total number of VOC staff in the Persian directorate hovered around 100 until 1742, after which date the number declined due to death and non-replenishment of staff. Most of the staff was based in the factory in Gamron, where the VOC had a large fortress-like factory. It was well-armed with thick walls sufficient to withstand an attack by a foe having artillery, while it could repulse such an attack using its own canons and mortars as well as muskets with which its military was armed. In normal times, until 1721, there had been no military in the factory, but the insecurity in the town and environs as a result of the Afghan occupation had changed that. The continued presence of soldiers in the factory was due to the insecurity created by the misrule under the last Safavids and under Nader Shah. The VOC could not rely on the authorities to provide protection, because they themselves were the cause of the insecurity.

Table 1.1: Number of staff in the VOC Persian Directorate during 1739-1747

Year	Total staff	Gamron	Isfahan	Basra	Bushehr	Ship's crew
1739	108	96	3	7	2	
1740	108	n.a.	n.a.	n.a.	n.a.	
1741	103	96	2	4	3	25 de Valk
1742	100	92	2	4	2	
1743	79	69	3	4	3	3 de Valk
1744	77	55	3	6	2	16 de Valk
1745	82	70	5	5	2	
1746	77	30	1	4	2	40 Oosterhout

Source: VOC 2477 (12/05/1739), f. 148; VOC 2511 (31/07/1740), f. 1440-41; VOC 2517 (15/04/1741), f. 2221; VOC 2583 (31/12/1741), f. 118-19; VOC 2680 (30/06/1743), f. 195; VOC 2680, Resolution Gamron (21/07/1744), unfoliated; VOC 2680, f. 187; VOC 2705 (31/07/46), f. 128.

The higher number of staff in Isfahan in 1745 is due to the fact that the council at Gamron had sent an investigative committee to Isfahan to examine the agent's activities and to close down the factory. These figures do not tell the entire story, because they do not say anything about the condition the men were in. For example, in December 1741 the director in Gamron reported that the soldiers in the factory were very weak; on August 31, 1741 he reported that only 18 men were

---

842 (Aalmis left Gamron on 04/06/1739 to become 'second' in Isfahan). VOC 2510, f. 211; VOC 2705 (31/07/1746), f. 129.

16. VOC 2416, Memorandum Clement to van Loon (11/06/1736), f. 1077; VOC 2416, Resolution Gamron (28/02/1736), f. 839.

able to carry arms.[17] Also, most of the staff was not military but commercial and administrative in nature. Only Gamron had a military presence; the other VOC factories only had commercial staff. Sometimes, in case of need, the factory at Gamron also would rely on the crews and the cannons of Dutch ships lying in the roadstead for protection.

Table 1.2: Breakdown of VOC staff in the VOC Persian directorate by profession

Year	Total	Commercial/ Administrative	Military	Maritime	Various
1740	108	42	43	6	17
1741	108	45	33	8	17
1744	77	23	16	4	7

Source: VOC 2511 (31/07/1740), f.1440-1; VOC 2517 (15/04/1741), f. 2221; VOC 2680, Resolution Gamron (21/07/1744), unfoliated; VOC 2680, f. 187.

As to the reliability of the information offered by the VOC documents I submit the following. The Dutch were very wary of rumors and they, therefore, always tried to verify them. If this was not possible they explicitly stated so. All other information was referred to a known source (e.g., VOC staff member, merchant, government official) and often was supported by documentary evidence (e.g., letters from government officials, local chiefs as well as royal edicts). The few surviving Diaries (Isfahan, Gamron, and Basra) or its extracts provide firm dates as to a multitude of events, while these also show how the Dutch sifted and selected the information that they received and passed on to their superiors. The fact that the information was not vetted or written down by one person, but was for the use of the entire council of the trading station, also meant that more rather than less information was recorded. Also, the VOC documents were never meant to be read by people outside the Company, and therefore, in my opinion, this information can be relied upon to a great extent, as the reporters had no reason to censor their reports, because of what readers outside the Company would say or think. Nevertheless, the information was gathered and interpreted by Dutchmen, who, moreover, gave their own 'spin' to some events, so as to, e.g., justify their own actions, which they believed would not find favor with their superiors. However, given the fact that these superiors had other sources of information to verify the news received from Iran (captains from returning ships, returning staff, private letters from dissenting staff, etc.) the reporters had to be careful not to overdo their spin. Nevertheless, the information in the VOC documents is one of the most important sources of information for this terrible and bloody period of the history of Iran, which I hope will contribute to a better understanding of this period.

17. VOC 2583 (31/12/1741), f. 118-19.

CHAPTER ONE

THE SITUATION AS SEEN FROM ISFAHAN

THE BEGINNING OF NADER'S CAREER

Old Khorasani natives had told the Dutch that Nader Shah was born as Nader Qoli to poor parents. Although he later would maintain that his family was a noble one, people who had known him in his youth denied this and the Dutch considered them more reliable as source than Nader himself. Nader Qoli left his family as a child and served a local Khorasani nobleman, Baba Khan Beg (Baba Chan Beek), as *jelowdar-bashi* (chief of the forerunners), until his 26th year. Because he was an intelligent youth his master soon employed him as a valet, but Nader Qoli was not accustomed to such a good life and indulged in excesses. He started to steal and had been caught red-handed a few times, so that finally his master ordered to give him the bastinado. As a result of this beating he became lame on his right side, which in 1740 still was noticeable when he walked. Nader Qoli was dismissed from his master's service and he, not knowing what to do, went from one village to the other living as a highwayman. He had a few comrades with him, who elected him as their chief. After some time his band had increased to 150 men, which induced him to more daring deeds. Nader Qoli then started a career of highway robbery and held up caravans. He took the villagers along the roads into his service who served him loyally, because he paid promptly.[1]

After the Afghan invasion Nader Qoli was living in the Qajar area (Astarabad). Ostensibly he was willing to change his career of highwayman to find his fortune in war. With his band of now 500 experienced men he went to Mashhad and offered his services to the Safavid pretender to the throne, Tahmasp Mirza. This offer was on condition that the prince would appoint him E`temad al-Dowleh or grand vizier, when he would accede to the throne, and after Nader Qoli would have shown him his prowess by conquering Seistan and having expelled the Afghans. The prince, after consultation with his counselors, agreed to these conditions and bestowed on him the name of Tahmasp Qoli Khan. The latter then marched with his robbers

---

1. VOC 2584, Beschrijvinge Wegens d'Opkomst des Persischen Opwerpeling Welie Mahamed off Sjah Nadir. (henceforth cited as Beschrijvinge), f. 1882-83.

to Seistan and conquered that province in a short time, after which feat he returned with a considerable booty to Mazanderan.[2]

[I have described the events leading up to the defeat of the Afghans by Tahmasp Qoli Khan and the arrival of the victorious Safavid army in Isfahan in the prequel to this publication, *The Afghan Occupation of Safavid Persia* (Paris-Leuven, 1999)]

NADER'S ARRIVAL IN ISFAHAN

It was only a few days after the reconquest of Isfahan, viz. on December 9, 1729 that Shah Tahmasp II arrived in his capital city. The day before, the Dutch had gone to welcome him in Gezd (Geds), a village three German miles outside Isfahan. The shah received them well and talked during one hour with them. Although the English also were received they were given leave to depart as soon as they had presented themselves. The shah entrusted the administration of the kingdom, as well as his royal seal, to the *qurchi bashi*, Tahmasp Qoli Khan [the later Nader Shah, whom I refer to as Nader throughout in what follows]. Nader sent for the VOC dragoman on January 4, 1730 and asked for the royal decree in which the VOC privileges had been granted. He, of his own accord, ordered the *vaqaye`-nevis*, or secretary of state, to renew verbatim the privileges granted by Shah Soltan Hoseyn on August 29, 1722 as well as to confirm all other privileges in another decree (*raqam*). These favors were indeed confirmed by the royal seal on January 7, 1730.[3] Shah Tahmasp II whole-heartedly agreed with this decision, as he told Schorer, the chief of the VOC factory in Isfahan, during an audience in February 1730. Before he could even list the Dutch complaints and claims Shah Tahmasp II told Schorer that the VOC had to accept the financial loss it had suffered during the Afghan occupation. As soon as he would be able to he would repay his father's loans as well as the money taken from the Dutch by the Afghans. Shah Tahmasp II wanted to do it right there and then, but as everybody knew the Afghans had taken everything away so the Dutch had to exercise patience.[4]

In the beginning it was apparently not clear to the Dutch what function Nader held. They referred to him as *qurchi-bashi*, as *qollar-aghasi*, and even as E`temad al-Dowleh or grand vizier, which functions he seemingly actually held at some time or other.[5] The confusion about the functioning of the bureaucracy also was prevalent among some Persian officials such as Mohammad Zaman Beg (Mhamed Zamoen Beek) from Shiraz, who came to visit Schorer to ask him how the governorship of Lar and Gamron and the *shahbandar*ship had been organized in the past. Schorer told him that normally Lar and Gamron were under one governor, while the *shahbandar* was responsible for the collection of the import and export duties of both Gamron

---

2. VOC 2584, Beschrijvinge, f. 1993-94.

3. VOC 2168, Schorer to de Cleen (09/01/1730), f. 186-90. Nader also ordered that the EIC had to pay a fine of 320 *tuman*s and had to give up their horses to make a distinction between the Dutch and the English.

4. VOC 2168, Schorer to de Cleen (25/02/1730), f. 191-94.

5. VOC 2168, Schorer to de Cleen (01/09/1730), f. 189; Ibid., Schorer to de Cleen (30/03/1730), f. 205, 208-10.

and Kong. At his request Schorer wrote a note about this for the elucidation of Nader and Mohammad Taqi [Shirazi], who was the latter's main adviser.[6]

Nader ordered the Dutch to take up residence again in the VOC factory, which they visited on January 5, 1730 and found to be inhabitable. The buildings were in a bad state; the doors and windows had been taken away and burnt, while the walls were without plaster. Soon repairs were executed so that some rooms were fit to live in and the big hall was prepared to be able to receive visitors. Schorer and his staff moved into the factory on February 3, 1730. The 4,000 *tumans*, which they had buried in 1727 before having to vacate the building, were not found, however.[7]

The Dutch were shown much respect and honor by Nader, who acted as if he was an enemy of the English. He asked Mirza ʿAli Naqi, the royal physician, how the Dutch and the English had behaved during the Afghan occupation. Mirza ʿAli Naqi, a friend of Schorer's, praised the Dutch and criticized the English. Nader then said in the presence of the VOC dragoman that he had to show the shah and the population who were friends and who were enemies of the Crown. He immediately sent some tax collectors to the English to demand 3,000 *tumans* (Dfl. 127,500) from them. They had to pay that same day otherwise their chief would get the bastinado until the nails would fall off his toes. A courtier intervened and said that the English could not pay that much money, where upon Nader asked the VOC drago-man whether this was true. He replied that he did not know; he only knew that the English had not suffered extortion from the Afghans and had given only trifles to them of their own free will. Nader therefore ordered the tax collectors to get as much from the English as they were able to and to carry it back on the EIC horses, which had to be confiscated. This order was executed on March 20, 1730. The tax collectors stayed for three days with the English, who gave them amply to eat and drink. In exchange for this treatment only their servants and dragoman were beaten. On the third day they took the EIC resident outside to beat him as well. Through intercession by the *moʿayyer-bashi* (chief assayer), Hasan ʿAli Khan, the English were let off with a payment of 350 *tumans* and loss of their horses. Nader said that they had been punished sufficiently, and the population had seen how he treated good and bad actions. He took the last remaining horse of the English on that occasion and gave it to one of the tax

---

6. VOC 2168, Schorer to de Cleen (30/03/1730), f. 207-08. He also could have asked Safi Qoli Khan (Seffie Coelie Chan), the chief porter of the royal court at that time, who had been governor of Lar and Gamron in 1717. VOC 2168 (25/02/1730), f. 193. Mohammad Taqi Shirazi was one of Nader's main confidantes, and after 1736 became the most powerful man in the kingdom after Nader Shah. The need for information on how to manage the state was indeed felt at the highest levels of government. In 1731, the secretary of state therefore wrote a manual outlining the organization, functions, titles and remuneration of the Safavid bureaucracy, of which an incomplete text has survived and which has been published and edited by Yusof Rahimlu as Mirza Naqi Nasiri, *Alqab va Mavajeb Dowreh-ye Safaviyeh* (Mashhad, 1371/1992), and which has been translated into English and provided with commentary by Willem Floor as *Titles and Emoluments in Safavid Iran* (Washington DC: Mage Publishers, 2008) On the organization of the Safavid state in general see Willem Floor. *Safavid Government Institutions* (Costa Mesa: Mazda, 2001) and Willem Floor and Mohammad Faghfoory, *Dastur al-Moluk* (Costa Mesa: Mazda, 2006).

7. VOC 2168, Schorer to de Cleen (30/03/1730), f. 208-09, 222. As under Ashraf's rule, Nader detailed a guard of three soldiers to the Dutch factory to protect them from molestation by his own troops. The Dutch had to pay these soldiers, who were Qajars, three *mahmudis* per day and per person. VOC 3168, f. 579-80.

collectors. Nader also told the EIC dragoman that his masters henceforth might come on foot to see him.[8]

NADER DEPARTS FROM ISFAHAN

Nader left Isfahan on January 8, 1730 with his army consisting of 20,000-25,000 regular troops to destroy Ashraf Khan, the other Afghans leaders and their troops. Before he left he had asked Schorer to write to Gamron to ask Leendert de Cleen, the VOC director, to detain fleeing Afghans and to prevent them from escaping to the islands. It was said that Ashraf Khan had fled with about 300 men to Baluchistan, though others said to Qandahar. Soon the first captured Afghan families were brought to Isfahan, all of whom were made slaves. Amongst these were the mother, wives and children of Mahmud Khan and some of Ashraf Khan, as well as Sayyed Sadeq. The heads of Mullah Za`fran and the chief priest Miyanji were also brought back in victory.[9]

In Nader's absence he was represented by his *vakil* (agent) Tahmasp Beg Jalayer, a native of Zamindavar province. He was a brusque, bad-tempered man, according to the Dutch, who acted like a buffalo. He had ordered two tax collectors to demand 150 *tuman*s from the VOC Banyan broker, which was the latter's quota allotted by the chief of the Banyans of Isfahan, who had been ordered to contribute to the war effort. When these tax collectors came to collect on May 15, 1730 Schorer protested, for even the Afghans had not demanded payment from those in the service of the Dutch, something from which they were exempted by royal decree. Tahmasp Beg, however, did not care about the royal decrees and gave orders to collect the money, even by force if need be. Schorer therefore addressed himself to Havids Beek,[10] the *mehmandar* (conductor of ambassadors) who was *soltan* of the Bakhtiyari Lurs. Schorer threatened to leave to Gamron if the decree would not be respected. Havids Beg went to see Tahmasp Beg and reported that if the latter would get 110 *tuman*s the VOC native servants would be exempted from paying their contribution. If Schorer refused, however, he would spare nobody and take the money by force. Havids Beg advised Schorer to give in and to accept the offered order (*ta`liqeh*) exempting the servants from all quotas, although he gave as his personal opinion that Tahmasp Beg did not respect anybody's seal, not even his own. He also said that he believed that the situation would get worse in Isfahan and advised Schorer to leave altogether. Schorer faced with this situation gave in and paid the money. As a consolation, he reported that the English had been ordered to 'lend' 1,100 *tuman*s. Havids Beg told Schorer in confidence that he expected a conflict between the shah and Tahmasp Beg any moment. The latter acted without even consulting the shah and only did his best to ruin the shah and the city of Isfahan at his master's orders. The royalists were only waiting for information from the army for it was rumored that Nader had died, or had been imprisoned. Nader was said to covet the crown and that he wanted to become shah. If this news proved to be true the royalists would

---

8. VOC 2168 (30/03/1730), f. 213-26.

9. VOC 2168 (30/03/1730), f. 220.

10. I have not been able to identify this name or find any particulars about this person bearing that name in Persian sources; "Havids Beek, zulthan der Bagtiaerissen Looren, defroyeermeester." VOC 2253 (01/06/1730), f. 892. The name also occurs as Havids Sulthoen. He was *kalantar* of Qomisheh and died in October 1732, poor as a beggar and childless. VOC 2416, van Leijpsigh to Koenad (13/10/1735), f. 2255; VOC 2322, Buffkens/E. Sahid (Isfahan) to de Cleen (22/03/1733), f. 334.

attack Tahmasp Beg and his men, an event which he expected within the next 10 days. Havids Beg advised Schorer to move at least to Jolfa.[11]

SHAH TAHMASP II TRIES TO RULE

To the joy of the population Tahmasp Beg left on June 17, 1730 to Kuhgilu, at Nader's orders it was said. The latter charged Hasan `Ali Khan, the *mo`ayyer-bashi*, with the governorship of Isfahan. He was not allowed to do anything without the foreknowledge of the shah. The new governor was a Persian and a friend of the shah, so one hoped for the better. Also, Mir `Abdol-Qasem (Mier Abdoel Cassum) was appointed as the new *sadr* or chief of the religious administration.[12] It was left to the shah to choose additional members of the royal council. The council members did not want to interfere with military matters, because they preferred to see how the clash between Nader and the Turks would end. Meanwhile, the shah continued to show his friendship for the Dutch, while he remained cool towards the English. On June 23, 1730 the shah sent for Schorer to come to Jolfa where he was regaled at the *kalantar's* house. Schorer was told to sit near to the shah; the rest of the company had to remain standing. He said that his father had not had a better friend than the Dutch, which was the reason why he loved them so much. The shah asked Schorer about Europe, Batavia, trade and the VOC ships in Gamron. He personally poured a drink for Schorer from his own bottle of brandy. After one hour the shah left and ordered Schorer to make merry with the quarter chiefs (*kadkhodas*) of Jolfa that day and then rode to the *Hazar Jarib* garden.[13]

Shah Tahmasp II, who was described as a well-built man, and was said to be sensible for his age, which was 28 years, was a greater lover of Bacchus than of Venus the Dutch believed. He asked them for alcoholic drinks as well as for a fluorescent liquid which, if put on one's face, clothes or carpets, yielded a bright light. The Dutch asked Joseph Hermet, a French physician, whether he knew this liquid and whether he could make it. According to Hermet, the liquid was called *fosserorium*,[14] and though he never had made it he would try. During Ramazan the shah left with his wives to the pleasure gardens outside Isfahan, where he amused himself *inter alia* with all kinds of weapons.[15]

Tahmasp II had asserted his own position by appointing Mirza Rahim as E`temad al-Dowleh or grand-vizier, who until then had exercised this function provisionally. Mirza Rahim was 45 years at that time and a very good friend of presents, Schorer wrote. Since he had been ordered not to give any presents he tried to flatter Mirza Rahim with words. The shah, mean-

---

11. VOC 2253 (01/06/1730), f. 891-96.

12. On the role of this official see Willem Floor, "The *sadr* or head of the Safavid religious administration, judiciary and endowments and other members of the religious institution," *ZDMG* 150 (2000), pp. 461-500.

13. VOC 2253, Schorer to de Cleen (01/07/1730), f. 899-905. On the occasion of `eyd al-fetr the shah sent a small cross and three rings to Schorer. VOC 2253, Schorer to de Cleen (01/06/1730), f. 896.

14. I have been unable to identify this term. Either I have misread the original or it is a copyist's error. Most likely reference is made to *vibro (photobacterium) phosphoreum*; a liquid culture of the vibro bacteria combined with oxygen produces a sustained bluish-green glow.

15. VOC 2168 (30/03/1730), f. 219; VOC 2253, f. 658.

while, had expressed the wish that Schorer would leave for Batavia to inform the governor-general of his affection for the Dutch and his promise to repay his debts to the VOC.[16]

Shah Tahmasp II confirmed his appreciation for the Dutch by granting Schorer an audience when he was feverish and gave him a decree ordering the customs-master or *shahbandar* of Gamron to pay the 5,000 *tuman*s which his father had assigned to the customs revenues to [partially] pay off the Dutch loan. The English received a similar decree for 3,000 *tuman*s, which they had lent his father. The shah told Schorer, whom he entrusted with presents and a letter for Batavia, that he trusted nobody better than the Dutch. Moreover, in the presence of the leading courtiers, the shah said that he would repay the Dutch twice the amount for all they had suffered and done, for he was very pleased with them. However, he did not keep his promise to visit the VOC factory, which Batavia undoubtedly welcomed in view of the high costs it would have entailed.[17] Schorer's voyage to Batavia probably also put an end to plans which shah had, viz. to send an ambassador to Batavia. Mirza Taqi, the *monshi al-mamalek*, had sounded Schorer about this idea and had asked whether an ambassador or a letter would be better. Schorer had pointed out that nobody in Batavia spoke Persian, the journey was difficult, and a letter would therefore be preferable. Mirza Taqi reacted that in that case he would advise that a letter would be sent. Schorer took his leave from the shah on October 2 and left Isfahan on October 8, 1730.[18]

NADER DEFEATS THE OTTOMANS AND THE ABDALIS, AND SHOWS HIS AMBITION

In February 1730, the Turkish governor of Baghdad, Ahmad Pasha, had sent an envoy to the shah to congratulate him with his accession to the throne. Shah Tahmasp II in return had sent an ambassador to the Turkish court, viz. Mohammad Reza Khan, brother of the former grand vizier, Mohammad Qoli Khan Shamlu (1720-22). However, Nader, after his campaign in the Kuhgilu area, attacked the Turkish forces and defeated them. He retook the provinces of Hamadan and Kermanshah and a large part of Kurdistan, which enhanced his power. A letter from Armenians in Hamadan, dated June 29, 1730 confirmed his victory and the recapture of Hamadan. The Turks had lost many troops and two pashas. The governor, `Abdollah Rahman Pasha, had fled with the loss of all his property. On June 19, 1730 the *monshi al-mamalek*, Mirza Taqi Shirazi and other officials, returned to Isfahan with the two captured Turkish pashas. The shah set them free and gave them robes of honor.[19]

---

16. VOC 2253, Memorandum Schorer, f. 658. The Dutch congratulated the grand vizier with his appointment on October 2, 1730. Mirza Rahim's macebearer was Tahmurath Beg (Tamoeras Beek). VOC 2255 (28/01/1731), f. 2260, 2271.

17. VOC 2255, van Leijpsigh to de Cleen (28/01/1731), f. 2222-24; Ibid. (23/09/1730), f. 2194-97.

18. VOC 2253 (01/07/1730), f. 860; Ibid., letter Tahmasp II to de Cleen, which arrived with Schorer on 09/12/1730, f. 571-74 ("Schorer left at his [i.e. the shah's] command to inform Batavia"); Ibid., Hadje Calb Alie to de Cleen, f. 575-78 (with robe of honor); VOC 2254, de Cleen to Miersa Mhamed Rahiem, grand vizier (14/06/1731), f. 1285 (reports Schorer's departure for Batavia). The traditional rivalry between the EIC and VOC again manifested itself, when Mirza Taqi, attracted by EIC presents, paid his first return visit to the English factory. VOC 2255, f. 2355.

19. VOC 3168 (30/03/1730), f. 218; VOC 2253, Schorer to de Cleen (01/07/1730), f. 899-901, 857. Mirza Taqi (Miersa Tagghie) was not only *monshi al-mamalek*, but he was also described as Nader's all-do (*albeschik*). One of his clerks was Mirza Baqer (Miersa Backer). VOC 2253 (01/06/1730), f. 898.

After the war with Turkey, Nader moved to Khorasan where he defeated the rebellious Turkmans. He then dealt with the Abdali Afghans who had made common cause with Hoseyn Khan Ghalzai. They had massacred some 12,000 men, women and children (they even cut open the bellies of pregnant women) and had enslaved many people and left with a large booty. Nader subjected them again and made preparations for a war against the Russians, though it was also said that he intended to move against the Uzbeks in Orgenj. Nader's troops meanwhile were misbehaving in Mashhad. The soldiers raped many women and girls, against which he took no measures. In fact, wherever he went he fleeced the population and sent all his proceeds to Khorasan. It was said that the Amberloes[20], a tribe living between Qazvin and the forests of Mazanderan, had rebelled because of his treatment of them. Because of their armed incursions from their mountains the Russians had sent troops to destroy them.[21]

Before Shah Tahmasp II left Isfahan on October 31, 1730 he had received a Turkish envoy sent to obtain Nader's confirmation of the peace treaty. The shah had given him leave to depart with the message that if his master wanted peace with Persia he had to return all conquered territory, as well as those Persians that had been enslaved, and to pay an indemnity for all war damage that Persia had suffered. Otherwise the war would continue. The reaction of the Turks was not known at that time; it was said that Ahmad Pasha was collecting troops near Baghdad, but also that he was sending friendly letters to the shah. Information from Erevan, Tiflis and Nakhjevan had it that the few Turks who still were there feared the Persian troops and were sending their slaves and property deep into Turkish territory.[22]

Nader was still in Mashhad in January 1731 when a son was born to his wife, the shah's sister. Both he and his oldest son (by another wife), Reza Qoli Khan, carried on a great state. Especially the latter's, whose entourage was even more richly dressed than that of the shah. When Reza Qoli Khan went out riding 14 horses rode before his with golden saddles and reins studded with jewels. He was married to the youngest sister of the shah. Nader was said to have send his son with only 8,000 men to join the shah, for he himself would go to Herat where the Abdalis were collecting a large force. He was said to intend to do so to put the shah in a position where he had to ask Nader for help to show that the reports about him, that he wanted to declare himself independent, were all lies. It was also rumored that Nader carried the *jiqeh* (royal plume) in Mashhad on the right side. People asked him why he did that for it was not fitting for a commoner to do so. Did he have plans to become shah himself? If that was case he was told they would take appropriate measures. Out of fear for his life Nader had taken off the *jiqeh* and said that he was but a slave of the shah.[23]

TAHMASP II IS DEFEATED BY THE OTTOMANS

Before the shah's departure his 7,000 troops had to be paid by the population of Isfahan. The Moslems had to pay 4,000 *tuman*s, the Armenians 600, the Indians 300 and the destitute Jews

20. For a discussion of the ʿAmarlu, a Kurdish tribal group, see Gmelin, S.G. *Reise durch Russland*, 4 vols. (St. Petersburg, 1774), translated into English and annotated by Willem Floor as *Travels through Northern Persia 1770-1774* (Washington DC, Mage Publishers, 2007), pp. 353-54.

21. VOC 2255 (28/01/1731), f.2280-82.

22. VOC 2255 (28/01/1731), f. 2291-93.

23. VOC 2255, van Leijpsigh to de Cleen (28/01/1731), f. 2281-2; VOC 2584, Beschrijvinge, f. 1958.

100 *tuman*s. As a result of this operation Isfahan was an emaciated city, Nicolaus van Leijpsigh (Schorer's successor) reported. Against the will of his advisers, he had the third day's fever, the shah left to the village of Tirun-Karvar (Thierom Karvar) at one German mile west of the city. On November 6, he suddenly decamped from there going towards Hamadan. On January 16, 1731 news was received in Isfahan that the shah had taken four forts held by 12,000 Dargazinis, Afghans and Turks. He was said to have moved from Hamadan to Sinneh (Sien) and intended to go from there to Tabriz. He had appointed Mohammad Khan Baluch as general (*sardar*) of his army, who had shown much courage during the capture of the forts. At that time his army had grown to 30,000 men. During his stay in Hamadan the shah had almost been killed when the *jabbehdar-bashi* (chief of the arsenal) had gone into a powder house containing 2,000 *mann* of gun-powder, left by the Turks, with a burning water-pipe. The powder had exploded and about 2,000 people were said to have been killed, and many houses had been ruined close to the one the shah had been staying in.[24]

The area from Hamadan to Borwarie[25] had been ravaged by the plague, 200,000 people were said to have perished. The plague was also said to have scoured Kashan, Baghdad, and Kermanshah. The survivors had fled into the mountains, also out of fear for the cruelty of the Turks. Many even came to Isfahan, Shiraz, Qazvin and Soltanabad.[26] In Isfahan, people suffered from the effects of a drought, the most serious one in human memory. Until January 5, 1731 no snow or rain had fallen, but fortunately on that day heavy snow fell. People were happy notwithstanding the fact that due to intense cold many people and animals died of the worst cold they could remember. As a result of these natural calamities life in Isfahan was very expensive during the first quarter of 1731. This situation was aggravated by the fact that the *na'eb* (deputy governor) of the city (the chief eunuch Agha Jamal) had sent people to the villages to stop any food coming from there. This enabled him to sell the grain from his and that of his friends' warehouses at high prices. The bakers, butchers and the like had to give rich presents to be allowed to sell at prices, which they fixed themselves. Bread (not of pure wheat flour) was sold at 4 *mahmudi*s per *mann-e shah* of 12 lbs. or 5.96 kg. Meat was sold at 8 *mahmudi*s and rice at 7 *mahmudi*s per *mann-e shah*. The population was grumbling against the *na'eb*. Seeing that their low-key protest had no effect, they on April 11, 1731 threw stones at him, but he was able to save himself by fleeing into the royal palace where the stones nevertheless followed him. Out of fear he sent messengers to the villages to send food to the city. Another eunuch, Agha Kamal, secretly informed the shah about the situation. The *na'eb* meanwhile was repairing the royal palaces and pleasure gardens and every week urged the laborers to hurry up.[27]

---

24. VOC 2255 (28/01/1731), f. 2285-87.

25. Burvari, the Armenian name for Barbarud, near Borujerd.

26. VOC 2255 (03/11/1731), f. 1866.

27. VOC 2255, van Leysigh to de Cleen (20/04/1731), f. 2318-21. The deputy (*na'eb*) of the shah in Isfahan during his absence was the *nabab* Mirza `Ali Naqi, who was also his brother-in-law and his physician. However, when he left Isfahan with the shah, the latter had appointed Agha Jamal as his deputy. Ibid., f. 2308, 2311. `Ali Naqi in his turn also had a deputy, Hajji Mohsen, who had been taken prisoner by the Turks and therefore was replaced by the eunuch Hajji Kalb `Ali. VOC 2255, van Leijpsigh to de Cleen (03/11/1731), f. 1844. It was said that Mirza `Ali Naqi, the *vaqaye`-nevis*, had died in Qazvin of his wounds suffered in battle against the Turks. Also, that the grand vizier had been dismissed. Ibid., f. 1867. Hajji Kalb `Ali's deputy was Mirza Taher. VOC 2255 (28/12/1731), f. 1889.

Shah Tahmasp II had ordered that nobody in his army was allowed to have pistols, saddle-coats (*shabrakken*) or straps (*japrassen*) on their coats. The purpose of this order was to make the Persian soldiers distinguishable from Turkish spies who might be in the army. The shah believed that no Turk would ever travel without these trappings, or that they might wear other clothes. He also had given orders not to slaughter lambs under six months of age in those areas where lambs were killed very young. The reason for this order was that the shah had observed that one of his soldiers spent most of his pay on clothes lined with lambskins. He became very angry and said that he had not paid the soldier to buy clothes, but to earn money for his family and that he should fight in common soldier's clothes. The soldier was given the bastinado and died. The shah also ordered the *ordu-bazar* (the army train) to leave, for he had seen that a soldier had to pay 1.5 *mahmudi*s for one melon about which the shah was very angry. Henceforth the soldiers had to satisfy themselves with wheat and barley provided for by the shah. Other orders sent by the shah were that henceforth luxurious fabrics were neither allowed to be woven nor golden or silver female jewelry be made. Jewelry and the like had to be brought to the Mint to be melted and coined. Also, that precise registers had to be kept of which foreigners entered and left towns, while the *kadkhoda*s (heads of town quarters) were ordered to keep an accurate journal of what happened in their quarter such as "fights, drunkenness, prostitution, flimsy lawsuits, marriages, births, deaths and the like." A copy of these journals had to be sent regularly to the shah, who was also reported to have appointed informers to verify the implementation of these orders.[28]

After having received news that Ardabil had been retaken, while the Turks had vacated Nakhjevan of their own accord, it was expected that Shah Tahmasp would attack Erevan. On September 22, 1731 information of Shah Tahmasp's defeat was received in Isfahan. Many people wanted to flee and sell their furniture because they believed the Turks were coming. The English prepared pack animals to leave the city as well, because they did not want to suffer the experience of another occupation. Horne, the EIC Resident, asked van Leijpsigh what he was going to do. The latter replied that the Dutch would stay; for if the Europeans would flee it would show the population that there was no hope any longer and that would put them into a difficult position.[29]

The shah almost had been made prisoner when he, with 100 men, had come to the relief of the baggage train that was being attacked by 8,000 Turks. A heavy thunder separated the fighting parties and made a hasty flight possible. During the crossing of the river Aras the shah almost had drowned. Because of that event everybody was obliged to celebrate for one day, "which costs us a lot of money," van Leijpsigh grumbled, although the shah was very pleased with it. After his defeat the shah was said to have gone to Qom, but later it was said to Tehran, where he still had an army of 15,000 men. Many of the fugitive soldiers were infesting the roads. The shah did not send for help to Nader at that time. He ordered the *beglerbegi*

---

28. VOC 2255 (28/01/1731), f. 2289-91 ("vegterijen, dronkschap, hoererijen, vlase [?] processen, huwelijken, kindergeboorten, sterfte.")

29. VOC 2255 (31/11/1731), f. 1832-33, 1861-63, 1869-70. Ahmad Pasha was said to have had 200,000 men, but according to others only 40,000. He was said to favor war, based on the Turkish-Afghan treaty. Tahmasp II had first refused to give battle. When he finally did he was defeated. The Turks then were inclined to conclude a peace treaty with the shah. They feared Nader, but it was unclear whether the shah had asked for his help. The Turks had arrested the Persian envoy to Istanbul, Reza Qoli Khan, at Kirkuk [?] (Carcouw); VOC 2584, Beschrijvinge, f. 1962-63.

of Fars, Mohammad ʿAli Khan, to go to Shiraz and recruit new troops, while Hasan ʿAli Khan, *moʿayyer-bashi* (the assayer of the Mint) the *farrash-bashi* (chief of the royal menial servants), and the *nazer* (high steward of the royal household) were ordered to prepare equipment, clothes and boots for the shah's army. To pay for the new equipment the shah had given orders not to extort more money from the population of Isfahan, although the *moʿayyer-bashi*, who had been again appointed governor of Isfahan, was busy robbing them of their last possessions. The shah therefore had instructed the *nazer* to "appropriate the revenues of which the mullahs live and which, we are assured, amount to more than 100,000 *tuman*s per year to pay the troops with." *Sardar* Mohammad Khan Baluch was ordered to collect the revenues of Qazvin, Qom, Tehran, Saveh, Kashan and Isfahan. The population of Qazvin, moreover, had been charged with a fine of 400 *tuman*s as a punishment for the riots, which had broken out there, after the news of the shah's defeat had become known. As a result of this it was said that, about 3,000 families had moved to the Russians in Gilan. During the riots people had even attacked the shah's harem, but worse had been prevented by the courageous defense put up by the eunuchs.[30]

Mohammad ʿAli Khan[31] returned from Shiraz with 2,000 men on July 5, 1731. He was ordered to proceed with the *moʿayyer-bashi* to Hamadan to watch Turkish movements. The *moʿayyer-bashi* behaved in a very oppressive manner taking what he could lay his hands on. The Armenians had to pay him twice an amount of 600 *tuman*s; the Banyans had to pay 300 *tuman*s and the Moslems 1,400 *tuman*s. This money was taken or 'borrowed' by force. He also had made it known that henceforth the Afghan coins would not be legal tender any more, which resulted in a total standstill of the little trade that still existed, for most of the Persian Safavid coinage had already been exported.

Meanwhile, the shah had returned to Isfahan on November 30, 1731 preceded on November 19 by Mohammad Khan Baluch, who left again for Shiraz on December 16 to destroy the Sunnis led by Sheikh Ahmad Madani. On December 5, 1731 van Leijpsigh was received in audience by Shah Tahmasp, who first asked about Schorer's demise about which he was sad and then asked whether the Dutch had cannon casters, carpenters and the like which he badly needed. The Dutch, however, were unable to help him.[32] After his defeat Shah Tahmasp II kept most of his ministers in their posts. The shah offered the eunuch Kalb ʿAli the function of royal treasurer, but he declined; he then was appointed *jabbehdar-bashi*. Mirza Naqi, the *vaqaye'-nevis* had died, but no successor had been appointed for the time being.[33]

An envoy from Ahmad Pasha had been held up at the shah's orders at Tehran, who sent the former *qurchi-bashi*, Mohammad Reza Khan, as his ambassador to discuss peace with the Turks and to return with the envoy to Hamadan. The Turks had demanded that they would keep all territory on their side of the Aras, while Persia would keep the land on the other side.

---

30. VOC 2255 (03/11/1731 + appendix 02/12/1731), f. 1832-33, 1850-54.

31. On June 11, 1730 Schorer reported that Mohammad ʿAli Khan had arrived in Isfahan as *beglerbegi* of Fars with a jurisdiction and authority just like Lotf ʿAli Khan in 1717. VOC 2253, Schorer to de Cleen (01/07/1730), f. 901.

32. VOC 2255, van Leijpsigh to de Cleen (28/12/1731), f. 1893-94.

33. VOC 2255, van Leijpsigh to de Cleen (28/12/1731), f. 1891-92. Later it was reported that "Miersa Takie, the vakanevies," was appointed vizier of Rasht. VOC 2322, van Leijpsigh to Koenad (22/03/1733), f. 389.

The Dutch hoped for a speedy peace, for that would mean that Turkish and Greek [-Orthodox] merchants would come again to Isfahan. Finally, on January 29, 1732 the *naqqareh*s or kettle-drums were beaten because of the conclusion of peace with Turkey. The conditions were that Turkey would keep all territory on yonder side of the Aras as well as the towns of Kermanshah and Hamadan, while Turkish-held territory on this side of the Aras would be returned to Persia after three years. Ahmad Pasha had promised that he would try to induce the Porte to reduce the three-year period.[34] After peace had been concluded with the Turks, the shah again asked the Dutch and English for cannon casters, carpenters and other artisans. Meanwhile, Mohammad Reza Khan, the Persian envoy, had been received with much pomp in Baghdad.[35]

It was also reported that a treasure of 40,000 *tuman*s had been discovered in the palace. On February 17 and 23, respectively, Reza Qoli Khan and Mohammad Qoli Khan, the deputy *qurchi-bashi*, had returned. The latter had been sent to Istanbul in 1729. After the shah's defeat he had been sent to Ahmad Pasha, and the former to Istanbul. The shah and Nader held Mohammad Qoli Khan in high esteem. He had been accompanied by some Afghans, who had been killed by robbers en route, but according to some, at the shah's orders. It was further reported that the shah had reappointed ʿAbdol-Baqi Khan as governor of Kermanshah, as well as the former governor of Hamadan to their same positions. Vali Mohammad (Welie Mahmet), at the request of the population of Tabriz, had been appointed governor of that city. However, Nader opposed his appointment and therefore, Bisetun Khan Afshar Urumi (Biesietoen Chan), who had been governor there previously, was reappointed. The chief gunner, Mohammad Qoli Khan (Mhamed Coelie Chan), was appointed as deputy *divan-begi*, while his brother, Naser ʿAli Beg (Neseralie beeck), as deputy chief gunner. Mohammad ʿAli Beg (Mahmed Alie Beek) became *darugheh* of Isfahan. The post of royal huntsman was unoccupied, because the holder of that office, ʿAli Mardan Khan, when he was dead drunk, had fallen of a terrace and had died. He was a good friend of the EIC, who thus lost an important support, because he was a drinking friend of the shah and had more access to the shah than anybody else. The shah was very sad about his demise and had given orders to take his corpse to Karbala to which end he gave 150 *tuman*s from the royal treasury.[36]

NADER'S ACTIVITIES IN KHORASAN AND SUSPICIONS ABOUT HIS LOYALTY.

In April 1731 it was reported that Nader's brother, Ebrahim Khan, had been defeated by the Turkmans and had lost 4,000 of his 7,000 troops. Nader therefore had taken the field himself against them. He defeated them and took their most important leaders as prisoners to Mashhad. Meanwhile, he was forming a large army to move against Herat. Hoseyn Khan Ghalzai was said to have collected an army of 60,000 to 90,000 men and allegedly had been proclaimed shah. Seydal Khan had been appointed as his *sepahsalar*.[37]

---

34. VOC 2255 (28/12/1731), f. 1882; Ibid., (29/01/1732), f. 1907-08.

35. VOC 2255 (11/01/1732), f. 1904.

36. VOC 2255 (30/05/1732), f. 1981-85.

37. VOC 2255 (20/04/1731), f. 2313-14.

Rumors about Nader's alleged disloyal behavior were still strong. He was said to have sent orders to Kerman not to pray any longer in the *khotbah* for the shah's welfare and health. He further had summoned 12 brocade weavers from Isfahan, which the *na'eb* of Isfahan, who was a partisan of his, had sent. The latter was also preparing a gold and jewel-studded saddle for a led horse and a shield of pure gold studded with jewels. It was also said that Nader was minting coins in Mashhad on which the name of one of the Moslem prophets named Shah-e Najaf (Sjah Nejef; i.e., Imam Hoseyn) was struck. He also had changed his seal and had arrogated to himself a more important honorific, viz. *vali* of Khorasan, so that, according to many, it was clear that he wanted to become shah, the more so since he had married the shah's sister. Others (his partisans), however, maintained that Nader was upset by the fact that the shah listened to flatterers who told the shah that he was a rebel. He therefore stayed away from court until the shah had sent these people away as he had requested already many times.[38]

On October 27, 1731 a loud yelling on the royal square followed by the beating of the kettledrums, which was continued for three days, heralded the fact that Nader had defeated the Abdalis and had retaken Herat and Farah. It was also rumored that he shortly would attack the Turks at Hamadan. The Dutch, however, hoped for peace for this was what the country needed. After his victory Nader had appointed Allah Yar Khan as governor of Herat. The latter defected to the Abdalis, however, and defeated Nader who lost 10,000 men. Nader then regrouped his dispersed troops and retook Herat. He then sent for Mahmud Khan Ghalzai's sister from Qandahar to take her as his wife, but it was unknown whether she would come. On May 16, 1732 a cousin of Nader returned to Isfahan to report on the conquest of Herat on the occasion of which again the kettledrums were beaten for three days. It also became known that Ahmad Pasha had sent an envoy to Nader to get his agreement to the treaty with the shah. Nader kept the envoy for two weeks and then gave him 100 *tuman*s cash and 15 horses as a present and instructed him to tell his master that he himself would come to Baghdad to discuss peace or war. It was said that he also had written to the shah that he was not pleased with the treaty and therefore had decided to challenge the Turks himself.[39]

Nader sent for the *mo'ayyer-bashi*, the *farrash-bashi*, and the *khalifeh al-kholafa* and therefore Shah Tahmasp sent them to Herat on March 23, 1732. Messengers went to and from Isfahan and Nader, but the Dutch were unable to find out what the nature of their messages was. On June 3, 1732 when the *mo'ayyer-bashi*, the *farrash-bashi* and Mirza Kafi, the *kholafa*[40] returned from Herat, the Dutch learnt that Nader was at Mashhad and had requested the shah to lead his troops to Qazvin or to send these under the command of *beglerbegi* Mohammad 'Ali Khan to him and to transfer to him full authority for a period of four years to deal with the Turks properly. It was unknown what the shah had replied to the last request. People believed that the three officials were plotting to depose the shah. These suspicions were allayed when the three returned with large costly presents for the shah, viz., 10,000 *tuman*s in cash, some

---

38. VOC 2255 (20/04/1731), f. 2315-16.

39. VOC 2255 (03/11/1731 + appendix 02/12/1731), f. 1871-72; Ibid., (28/12/1731), f. 1892-93; Ibid., (30/05/1732), f. 1986–87.

40. On this person and his function see Willem Floor, "The khalifeh al-kholafa of the Safavid Sufi order," *ZDMG* 151 (2003), pp. 51-86.

fine horses, camels and mules taken from the defeated Abdalis. But it served only to blind the shah against their designs.[41]

The Dutch bemoaned this news for it meant the end of peace. They suspected that Nader wanted to continue the confused state of the country on purpose to serve his personal interests. For if there were no enemies anymore he could not act the 'bravado' *vis à vis* the shah as he had been doing these past few years. He was also believed to have sent a delegation of 10 men to the Russians in Gilan ordering them to leave the country or else he would force them to do so. His army at that time was estimated to amount to 120,000 men, amongst whom 15,000 Abdalis. He was said to have sent an envoy, an Afghan, to the Turks with 5,000 men (Afghans and Afshars) to declare war on the Turks. Nader was approaching Isfahan and was believed to be at 22 day's journey east of Isfahan. Shah Tahmasp prior to all this information had sent Ahmad Pasha a costly robe of honor, a Turkish turban with feather and jewels as a present. But he changed his mind and made preparations for war and summoned *sardar* Mohammad Khan Baluch to Isfahan. Nader was also said to have allowed the Afghan, Allahyar Khan Abdali (Alla Jaar Chan), to flee with 300 other leading rebels. Also, that the son that had been born to him by Mahmud Khan Ghalzai's sister, who was named Almas Khan, had been appointed as governor of Qandahar. During his minority, his mother's brother would act as his *na'eb* or deputy.[42]

In June 1732, six Georgians sent by the prince of Imeret'i, came to offer their lord's submission if the shah would protect him against the Turks. They had not yet received a reply, but were defrayed at 15 *mahmudi*s per day.[43] On July 8, 1732 Shah Tahmasp went to Ben Isfahan and from there on July 9 to Najafabad, whence he continued to Mohammadiyeh (Mahmadiya) with 22,000 men on July 16. There he inspected the troops and gave Mohammad 'Ali Khan (who had arrived from Shiraz on June 30) leave to go to Nader.[44] The war was expected to start in September notwithstanding the fact that Ahmad Pasha had written that he would induce the Porte to return the towns on this side of the Aras within three years. He also asked that a Persian ambassador be sent to Istanbul and not to adopt Nader's hostile line. He finally asked to wage war, if it had to come, not near Baghdad but in Azerbaijan, for he did not want to break his word with regards to the concluded peace. To show his good will he put on the shah's robe of honor with much ceremony four German miles outside Baghdad.[45]

IRAN'S RELATIONS WITH RUSSIA

Apart from Turkish troops on Persian soil there were also Russian troops. The latter gave no indication in December 1730 that they had any intention to vacate Gilan. Shah Tahmasp II forbade Nader to take action against them, for he did not want a conflict with Russia. It was rumored

---

41. VOC 2255 (30/05/1732), f. 1985; VOC 2584, Beschrijvinge f. 1963. The *mo`ayyer-bashi* had been a supporter of Shah Tahmasp II, but he became the shah's enemy because of his beautiful wife. The shah wanted to see her, which the *mo`ayyer-bashi* did not want to allow him. Shah Tahmasp then arranged to view her anyway by stealth.

42. VOC 2255 (30/05/1732), f. 1988-90.

43. VOC 2322 (26/07/1732), f. 297vs.

44. VOC 2322 (26/07/1732), f. 281vs-82vs. Van Leijpsigh also reported that, "if the shah protected him [i.e., the prince of Imeret'i], he would kick out the Turks." Ibid., f. 287vs.

45. VOC 2255, van Leijpsigh to de Cleen (30/05/1732), f. 1981-85.

that during Tahmasp Beg's rule of Isfahan that Shah Tahmasp had in secret contacted the Russians promising them Gilan if they helped him against foreign aggressors and rebels. There was talk that a large embassy would come, but finally only one dragoman came. In September 1730, a messenger from the Russian general in Gilan came to court; the purpose of his mission was unknown. According to information received by the Armenians, the Russians were being reinforced by a considerable number of fresh troops towards the end of 1730.[46]

The Persian ambassador to Moscow, Mirza Ebrahim returned having achieved nothing. Russia did not want to return Gilan, but nevertheless wanted to live in peace with Persia.[47] Prior to Shah Tahmasp's departure to Erevan he received a Russian ambassador in Tabriz, who received a cool welcome at first, but later was given the VIP treatment. Mirza Ebrahim accompanied the ambassador and both returned to the Russian commander at Rasht to discuss peace between the two countries. Russia was said to be prepared to return all Persian territory with the exception of Baku, Darband, and Niyazabad or Nisovaya (Niasawaar). It preferred however to see first what the outcome of the Persian campaign against Turkey would be, while reinforcing its forces in Gilan at the same time.[48]

On January 29, 1732 a Russian ambassador arrived in Isfahan who was received by the shah on the same day.[49] The only presents he had were six falcons and three casks of brandy, which was not appreciated at all. The shah kept the ambassador standing for 1.5 hour without asking him anything and finally gave him leave to depart. In the beginning the ambassador was considered to be a spy, which was the reason why he had some guards posted at the gate of his house. He was not allowed to go outside of his house either. The shah gave orders to stop the supply of his daily allowance, while he was given an open unsealed letter for his master. The ambassador was forced to live at his own expense for a few days. Then the letter was taken back and he was given 200 *mahmudi*s (Dfl. 95) per day. He was finally given leave to depart with a sealed letter and a present of 200 *tuman*s and received a civil treatment. The ambassador was even received twice by the shah (on March 19 and April 2, 1732) and left for Gilan on the day of the last audience. The ambassador left two of his men behind. The Dutch did not visit him, because the court considered the man to be a spy. According to Kalb `Ali, the eunuch, it was still uncertain what territory the Russians would return. Meanwhile, many rich merchants with their families had left Gilan for Baku and Darband to stay out of the hands of the money-hungry Persians.[50] In July 1732, van Leijpsigh reported having learnt that the Russians had returned Baku and Darband and that the Persian army was marching on Shamakhi and Shirvan to retake these towns from the Lezgis.[51] The Lezgis had marched with 15,000 men against the Armenians who, despite being only 3,000 strong, had defeated them with loss of much life, baggage and artillery. Afterwards it was said that the Armenians, Georgians and

---

46. VOC 2255, van Leijpsigh to de Cleen (28/01/1731), f. 2284-85.

47. VOC 2255, van Leypigh to de Cleen (20/04/1731), f. 2318. Mirza Ebrahim had been the assistant of Mirza Rabi`a, the well-known *mostowfi-ye khasseh* around 1700.

48. VOC 2255, van Leijpsigh to de Cleen (03/11/1731 and 02/12/1731), f. 1860-61.

49. VOC 2255, van Leijpsigh to de Cleen (29/01/1732), f. 1908.

50. VOC 2253, van Leijpsigh to de Cleen (30/05/1732), f. 1972-76.

51. VOC 2322, van Leijpsigh to de Cleen (26/07/1732), f. 284.

Lezgis had agreed to join forces and had defeated the Turks at Tiflis, which they took. Later it was said that the Lezgis had enslaved 13,000 Georgian families.[52]

THE FALL OF TAHMASP II

In December 1731, van Leijpsigh reported that the country had been totally sacked, while the shah was having all buildings in Isfahan repaired. He, in particular, devoted his time on the Sa'adatabad garden in which he had much pleasure, and which had become very beautiful. Shah Tahmasp also spent a lot on his public council for which he had much gold and silverware prepared. To celebrate the rehabilitated pleasure garden of Sa'adatabad he ordered to prepare all kinds of fireworks. This occasion was the scene of the customary rivalry between the Dutch and the English. The Dutch had their tent pitched near a wooden bridge and the Armenian merchants. The English had been allotted a site close to Pol-e Khvaju together with the Banyan and the Jewish merchants. This the English did not like and on December 28, 1731 they bribed the servants of the mo'ayyer-bashi to strike the Dutch tent and put theirs in its place. Van Leijpsigh protested to Kalb 'Ali, one of the harem eunuchs, who reported it to the shah. The latter then ordered to pitch the Dutch tent near his talar or open hall, which never before had been permitted to any royal counselor or ambassador, for one could look from that site straight at the royal harem. That same evening the shah sent for van Leijpsigh and told him to sit near to him and gave him five times to drink from his own golden wine goblet, which was quite a lot van Leijpsigh remarked. The next day he had his servants pay the Dutch much respect and on December 30, 1731 honored them by coming on foot to their tent and later sent a bowl with fruit to show his appreciation. Despite these favors shown to the Dutch the shah did not visit the VOC factory although he passed it twice on January 28, 1732, while the entire VOC staff was lined up with presents. The shah stopped to talk with Van Leijpsigh, which was considered quite an honor too.[53]

On April 10, 1732 a conspiracy against the shah's life was discovered. The royal slave (qol) Bijan Beg, who called himself the shah's brother, had organized it. Under torture (bastinado) he confessed to be the son of Allahverdi Khan, a slave of Shah Soleyman. The other participants in the conspiracy were a Kurdish chief, an Afshar chief, the Afghan Ja'far Khan, the last Afghan governor of Shiraz, Mirza Mohammad, the jabbehdar-bashi and two eunuchs of the royal harem who were supported by about 4,000 men, both officers and soldiers. One of the shah's slaves had pretended to join the conspiracy, but feigning that he had forgotten his seal to confirm their pact he went home to fetch it. However, he went straight to the house of the Royal Master of the Hunt (shekarchi-bashi), who immediately informed the shah about the conspiracy. Shah Tahmasp II ordered their arrest and had the matter investigated. The leaders of the conspiracy were all publicly beheaded, Ja'far Khan's body was burnt, and those of the others were thrown as prey to lions and other animals. The women of the pretenders were put alive in bricked chimneys to die. The conspirators had already divided the booty amongst themselves, and each one of them had been allotted part of the city to do with as he liked.

---

52. VOC 2255 (03/11/1731), f. 1863; Ibid., (30/05/1732), f. 1991.

53. VOC 2255 (28/12/1731), f. 1891; Ibid., (11/01/1732), f. 1901-03; Ibid., (30/05/1732), f. 1959-62. The two rival European Companies continued to cast aspersions on each other and organized parties for the courtiers to sway them to support the one or the other view. See, e.g., VOC 2255 (28/01/1731), f. 2222-40. For a list of the cost and prices of firewood, wines and fireworks see VOC 2254 (09/07/1732), f. 879.

As a result of this event Shah Tahmasp II was more cautious about his eating, drinking and riding habits. He employed more tasters and guards, and only went out riding accompanied by a great suite of cavalry and infantry. Formerly he was very careless, he drank and ate what was put in front of him and he did not care whether he was guarded or not. He sometimes rode to the pleasure gardens situated at five miles outside Isfahan accompanied by only three horsemen. However, after the conspiracy, he had become so frightened that he used to fire guns with balls four to five times per week from the *Hazar Jarib* gardens at the tomb of the famous Afghan sorcerer Dara Shah (?).[54] In mid-May one of the cannons burst and Shah Tahmasp was almost hit by a piece of metal. He then ordered the fine building in Shahrestan (Serrestoen; a suburb of Isfahan) to be demolished.[55]

Nader was at Semnan at the end of May 1732 with 80,000 horse and 40,000 foot. Shah Tahmasp was at Sar-e Chashmeh at seven leagues from Isfahan. Nader was said to intend to go in person to Baghdad. He also sent 6,000 men to Kerman, who had to go from there to Shiraz via Kuhgilu with other troops to take Basra. Mohammad Khan Baluch returned to Isfahan with his troops when Nader had dismissed him as *beglerbegi* of Kuhgilu. Meanwhile fights had broken out between the population of Qazvin and Nader's troops because they had raped some Qazvini women. Each side lost about 75 dead and the Qazvinis said that they would not suffer the presence of Nader's troops anymore.[56]

On August 1, 1732 Shah Tahmasp returned from Sar-e Chashmeh to Isfahan. It was said that at Sar-e Chashmeh the shah had intended to flee to the Bakhtiyaris and from there to Kuhgilu and on to the Turks to ask for help against Nader. The *mo`ayyer-bashi* and the *kholafa*, however, had talked him out of it with flatteries.[57] He sent the *mo`ayyer-bashi*, the *kholafa* and other officials to welcome Nader, and on August 9, with the agreement of the latter, Mohammad Reza Beg left as ambassador to Ahmad Pasha. His message was that the shah allowed the Turks a period of three months in which to return the Persian cities, the conquered artillery and those Persian subjects who had been enslaved, if not war would follow. On August 26, 1732 Nader accompanied by 32,000 men arrived in the *Hazar Jarib* garden. It caused much talk under the population that he camped in the *Hazar Jarib* garden, for it was against the shah's orders that any of the grandees, *sardar*s, and ministers coming to court to strike camp there without having first made their *salam* at the `Ali Qapu and having been given leave to depart by the shah.[58] The Dutch welcomed Nader when he passed through the bazaar, he only said: "be welcome." That same day, all classes of the population presented him with costly presents. Two days later, accompanied by 3,000 men, he went to pay his respects to the shah at the Sa`adatabad garden, where he only remained for 15 minutes. That same afternoon Nader [or as he was still known at that time: Tahmasp Qoli Khan] dismissed most of the ministers, and with the exception of the *beglerbegi* Mohammad `Ali Khan and the *sardar* Mohammad Baluch Khan, he all imprisoned them. He also appointed tax collectors to confiscate all their

---

54. I have been unable to identify this person or his tomb; the latter is neither mentioned in Honarfar's *Ganjiheh* nor in Mehrabadi's *Athar*.

55. VOC 2255 (30/05/1732), f. 1977-81.

56. VOC 2322 (26/07/1732), f. 283vs, 288.

57. VOC 2322, f. 293.

58. VOC 2584, Beschrijvinge, f. 1971-72; VOC 2322 (12/09/1732), f. 289vs.

property. After a few days he all released them and gave the *mo`ayyer-bashi* and the *kholafa* a robe of honor. They all were sent to various parts of the country with their families under escort of soldiers.[59]

Nader, who had planned a coup with his partisans, invited Shah Tahmasp II to visit him in the *Hazar Jarib* garden on September 1, 1732, to which he consented. One of his slaves, Bijan Beg who had discovered the plot by his alleged brother warned the shah not to go there since he had heard that something treacherous had been planned. However, Shah Tahmasp II chose to ignore his warning for if "his Baba Khan (Baba Chan) intended to do this there was nothing he could do about it." He instructed Bijan Beg, however, to be on his guard during the visit and when he gave the order, in case of treason, to kill Nader immediately. The latter regaled Shah Tahmasp II luxuriously with a meal richly accompanied with wine of which the shah was a great lover. As a result of excessive drinking Shah Tahmasp II got drunk, as had been intended, and Nader had him disarmed and taken into the harem. The shah had fallen into a slumber and Nader sent for all army commanders to see their shah, to make them understand what kind of problem he had on his hands, and that such a drunkard could not any longer rule Persia. He asked them to make this known to the army as well as the fact that he would act as regent of Persia until such time that the shah would have bettered his life. The army commanders agreed to this. Nader also ordered the execution of Bijan Beg. He had been standing behind Nader during the visit and twice had asked the shah for a sign to kill him in the full meeting, but each time the shah had waved him away.[60]

NADER BECOMES REGENT — HIS FIRST ADMINISTRATIVE, POLITICAL AND FISCAL ACTIONS

At ten o'clock of September 2, 1732 Nader proclaimed Shah Tahmasp's son as the new king under the name of `Abbas III. The latter had been born on July 5, 1732.[61] Nader would be regent until the new king would come of age. On September 4, 1732 Tahmasp Mirza (as the former shah was now known) accompanied by his mother, some wives, eunuchs and servants in 12 *kavajeh*s or litters was sent under escort of 800 horsemen to Kalat via Yazd. On September 8, 1732 the new child-king was formally proclaimed king in a public royal council meeting presided over by the shah in his cradle. The *khotbeh* was read, a new seal and coin were made, while candy was distributed. Qasem Khan Shamlu, governor of Qom, was appointed as the shah's governor. He married one of the shah's aunts and took up lodgings in the royal palace. The army moved into Isfahan, and to all towns new governors were sent.[62]

Nader gave the governorship of Isfahan and its dependencies for 80,000 *tumans*, or 10,000 more than the usual amount, to Mir Abu'l-Hasan, whom he also gave one of the former shah's sisters as wife. In 1733 he ordered him to be strangled in Qom, allegedly because Mir Abu'l-Hasan had been a weaver and Nader, learning this, did not consider him to be fit

---

59. VOC 2584, Beschrijvinge, f. 1973-76; VOC 2322 (12/09/1732), f. 290r-vs.

60. VOC 2584, Beschrijvinge, f. 1973-80; VOC 2322 (12/09/1732), f. 291.

61. VOC 2322 (26/07/1732), f. 284. His mother was a daughter of Fath `Ali Khan Daghestani, the grand vizier (1715-20) of Shah Soltan Hoseyn.

62. VOC 2584, Beschrijvinge, f. 1980-82; VOC 2322 (12/09/1732), f. 291-vs; VOC 2322 de Cleen to Batavia (30/09/1733 + appendix 30/11/1733), f. 27.

to be related to a king.[63] The new governors started their administration by extorting a lot of money from the population. In Isfahan, the Moslem population had to pay 10,500 *tuman*s, the Armenians 1,000 and the Banyans 500 *tuman*s. Many were unable to pay and died as a result of the bastinado. Even nobles like Mohammad Zaman Khan, brother of ʿAli Mardan Khan, the ambassador to India, died as a result of such a beating. Many people had already fled from Isfahan to Yazd and elsewhere on hearing the news of Nader's coming to Isfahan for he respected neither his word nor loyalty.[64]

On September 1, 1732 a Russian agent, Semen Avramov (Simon Abrahimts) arrived in Isfahan and was given a daily allowance of 150 *mahmudi*s. He had previous acquaintance with Nader and told van Leijpsigh that, "the general can form a good army and defeat an enemy and subsequently totally ruin the country sparing neither merchant nor foreign friends." He had personal experience with this policy, for, when in Mashhad, Nader had twice taken everything from him.[65] [The Russian agent's view was very insightful, as future events show.]

The Dutch did not escape the impact of the new government either. Already on August 28, 1732 Mirza Taqi [Shirazi], the *monshi al-mamalek* informed the Dutch in Isfahan that he expected them to pay 4,000 *tuman*s. The dragoman was able to get this demand reduced to 500 *tuman*s. Mirza Taqi advised to pay without demurring, for Nader was in the habit to double the amount if one pleaded for its reduction or exemption. He drew their attention to the English, who had given Nader a present of 200 *tuman*s consisting of cloth and crystal. The latter had looked disapprovingly at it and said why don't they give horses. He had ordered Mirza Taqi to inspect the new English present before accepting it, and the latter added ominously, that this is only the beginning! Mirza Taqi also said that tax collectors would be sent to Gamron to collect money willy-nilly from the Companies there. Whatever argument the dragoman raised against a Dutch contribution it was to no avail. Mirza Taqi replied that Nader needed money for his troops now. Already on August 29, 1732, four of Nader's servants had brusquely asked van Leijpsigh what present he had prepared for their master. They told him that they had orders to take 300 *tuman*s from him by force. Van Leijpsigh told them they could take his life and clothes, for he had no money. They left after one hour, promising to return the same evening. Through a friend, the Moslem merchant Aqa Sayyed (Aga Saijit), who had influence with Nader, the Dutch were able to bring about that Mirza Taqi himself came that evening.[66]

Mirza Taqi advised van Leijpsigh in his own interest to pay. He inspected the present, which the Dutch had prepared (chintzes, porcelain, and rarities). Mirza Taqi said that his master preferred horses and mules, and that textiles and the like would be valued at one-third of their value, so that the Dutch would loose a lot of money. Van Leijpsigh said that he had three horses in the factory and Nader was welcome to them; he had no money to buy other horses. Mirza Taqi promised to get the amount reduced to 200 *tuman*s, but then the Dutch

63. VOC 2584, Beschrijvinge, f. 1993-94.

64. VOC 2584, Beschrijvinge, f. 1982-83; VOC 2322 (12/09/1732), f. 292; VOC 2322 de Cleen to Batavia (30/09/1733 + appendix 30/11/1733), f. 27vs.

65. VOC 2322, van Leijpsigh to de Cleen (12/09/1732 and appendix of 28/10/1732), f. 292. Avramov had been secretary to Ambassador Artemii Petrovich Volynski. Bushev, P.P. *Posol'stvo Artemiya Volynskogo v Iran v 1715-1718 gg.* (Moscow 1978), index.

66. VOC 2322 de Cleen to Batavia (30/09/1733 + app. 30/11/1733), f. 28-29vs.; VOC 2322 (12/09/1732), f. 294-vs.

had to pay. If they could not buy horses he would supply them and they could pay him back in three months. He selected a few chintzes, porcelain and rarities and told van Leijpsigh to be at Nader's palace with the goods and the three horses. The next day Nader refused to accept the presents and yelled at Mirza Taqi that he had ordered to take 200 *tumans* from the Dutch. Van Leijpsigh then supplied 10 horses and 12 mules at a cost of 158½ *tumans*, which were assessed at 106½ *tumans* only, or 52 *tumans* less than the amount for which Mirza Taqi had sold them to the Dutch. The remainder (93.5 *tumans*) they had to supply in cash, so that including the loss on the money transfer, the cost of borrowing money, and the usual 15% to the tax collectors (32 *tumans*) for their trouble, the Dutch paid 400 *tumans* in total, of which Nader only received 200 *tumans*. Because Leendert de Cleen, the VOC director in Gamron, expected more extortion, in October 1732 he decided to execute the decision taken on July 7, 1730 and to recall the VOC staff from Isfahan, the more so since Batavia had approved that decision on October 5, 1731. Exactly one year later de Cleen ordered the staff in Isfahan to depart for Gamron. Only the two interpreters and Joseph Sahid had to remain behind to report how things developed.[67]

Since Shah Tahmasp's removal Nader had not left the royal palace. Every time he devised new ways and means to oppress the people. He ordered that all landed property, houses, gardens, trees, orchards and farm animals had to be inventoried. All doors and windows of the Farahabad palace were collected and put into storage. It was also said that he would demolish the *talar* or open hall, which Shah Tahmasp had built in Sa`adatabad. Nader, who now called himself Tahmasp Khan (Tamas Chan), further ordered the large amount of jewels, gold and silverware, costly cloths and clothes in the royal palace to be inventoried and packed. The gold and silver, however, had to be melted. He paid his soldiers munificently, removed all books from the royal library and distributed the books and the pictures among the troops. He also ordered to count all Armenians and Banyans who then were ordered to pay money, while he also demanded his share of their daughters.[68]

In October 1732 Nader ordered the police officers (*ahdath*) to take all *nabab*s (Safavids male descendants in the female lines), *khankhan*s (chanchans; or sons of khan's), nobles and *qollar* (royal slaves) and their families to Qazvin. The royal harem with the baby-shah would follow. All eunuchs, with the exception of 15, were dismissed, and were given leave to go to Shah `Abdol-`Azim, Qom and Shah-e Cheragh (Shiraz) to spend the rest of their days in devotion. At mid-October the whole royal palace had been emptied and everything had been taken to Qazvin. Nader forced the population of Isfahan to buy the entire contents of the royal workhouses (from butter down to spices). Those unwilling were laid under the sticks. Nader also collected the revenues of the city and it dependencies, which they impossibly could pay, because the villages were all destitute and ruined. Before Nader left Isfahan he gave the last three sisters of Shah Soltan Hoseyn away in marriage; one to his brother Ebrahim Khan, one to Mirza Abu'l-Qasem, and one to Rahim Khan Gerayli (Rahiem Chan Geraaijlie). On October 5, 1732 the baby-shah left to Qazvin on the occasion of which Nader granted robes of honor

---

67. VOC 2322 (12/09/1732), f. 293 vs-302 vs; VOC 2584, Beschrijvinge, f. 1983-84; VOC 2322 de Cleen to Batavia (30/09/1733 + appendix of 30/11/1733), f. 29-31 (the 320 *tumans* borrowed in Isfahan cost 400 *tumans* in Gamron). The order to depart was not executed, because van Leijpsigh was not allowed to depart.

68. VOC 2322 (appendix 28/10/1732), f. 205-vs; VOC 2584, Beschrijvinge, f. 1984.

to many of his troops during a public *majles* or meeting. He himself left on October 13, 1732 via Golnabad, Sa`adatabad, Koh-e Soffeh and Najafabad to attack the Bakhtiyaris who had killed the governor that he had sent them. Meanwhile rumors circulated that Khorasan was up in arms against him, while Uzbeks and Turks were invading that province.[69]

Nader and a number of courtiers, such as Mohammad Rahim Khan (Mhamed Rahiem Chan), and the *khalifa al-kholafa* Mirza Kafi, had received a Russian envoy during four consecutive days. The envoy had given Nader four mirrors and furs, of a value of 150 *tuman*s, and a letter from the Russian general. On October 23, 1732 Mirza Kafi had been at the envoy's house to prepare papers that would be sent to the Russian commander at Baku. Nader also was said to have ordered to pay the arrears of Mashhad of 900 *tuman*s and 90 *tuman*s as a gift for the Russian general, of which 20 *tuman*s had already been paid. The envoy's defrayment was still being organized, while he was given the choice of residence in Isfahan or Qazvin. It was expected that he would reside in Isfahan, where he was staying in the house in which the French consul Gardanne had lived for some months during Ashraf's reign.[70] Nader also informed the *sharif* of Mecca, who had come to Isfahan to accompany in person the *hajj* caravan, and who in the past had received an annual present from the shah, that he had to leave, for he himself would pay a visit to Mecca to give him his annual present. Because of this and other events the *nabab* could not sleep since his appointment. However, he was sound of mind enough to remind the Dutch that the Russian envoy had gifted him thrice, the English twice and the Dutch not even once. To correct this unequal treatment van Leijpsigh had a present prepared for him.[71]

Since he had left Isfahan, Nader was fully occupied at Shushtar with the Arabs and the Bakhtiyaris who were said to cooperate with one another. In early October 1732 orders arrived in Isfahan to send Nader some cannons and ammunition. It was also said that many of his men and animals had died because of the cold.[72] Via the Bakhtiyari region and Shushtar, which suffered his fury, Nader marched to Baghdad and started its siege. Mohammad Qasem Beg, Hasan `Ali Khan's *nazer*, and the *mo`ayyer-bashi* told van Leijpsigh that Persian troops had plundered everything as far as Kirkuk and had enslaved 12,000 Turkish troops of which nine important leaders were brought to Isfahan on February 9, 1733 to be shown to its people. They were imprisoned in the citadel. Nader at the same time was preparing some vessels to ferry his troops across the river at Baghdad. Ahmad Pasha remained inside the city, which confirmed people in their opinion that a big Turkish army was approaching. A Frenchman, Lazare, arrived in Isfahan on October 26, 1732 who had traveled via Erzerum and Tabriz and left for Baghdad on December 27, 1732. It was said that he carried a letter from the prime minister of France. He received a daily allowance of 17 *mahmudi*s and a half *mann-e shah* of food per day. Later it was said that Nader had appointed him as overseer of the vessels to ferry the troops across the river and had promised him that he would send him back with a satisfying reply after

---

69. Ibid., f. 1985; Chan Jan son of Aslamas Chan gave Nader a present of 1,000 *tuman*s, as a result he and his father were still free. VOC 2322, van Leijpsigh to de Cleen (appendix 28/10/1732), f. 306 vs-307, 334vs-35vs.

70. VOC 2322 (28/10/1732), f. 307vs-309.

71. VOC 2322 (22/3/1733), f. 378vs-79. It is highly unlikely that the *sharif* of Mecca had come in person to Isfahan; it is more likely that this was one of his representatives.

72. VOC 2322, van Leijpsigh to de Cleen (20/11/1732), f. 911.

the victory. It was also generally said in Isfahan on February 2, 1732 that Nader publicly had sworn on the Koran to the army commanders that after the conquest of Baghdad he would restore Shah Tahmasp to power. On February 4, orders arrived to send him 400 carpenters and 500 smiths, which order was executed on February 11. On June 28, 1733 the *darugheh* of Isfahan quietly left Isfahan to complain about the excessive extortion of the population, which, instead of 24,000 *tuman*s, had to pay 50,000 *tuman*s.[73] It therefore was not uncommon to see even members belonging to great families go begging in the street for all people were ruined due to the taxation and exactions. For at that time there was nobody who was willing to give money for a house; on the contrary there were many who were willing to abandon house and hearth to move elsewhere, if only they would not be prevented from doing that or from being betrayed. Some people even committed suicide, just to be free of the continuous extortion and violence in early 1733. Because the Dutch did not expect any change for the better as long as the warlike operations continued in Persia van Leijpsigh advised that it would be better to abandon the Isfahan factory.[74]

On December 28, 1732 John Geekie the new EIC chief arrived in Isfahan. His predecessor William Cockill left on January 4, 1733 with their dispenser Mr. Rhee and with the fortune hunters the Italian Count Cherubin and M. Laporterie, who had come to Isfahan in February 1732 to seek service in Persia as engineers. However, apart from nice words they were not offered anything, and like so many others, they had become tired of it and left. The relationship with the English was good and van Leijpsigh wanted to keep it that way.[75]

NADER'S INQUIRY INTO THE LEGAL POSITION OF THE VOC

After Nader's departure for Baghdad, it was said that the Russian envoy had been able to influence Mirza Taqi (*monshi al-mamalek*) and the *kholafa* with rich presents to recommend Nader to examine the trading privileges of the Dutch and English. The idea being that he should revoke them and grant these privileges to Russian merchants. For these were richer and had greatly served Nader in the past. The Dutch and English only imported rags (i.e., textiles), which Persia could do without, while they exported large quantities of specie, which it needed. This had the desired effect and led to a thorough questioning and examination of the Dutch and English. Nevertheless, the Russian envoy only received 70 *mahmudi*s in copper money per day and only after much difficulty. The governor of Isfahan, the *nabab*, who was Nader's brother-in-law, had informed the Russian envoy to write to the empress that she had to ready her arms for Nader intended to wage war on her.[76]

On September 26, 1732 late in the evening, Havies Sulthoen, the *mehmandar-bashi*, came to the Dutch factory with orders from Nader to appear before him the next day at two hours p.m. The Dutch prepared a present consisting of spices, chintzes, Yazdi fabrics and shawls (total value 2,800 *mahmudi*s). On arrival the Dutch displayed the presents below the *talar* or verandah where Nader was seated. He looked at them and told his macebearer that

---

73. VOC 2269, Spahans Dagregister, f. 6607r-vs.

74. VOC 2584, Beschrijvinge, f. 1994-95; VOC 2322, van Leijpsigh to de Cleen, f. 389; VOC 2322 (22/03/1733), f. 362vs, 365 vs.

75. VOC 2322 (22/03/1733), f. 363 vs-64.

76. VOC 2322 (22/3/1733), f.364 vs-365.

van Leijpsigh was welcome and that he thanked him for the presents. If he had any requests he only had to tell Mirza Taqi. Then the Dutch were allowed to return to their factory. The Dutch preferred to wait to see what would happen with the EIC requests. On October 10, Mirza Taqi sent for the VOC interpreter to come and see him with the Dutch decrees. He told Joseph Sahid that Nader had instructed him to read them, after which he would inform the Dutch about his decision. Two days later the Dutch and the English agents as well as the Russian envoy, were sent for by Mirza Kafi Nasiri, the *kholafa*.[77] He told the Dutch and English agents that he had summoned them at the orders of Nader to discuss their treaty rights and that the Russian agent was there to act as a witness. The *kholafa* then sent for ʿAli Qoli Beg, the Portuguese renegade priest,[78] who had informed Nader that the Dutch had not fully respected the shah's rights in the past. The *kholafa* told van Leypsigh that he had been charged to examine their privileges. Nader wanted to grant them a new decree, whose privileges would be based on the one that the Dutch had concluded with ʿAbbas I. Van Leypsigh insisted that Nader should respect the text of the decree as granted by Shah Tahmasp II and confirmed by himself. ʿAli Qoli Beg then was asked to speak, who submitted that the Dutch had an obligation to buy 300 cargas of silk per year at 48 *tuman*s per carga and to give a present (*pishkesh*) in recompense for toll-free trade up to 20,000 *tuman*s per year. In this way the royal court had enjoyed an annual benefit of 12,000 *tuman*s, but after a few years the Dutch had only bought 100 cargas of silk at 44 *tuman*s on the basis of new privileges that had been negotiated with corrupt ministers. Moreover, in case the court delivered no silk the Dutch were not required to give the annual present. ʿAli Qoli Beg furthermore said that he had discovered that in 1712 the Dutch had paid 22,000 *tuman*s less to the royal court, because of their illegal export of specie. He therefore submitted that no money had been taken from the Dutch and that therefore a new treaty needed to be concluded.[79] The *kholafa* then said that all decrees granted by Shah Soltan Hoseyn were null and void as of now. Van Leijpsigh reacted that he had not been authorized to discuss that issue, about which he would have to report to Gamron, and repeated again his request that Nader respect his own recent confirmation of the decree. As to the fraud alleged by ʿAli Qoli Beg, van Leijpsigh said that the Dutch were no thieves and nobody had been shortchanged by them in the past. The *kholafa* said that the decrees had to be fetched from the *monshi al-mamalek* so that he could study them. Van Leijpsigh promised to do so. ʿAli Qoli then intervened and said that the Dutch had built a factory in Gamron, although foreigners were not allowed to build a fort in Persia. Moreover, that the Dutch had razed another fort in Gamron, which traditionally had been a refuge for the Moslem population. Furthermore, that after the flight of the Afghans the Dutch had taken possession of the citadel and had appropriated the best goods, which they had found there, and had only returned valueless items. The *kholafa* said that he had not asked ʿAli Qoli to come for these matters, but only on the matter of the privileges of the Europeans in Persia. He added that "The kingdom was in disorder and everybody had to strengthen his house to beat off the rebels. Nader has better knowledge about this than you."

---

77. On this person and function see Floor (2003).

78. For the story of this convert see Francis Richard. "Un Augustin portugais renégat, apologiste de l'islam chiite au début du XVIIIᵉ siècle," *Moyen Orient & Océan Indien* 1 (1984), pp. 73-85.

79. As to the terms of this treaty, the composition of the so-called treaty goods and the claim of payment for exported coins see Willem Floor, *The Commercial Conflict between Persia and the Netherlands, 1712-1718* (Durham University: Occasional Papers no. 37, 1988), pp. 3-4.

`Ali Qoli Beg could not be stopped, however, for he then started to harp on the nature of the VOC imports, which were only rags and tree bark that Persia could well do without and thus save its coin. The *kholafa* commented that if this were true he was right. Van Leijpsigh pointed out that previous shahs had all done quite well with the Dutch imports of fruits, rags, tree birch etc. as `Ali Qoli Beg preferred to call them. If not, they would not have invited the Dutch to come nor would they have suffered them for such a long time. The *kholafa* did not reply and only said that he wanted the royal decrees, which van Leijpsigh promised to obtain from the *monshi al-mamalek*.

The *kholafa* then started to question the EIC agent Cockill about the EIC rights. Geekie said that the EIC rights had been granted after the conquest of Hormuz, which rights were half of the revenues of Gamron (though they usually only received about 1,000 *tumans*), as well as free trade exempt from imposts. He wanted a confirmation of these rights. The *kholafa* told him as well to bring him the decrees, after which he dismissed the Dutch and English, though the Russian envoy stayed behind. The Dutch sent *kholafa* their decrees, who, after having read them, informed them that he would inform Nader as to their contents.

The *kholafa* called the three representatives again on October 16, 1732 to inform them that at Nader's orders they all had to go to the royal palace to discuss their decrees with the eunuch Agha Kamal, in the presence of the *kalantar* of Isfahan, Mirza Fathollah (Miersa Faatulla). Van Leijpsigh and Geekie went to the palace, where they later were joined by the Russian agent and `Ali Qoli Beg. The *kholafa* then told them that he would presently inform them about Nader's wishes. After having first discussed matters with Geekie he turned to van Leijpsigh who told him that in Isfahan he only had the royal decrees that had been confirmed by Nader. However, he could not discuss them, because he had not been authorized to do so. `Ali Qoli Beg then was invited again to relate his view of the Dutch privileges, after which the *kholafa* asked one of the clerks who was present to read out aloud the text of the main royal decree. The *kholafa* then asked van Leijpsigh why the Dutch had not bought 100 cargas of silk three years ago as they were obliged to do. Van Leijpsigh replied that the former Dutch agent, Schorer, had departed for Batavia with the new royal decree to obtain the approval of the governor-general. However, his ship had perished, so that unfortunately he has as yet received no orders and therefore could not trade in silk. Moreover, it would be ridiculous in view of the fact that he could not ask the shah to deliver silk that he did not have, for Gilan was in Russian hands. The *kholafa* reacted that his words were mere pretexts. The Dutch should have asked for silk to be delivered and if the royal court had been unable to do so there would have been no reason to have their present meeting, because now he had the right to demand the present (*pishkesh*) of the last three years. For maybe the royal court had bought silk at a loss from private merchants with a view to deliver it to the VOC. The Dutch had broken the agreement, which therefore was annulled. Besides, Nader did not want to hear anymore talk about Shah Soltan Hoseyn's decrees, for his ministers had deceived him, thinking only about lining their own pockets. The *kholafa* then asked how big VOC trade had been during the last three years. Van Leijpsigh replied that he did not know, because trade was carried out in Gamron, but he was afraid that it did not amount to much as the merchants there had been ruined. The *kholafa* then said that he would ask the governor and *shahbandar* of Gamron for that information. He then asked the Russian agent what the price of silk was in Rasht at that moment.

Semen Avramov replied that when he was there it was 60-70 *mahmudi*s per *mann-e shah*.[80] The *kholafa* made a quick calculation, using the price of 60, and said to his fellow courtiers that this represented a large sum due to the court and that this should be discussed. He also asked van Leijpsigh whether he had any comments, who answered that he would write to Gamron for instructions. However, 'Ali Qoli Beg, the renegade Portuguese priest, insisted that the VOC had to pay 22,000 *tuman*s. In 1714 Shah Soltan Hoseyn had taken 14,000 from the Dutch agent Macare as a partial payment, so that 8,000 *tuman*s remained to be paid. Van Leijpsigh reacted that if that were true how then it was possible that on the IOU the court had written that silk had been delivered as repayment of the loan. The *kholafa* asked van Leijpsigh how much the VOC had lent to Shah Soltan Hoseyn and for what reason. Van Leijpsigh replied that the VOC had lent 17,000 *tuman*s during the siege of Isfahan to pay the troops and therefore the Dutch had given him the money. "Had they done wrong in doing so as friends, and was it because of that reason that he was now treated in that manner," to which question he received no reply. The *kholafa* only observed that with the death of Shah Soltan Hoseyn his decrees had become null and void. Van Leijpsigh then asked whether this also applied to the royal debt to the VOC, because Nader did not want to pay it. If that was the case he asked leave to depart for Gamron. The Europeans then were offered lunch, during which time Nader was informed about the discussion. After lunch they each returned to their factory, though the Russian stayed for another half hour.

In the evening the *kholafa* informed the VOC dragoman that Nader (who had been seated behind the door of an adjoining room during the discussion) had ordered that the Dutch had to pay the annual present over the past three years to the *shahbandar* in Gamron. Van Leijpsigh considered this ridiculous and therefore went that same evening to the *kholafa*'s house and told him that he had no authority to do so and would not leave the factory until this matter had been properly resolved. The *kholafa* said that he would see what he could do. Fifteen minutes later one of his servants told van Leijpsigh that he was summoned to come and see Nader. He then rode to the palace where he did not see Nader, but the committee of three, which said that since he could not issue orders he had to sign an IOU promising payment of three year's of presents by New Year of 1733 in cash or in kind. Van Leijpsigh said that this was impossible and that Nader had best do right away what he had in mind rather then wait for another five months. The *kholafa* replied that if van Leijpsigh persisted in this manner things would only become worse for the Dutch and therefore it would be better to sign the IOU. Because if he refused to sign Nader surely would force him to sign it by giving him the bastinado. The *kholafa* then told him that he would send a servant to the Dutch factory with the IOU on October 17, 1732. Seeing that his opposition was of no use and to win time and get orders from Gamron van Leijpsigh acquiesced in the matter. The *kholafa*'s servants came very early the next morning and did not even allow van Leijpsigh to properly dress himself and forced him to sign immediately.

But the royal court was still not done with him, for van Leipsigh was sent for by Mir 'Abdol-Qasem (Mier Abdol Cassum), the governor of Isfahan, which city he held with 1,000 men. The governor told him that since there was nobody who could read Dutch van Leijpsigh

---

80. At that time, *kadkhoda-pesand* raw silk was sold in Isfahan at 20 *mahmudi*s per *mann-e shah* or 28 *tuman*s more than the court was allowed to charge the VOC (viz. 44 *tuman*s per carga of 36 *mann-e shah*). VOC 2322 (28/10/1732), f. 333vs.

had to write the Persian translation of the royal privileges next to the Dutch text and to affix his seal to the IOU. Moreover, a group of Armenians had to seal the IOU and act as security. Van Leijpsigh told him that he was surprised by this behavior. If the governor wanted to have a Persian translation then he had better write it himself, while he could not demand Armenians, who had nothing to do with the entire affair, to act as security and seal the document. The governor agreed to that, but insisted that the VOC interpreter seal the IOU and that the VOC brokers be security for van Leijpsigh, to ensure that he would not leave Isfahan. Van Leijpsigh was very disturbed about this turn of events, for it was clear that Nader wanted to harvest what he had not even sown, and he feared the violent treatment that would be in store for him. He also expected that Nader would make trouble for the Dutch in Gamron, whither he would sent Wakhtang Mirza as collector (*mohassel*) to demand the present (*pishkesh*) as well as to deal likewise with the English.[81]

Van Leijpsigh characterized the nature of the discussion with the court officials and Nader as follows: "If it is to his advantage he [Nader] refers to the decrees obtained by Ketelaar [in 1717]. When it is to his disadvantage he says that the decrees are void, without paying attention to the curses that are called upon him in those decrees [for breaking them]. This rebel is surrounded by flatterers and maligners." Van Leijpsigh, without approval from Gamron, paid a visit to Avramov to draw his attention to the excellent relations between the Netherlands and the Tsar Peter I; he hoped that this be reflected in Persia as well, what the agent promised to do. The Russian agent told van Leijpsigh that he had said to Nader that it would be better to keep the Europeans as friends rather than to treat them in this way and he promised van Leijpsigh that he would discuss the issue with Nader again. The fact that on November 10, 1732 Nader sent Ahmad Khan as an envoy to Russia with a large present consisting in pearls, precious stones, 3-4 lions, 2 tigers and 4-5 monkeys was interpreted as a sign of Nader's fear for Russia's power. Avramov had discussed the matter with Nader (as he told van Leijpsigh when riding by the Dutch factory), who said that he knew well that the Dutch had neither goods nor money in Isfahan, reason why he had demanded an IOU. However, he would never relinquish his claim on the annual treaty goods (*pishkesh*). At the Russian's suggestion van Leipsigh wrote to Nader asking for the return of the IOU, but he received no immediate reply.[82]

The governor of Isfahan constantly pestered the Dutch about presents for Nader in connection with the outstanding dispute about their privileges. He threatened to demand from him the money which Nader had assigned on the Europeans from Gamron and on January 20, 1733 he sent his steward (*nazer*) to tell van Leijpsigh that only a few days were left before the IOU would become due. The Dutch were instructed to pay on time, to have the goods ready for transportation to Baghdad or at least its corresponding value. At least half of the payment had to be in cash anyway, for Nader needed that badly. Van Leijpsigh replied that he still had not received a reply from Gamron and that there was still three months time. Moreover, he had sent Nader a letter about this issue, so he asked the governor to have patience. The governor said that he would not wait, and, if need be, he would confiscate the VOC factory and its contents, for he was lord and master in Isfahan. Maybe, he would not even allow van Leijpsigh

---

81. The description of the discussion resulting in the demand of the IOU is based on VOC 2322, van Leijpsigh to de Cleen (12/09/1732 + appendix 28/10/1732), f. 312vs-332vs, unless otherwise indicated.

82. VOC 2322 (28/10/1732), f. 313-333 vs.

the only thing he then possessed, his life. The governor meanwhile also threatened the Banyans who stood security for the payment of the Dutch IOU. The latter however pointed out that this only held in case van Leijpsigh fled or left and then only on the date due. Van Leijpsigh asked to speak to the governor himself who did not consider this necessary since his wishes had been made known by his *nazer*. He informed van Leijpsigh that if he would pay him 6,000 *tuman*s (half the amount due) he would induce Nader to grant a respite for the remainder. Van Leijpsigh replied that he did not even have 50 *mahmudi*s, to which the governor only uttered threats. Van Leijpsigh therefore visited the governor on January 21 himself and was received friendly. He listened to van Leijpsigh's arguments and said that Nader would never accept these. As a friend he advised him to pay. For in case of non-payment Nader would become angry and sent him 30 rough Khorasani soldiers to get the money by whatever means. He added: "Do not you know that the *vakil* does not care at all that the country becomes a ruin or whether trade is carried on. The only thing he cares about is whether his troops are well dressed and kept." In order to prevent any further trouble van Leijpsigh gave the governor a present, after having received a reminder to that effect and he sent a letter to Nader. He also asked `Ali Mardan Khan, the ambassador to India, who had arrived in Isfahan on March 12, to intercede for the Dutch. Because the road between Isfahan and of Baghdad was unsafe due to troops and robbers his messenger left with the governor to Baghdad.

On November 13, 1732 the Dutch in Gamron decided to transport Mohammad `Ali Khan, Nader's ambassador to India to make Nader more amenable to their needs, also because the English had offered to do so. Because van Leijpsigh had informed de Cleen that there was a plan to arrest the chief of both the EIC and VOC (the English had the same information) the chiefs did not welcome Mohammad `Ali Khan in person when he arrived in Gamron on December 18, 1732. `Ali Mardan Khan returned from India with a Moslem ship on December 28, 1732. At that time, Wakhtang Mirza had also arrived in Gamron. It was his task to collect the treaty goods from the Dutch as well as to discuss the dispute with the EIC about their share in the customs revenues. De Cleen used that opportunity to discuss the outstanding issue with all of them (including the new and old *shahbandars*) to induce them to write a letter to Nader supporting the Dutch position. The inducement included presents and horses which were in short supply. The Dutch indeed received the required letters, stating that the Dutch were right in their interpretation of the royal decrees, and which were forwarded to Isfahan on February 4, 1733. Van Leijpsigh reported that Nader disagreed with that interpretation, but that he would not insist on payment, but given the Dutch friendship for the shah and their services to his ambassador, he granted them the treaty goods and would return the IOU. However, it was necessary to reach a clear agreement about the payment of customs duties and other imposts.[83]

On April 8, 1733 the messenger returned with Nader's reply. Van Leijpsigh was not to be molested for as long as he had not received a reply from Gamron. However, the moment this would arrive they were allowed to collect the money immediately. Moreover, van Leijpsigh was urged to speed up the matter. The messenger told van Leijpsigh that none of the courtiers (`Abu'l-Qasem, the *khalifeh*, and Mirza Taqi) had dared to put the request to Nader. It was only the French adventurer Lazare, who had much influence with Nader, who had done so. In reaction, Nader had written his decision (*ta`liqeh*) on the petition. Van Leipsigh therefore decided

---

83. VOC 2322 de Cleen (30/09/1733 + appendix of 30/11/1733), f. 30vs-42vs, 45-46.

to send the interpreter, Joseph Sahid, to the army camp in Baghdad with presents for Lazare. Sahid reported that food was difficult to get en route and twice as expensive as normal.[84]

On arrival in Baghdad, Joseph Sahid contacted `Ali Mardan Khan, because M. Lazare was absent. He told Sahid that he had discussed the issue with Nader, who after having explained the issue to him, had replied that he would not make things too difficult for the Dutch. `Ali Mardan Khan then informed him that the VOC interpreter was in Baghdad. He told Sahid that Nader knew neither mercy nor pity, that he was mercurial, and that he was wroth to let even one *mahmudi* go. It was better to await Lazare's return, because none of the courtiers or counselors had the nerve the raise the subject with Nader. When Lazare returned early June 1733, he organized an audience for Sahid with Nader, who was only attended by the *mo`ayyer-bashi* and Mostafa Khan. Sahid gave de Cleen's letter as well as the request by Wakhtang Mirza to the receiver of requests (`arz-begi). Nader said that the Dutch had written him already several times, but that he had not yet replied. He would read the documents and send for them in two days' time. He told Sahid that he would not be unreasonable. After four days a public crier (*jarchi*) came for Lazare and Sahid with orders to join Nader. Also present were the *mo`ayyer-bashi* and Mirza Taqi Shirazi. Nader asked Joseph Sahid to state what was in the request. Mirza Taqi was then ordered to read Mohammad `Ali Khan's and Wakhtang Mirza's requests. Joseph Sahid added that the meaning of decrees was clear, viz. that the treaty goods were only due when silk was supplied by the shah. Since the Russians held Gilan there was no silk. Nader then asked: "what is the quantity of and in what do these treaty goods consist?" Mirza Taqi read the list aloud and Nader asked: "what is their value in cash?" Joseph Sahid replied that at the time of the issuance of the decree the value was 500-600 *tumans*. Nader then asked Mirza Mehdi to read their request aloud so that he might know what the Dutch exactly wanted. Nader said that he had a positive opinion about the services that the Dutch had rendered, while others also had written in a positive sense about them. However, he started to laugh when it was read that the Dutch would depart from Persia if the court did not respect the latest decree. Nader said: "what kind of pretext is this? They have always been here and have always traded with us, for there always has been friendship between them and the shah. These treaty goods are a trifle, I will write that we will return the IOU." Lazare in addition mentioned that the Russian agent also had maligned the Dutch. Nader then replied: "what a shit is this Simayun; it is none of his business, why should I listen to him?" Lazare pointed out that Simayun (Semen Avramov) had come to trade and therefore wanted to oust the other Europeans. Nader reacted: "What can he import, but some leather? We know quite well who is of more use to us." Nader then addressed Joseph Sahid and said, "I give up my claim and will give orders to return the IOU. However, once Gilan is again in our possession, does that mean that the Dutch will give me the treaty goods?" Lazare then replied that if the court would supply silk the Dutch would give the goods. Nader then said let them come and buy silk in Gilan and give me the goods. The *mo`ayyer-bashi*, to make things difficult, suggested that Nader, while relinquishing the IOU, would need a commitment for this year's treaty goods. Joseph Sahid said that this was not proper to which Nader acquiesced. He then asked how much silk the Dutch would buy. When he was told that the silk would be delivered in cargas of 36 *mann-e shah*, he calculated that this would be 72 *mann-e Tabriz*. As to the price, Joseph Sahid pointed out that

---

84. VOC 2322, Van Leijpzigh to de Cleen (appendix 28/10/1732), f. 312vs-326; Ibid, idem to idem (22/03/1733) f. 370vs-76 vs; VOC 2322 (01/05/1733), f. 396 vs.

the royal decree had fixed the price at 44 *tumans*. Nader once again made a calculation and said that this would result in 80 *mahmudi*s per *mann-e Tabriz*, but Sahid said that it would be 60 *mahmudi*s. Nader then asked which quality silk the Dutch wanted, to which Sahid replied that this also had been stipulated in the decree. "How is that realized?" asked Nader, to which Sahid pointed out that this was done on the basis of a sample as stated in the decree. Nader then said that he would write to Gamron that de Cleen (the VOC director) had to send people to Gilan immediately and to deliver the treaty goods in Isfahan. Joseph Sahid then pointed out that it was the custom that the goods were transported to Isfahan after the silk had been delivered there. Nader ordered to check whether the decree stated as much. He further said: "why should not we agree upon a new treaty text, do away with the treaty goods, and fix an annual gift?" Joseph Sahid said that he was but the interpreter and could not negotiate a treaty. Nader then said to Mirza Taqi Shirazi: "Thamas Miersa is about to come here and I will leave for Khorasan, we therefore will send them a non-committal reply." Later the Dutch might finalize the text with Tahmasp Mirza in any manner they liked, which words he repeated twice. However, Nader insisted on the Dutch buying silk in Gilan and delivering their merchandise in Isfahan. Joseph Sahid submitted that it was impossible for Gamron to send 4,000 *tumans* to buy silk, to have staff available to buy silk, and to deliver the goods. Nader then wanted to know why this was not possible. Sahid pointed out that Gamron was ruined, the roads were unsafe, and pack animals were difficult to get. In the past, the VOC normally had a turnover of 20,000 *tumans* per year, but this was not anymore the case. Nader then said that the Dutch had to send someone with plenipotentiary authority to negotiate new terms, after which he gave Sahid leave to depart. The next day, the requests were returned to Sahid with Nader's decisions written on them.[85]

Van Leijpsigh threw a party to celebrate the good news that he had received on July 1, 1733. He reported that Nader wanted Gamron to write to Batavia to send a plenipotentiary to discuss the Dutch rights and demand new decrees to avoid future misunderstanding, for he still insisted on payment of the treaty goods if there was no silk trade. However, because of the friendship between the two nations and the services rendered he wanted to make a gesture. The English had received a similar order. The IOU had not yet been returned because the officials wanted to see the original apostil (*ta`liqeh*).[86]

THE SIEGE OF BAGHDAD AND CONTINUED FISCAL OPPRESSION

The royal palace was deserted by April 25, 1733 when Agha Kamal left with the princesses and the other women to Qom. Only gardeners and doormen lived in it. The entire stores of the royal workshops (butter, firewood, wheat, barley, medicines, spices, tents and other textiles) were forced upon the inhabitants of Isfahan and the Banyans who had to buy this; they were encouraged to do so by receiving a sound beating. In Isfahan there was no trade anymore, for nobody had any money. The *`abbasi* had a value of 3.5 *mahmudi*s and the ducats had a value of only of 25-25.5 *mahmudi*s copper money.[87]

---

85. VOC 2322 II (16/06/1733), f. 16-18, 20-37.

86. VOC 2322 (03/07/1733), f. 403-04 vs., Ibid. (10/07/1733), f. 905-07 vs; VOC II 2322 text of the ta`liqeh, f. 15.

87. VOC 2322 (appendix 28/10/1732), f. 334; Ibid., (01/05/1733), f. 401 vs.

On July 12, 1733 tax collectors arrived in Isfahan to demand 24,000 *tuman*s, although they took 50,000 *tuman*s, about which the *darugheh* of Isfahan was so incensed that he went to Nader's army camp to lodge a complaint. The city and villages were almost empty of people (many of whom had fled) so that hardly anybody was seen in the streets. On July 17, 1733 the Dutch reported that in the past days money had been taken by force from the people in Isfahan and that even officials received the bastinado. The tax collectors made it known that 1 `abbasi` white money had to be accepted without any agio and that 10 *paisa*s of copper money only valued 4 *paisa*s. Further that bread had to cost only 1 *mahmudi*. "The authorities have gone mad" the Dutch commented, "for everything is getting more expensive. For one `abbasi` was equal to 80 *paisa*s and is now equal to 100 *paisa*s. Bread is now 10 *paisa*s per *mann* higher in price, for the *mann-e shah* is bought for 40 *paisa*s and because now 10 *paisa*s have to be accepted at the value of 4 *paisa*s the price of one *mann-e shah* is 50 *paisa*s." This of course was impossible and the money-changers immediately left.[88] Nader also used other means to get money of which the Dutch relate one interesting example. Someone in Isfahan borrowed 20,000 *tuman*s and bought hoof irons and horse shoes with it. He then went to Nader's army at Baghdad to sell them, where there was a great need for them. He was able to make 150,000 *tuman*s. As soon as Nader learnt about this he sent for the man. He asked from whom he had borrowed the 20,000 *tuman*s. Having learnt the moneylender's name Nader immediately sent a courier (*chapar*) to Isfahan to demand the IOU and inform the man that the 20,000 served to pay off his taxes. He finally took 145,000 from the merchant who had to be satisfied with 5,000 *tuman*s.[89]

Meanwhile, Ahmad Pasha continued to fire his cannons at the besieging force. The Persian army before Baghdad numbered 300,000 men according to the VOC dragoman. Of these only 100,000 were actually soldiers, 80,000 horse and 20,000 foot, and all were battle hardened. The remainder consisted of servants, Turkish slaves, traders and artisans. There was a lot of food and fodder, although not as cheap as it should be, he commented. A quantity of 12 *mann-e Tabriz* of wheat cost 200 *mahmudi*s and even at that price it was difficult to get. Joseph Sahid was convinced that Baghdad would shortly fall, while Basra was also besieged.[90] The situation in Baghdad, which was tightly contained, was the reverse. Hunger was the great problem of which 60,000 people died during the siege. The price of 70 lbs. of wheat or barley during the siege was 8,000 *mahmudi*s (Dfl. 340), while Ahmad Pasha still had only two horses. (After the Persian defeat the price of wheat fell to 18 *mahmudi*s). The hunger became so serious that on June 1, 1733 or thereabouts Ragoel Effendi[91] came to parley with 25 persons with Nader. Three days later the latter sent some negotiators to the city who returned with Ragoel Effendi and Ahmad Pasha's son-in-law. After their talks Nader sent Mirza Taqi Shirazi to Ahmad Pasha as his deputy. The Turks promised to return all Persian slaves in Baghdad; they further would pay a substantial amount of money and would return all that which had been taken from the shah. Further 200 leading citizens would serve as hostages until they had written to the Porte

---

88. VOC 2269, Spahans dagregister, f. 6608-vs.

89. VOC 2584, Beschrijvinge f. 2004-05. The Dutch called Nader a 'Nero'. VOC 2322, de Cleen to Batavia (30/09/1733 + appendix of 30/11/1733), f. 129 vs.

90. VOC 2322 II. Joseph Sahid to van Leijpsigh (16/06/1733), f. 16, 20, 37-41; VOC 2584, Beschrijvinge f. 2002.

91. I have been unable to identify this person.

to return all Persian territory and all Persian slaves held on Turkish territory on the condition that Nader would withdraw to Kermanshah. The border between Persia and Turkey would be the same as before, and only then Nader had to return the hostages. The latter reacted: "Baghdad is already mine; they had better deliver it to him, in which case he was willing to discuss a general peace agreement as well as other disputes." As a result of that situation each day some 10 to 20 Janissaries and others deserted Baghdad. Mohammad Rahim Khan, with some troops, was sent to reconnoiter the approaching Turkish relief force. He went about 70 German miles north of Baghdad and did not find the approaching army. The Persian force plundered what they could lay there hands on and enslaved many people. The Frenchman Lazare also was in his company, and only returned to Baghdad at the beginning of June 1733. He was well received by Nader, who took off his own *kurdi*, or sleeveless overcoat, made of heavy yellow broadcloth, and gave that as a present to Lazare. Mohammad Rahim Khan fared less well. He was demoted and was sent to Khorasan. The only courtiers which were still in Nader's good graces were the *mo'ayyer-bashi* and Mirza Taqi. But Persian territory was not treated differently. For example, Nader sent some troops under a *sardar* to Kermanshah who pillaged that town, enslaved its population, and took all food supplies with them, which greatly relieved the army's situation. In November 1732, some cannon and ammunition was sent to Baghdad where it was said that many soldiers and animals had died because of the cold.[92]

NADER'S DEFEAT AT BAGHDAD

Both before and after Nader's defeat at Baghdad the Bakhtiyaris had closed all roads around Isfahan and plundered all coming and going traffic. They even killed *rahdar*s or road-guards at Urchini, at six German miles from the city. In September 1733, the situation on the roads had somewhat improved.[93]

Nader did not want to maintain the peace with the Porte and had sent a message to Ahmad Pasha that he had to prepare himself, for the peace was at an end and he would come to pay him a visit. Ahmad Pasha informed Istanbul and asked for reinforcements, which arrived in the form of 50,000 troops plus an equal number en route from Erevan. However, these had orders not to advance further because of the approaching winter. In the summer of 1734 these troops would be strengthened by troops from Europe and then the combined force had to attack Nader. It was further rumored that Tahmasp II had apologized for Nader's behavior.[94] In fact, on September 2, 1733 the "former vakanevies (*vaqaye'-nevis*), Mirza Qeyas? (Miersa Keyraas) informed van Leijpsigh that he had received a letter from the *kholafa* (gollofa) from Mazandaran. In that letter the *kholafa* had written that the shah [Tahmasp Mirza] was hunting, that he a good steward, 30 servants, and that there were no guards. The shah had already sent for his family from Mashhad. Tahmasp Khan (Tamas Chan =Nader) also was said to have given orders to bring the rest of the family to Mazandaran, including the little 'Abbas III.

---

92. VOC 2322 (29/11/1732), f. 911 vs.

93. VOC 2322 II (11/09/1733), f. 236.

94. VOC 2322 Hey to de Cleen (27/08/1733), f. 416vs-417.

Tamas Chan [=Nader] also had had told the shah that he had not forgotten his promise to put him on the throne again, but he first had to resolve the problem with the Turks."[95]

Nader abandoned the siege of Baghdad on the approach of the Turkish relief force, which was said to be 250,000 men strong. He had left Mohammad Khan Baluch in charge of the siege with 15,000 men, and moved against the Turkish relief force with 150,000 men. The battle was engaged on July 17, 1733. The Turks retreated faced with Nader's fury and abandoned their artillery. However, after fierce fighting, which lasted till after sunset, the Turks were able to force Nader, who himself had fought like a lion and had received two wounds, to withdraw and flee under the protective cover of the night. When Mohammad Khan Baluch learnt about the battle's result from fleeing soldiers he moved with 4,000 cavalry to Shushtar leaving 12,000 foot soldiers, 12 fieldpieces and many supplies in his camp at Baghdad. When Ahmad Pasha learnt this from deserters he ordered a sortie, which was able to kill the Persians and to return safely with their booty in the city. During the siege as many as 60,000 people had died of hunger. Topal Pasha, the *sar`askar*, arrived at Baghdad and held discussions with Ahmad Pasha. He sent a certain Fulad Pasha (Polat Basha) with 50,000 horsemen to Kermanshah to secure that town and to destroy Hamadan and environing settlements. After three days Topal Pasha returned with his army to Kirkuk to await further orders from the court.[96] The news of Nader defeat was received on July 27, 1733 in Basra.[97]

THE BASRA INTERMEZZO

On July 26, 1732 van Leijpsigh had reported that Nader not only intended to march against Baghdad but he also had designs on Basra. He was said to have sent 6,000 men to Kerman in order to march via Shiraz and Kuhgilu against that town recruiting more troops en route. He immediately informed the VOC factory in Basra about this news. This news was also confirmed from Kerman, through which town these 6,000 men indeed passed as well as from Basra whence it was reported on December 15, 1732 that it was said that Nader had written to Hoveyzeh and Dowraq to join their forces and attack Basra. He would send them a khan to assist them. One day later the Dutch wrote in their diary that the Armenian merchants in Basra had received secret orders from their principals in Isfahan to leave that town at the orders of Nader. These rumors also reached the ears of the Turkish governor who on January 2, 1733 ordered the population to arm itself in connection with an expected attack from the Persians who were preparing themselves at Hoveyzeh.[98]

On January 3, 1733 orders from Nader were received to seize all ships and vessels at Bushehr to use them for action against Basra. He was also said to have appointed already a gov-

---

95. VOC 2269, Spahans Dagregister, f. 6611. See also VOC 2323, f. 970 (March 1) where the same *kholofa* told on February 28, 1733 after his return in Isfahan that Tahmasp Mirza would be reinstated on the throne and that Nader had sent for him to that end.

96. VOC 2322 Hey to de Cleen (19/08/1733), f. 427-8; VOC 2322 Hey to de Cleen (05/08/1733), f. 425.

97. VOC 2269, Extract Daghregister Bassoura, f. 6612; VOC 2322, Hey to de Cleen (05/08/1733), f. 425; VOC 2584, Beschrijvinge, f. 2007-08.

98. VOC 2322, Dames Hey (Basra) to de Cleen (15/12/1732), f. 423-vs; VOC 2269, Extract Daghregister Bassoura, f. 6612 (16/12/1732 and 02/01/1733).

ernor of Basra, viz. Agha Jamal, his *na'eb* who was in charge of the royal harem, which was at Qom at that time. On January 25, 1733 it was reported that the Persians had abandoned their plan to attack Basra and were enslaving a lot of women and children in Hoveyzeh, who were sold for 15-20 *mahmudi*s per person. However, from April till mid-May 1733, a Persian force supported by rebellious Arabs constantly threatened Basra. On April 1, 1733, villagers fled into Basra because Bin Milaan[99] and his rebels had reached the village of Jesagier [probably the Jazayer district] at 15 German miles from Basra. The headman, Mier Nama, fled because, contrary to his people, he refused to join the rebels, which they did out of fear of being plundered and murdered. The headman reported that Bin Milaan had orders from Nader to take Basra and appoint Mullah 'Ali as its governor. After the threatening moves subsided somewhat the rebels sent an order from Nader to one of the local Arab chiefs, Mohammad Mane' (Mhamed Mana), in which he was offered the governorship of Basra, if he joined forces with Mir Sa'id Khan (Mier Saed Chan), the Arab commander of the Persian force in Jesahier (Jazayer district). Mohammad Mane' took Mir Sa'id Khan prisoner when he had made him believe to accept his offer on July 9, 1733. That same night he took Mir Sa'id Khan into Basra. This put an end to the Persian threat, or so it was believed, for the news of Nader's defeat at Baghdad was received on July 27, 1733 in Basra.[100] However, Nader marched to Shushtar after his defeat at Baghdad to suppress the Mohammad Khan Baluch and Sheikh Ahmad Madani revolt. On January 14, 1734 the Dutch factory at Basra recorded in its journal that, "Molla Mhamed prince of Havize received information that Tamas Chan had arrived there [i.e., Hoveyzeh] and marches on Shushter and then on the Gaab [Cha'b or Ka'b Arabs] inhabitants of the island of Qobban (Gaban)[101] as well as on other Arabs to enforce their obedience." On January 20, 1734 the same source reported that, "according to information from merchants from Suster, Tamas Chan has pardoned the rebels with the exception of the Tjaabs [Ka'b Arabs] against whom he has sent a certain Chan Kasom Chan with 5,000 men to destroy their Sheikh Farajollah (sjeeg Ferae houla)." Nader also sent a letter to the *motasallem* of Basra, which was received on January 26, warning him not to give protection to any of the Arabs whom he was pursuing. Also to send him five galleys well-equipped with crews and military supplies. In reply the *motasallem* sent on January 26, 1734 a certain Khalifeh Efendi (Galiff Evendi) with five galleys towards Haffar (Affaar) where Nader's troops were said to be. On January 31, the *motasallem* sent the grains and butter that Nader had demanded. On February 5, 1734 a vessel from Bushehr brought news of the total defeat of Mohammad Khan Baluch and his supporters. Two days later the Persian khan at Qobban (Gaban) sent a letter to the *motasallem* asking him for food and fodder. On Febrary 10, 1734 five galleys left Basra for Qobban with food supplies and fodder. On February 13 and 14 news was received in Basra that the Persian troops had chased the

---

99. I have not been able to identify this person. He probably is a chief of the Bani Lam, see S.H. Longrigg, *Four Centuries of Modern Iraq* (London, 1925), p. 156.

100. VOC 2269, Extract Daghregister Bassoura, f. 6612-12 vs (on f. 6613 reaction of the *motasallem* of Basra regarding the Persian attack); VOC 2322, Hey to de Cleen (05/08/1733), f. 425; On July 12, 1733 tax collectors arrived in Isfahan to demand 24,000 *tuman*s, and even government officials were given the bastinado to get money, for the city and villages were almost empty of people (many of whom had fled). VOC 2584, Beschrijvinge, f. 2007-08.

101. On these events and the Ka'b Arabs see Willem Floor, "The Rise and Fall of the Banu Ka'b. A borderer state in Southern Khuzestan," *Iran* (2006), p. 277–315.

Ka`b (Tjaabs) and other Arabs into a castle at Qobban, where they were besieged. The Arabs had released Persian prisoners of war.[102]

CONTINUED MILITARY OPERATIONS AT BAGHDAD AND FISCAL OPPRESSION

On July 27, 1733 van Leijpsigh learnt that the officials had to leave Isfahan at Nader's orders and he therefore tried to get the IOU back from the governor. Mirza Rahim was willing to do so, but the *mostowfi* could not find the document. On August 2, 1733 when he visited the new governor Ebrahim Khan (the ex-*nazer* of Shah Tahmasp) he again asked for the document, the same day that the news of Nader's defeat and flight was received. The officials present all claimed that the document was not in Isfahan, but that Mirza `Abdol-Qasem had it, who would soon be in Isfahan. Nader was said to have attacked Turkish forces with fury, but had been repulsed and lost 50,000 men and all his baggage and artillery. He was said to have withdrawn to Hamadan where he ordered Laporterie to cast 20 cannons and 2 mortars. Moreover, money had to be collected from the population. However, this time most villagers shot at the tax collectors with real bullets. On August 2, Nader's chief gunner, `Ali Khan Beg, arrived in Isfahan to have new cannons cast, while the *mo`ayyer bashi* and *darugheh* and other officials were collecting tents and clothes, with which they left for Hamadan on August 4, 1733. Nader sent for new troops from Khorasan and allowed only his own *chapars* to move over the roads.[103] In August 1733, an Afghan with 15 men arrived from Hamadan as envoy from Nader to Hoseyn Khan Ghalzai. He was said to offer him Kerman, Yazd, Shiraz and other lower lands in exchange for troops. At the same time it was rumored that the Bakhtiyari-Lors had accepted a king, whose name was `Ali Shah (Alie Sjah). They had already started to collect the royal revenues in the surrounding villages.[104]

It was said on August 5, 1733 that Nader was at Bohrez (Bohris) at 8 [German] miles from Baghdad. He had lost only 500 of his horse, but all his foot (40,000) including his baggage, clothes, artillery and animals. On the other side of the bridge 15,000 men had remained, commanded by Khan Jan, Mohammad Khan, Mohammad Reza Khan, and Mohammad Rahim Khan. On August 6, 1733 the *mo`ayyer-bashi* and the *darugheh* arrived with orders to inspect the accounts of the officials and to recruit troops to get tents, artillery, clothes and other baggage ready and to depart from Isfahan after 40 days. Nader had dismissed the whole *ordu-bazar* and kept only some sword sharpeners, blacksmiths and saddle makers.[105]

The *mo`ayyer-bashi* ordered to open all shops and he demanded 90,000 *tuman*s in cash and 10,000 tents from the inhabitants of Isfahan. For the new cannons, still to be cast, he assigned 2,000 *tuman*s on the inhabitants, to be paid to the *tupchi-bashi*, `Ali Khan Beg. The *mo`ayyer-bashi* allegedly had said that Nader only had 10,000 men with him and that many of his soldiers had perished of thirst during their flight. Nader also had sent some men to the former Shah Tahmasp to bring him to Mazanderan. On August 14, 1733 it was reported that

---

102. VOC 2323, Extract Bassouras Dagverhaal, f. 2041-51.

103. VOC 2322 II (11/09/1733), f. 236-41, 249; VOC 2269, Spahans Dagregister, f. 6608 vs (03/08/1733).

104. VOC 2322 II (11/09/1733), f. 250.

105. VOC 2322, de Cleen to Batavia (30/09/1733 + appendix 30/01/1733), f. 62vs-64; VOC 2269, Spahans Dagregister, f. 6609 vs-10 (05 and 06/08/1733).

Nader had put a Turkish envoy, who had offered peace, on a donkey after having him ridiculed by his army. He sent him back with the message "in three months time I will be back, and then I also will take Istanbul itself."[106]

Nader was unperturbed, for when some officials drew his attention to the sorry state of the people and pointed out that they would not be able to pay what had been demanded from them, he replied: "if they are not able to pay I want you to get it from them willy-nilly. If not, I'll send 500 horsemen to sell them with their wives and children to get my money. Now I also want to have an additional 13,500 *tumans* for the horses who have died during the [1733] Baghdad siege." The officials seeing that things only would get worse if they pressed the matter dropped it and executed Nader's orders. Another example of Nader's callous attitude was that having heard that people were talking about his tyrannical behavior he asked one of his courtiers: "How is it that they talk so much about me, for I have not come to leave the country in peace and quiet, but to turn everything upside down, since I am not a human being, but I am God's wrath and punishment," with which the Dutch reporter concurred.[107]

On September 11, 1733 Khan Jan (also called Aslamas Khan) returned to Isfahan to recuperate for a few days. At that time Mirza Taqi bypassed Isfahan coming from Shiraz via Najafabad to proceed to Hamadan to reinforce Nader with money and 2,000 men. The *vakil* Tahmasp Beg Jalayer also had joined Nader about that time coming with only 150 men from Khorasan. Nader, meanwhile, was making plans to attack the Turks and fortified Hamadan. In Isfahan he had chains made to be used for striking a bridge over the river near Baghdad [f. 876].[108]

On September 14 the *tupchi-bashi*, `Ali Khan Beg, accompanied against his will by Laporterie, a Flemish adventurer, left Isfahan with 22 pieces of cannon and 2 mortars. That same day rumors circulated that the former Shah Tahmasp II was collecting troops and that coins had been struck in his name. The next day the *kadkhoda*s of Isfahan were arrested to ascertain who had brought the new `abbasi of Shah Tamasp into the city; though it was believed that the money had been struck in Isfahan itself. On September 16, 1733 the counterfeiter was caught and taken to Ebrahim Khan, the governor of Isfahan. The man claimed that he wanted to find out whether people still supported Shah Tahmasp's cause and to encourage the undecided. However, he had experienced that nobody cared for Shah Tahmasp anymore and he regretted his deed. Ebrahim Khan had laughed about this and let him go. Whether the governor really considered it a laughing matter, or that he wanted to be on the safe side is unknown. However, at that time rumors persisted about the growing army of Shah Tahmasp, which fell only 20,000 short of Nader's army of 70,000 that faced with a Turkish army of 600,000. [f. 877-78]. [Although these data are, of course, unreliable it shows the uncertainty that prevailed about the real military-political situation]

---

106. VOC 2269, Spahans Dagregister, f. 6610 (06/08/1733).

107. VOC 2584, Beschrijvinge f. 2006-07.

108. The description of the events from September 13, 1733 till July 3, 1734 are all based on VOC 2323, Extract van 'tSpahans Dagregister (Summary of the Isfahan Diary) unless otherwise stated. For easy reference the relevant folio numbers have been given in the text. The dates also serve as an easy reference guide.

UNCERTAIN SITUATION AND OPPRESSION
IN ISFAHAN

On September 26, 1733 rumors were circulated in Isfahan that the *vakil*, Tahmasp Beg, would come to the city. On hearing this rumor many people fled the city out of fear to be exposed to his tyranny once more. It moreover was said that he had orders to levy a contribution of 8,000 *tuman*s from the population of Isfahan and 7,000 *tuman*s from the leading officials (Mirza Fath-ollah 4,000, Mirza Qasem 2,000, Gholam Reza 1,000 and from the *mostowfi* also 1,000 *tuman*s). It was also said that he had orders to confiscate the property of 'Ali Mardan Khan Feyli. A lot of other rumors were circulating at that time about Nader's killings of officials, of demotions, appointments, his own military position and that of the former Shah Tahmasp. The Lurs, although having left the area around Isfahan, were still in revolt, in which they were joined by the Ardalan Kurds. Apparently the support for the ex-shah was still considerable, for it was also reported that Mirza Taqi was arrested by Nader when he put about that Nader had intentions to become shah himself, which rumor would have had led to an uprising by the army, if he had not stopped his mouth [f. 881-87].

On October 17, 1733 the new *kalantar* of Isfahan[109] and the other officials and *kad-khoda*s returned from court having been totally fleeced. Because the *kadkhoda*s had praised Nader and had said that they were but his slaves, and that they were even prepared to sell their wives and children for him if they had no money anymore they had been given robes of honor. The news of Tahmasp Beg's coming was confirmed, and also that he had orders to levy 8,000 *tuman*s from them; many people therefore left Isfahan. Houses to quarter the *vakil*'s men were emptied of the people living there, while the population also had to provide carpets, bedding, pots and pans to which every family had to contribute [f. 890-91].

Tahmasp Beg also had orders to stock supplies for three months for the coming winter and to prepare a campaign against the rebellious Sunnis in Fars. Before Tahmasp Beg entered Isfahan he had killed the population of two villages outside Isfahan, whom he wrongly believed to be Bakhtiyaris. At sunset October 22, 1733 Tahmasp Beg entered the city and made it immediately public that henceforth he had to be called *sardar* and anyone calling him *vakil* would be fined two ducats (Dfl. 894). The next day the kettledrums were beaten because Nader had scored a small victory over the Turks at Kirkuk [f. 892-95].

Meanwhile the *sardar* was busy making an inventory of what he needed and to collect it from the population. It was estimated that Isfahan and its dependencies had to supply some 10,000 *tuman*s in value, including some arrears from other places. The *sardar* had also been appointed *beglerbegi* of Fars, Qandahar, and Iraq. Because the kettledrums were still beaten on October 24, 1733 the population presented the *sardar* with sugar and candies but he did not want to receive it. He said that he had not come to ruin the city, but to make it flourishing again. He only wanted the annual revenues and nothing else, i.e., as much as had been fixed in the days of Shah 'Abbas I. Meanwhile the population had to exert itself to buy grain from the royal granaries with cash. He gave orders that the price would be fixed at 16 *paisa*s for one *mann* of wheat and 10 *paisa*s for a *mann* of barley on the condition that the price of bread

---

109. This probably was Mirza Mohammad Hoseyn (Miersa Mhamed Hossein), son of Mirza Rafi`a, the author of the *Dastur al-Moluk*. The *kalantar*'s steward (*nazer*) was `Ali Naqi Beg (Alie Naggie Beek) "a great scoundrel." VOC 2477, f. 605, 636.

would be respectively one *mahmudi* for wheat bread and 3/5 *mahmudi*s for barley bread. But the Dutch did not believe his good intentions [f. 896-98].

Already on October 26, 1733 the *sardar* made public that all shopkeepers had to open their shops and be present. Those failing to do so would be arrested, while their property and house would be confiscated. He himself was said to amuse himself with some 20 prostitutes whom he had sent for. The peasants who the *sardar* was recruiting as an army to be used against Mohammad Khan Baluch were an additional burden on the population. This decree had the desired result, for on October 28 all shops and bazaars were open. That day the *sardar* also made public that henceforth the double *paisa* had to be accepted as one normal *paisa* and that silver and gold specie, whether Afghan or Safavid coins, were equally current and interchange-able at the rate of exchange of one ducat for 15 *mahmudi*s without having the right to demand agio for good coins. The collection of money meanwhile was progressing slowly but certainly. The Armenians had not paid their quota yet and therefore were beaten. At the same time it was rumored that the *sardar* intended to assign another 20,000 *tuman*s on the population. The *sardar* also made other preparations for the coming military operations, such as the casting of 45 cannons [f. 899-902].

On November 11, 1733 the kettledrums were beaten in Isfahan because Nader had defeated Topal Pasha at Kirkuk, who was seeking peace.[110] In general, people did not believe it, and said it was only a lie to mislead those who had declared themselves for the ex-shah such as Mohammad Khan Baluch. From several sources the Dutch received conflicting information about the battle and they found it impossible to evaluate these reports. Despite his bravura the *sardar* did not feel secure either for on November 14 he made it public that all arms had to be brought to him or to be sold to the soldiers on pain of death and confiscation of property. On November 17 the soldiers were taking all horses, mules and donkeys from their owners by force. Because it was cold they also plundered the people in search for furs, and coats as much as possible. People therefore when going abroad left these items at home [f. 903-08].

On November 19, 1733 the kettledrums were beaten. Nader was said to have won a decisive battle against Topal Pasha, who had died. His son and 4 pashas were said to be prison-ers. The Turks had suffered 15,000 dead and 12,000 prisoners, while all their artillery had been taken and Kirkuk destroyed. But there was nobody who believed it. An official illumination and beating of the kettledrums was ordered as of November 20. It was said that the *sardar* had been ordered to collect 30,000 *tuman*s because of the victory. The kettledrums, which people laughed at, only stopped at sunset on November 26. The old fortress was also repaired and the laborers who had cast the cannons were given one *mann* of wheat per day as wages. The *sardar* also ordered that it was forbidden for married women to be outside their homes [f. 908-11].

On November 25, 1733 the *sardar* assigned 8,800 *tuman*s on the population of which the Armenians had to pay 700 and the Banyans 350 *tuman*s. The population was also pressed to bring the newly cast cannons outside the city. Meanwhile the taking of riding and pack-animals by force continued unabated. It was also said that Nader had ordered to make a new

---

110. At the end of September 1733 Nader had marched via inaccessible roads and attacked the Turks, who had not expected him, about mid-October and defeated them. The Turks were sleeping and Nader had attacked at night. He killed many of them amongst whom Topal Osman Pasha. VOC 2584, Beschrijvinge f. 2008-09.

tax assessment of Isfahan and to levy revenues in accordance with that, in addition to that which had already been taken. The Armenians were ordered to deliver 30 horses and mules, 40 matchlocks, 40 swords, bullet-bags and powder-bags within 10 days. It was also said that the *kadkhodas* of Isfahan had been imprisoned as security that the money would be paid by the population and that the animals and guns would be supplied. From the surrounding villages as many horses and donkeys were being brought as was possible as that time [f. 911-13].

The *sardar* also dismissed the peasants whom he had recruited as soldiers and took everything from them, such as clothes and guns, which he had given to them. Tax collectors, moreover, were appointed to demand the one *tuman* back, which had been given to them, while they also had to pay 120 to 150 *mahmudi*s extra for their dismissal. The lead that he had demanded from the apothecaries in a great hurry he returned to them and he also demanded the return of his money, which they did. The whole population continued to suffer under the burden of the tax collectors' demands for money and animals. An additional burden was the *sardar*'s order to repair the city walls [f. 913-15].

The citadel was filled with supplies and the peasants and others who could not pay cash were forced to cut their fruit trees to sell it as firewood to get money. In this way this city finally will be turned into a desert, van Leijpsigh commented. On December 3, 1733 Ughurlu Khan, governor of Qazvin, arrived in Isfahan. Two khans from Qom and Tehran and 500 men accompanied him. They were a certain Mohammad Qoli Beg, who would be appointed as governor of Isfahan, and Ughurlu Khan, who would become *kutval* and stay in its citadel. The quotas of money to be paid meanwhile were beaten out of the poor people. The *sardar* also claimed all income of the bathhouses and of the shops of the rice-huskers, so that their owners did not get one penny. A lot of violence was also used in the commandeering of houses from their owners, which made the Dutch comment that the situation was lamentable. The *sardar* who did not want to keep the confiscated goods of those killed or degraded, forced such goods as carpets and textiles on textile sellers and carpet weavers in exchange for cash. Those who refused or even showed unwillingness to do so were given a sound beating to change their mind in addition to which they were fined. Because rumors had it that Nader had suffered a considerable loss in men, that Mohammad Baluch's party grew in strength, and that Kerman was on the point of surrendering, people in Isfahan began storing food out of fear for a siege. The stocking of the citadel also continued. A few rowdies (loeties; *luti*s) who wanted to make use of the confusion were caught in Isfahan. To be better prepared the *sardar* gave orders to make 14,000 swords. The confiscation of animals continued unabated. The Armenians had to deliver their assigned part on December 8. The *sardar* meanwhile had given orders to distribute 600,000 *mann* of unhusked rice from the royal granaries in the city at a price of 2 *mahmudi*s in cash. People feared a great dearness of rice next year because the greater part of the lands had not been sown because the peasants could not work on them [f. 916-21].

Meanwhile new troops arrived in Isfahan, such as 500 men under Mostafa Khan, who was said to have orders to attack the Lurs. The governor of Golpeygan, `Ala Aqa, arrived with 200 men. These troops regularly got supplies, for the *sardar* also repeatedly made it known that he would march. To get more money, he, on December 11, again forced people to buy wheat from the royal granaries at 22 *paisa*s. However, this time he also forced them to sell it back to him for 18 *paisa*s. There was no news about the whereabouts and situation of Nader in Isfahan.

What increased the insecurity and uncertainty was the fact that the small, armed groups, which the *sardar* sent out to reconnoiter or to punish a village, returned, having received a sound beating while some troops also deserted. The *sardar* therefore increased the guards around his residence and allowed only Khorasani soldiers to guard the royal palace [f. 922-26].

On December 16, 1733 the *sardar* again by force distributed unhusked rice among the population. The Armenians had to 'buy' 50,000 *mann* at 1/5 *mahmudi*. Horse dealers (brokers) were fined 50 horses and in addition had to buy 20 of their own old horses at 10 to 15 *tuman*s a piece. On December 17 the *sardar* ordered to empty all houses within the so-called 'Afghan walls'[111] for Mohammad Qoli Beg, who was said to arrive the next day with 6,800 men. If they were not evacuated by that time it was made known nobody was allowed to take anything out of it anymore. The Dutch, though their factory was within these walls, were allowed to stay, however. The walls of the 'Afghan city' were ordered to be repaired and all holes and entrances be filled up. On its bulwarks cannons were put, on its walls guards, while water was let into its moat. The repair works had to be done by the soldiers themselves [f. 927]. The crying people were put out of their houses, but the authorities mocked them and received one another at parties at the expense of the population. Some servants of Mohammad Qoli Beg, who was Nader's uncle, had already arrived to prepare the *mo'ayyer-bashi's* house for him. The *sardar* ordered his troops to move to Khvaju and prepare a house for him there [f. 929].

On December 19, 1733 the *sardar* gave orders to empty the shops of the textile sellers, for he intended to march on December 21. Mohammad Qoli Beg arrived that day with 300 miserable looking horsemen. On December 21, about 3,000 Kurdish troops arrived, while on the next day the *sardar* allowed the recruited peasants to leave after having taking everything from them. He also allowed the people to return to their houses. On December 23 the *sardar* demanded 200 horses from the people of Isfahan, while he ordered the villages to supply him with 100,000 *mann* of straw and the same quantity of firewood as well as all revenues in grains and to bring these into the citadel. The soldiers used a lot of violence, and took women away, while they also stole all they could when going into the houses. On December 25 the *sardar* ordered to prepare 2,000 big matchlocks or *jazayeri*s, viz. 1,000 with golden and 100 with silver inlay which had to serve for the shah it was said. On December 26 the *sardar* again commandeered houses for 1,100 men from Baghdad commanded by Besitun Khan's son. Supplies were still being brought into the citadel. The newly arrived soldiers plundered a caravan at Qomishah. The *sardar* announced that he would leave in six days for Shiraz and had selected Mirza Gholam Reza's house as his first halting station (nackel mackein; *naql-e makan*). After a courier (*chapar*) had arrived coming from Nader on December 27 the *sardar* sent tax collectors into the villages to collect the revenues in grain and to bring these fast into the citadel. He also made it known that all troops had to leave the city by the next day and that the city of Isfahan had to prepare the supply train (*ordu-bazar*) for the army. Meanwhile, the forceful requisitioning of houses, the burning of their doors and windows continued. Rain and snow would make a complete ruin of the city the Dutch prophesized. Rumors moreover, had it that Nader would give Isfahan as 'alladaad' (*allahdad*; free for all) to his army [f. 930-34].

---

111. This term refers to the walls around a city quarter in the center of Isfahan that Ashraf had constructed in 1727. For details see Floor, *Afghan Occupation*, p. 250. For a picture of the remains of these walls see Sirus Shafaqi, *Joghrafiya-ye Esfahan* (Isfahan: Daneshgah, 1352/1973), photo 25.

On December 29, 1733 the cannons had been taken outside the city, but the *sardar* postponed his departure with another four days and stayed in Khvaju. On December 31 he ordered to distribute the unhusked rice to an amount of 500,000 *mahmudi*s, of which the Armenians had to pay 50,000 *mahmudi*s at 14 *mahmudi*s per *mann*. The reason of the delay was said to be that the *sardar* could not bear to leave the Isfahan courtesans. Moreover, he feared that as soon as he had left that the population would close the city gates to him [f. 935-36].

On January 1, 1734 news arrived that Nader had made peace with the Turks. The next day the *sardar* mounted up, while the guards at the gates were doubled. His army numbered 8,000 men who were said to be accompanied by 4,500 tarts dressed in male attire. The heavy cannons were difficult to move and were taken back to the citadel. On January 9, the new governor forbade the Moslems to drink wine and brandy and ordered them to fast and pray for Nader's victory. He also continued to force, by means of the stick, the people to accept the unhusked rice, while food and fodder were continuously brought into the citadel. Many plantain trees from the royal gardens were cut to serve as firewood. On January 11 it was also made public that Moslems were not allowed to have parties or marriage parties without his permission. Even permission was needed for burying the dead for whom five *mahmudi*s per body had to be paid. The Banyans were forbidden to drink wine or brandy and they were not allowed to bring women into the caravanserais or to divert themselves. Because of the many conflicting rumors the governor increased the number of informers to find out who was in favor of which party in the city [f. 936-41].

A VICTORIOUS NADER RETURNS TO ISFAHAN

On January 28, 1734 the royal palace was repaired, cleaned, swept and covered with carpets. On February 17, all *mostowfi*s were ordered to go to Shiraz with the Fars accounts. Mohammad Qoli Beg was confirmed as governor, while the other governors such as Ughurlu Beg were ordered to return to their posts. Although many did not believe that Mohammad Khan Baluch had been defeated all signs pointed that way. On February 4, orders were given to sow clover and barley in all gardens for Nader's riding and pack animals when he would come in Isfahan. On February 16 part of his supply train (*ordu-bazar*) had already arrived in Isfahan. However, military operations had not been finished yet since on February 17, 1734 *chapar*s from Shiraz had ordered to fetch cannon-casters, while on the next day the apothecaries were forced with the bastinado to deliver 300 *mann* of tin and other materials necessary for cannon-casting. It was said this was necessary, because the river between Shushtar and Kuhgilu could not been crossed with cannons [f. 956, 958-59, 964-6].

Though Nader's victory over Mohammad Khan Baluch was made known on February 19, 1734 he still ordered the governor of Isfahan on February 25 to send him as soon as possible 5,000 *tuman*s in cash and some troops and horses. On February 27 an order from Nader arrived in Isfahan ordering to take back the money given as a present to the mullahs. This order was followed by another one on March 3 to collect the remainder of the royal revenues in Isfahan and to have these ready by New Year (*Nowruz*) at Qazvin. The order stipulated that the cash part had to be paid in cash and the kind part in kind. Moreover, all governors, viziers and other officials of all cities had to assemble there as well. On March 6 another order arrived, to sow clover in all *qoruq* areas (pasture land reserved for the royal herd) and gardens for Nader's pack animals. He also ordered to move all [Bakhtiyari] Lurs living in the villages around Isfahan to Khorasan and to burn and destroy their villages. The man put in charge of this operation was the former *darugheh* of Isfahan, Cheragh Beg. His successor was the *min-bashi* 'Askar, who also was *darugheh* of the Chahar Mahall [f. 966-80].

Nader also thought about other beings than his pack animals, for on March 20, 1734 orders were received to sow two times more rice than usual around Isfahan, because at Shiraz hardly any crops had been sown due to the rebellion. On March 27 an order was received to levy a tax on sheep, mares, cows and she-donkeys at a rate of respectively 1 *mahmudi*, 5 *mahmudi*s, 3 to 4 *mahmudi*s and 4 *mahmudi*s per year per head [f. 981-5]. Nader was reported to have lost his senses, because his thirst for blood seemed unquenchable, for so many people were reported killed in Shiraz and elsewhere. On his return from Shiraz to Isfahan Nader committed many cruel acts. The 4,000 families whom he had taken with him from Shiraz to be sent to Khorasan were not able to keep up with the army's pace. He then ordered to cut their knee tendons and then left them lying in the road to perish.[112] He, moreover, also had become an alcoholic and allowed his army also to drink wine. He gave full reign to prostitution and recommended it as a good thing to his soldiers. This may also explain the rumor, that somebody in Isfahan was said to have farmed the bordellos and wine-houses for 5,000 *tuman*s per year. To show how immoral he had become the Dutch reported him having said: "Who is God; I have declared all women to be common property." On his return in Isfahan he started to extort money and killing many people, which was a daily occurrence [f. 998-90]. He also, by force, had Armenian girls taken from Jolfa to enjoy his carnal lust with them.[113] Nader made his entry into Isfahan on April 28, 1734. He wore the *jiqeh* on the right side [f. 994]. Turkish envoys had arrived 10 days before; their *mehmandar-bashi* was Mirza Mehdi Kowkabi [f. 992-93]. On May 3, Nader sent an envoy to the Porte, named Mohammad Qoli Khan, to confirm the agreed upon peace. He first intended to take care of the Lezgis and then to march on Qandahar [f. 999, 1105].

BAN OF 'ASHURA FESTIVAL

In May 1734, Nader forbade the Persians to stage their annual Hoseyn-Hasan festival. "It was said, that when he issued this order he told the olama that if his subjects, because of their faith in two persons who hardly had done anything in their life, were prepared to cut their heads and beat their bodies and the like, he feared that they would kill themselves in the event he, who had done so much for them, would die."[114] Nader showed himself more lenient towards the Banyan community in Isfahan, which at that time only numbered 300 men, while under Shah Tahmasp II there still had been 800. The governor had claimed their previous head-money of 250 *tuman*s against which they protested. Nader then issued a decree stipulating that not more that 50 *mahmudi*s per person per year might be levied, while they also would be exempt from all

---

112. VOC 2584, Beschrijvinge, f. 2014-15.

113. VOC 2584, Beschrijvinge, f. 2016; VOC 2323, f. 990. On April 8, 1734 Nader behaved most improperly with prostitutes and young male dancers.

114. VOC 2584, Beschrijvinge, f. 2016. As part of his peace proposal to the Turks Nader promised to ban the cursing of the thirst three caliphs and to order that henceforth no more difference would be made between Sunni and Shi'a Islam. VOC 2416, Koenad to Batavia (10/12/1736), f. 381.

extraordinary taxes. On May 8 the *mo`ayyer-bashi* was again re-appointed governor of Isfahan, while he also was the royal court's steward or *nazer*. [f. 1100-01, 1105, 2022, 2027].

NEW MILITARY OPERATIONS RESULT IN NEW FISCAL DEMANDS

On June 14, 1734 Nader left Isfahan for Hamadan. En route he plundered and ruined all villages and towns. Nader even had sons kill their fathers, and if they refused he had them killed.[115] Although Nader had left, the town still could not breathe freely, for on July 3 the *mo`ayyer-bashi* demanded 1,000 camels from the population. He had to supply them to Nader's army and he forced the cameleers to deliver to him at half their price and to oblige them not to say anything against coming caravans to prevent them from making a round-turn [f. 2027].[116]

On October 26, 1734 the governor of Isfahan (the mahjar basjie; *mo`ayyer-bashi*) summoned van Leijpsigh and Geekie, the EIC agent, to receive an order from Nader addressed to them. The order concerned the demand to sell or supply ships to attack the Arabs in the Gulf. Van Leijpsigh also reported that it was rumored that Hoseyn Khan at Qandahar wore the royal aigrette and had a royal carpet (*masnad*) made and now ruled those parts as king. Also, Sorkhay Khan (the Sorgaeb) of the Lezgis was difficult to trap in his mountains.[117] Finally he (Casjil Sorgaab) fled with his wife, abandoning his treasury, to the Shamkhal (the sjamgaels). Nader then took Shirvan and plundered it and sent the entire booty to Khorasan. At Ganjeh he had attacked the Turks, who had a very strong castle there. Nader lost many men and animals due to fierce Turkish resistance and the severe cold. It was expected that this would harm his reputation, because Nader had become so full of himself that he thought that the whole world trembled before him. `Abdollah Pasha who had arrived with a large army at Tarwan [?] was said to have offered peace, but Nader had turned him down; he was not interested in making peace at all. Aslamas Khan or Jan Khan, son of Mohammad `Ali Khan, was said to have been send as *sardar* with 10,000 men amongst whom many Georgian nobles to Tiflis to recapture it from the Turks. It was also said that troops that Nader had sent to Triam [?] had been repulsed by the Turks. Reza Qoli Khan, Nader's son, had been put in charge of all the treasure that his father had collected in Khorasan. He was in Veramin in January 1735, with his entire family and everything else, including pots and pans. This was allegedly because the Turkmans had recently attacked Mashhad with 15,000 men, but Ebrahim Khan had defeated them with a loss of 4,000 men. Another reason that was mentioned was that the move was out of fear of the Qandahar Afghans, who allegedly also were on the move and preparing themselves to wage war on the Persians. Further ground for this supposition was the arrival of an envoy from Hoseyn Khan of Qandahar, a certain Hajji Adam (Hadje Adam), who had passed through Isfahan on September 24, 1734 on his way to the royal court. He returned to Isfahan on December

---

115. VOC 2584, Beschrijvinge, f. 2016-17; VOC 2323, f. 2022.

116. The description of the events from September 13, 1733 till July 3, 1734 are all based on VOC 2323, Extract van 'tSpahans Dagregister (Summary of the Isfahan Diary) unless otherwise stated. For easy reference the relevant folio numbers have been given in the text. The dates also serve as an easy reference guide.

117. VOC2357, van Leijpsigh to Hey (04/11/1734), f. 1103f, 1124. As to the content of the discussion regarding the ships and the follow up see Floor, "The Iranian Navy."

8, 1734. After 20 days he had been taken by a number of mounted guards to Tahmasp Qoli Khan in Kerman. Hajji Adam left very dissatisfied from Isfahan, but van Leijpsigh had not been able to learn the purpose and result of his mission. On November 15, 1734 the *mo`ayyer bashi* had been sent for by Nader and he appointed Fazel `Ali Beg as his *na'eb*. Meanwhile at Isfahan preparations were made for a national assembly at New Year in Qazvin. The *jabbehdar-bashi*, Ahmad Rahim Beg (Achmet Rachim Beek) had instructions to prepare golden cups of 200 *mann* for the carousal. To that end an enormous tent of 400 meters (*gaz*) length was being prepared. The cover was being prepared with red dye from Shamakhi. Reportedly, the purpose of the assembly (*majles*) was to proclaim Nader as *sepahsalar* of Persia and his son as grand vizier or E`temad al-Dowleh of `Abbas III, who would be sent for from Mazanderan. Further that Qazvin would become the royal residence. The former shah was said to have almost died, but he had recuperated. People had not given up hope that he would accede to the throne again, "may it happen the earlier the better, because otherwise we may only expect worse," van Leijpsigh commented. Geekie, the EIC chief, moved everything out of his house on January 10, 1735 and had it taken to the house of the Carmelites, Augustines and his interpreter in Jolfa. The move lasted three days. He even had taken the doors out of the rooms. On January 13 Geekie was sent for by the deputy governor, Fars `Ali Beg (Faars Alie Beek) (the governor had left for court on November 5, 1734). Geekie gave him the key of the house, because it belonged to the shah. Geekie told him that the house was empty, because he had been ordered by his masters to depart for Gamron immediately and that he had come to take his leave. The deputy said that Geekie could not leave for Nader was his master. He would inform Nader and told Geekie to send a request. The deputy governor therefore returned the key and told him to go home. Geekie said that he did not want to return to his house and therefore would go to Jolfa. The deputy agreed to that but told Geekie that he had to keep the key and that the EIC porter had to remain in the house. The EIC interpreter was made security in case Geekie would flee. The *kalantar* of Jolfa was also instructed to watch Geekie's movements.[118] Geekie left for Gamron on February 28, 1735.[119]

The people of Isfahan meanwhile had to pay for the victory at Shirvan. To that end a certain Hasan Khan Beg came with 100 tax collectors to collect 36,000 *tuman*s, of which Isfahan and its dependencies had to pay 9,000 *tuman*s. The people sold all their domestic utensils and the like with the pretext of going on a pilgrimage to Mecca with their family. However, Nader sent strict orders to all officials of those towns, which these people had to pass through to prevent them from making that journey and to force them to return. Nader stood in dire need for that money since he had lost 90% of his horses at Ganjeh and other riding and pack animals due to cold and fatigue. He sent for gun-powder, bullets and two cannon-casters. He intended to cast a very heavy ball in his camp of a weight of 16 *mann-e shah* and use it for bombardments.[120] Further, Khan Jan had defeated the Georgians at Tiflis. It was reported that

---

118. VOC 2357, van Leijpsigh to Hey (04/02/1735), f. 1137-40, 1141-46; VOC 2416, van Leijpsigh to Hey (04/02/1735), f. 1843-48, 1856. Geekie had sent in secret a courier to Nader with unknown objective. Since one month he had been preparing himself in secret to leave Isfahan, but the governor did not let him. He was desperate, according to VOC 2357, van Leijpsigh to Hey (05/11/1734), f. 122.

119. VOC 2357, van Leijpsigh to Koenad (03/06/1735), f. 1173; VOC 2416, f. 1903. Van Leijpsigh had recommended the deputy governor of Isfahan to allow Geekie to leave. VOC 2357, private letter van Leijpsigh to Koenad (28/02/1735), f. 1226.

120. A large part of the Bakhtiyaris who had been resettled in Khorasan had profited from this occasion

that they wanted to put Wakhtang Mirza (Vagtan Miersa) on the Georgian throne again. The *sardar* Tahmasp Qoli Khan had killed Hoseyn Khan's envoy with all his people. Pir Moham-mad Khan (Pier Mhamed Chan) had Ghani Khan (Ganni Chan) and 300 men killed.[121]

INDIFFERENT TREATMENT OF EUROPEAN REPRESENTATIVES

Aqa Mohammad (Aga Mhamed), the do-all (*albeschik*) of Nader arrived in Isfahan on May 12, 1735. At that time van Leijpsigh had not heard anything from Tahmasp Qoli Khan in reply to his requests. He said he had given them to Mirza Mohammad (Miersa Mhamed) the treasurer who had submitted them to Nader. However, he had not received any news about a reply. Van Leijpsigh reminded the council at Gamron what the *kholofa* had advised him in 1732, viz. to write Nader a letter and give him satisfaction otherwise the latter might give orders to bastinado the Dutch. The man behind the investigation of the Dutch privileges was the Russian resident, Semen Avramov (Simon Abrahamits) to find a pretext to damage the position of the Dutch and English Companies and to blacken their reputation with the greedy Nader. To that end he had given rich presents to Mirza Taqi, the *monshi al-mamalek*, "a brazen and also an avaricious person" and the *kholafa*, which is "what it is all about as far as the natives are concerned, without making any distinction between friend and foe." Thus, they sided with his point of view, i.e., the Dutch and English Companies were but importers of rags and exporters of money, reason why these should be expelled from Persia. This led to the investigation of the privileges. Meanwhile, the town was ruined and money scarce. Geekie had left Isfahan on February 28, 1735 against Tah-masp Khan's direct order and the English house, which was being occupied by their interpreter Joseph Hermet and five servants, was being claimed by the *nabab* Mirza Ebrahim and Avramov's wife, who wanted to live there. However, Tahmasp Khan refused both their requests.[122]

The Russian ambassador Golitsyn was first badly received in the royal council; Nader even grabbed him by his throat, but later he was well treated. The Dutch surmised that this may have been due to the Russian of support of men and ammunition (bombs, mortars) as well as food supplies by the Russian general. The result was the Russian withdrawal from Baku, Darband, Soelaag [?] Niazavar and Salian. It was further said the Avramov had returned once again. Van Leijpsigh commented that he hoped that the Russians would never get a foot on the ground in Persia, because it would be disadvantageous for the Dutch and English. However, Thamas Chan (i.e., Nader) was unreliable and it might well be that after they had delivered their part he would drop them.[123]

---

to return to their old hide-outs and were said to number 20,000 men and to have defeated an army that had been sent against them. VOC 2357, van Leijpsigh to Hey (02/04/1735), f. 1147-48; VOC 2416, van Leijpsigh to Hey (02/04/1735), f. 1856-57. Later it was reported that some of the remaining Bakhtiyaris, estimated at 800 men, were on the road again and pillaging in the Chahar Mahall and Peria area. VOC 2417, Clement (Kerman) to Koenad (Gamron) (29/06/1735), f. 2096; VOC 2357, private letter van Leijpsigh to Koenad (28/02/1735), f. 1128. It was said that Nader had lost as many as 50,000 men in the attack of the castle of Ganjeh. Also, that the population of some liberated Christian villages had been sent to Khorasan. VOC 2416, van Leijpsigh to Koenad (03/06/1735), f. 1956, 1961.

121. VOC 2357, private letter from van Leijpsigh to Koenad (28/02/1735), f. 1127-28.

122. VOC 2416, van Leijpsigh to Koenad (03/06/1735), f. 1905-18, 1935-37.

123. VOC 2416, van Leijpsigh to Koenad (03/06/1735), f. 1937-50.

Mirza Taqi had left for court on June 3, 1735 and returned on June 7 saying that he had orders from Nader to ride post-haste to Morchehkhvort (Mortjager) at 14-15 German miles from here. From his mace-bearer van Leijpsigh learnt that Nader had ordered him to return to his seat of government and only send clerks to court, from whom he would demand an accounting. Nader also had written that he would come to Qazvin at the beginning of winter, when he would send for him again. Mirza Taqi would leave on June 10 already to Shiraz.[124] Van Leijpsigh met with Mirza Taqi on June 9, 1735 who gave him a friendly welcome. He discussed Mohammad 'Ali Khan's voyage with him and the problems encountered about which Mirza Taqi was aware. He told van Leijpsigh that Nader had been informed, who gave him orders at Morchehkhvort to make the voyage during the next monsoon and to inform Safi Khan Beg (Zeffie Chan Beeg). At van Leijpsigh's request he dictated a letter to his first clerk, Aqa Ja'far (Aga Jaffer), for the ambassador and a certain Mohammad Zahid [?] Beg (Mhamed Zayit beecq). Mirza Taqi raised the issue of the important merchant Zeyn al-'Abedin. Van Leijpsigh pointed out that all interference in the market was an obstacle and bad for trade. It might even lead to the diversion of merchants to other markets, which would be negative for the Persian economy. Mirza Taqi said that he had been able to convince Nader to agree to a letter that put an end to Zeyn al-'Abedin's appointment and who had been ordered not to interfere with the merchants. He also had written such an order to Zeyn al-'Abedin and gave a copy to the Dutch. The next day Mirza Taqi paid a counter-visit to the Dutch factory. At that time Joseph Sahid, the dragoman, arrived and related that road guards had tried to collect road tax (*rahdari*) from a VOC caravan at Lar. This time the Dutch had been able to oppose payment, but they expected further problem in the future. Van Leijpsigh therefore asked Mirza Taqi, as governor of those parts, to issue an order to the road guards, in accordance with Dutch privileges. Mirza Taqi did so, while he also gave a letter ordering the *shahbandar* at Gamron to assist the Dutch in collecting debts. Also, two clerks of the treasury arrived with a written order from Nader to confiscate the houses of the EIC (in which their dragoman was still living) and the Russians and to repair them.[125]

NEW WAR WITH THE OTTOMANS

'Abdollah Pasha was said to march against Nader and had arrived at Erevan. A courier (*chapar*) returning from court told the Dutch dragoman that Nader had taken only 12,000 picked men to face the Turks who were coming to the relief of Ganjeh. The stink was terrible in the army camp due to dying horses and other animals, while also a kind of pest had broken out. It was reported that all of this had led to the raising of the siege of Ganjeh. Supplies were scarce and expensive in the army. At the same the Lezgis had recuperated again and were making preparations to retake Shirvan according to information received by Banyans from business relations in Shamakhi.[126]

---

124. VOC 2416, van Leijpsigh to Koenad (08/06/1735), f. 2059-60.

125. VOC 2416, van Leijpsigh to Koenad (16/06/1735), f. 2065-73, 2078.

126. VOC 2416, van Leijpzigh to Koenad (08/06/1735), f. 2062-63; Ibid., (16/06/1735), f. 2075; Ibid., (04/02/1734), f. 1849-50; VOC 2416, van Leijpsigh to Koenad (03/06/1735), f. 1956 (while storming the castle of Ganjeh, Nader was said to have suffered a damage of 50,000 *tumans*); VOC 2357, van Leijpsigh to Hey (04/02/1735), f. 1141; VOC 2416, Clement (Kerman) to Koenad (08/06/1735), f. 1899-1901 (information received on May 26 from a messenger than Nader had left Ganjeh and marched with 25,000 men against the Turks at Qars [?] (Chaser) to force them to end the siege of Ganjeh. Khan Jan with 15,000 had been sent to cut off all supplies; further a Russian army of 10,000 was in Baku and

After having arrived in Qars, where 'Abdollah Pasha had fled, Nader defeated him and took his artillery, when 'Abdolla Pasha sallied forth from the citadel. 'Abdolla Pasha then withdrew into the citadel. Nader laid siege for three days, but 'Abdollah Pasha stayed where he was. Nader believed that 'Abdolla Pasha would have waited for one year, which time he could not spare, so he decided to march to Erevan. However, he had not gone very far when he learnt that Fulad Pasha of Adana (Foelaar Bassja) with two other pashas and a large army, foot and horse, were coming to 'Abdollah Pasha's relief. The latter therefore took heart again and left the citadel to join forces with the relief-force. The joint force pursued Nader fiercely as far as Bagh Avard (Carbalagh Dheejaawoon) where the two armies gave battle on Sunday 27 Moharram 1148 (June 19, 1735). Nader defeated them with the loss of 30,000 men and 20 of their officers such as "bashas and degh bashas"; he also took 500 prisoners. 'Abdollah Pasha was killed during his flight by Rostam Beg, while Saru Mostafa, governor of Diyarbekr and son-in-law of the Soltan had been killed during his flight by Jalil Beg,[127] Nader had joined their heads to their corpses and sent these to the citadel of Qars and Erevan. Nader also captured many horses, camels, donkeys and fine arms. He informed Mohammad Taqi about this victory on 5 Safar 1148 [27 June 1735] when he was in Charbalaock D'heerje [?].[128] The kettledrums were beaten in Isfahan from July 13 till the evening of July 16, 1735 to announce his victory over the Turks.[129]

According to a report from Kerman, after a nine month siege of Ganjeh its commander said that if Nader wanted to have the citadel he first had to expel 'Abdollah Pasha who had come 6 months earlier with 150,000 men to Qars [?] (Chassan). If not, he intended to persist till the end with his defense. Nader decided to attack 'Abdollah Pasha. He had his generals take an oath that if he died or was defeated that they would go to Shah Tahmasp and they also had to swear loyalty to him. Nader detailed 8,000 men to prevent a Turkish break-through in case of defeat and marched on June 8 to 'Abdollah Pasha with 25,000 men. He left 12,000 men at Ganjeh and sent 16,000 men under Khan Jan to Georgia to cut off supply lines. Later he was again sent for by Nader to join him at Qars [?] (Chassan), because Wakhtang Mirza, who was at Darband with 30,000 Russian and Georgian troops, had asked for it. But before Khan Jan had joined him Nader had defeated 'Abdollah Pasha. The latter first had withdrawn into the castle, because he had no orders to give battle and had to wait for Hasan Pasha, the grand vizier who was approaching with a large army. Nader, who did not dare to attack the castle itself, induced him to give battle by cutting his supply lines. Some 50,000 Turks sallied forth from the castle and gave battle at a location at three hours distance from the castle. After one day of battle the Turks were defeated and then fled. 'Abdollah Pasha gave orders to return to the

provided assistance to Nader, on condition of restoration of Shah Tahmasp to the throne. Initially Nader had refused this, saying he did not need help, but at the advice of his leading officials he agreed that in case of victory he would discuss the modalities of Shah Tahmasp's return).

127. Jalil Beg Mish Most-e Khorasani, according to Mohammad Hoseyn Qaddusi, *Nadernameh* (Mashad, 1339/1960), p. 250.

128. VOC 2357, Tamas Chan to Miersa Taggie from Charbalaock D'heerje (received 27/06/1735), f. 913-15. Mohammad Taqi estimated the number of dead at 30,000 and as prisoners 20 officers and 500 soldiers. VOC 2357, Miersa Taggie to both Companies – for your eyes only (received 27/07/1735), f. 919. It was first offered to Koenad to read then the letter was taken to the EIC chief.

129. VOC 2357, van Leijpsigh to Koenad (20/07/1735), f. 1236 (this letter contains a very detailed account of the battle).

citadel. Many died on both sides during the battle.[130] After his victory at Qars [?] (Chassan), Nader in order to wait for new troops and to be closer to the siege at Ganjeh went to Erevan with 12,000 men at five miles from the citadel. `Abdollah Pasha learnt about this, and decided to attack him. He divided his army into four groups to attack Nader from all sides, and to catch him alive. Some deserters warned Nader in time. Because he saw no way to withdraw he sent all women, children, sutlers [*zoetelaars*] and the like away with 7,000 foot, and only kept his cavalry. He explained his troops the difficult position they were in, and told them it was death, imprisonment or victory. "Show me you are men who rather die than be prisoners", he said. "He would lead them as a father and sell his life dearly. He swore to die rather than to surrender." Nader then ordered to do away with the heavy baggage and they attacked the largest army corps led by `Abdollah Pasha and Mostafa Pasha, with sword in hand without firing a shot. They cut down everybody and almost penetrated into the camp of both pashas. Both had been deadly wounded, which lead to confusion in the Turkish army, which then fled leaving everything behind including the dead pashas. They fled to the citadels of Qasr and Erevan. It was said that 50,000 had fallen on the Turkish side and that Nader only suffered a loss of 700-800. He sent the corpses of the pashas to Erevan saying mockingly that he did not know how the Turks buried their dead. The cities in Persian were illuminated for three days; he further remitted a contribution that had been imposed, but demanded that new men be sent, e.g. 200 from Kerman and 300 from Seistan.[131]

Nader paid his troops on time and therefore they were loyal to him. Whether they won or lost Nader paid. In the former case, Nader said, payment served for recreation and encouragement. In the latter case it served to re-establish the poor taxpayer, who, roughly estimated, paid more than 250,000 *tumans* (Dfl. 10,625,000) per month for the upkeep of the 150,000 troops, who were dispersed over the country. They seldom attacked the enemy with more than 30,000-40,000 men. Since November 1734, Nader had a sum of 50,400 *tumans* exchanged at Dfl. 42.5 per *tuman*s or Dfl. 2,142,000. Since his last victory Nader acted very piously and said that he hoped that his friends would thank God and he ordered that Mirza Taqi to make this public throughout the country.[132] The same businesslike attitude Nader also displayed towards any request submitted to him. He would study it carefully to determine whether it was without any basis. For even as a soldier tried to cheat him about his pay, Nader knew how to compute with his rosary how much the man had been paid and for what purpose and thus made his experience pay in front of the troops, as had been reported by trustworthy people.[133]

Nader, to fill his depleted ranks after the Qars-Ganjeh campaign, ordered that new troops be recruited. Isfahan had to supply 200 men, which order was expected to lead to further ruin, for Nader also had ordered that each recruit had to be given three *tumans* as travel money and one horse. It was not allowed to deduct these costs from the regular taxes.[134] A

---

130. VOC 2416, Auwannes to Koenad (22/07/1735), f. 2104-08.

131. VOC 2417, Clement to Koenad (18/08/1735), f. 3081-85; VOC 2416, Clement to Koenad (29/06/1735), f. 2082-83.

132. VOC 2357, Koenad to Batavia (24/08/1735), f. f, 281-83.

133. VOC 2357 (24/08/1735), f. 268-69.

134. VOC 2416, van Leijpsigh to Koenad (29/06/1735), f. 2096.

courier (*chapar*) after 27 days travel from Nader's army arrived in Kerman on July 5, 1735 for *sardar* Tahmasp Qoli Khan, who was said to have orders to send for Pir Mohammad Khan and his troops from Herat to join Nader as soon as possible. It was also said that 40 *chapars* had been sent to recruit 30,000 men in and around Mashhad. On July 10, 1735 three *chapars* shortly after one another arrived to recruit 200 men, who had to leave immediately. It was therefore believed that Nader's victory at Qars [?] (Cassan) was not a major one.[135] Although Nader had defeated the Turks at Qars the plague had broken out at Ganjeh. It was believed to have caused the raising of the siege of that city. It was also rumored that Tiflis had been retaken by Khan Jan, who now was called Aslan Khan after his grandfather. Khan Jan, had been sent to Tiflis with 10,000 men amongst whom many Georgian noblemen to take it from Turks.[136] On September 16, 1735 a messenger arrived in Kerman reporting the conquest of the castle at Ganjeh, which resulted in another three-day illumination of the town. Nader then moved with part of his cavalry into Georgia to see whether he might conquer yet another town. The remainder of his army he quartered in Erevan. At the same time he ordered a fixed number for each city of notables such as mullahs, qadis, and *kadkhoda*s to come to court, although nobody knew for what purpose it was agreed it had to be something of great importance.[137]

MIRZA TAQI SHIRAZI SAYS NADER WANTS BETTER RELATIONS WITH VOC AND EIC

On August 25, 1735 van Leijpsigh and the dragoman went to speak to Mirza Taqi at the latter's request. When they came at his house Mohammad Latif Khan was also there, who had arrived in Isfahan on August 10, 1735. Mirza Taqi assured that Nader valued the friendship with the Europeans. He had received explicit orders from Nader to henceforth deal uprightly with the Europeans and give them satisfaction in all cases. Once he would be in Gamron he would examine the VOC privileges and give his report to Nader. Van Leijpsigh thanked both and congratulated Mirza Taqi with his new appointment, and told him that the Dutch always had most of their relations with his father, his grandfather and his great-grandfather. In reply Mirza Taqi promised to give the VOC satisfaction. He had with him four commands from Nader, two for the Dutch and two for the English (i.e., one for the Isfahan office and one for Gamron). He gave the one for the English in Isfahan to their dragoman Hermet who had been sent for. The other two copies he would take himself. The Persians asked Hermet why Geekie had left. Hermet replied because he was dissatisfied that the privileges had not been confirmed. Mohammad Taqi told him to see to it that an EIC agent would soon be back in Isfahan, for Nader had agreed to all privileges and he would grant even additional ones. The order that had been handed over was about the appointment of Mohammad Taqi as admiral (*kaptein ter zee*; probably *qaputan-bashi*) and governor of all seaports. Mirza Mohammad had been appointed as *shahbandar*, while Mohammad Taqi also had to prepare some ships and "goerabs" (*grab, gurab*; small sailing vessel) with the help of the Dutch and English. During the counter-visit on August 26, 1735 Mirza Taqi asked about trade and why VOC caravans did not come anymore. Van Leijpsigh replied that there was hardly any trade

135. VOC 2416, Auwannees to Koenad (22/07/1735), f. 2104.

136. VOC 2357, van Leijpsigh to Hey (04/02/1735), f. 1142. He was renamed Aslamas Khan, not Aslan Khan. Khanjan was the son of Mohammad `Ali Khan, a Georgian royal slave, the son of Aslan Khan.

137. VOC 2417, Clement to Koenad (21/09/1735), f. 3093-94.

and the fiscal burden was depleting the country. Mirza Taqi promised that everything would get better. Mohammad Zaman Beg (Mhamed Zamoen beecq), a cousin of Mohammad Taqi, would accompany Hermet to Gamron and would defray him en route. After Hermet had left Mirza Taqi urged van Leijpsigh to write Koenad to sell him two ships and other related matters.[138] Both Mirza Taqi and Mohammad Latif Khan left for Gamron on August 29, 1735.[139]

CONTINUED MILITARY OPERATIONS IN THE EAST, BUT PEACE IN THE WEST

Rumors were circulating at that time about a possible peace agreement with Turkey and the restoration of Shah Tahmasp II. For this unlikely event his supporters also found justification in Nader's preparations for a national assembly (*majles*), where according to rumor he would reinstate the former shah, which the Dutch did not believe. It was said he would ask the ex-shah for forgiveness and permission to fight the Taymanis (Taymenies), a Sunni tribe above Herat, who, having united with the Ghalzai Afghans of Qandahar, had defeated his *sardar* Tahmasp Qoli Khan. All important people had been ordered to be in Qazvin towards New Year (*Nowruz*); in all 12,000 people were expected. From Isfahan only 300 people would come such as all important mullahs, *shahzadeh*s (i.e. Safavid princes in the female line), *hajji*s, and important citizens. The Dutch therefore suspected that Nader would himself proclaim king in Qazvin. Nader had ordered the production of a very costly carpet or *masnad* worked with drawn gold and pearls. To that end pearl experts were sent to Bahrain. On each of the four corners it was to be fastened by four golden stones. Its total cost would amount to 20,000 *tuman*s or Dfl. 850,000.[140]

Nader's insatiable lust for money, which had paralyzed trade in Isfahan almost completely, manifested itself again in early October 1735 when he issued orders to confiscate the inheritances of Banyans during the last 12 years for which no heirs had come forward. For those inheritances where heirs were present 10% had to be paid to the Crown.[141]

Van Leijpsigh told various courtiers (`Ali Mardan Khan, Miersa Keyaas [?]) that if VOC staff was not treated in accordance with ancient custom that the Dutch would leave. They replied to have patience and that everything would turn out for the better. Mirza Qeyas [?] (Miersa Keyaas) and Mohammad Zaman Beg, both relatives of Mirza Taqi, wrote a letter to the latter requesting to treat the Dutch in a friendly manner. The preparations for the Qazvin *majles* proceeded and by 1736 nobody spoke about the restoration of Shah Tahmasp anymore. Towards the end of the year 1735 some participants had already left, but others were to follow later in December 1735. The feeling among the invited was one of uncertainty, for they did not know what Nader's intentions were or how they would have to react and so they all choose

---

138. On this part of the discussion see Floor, "The Iranian Navy."

139. VOC 2416, van Leijpsigh to Koenad (30/08/1735), f. 2186, 2189-97, 2216. It was also reported that a Russian resident had arrived in Rasht to promote their trade. Also that the *kholofa* would go as ambassador to Russia and was already en route. Ibid., f. 2212.

140. VOC 2416, van Leijpsigh to Koenad (13/10/1735), f. 2259-62.

141. VOC 2416, van Leijpsigh to Koenad (13/10/1735), f. 2231, 2263-64 ("there is much counterfeit money in circulation").

to play it safe and say 'yes and no' at the right time and at the right occasions. Nader had sent for many robes of honor and ordered Agha Jamal to bring his wife, the princess, to Kashan.[142]

The Turks had ceded Erevan, Tiflis and Ganjeh to Nader, while Ahmad Pasha had promised that he would propose to the Porte that a peace treaty be concluded. Nader had removed all inhabitants of Shamakhi and had ordered them to build a new city at four miles' distance in a swampy area, a certain way to make them die as animals the Dutch commented. Nader had regained all lost Persian territory by the end of November 1735 with the exception of Qandahar. This did not mean that all was quiet internally, for the Bakhtiyaris, who had been relatively peaceful for some time, had defeated a force of 3,600 Khorasanis which had been sent against them and continued to commit acts of hostility thereafter.[143]

At intervals Mohammad Taqi, Nader's do-all (albeschik), the governor of Lar, Amir Mehr 'Ali Soltan, the former admiral, Mohammad Latif Khan, and the new admiral Mohammad Taqi Khan passed through Isfahan in December 1735, but none stayed and moved on [presumably to court]. There was peace with the Georgians, but war with the Turks. The latter had made common cause with the Lezgis reinforced by 30,000 Tartars, but Nader defeated them; they lost 12,000 men. Then peace was agreed upon. New participants for the *majles* passed through Isfahan, but its location was not certain anymore. According to some, it would be in Qazvin and to others it would be in the Chal Moghan.[144] By March it was certain that it would be in the Chal Moghan, for Nader's envoys to Thatta returned to Isfahan with Mohammad 'Ali Khan's property on February 22, 1736 and went that way. The envoys (Zeffi Chan and Maijid Sayit) publicly praised the Dutch and vilified the English. Mirza Taqi was reported to have been out of favor and that he even had been strangled and his property confiscated. However, the contrary was true, because he had gained more influence than before with Nader. Mirza Taqi had deputized his brother as governor of the Garmsirat.[145]

The *sardar* Tahmasp Qoli Khan (serdaar Thamas Coelie Chan) had destroyed many of the Uzbeks, Baluchis and Taymenis and had captured much booty. He returned from Herat to Nader to attend the council meeting.[146] [From Kerman more details were reported about this news item] Tamasp Khan Jalayer also had joined Nader in Azerbaijan after having scored a devastating victory over Uzbeks, Baluchis and the Taymanis (Taaymemies), who had been supported by the Ghalzais. However, this was a dearly fought victory. One of the *sardar*'s subordinates, Esma'il Beg, lost apart from his own life that of one-third of his men, amongst whom Mir Heydar son of Mir Mehr 'Ali and many other *yuzbashi*s, or a total of 6,000 men. Tahmasp

---

142. VOC 2416, van Leijpsigh to Koenad (26/11/1735), f. 2280-81, 2288, 2290.

143. VOC 2416, van Leijpsigh to Koenad (26/11/1735), f. 2289-91.

144. VOC 2416, van Leijpsigh to Koenad (25/12/1735), f. 2296, 2306 (Amier Mheer Allie Sulthoen asked for a loan 40 *tuman*s at 20% interest, which was refused), 2309-10.

145. VOC 2416, van Leijpsigh to Koenad (08/03/1736), f. 2356, 2361, 2372-73 ("we also learnt that Mostafa Chan, governor of Lar had been beheaded, but that information needed confirmation"). Later van Leijpsigh reported that Mostafa Khan had not been beheaded and that Nader's farrash-bashi had seen him alive. VOC 2416, van Leijpsigh to Koenad (08/03/1736), f. 2385.

146. VOC 2416, van Leijpsigh to Koenad (08/03/1736), f. 2381.

Qoli Beg then attacked the Taymanis (Thaaymannies) with his entire force and defeated them, after which he pursued them as far as the Moghul border.[147]

VOC PRIVILEGES DISREGARDED

Despite promises, van Leijpsigh reported that Dutch privileges were totally and publicly disregarded. He considered Fars ʿAli Beg, the deputy governor, a selfish and a malicious person (*horzelkop*), who permitted that road duties were taken from a VOC caravan. Protests did not help neither did the order (tallega; *taʿliqeh*) from July 1734 nor the offer of a present. Fars ʿAli Beg told van Leijpsigh that he had orders to take road taxes from everybody. When the VOC caravan was being prepared the road guards came to inform the Dutch that they would not be treated as in the past, but now they also would have to pay road tax (*rahdari*), *gushi* (gouchi; tax on pack-animals), *mohrdari* (fee for the sealing of the bales), and *malek al-tojjari* (melik tujarie; fee for the chief merchant). The Dutch were given the warning in advance so that they would have the money ready for payment; otherwise the goods would have to remain at the road-guard house. The reason for this was that Nader had given orders to take road taxes from everybody, while the collection of road taxes was not farmed out anymore as in the past. Nader demanded a fixed amount from them, which they had to pay, irrespective of where they got it. The road guards even collected road tax from a transport of tobacco that had been brought three months ago for Nader himself. Van Leijpsigh told Fars ʿAli Beg that he was free to pay on behalf of the Dutch, because with such an imposition it was not possible anymore for the Dutch to stay who would depart like the English had done. They had always paid road taxes on the sly, but in the end they regretted that. The dragoman went to see Fars ʿAli Beg to ask for exemption in view of the VOC privileges granted in 1729 and which had been confirmed later. Fars ʿAli Beg replied: "Who are these road guards? I am a road guard and have to collect all imposts as ordered by Tamas Chan [=Nader] and to take road taxes from all coming and going merchants." The dragoman pointed out that it did not do to equate the VOC with simple merchants. Fars ʿAli Beg then asked that he bring him the royal order so that he might respect its contents. He was shown the royal order (*raqam*), and the orders (*taʿliqeh*) of 1734 and of 1735 issued by Mirza Taqi. Furthermore, the one issued on Mostafa Khan, the governor of Lar that had been given to give more security to the Dutch. Fars ʿAli Beg said after lecture of the documents that in the royal order nowhere road taxes were mentioned, which meant that a new order had to be issued. The orders (*taʿliqeh*s) were correct, and it was clear that the Dutch had received exemption from Nader. However, Fars ʿAli Beg had not received such an order. Nader needed money and was very attentive to his rights, and he did not dare to make an exception without an explicit order. He would write to the *moʿayyer-bashi*, while the Dutch were also free to lodge a complaint. Meanwhile, he advised the Dutch to pay road taxes, and if they would be granted exemption he would repay the money taken from them. Because the caravan had to depart van Leijpsigh gave in and paid, but he asked for a receipt for his books. Fars ʿAli Beg said that he did not give a receipt to anybody and he could not introduce new procedures. Everybody in town knew how much the Dutch had paid that should be sufficient. The total cost was Dfl. 27:12:9. Van Leijpsigh wrote a letter to Nader's treasurer asking him for a new order exempting the Dutch.[148]

---

147. VOC 2417, Clement (Kerman) to Koenad (18/08/1735), f. 3085; Ibid., Clement to Koenad (21/09/1735), f. 3095.

148. VOC 2416, van Leijpsigh to Koenad (08/03/1736), f. 2337-51.

PREPARATIONS FOR THE NATIONAL GATHERING
MEANS FISCAL OPPRESSION

The *farrash-bashi*, Mohammad Qasem Beg (Mhamed Cazum Beek), returned to Isfahan to make an inventory of the remaining tents, carpets and the like in the carpet and utensils department (*farrash-khaneh*). He told the Dutch that the *majles* would take place on New Year (*Nowruz*) and a fortnight later the decisions taken would be made public. The need for money continued unabated, and the Armenians still were bothered because they had not paid their quota. The Banyans received a break, because Nader repealed his earlier decree with regard to his reactive rights to their inheritances. However, others did not fare so well. Nader's agents extorted much money from the people in Bahrain using all kinds of pretext. Also, the Armenians in Isfahan continued to be pestered for money. Hajji Kalb `Ali (Calb Allie), Nader's trusted eunuch also hinted that it would be a good idea that van Leijpsigh gave a present for the shah. One of Nader's slaves, Emam Qoli Beg (Imoen Coelie beecq) was in Isfahan to make purchases and this was a good occasion to give a present of 100-150 ducats. Van Leijpsigh declined claiming that he had no money and that he needed permission from his director in Gamron. Nader finally broke the remaining resistance in the Caucasus by the Georgians and Lezgis. To weaken their resistance Nader transported 500 people from the villages around Ejmiatsin to Khorasan, where he also built churches for them. The *farrash-bashi* also confirmed the departure of Golitsyn and the *kholafa* to Russia. Kalushkin, the former's secretary had remained behind as Russian resident and was highly esteemed by Nader. Also remained behind some 20 military experts such as engineers, bombardiers, gunners and other trained military men who knew how to handle firework. It was also confirmed that Nader and his army had stayed for one month at Darband at the expense of the Russians, who had asked him to stay for three months. They offered to defray him and his army, but Nader refused. He told them that after the gathering that he had organized (at Chal Moghan) he would come back to be their guest. The Lezgis and Georgians had been subjugated, so that only the Afghans of Qandahar remained.[149] The Sorkhay Khan's[150] son was received with much honor at his court and Nader married Sorkhay Khan's daughter to confirm their union. Sorkhay Khan himself was too afraid to come in person to court.[151]

---

149. VOC 2416, van Leijpsigh to Koenad (08/03/1736), f. 2376-78, 2381-85 (f. 2381, in Turkey many young Armenians were enslaved and sold across the border where their Armenian co-religionists bought them free for sometimes as much as 10-12 *tumans* per person). The memory of these constructions may have lingered on in names of villages such as Tepe Kalisa, see C.E. Stewart, "The Country of the Tekke Turkomans, and the Tejend and Murghab Rivers," *Proceedings of the Royal Geographical Society* IX (1881), p. 530. However, Rawlinson pointed out that the word *keliseh* may be in most cases from the Turkish *keleh-kelesi* rather than from the Greek *ekklisia*. Lessar, P.M. "Second Journey in the Turkoman Country-Askabad to Ghurian near Herat," *Proceedings of the Royal Geographical Society* I (1883), p. 15.

150. Sorkhay Khan, the title of the chief of the Ghazi Qomoq tribe in Daghestan. For more information on these events see Abbas Qoli Aqa Bakikhanov, *Golestan-e Eram* (Baku, 1970) translated into English by Willem Floor & Hasan Javadi as *The Heavenly Rose-Garden. A History of Shirvan & Daghestan* (Washington DC: Mage Publishers, 2008), p. 123-32. According to Lockhart, *Nadir Shah*, p. 95, it was not his daughter, but the Usmi's daughter. The Usmi was the title of the chief of the Qeytaq, an ethnic group in in Daghestan and an ally of Sorkhay Khan. On the Usmi see Willem Floor, "Who were the Shamkhal and the Usmi?" (forthcoming).

151. VOC 2416, van Leijpsigh to Koenad (08/03/1736), f. 2384-85 (the Sorkhay, chief of the Lezgis had come to court); VOC 2416, van Leijpsigh to Koenad (16/03/1736), f. 2397.

Nader (Thamas Chan) had taken the Saffar castle, but was about to withdraw from Erevan, according to news received in Kerman, which further confirmed the conclusion of a one-year cease-fire with the Turks. Further that Russia would withdraw its troops from Baku, Darband and Georgia on secret conditions. The Russians had given Nader royal honors, and he had invited them to come to Qazvin and bring him some horses, mules and camels. The Russian ambassador who was highly respected by Nader was expected in Qazvin, where the royal palace had been embellished. It was widely believed that Nader himself, his son or his grandson (whose mother was Shah Tahmasp's sister) would be crowned as shah, in which case Nader would become his regent, who would then appoint Mirza Reza as grand vizier, whom he greatly respected. These dynastic rumors were somewhat countered by news from August 1735 when it was reported that a messenger from the former shah had brought Nader a document. Nader had asked the messenger who had sent it him to which he had replied 'Tahmasp Mirza'. Nader then had become furious and had the messenger given the bastinado so that he almost had died and had further ordered to have his tongue taken out. He then said to the messenger: "What do you call the king, Tahmasp Mirza? That is your and mine king." He then gave orders to make it known that it was not permitted to speak of Tahmasp Mirza, but only of Shah Tahmasp on pain of beheading. This news was not confirmed by subsequent reports.[152]

Through their couriers the Dutch learnt that Nader had erected the big tent which he had made on the Ramazan holiday (i.e., `eyd al-fetr` or February 13, 1736). He had his assembly (*majles*) there, and also received the Turkish ambassador Ganj `Ali Pasha and the Russian ambassador Golitsyn (Galitskin). During the *majles* there had been also an ambassador of the Baluch above Qandahar, as well as several bishops from Üch Kalisa (Utsjkalisa; i.e., Ejmiatsin).[153] Ahmad Pasha sent Nader a beautiful horse that had belonged to Timur Pasha the governor of Erevan, whom he had beheaded at the Porte's instructions. Supplies were in short supply in Nader's army and bread cost there 10 *mahmudis* per *mann-e shah*. Nader had distributed 12,000 male and female slaves (Armenians, Georgians, Turks, and Daghestanis) among the invitees to win them over, the Dutch commented. He further had the *molla-bashi* strangled, claiming that this was a punishment, because he had come too late. According to the VOC-messengers, the real reason was that during the *majles* Nader had asked those invited to appoint the person whom they wanted as shah, for he himself wanted to spend his days in devotion in Kalat. The *majles* then stated that it wanted nobody else but Nader, for he was their protector. It was believed that by New Year (*Nowruz*) this matter would be settled, for the Porte had made it clear it only wanted to make peace with the shah. Nader appointed `Abdol-Baqi Khan as his ambassador to the Porte, who was accompanied by Mir `Abdol-Qasem, the rascally Afghan Sayyed Sadeq, and some of the leading mullahs.[154]

---

152. VOC 2417, Clement to de Cleen (15/10/1735), f. 3110-24.

153. For the account by the Armenian patriarch of these events see *The Chronicle of Abraham of Crete* translated and annotated by George A. Bournoutian (Costa Mesa, 1999).

154. VOC 2416, van Leijpsigh to Koenad (16/03/1736), f. 2393-98 ("Nader's princess wife who had left Isfahan in December 1735 was still with her sister, the wife of the abovementioned Miersa Abbul Cassum [the *farrash-bashi*] in Qamsar near Kashan. She will not go to Kalat. Aga Camal had died and H.H. [i.e. Nader] will be pleased about that.")

FINALLY, NADER SHAH

Prior to the Chal Moghan meeting Nader had summoned his four most important generals, to wit: Ebrahim Khan, his brother, Pir Mohammad Khan, governor of Herat, Thamasp Qoli Khan, *sardar*, and Mohammad Taqi Shirazi. Nader pointed out to them that the kingdom needed a king to conclude a peace treaty with the Turks and to rule the country. The general assembly had to choose the next king in all freedom. It was said that they all had replied that Nader was their sole choice.[155]

During the Chal Moghan gathering Nader asked the participants to elect their shah, he wanted to withdraw to enjoy his old age. Those gathered asked him to become their shah, as he had wanted, for he was their protector. Nader then asked that they seal a document stating that they all elected him out of their own free will without force having been used. To this they agreed and he was loudly hailed as shah. He then ordered that henceforth he would be known as Nader Shah or *Vali Ne'mat*. The Dutch learnt from participants that his troops had been armed with cudgels with the clear intention to kill all those present if they had not elected him as shah.[156]

On New Year, March 21, 1736 the news of the election of Nader as the new shah was made known in Isfahan which was followed by the beating of the drums which only lasted three days and there was no illumination, for all this would be done when he would come to Isfahan. Nader had given orders, however, not to call him Shah but *Vali Ne'mat*. One day after his crowning Nader did not use the specially made *masnad* anymore and just sat on the ground as usual. There was no illumination in Kerman nor were clarions blown, which things were customarily done when a king was crowned. His money did not bear the title of king, as was customary, but just Nader. His seal had the text: *negin-e dowlat din bas keh rafteh bud [a] z jay/ beh nam-e Nader-e Iran qarardar khoday* (negiene, douleth, dien baskieraffta boedse jhay, beher nouw nadder, iroen karaer dhaar ghoday), of "the immeasurable costly jewel of religion that had been moved much from its place, God has put solidly in its place in the name of the Persian Nader." On his money the following text had been struck: *sekkeh bar zar kard nam-e saltanatra dar Jahan/ Nader-e Iran Zamin o Khosrow-e giti-setan* (zikke bher sherke heerd no-emhe selthenet Rhaderh jehoen nadderhee iroen samien nogosrouwhee githie zultoen) or "this silver has been coined in the name of the greatest on earth and of him who purifies it from its enemies, whose equal is not found on Persian soil."[157]

THE RUSSIAN EMBASSY

Van Leijpsigh reported that Golitsyn had been brought to Nader as a prisoner. Later it was said that he was treated with all respect and friendship. Maybe because the Russian general at Darband had sent Nader ships with food supplies when he had a shortage of them during the siege of Ganjeh. This was deemed credible, because the Russian resident, Semen Avramov's wife had to select two black (*kaffersche*) women at Nader's instruction. The Russian general had asked for the two

---

155. VOC 2368, Koenad to Batavia (19/03/1736), f. 22.

156. VOC 2584, Beschrijvinge, f. 2018-20; see also Brosset, *Collection d'Historiens Armeniens*, vol. 2, p. 328.

157. VOC 2417, Clement to Koenad (29/04/1736), f. 3170-71.

women. Safi Khan Beg (Saafie Chan Beek) was in charge of Golitsyn's defrayment.[158] Meanwhile, the two Persian ambassadors (Gollofa Miersa Kafi and Miersa Keyas, the former *vaqaye´-nevis*) returned from Russia. They had been sent by Shah Tahmasp II and were related to one another. The Georgian prince Wakhtang Mirza with his son Shah Navaz Khan (Sjah Nerwaaschan) had arrived from Moscow to Baku. Nader had assigned Safi Khan Beg to see to their defrayment and to invite them to him. Whether they would do that remained to be seen, van Leijpsigh observed.[159] The Russians did not receive the daily defrayment of 70 *mahmudi*s (Dfl. 29:15) anymore and the sub-lieutenant of the few soldiers they had there was forced to borrow money in the bazaar for their living expenses by drawing a draft on Baku. Nader had offended Golitsyn (Galotskien)[160] twice in the royal council; he even had taken him by the throat and expelled him from the council. Van Leijpsigh did not know why. Later it was said that he was treated with all respect, which maybe was due to the Russian general's commitment to supply Nader with men, ordinance (bombs, mortars) and food supplies. This was followed by the total withdrawal ("left this earth with cat and dog") from the towns of Baku, Darband, Niazawaar, and Salian. Nader allegedly had promised to refuse to make peace with the Turks and to push them back to their borders. In exchange Russia would send troops and military supplies. Golitsyn was still at court in May 1735. The resident Semen Avramov had also gone to Nader. Van Leijpsigh hoped that the Russians would never gain permanent access to Persian soil, because it would be disadvantageous to both the Dutch and English Companies. "However, Tamas Chan (=Nader) is untrustworthy and it is quite possible that he leaves them in the lurch once the work has been done." Nader had ordered diamonds, rubies, and pearls as a present for the empress of Russia. Pearls of 16 *habba*s were not for sale; the jewelers and the chiefs (kadchodas; *kadkhoda*) of Jolfa were given the bastinado.[161]

Semen Avramov (Simon Abrahamitsz), who had returned to Russia, on arrival in St. Petersburg was immediately beheaded and quartered as a traitor at the empress's orders. This was due to Golitsyn who had accused him in letters of having secretly accepted rich presents from Nader (Thamas Chan) and above all to have represented his own rather than the empress's interests. It had further been the Russian plan to install Wakhtang Mirza on the throne of Georgia and in this manner keep Nader out of there. The latter prevented this by quickly sending his own troops to Georgia. Golitsyn suspected that Avramov had supplied Nader with the information about this plan. Nader was said to be very depressed about his death and to have thrown his hat on the ground while saying that he had now lost a great friend and his right arm. He was said to have cursed Golitsyn and to have further denied him permission to appear before him, while telling him to get lost and returning the bombs that the Russians had given him. Golitsyn therefore was forced to return without having received an answer. He was

---

158. VOC 2357, van Leijpsigh to Hey (04/02/1735), f. 1142, 1145-46; VOC 2416, van Leijpsigh to Hey (04/02/1735), f. 1854.

159. VOC 2357, van Leijpsigh to Koenad (28/02/1735), f. 1127; VOC 2416, van Leijpsigh to Hey (04/02/1735), f.1841, 1854-55. The *kholofa* and Mirza Qeyas were both members of the influential Nasiri family, which had held the function of *vayaye´-nevis*, of *kholofa*, the governorship of Qarajehdagh and the management (*towliyat*) of the Sheikh Shehab al-Din shrine, and other functions as a kind of hereditary apanage. Nasiri, *Titles*, pp. 9-10, 47-49.

160. Prince Michael Mikailovich Golitsyn was a member of the War College; from 1740 to 1745 governor of Astrakhan and Russian ambassador to Persia between 1745 and 1748.

161. VOC 2357, van Leijpsigh to Koenad (03/06/1735), f. 1836-41; VOC 2357, private letter van Leijpsigh to Koenad (30/03/1735), f. 657.

said to be at Soulaag [?], a location that had belonged to the Cherkes in the past. Golitsyn had returned it to them and another part to the Persians. This he had written to the sub-lieutenant (propoletjiek; sic, properly пропрщик) of the small group of Russian military in Isfahan with orders to decamp immediately and to take Avramov's wife with him. Nader wrote her a very polite and consoling letter and ordered the deputy-governor of Isfahan to give her 63 *tuman*s (Dfl. 2,667:10) to defray her for a period of three months, which were not given to her. He also had to appoint an escort (*mehmandar*) and to arrange for her pack-animals and defray her during her journey to Rasht where she would embark on a ship. It was further reported that Nader after Avramov's death had ordered to collect henceforth and retro-activily customs duties and other taxes from Russian merchants in Rasht and elsewhere in N.Persia. He also was said not to want to have another Russian agent in Isfahan.[162]

[After the Turkish defeat at Kars] Golitsyn reportedly had received leave to depart. He had induced Nader not to make peace with the Turk without permission from Russia. Hasan `Ali Khan, the *mo`ayyer-bashi*, was said to be send as ambassador to Russia.[163] It was said that a new Russian resident would come. Golitsyn had traveled to meet up with the *kholafa* to return together to Russia. The *kholafa* was said to depart with 1,000 men.[164] Golitsyn had left for Russia, while the *kholafa* was still in Darband waiting for the elephants. Van Leijpsigh wrote that it was unclear to him what the purpose of this embassy was. Nader reportedly also had send letters to six other European kings that the *kholafa* has to present. The contents of the letters were that he wanted to maintain the old friendship as in the past.[165] [Meanwhile, the Persian envoys to Divel had returned] with amongst other things two elephants, which Nader intended to send as a present to the Russian empress. The *kholafa* allegedly also had a letter with him for the emperor in Vienna that he has to present in person. Golitsyn had left a resident behind named Ivan Kalushkin (Kaloetskie), who had been his secretary. It was also reported that the Russians had defrayed Nader for one month at Darband. The Russians had asked him to stay three months at their cost, but he had refused. Nader had told them that after the meeting [at which he would be acclaimed as shah] he would return for three days to be their guest. Nader held the Russians in great esteem. Golitsyn also had left behind 20 engineers, bombardiers, gunners, and people who were expert in handling fireworks.[166]

CHANGES AFTER THE CORONATION

It was said that Shah Tahmasp had been taken to Sabzavar and received a stipend of 7,000 *tuman*s per year. He was said to be in Hazar Jarib in Mazandaran, while others said he was in Sabzavar. `Abdol-Baqi Khan and his suite, consisting of Mir`Abdol-Qasem (Mier Abdul Cassum), Sayyed Sadeq (Seyit Sadeg), the qadi and other olama, had left for Istanbul in the company of the Turkish ambasasador Ganj `Ali Pasha (Gens Allie Patchia) with the election document to make it clear to the Porte that the Persian subjects had chosen their new shah out of free will. Moreover, that

---

162. VOC 2416, van Leijpsigh to Koenad (29/06/1735), f. 2086-91.

163. VOC 2416, van Leijpsigh to Koenad (06/06/1735), f. 2075-76.

164. VOC 2416, van Leijpsigh to Koenad (01/09/1735), f. 2263.

165. VOC 2416, van Leijpsigh to Koenad (26/11/1735), f. 2290-91.

166. VOC 2416, van Leijpsigh to Koenad (03/08/1736), f. 2357-58, 2384.

henceforth no difference would be made between the Turkish and the Persian religion and that every subject was free to follow the [Moslem] religion of his liking, something that greatly upset the Persians. In this way Nader wanted to induce the Turks to make peace and acknowledge him as shah. Nader was expected to come to Isfahan in June 1736. He further ordered to strike a new coin and to supply him with 20,000 strong jarabs (*jurab*) or shoes for his soldiers so that they could easily climb the mountains of the Baktiyari Lurs (Bagtiarisse Lorren) and destroy them. Nader's son, Reza Qoli Khan had been appointed as prince or *vali* (walie) of Khorasan, and his brother Ebrahim Khan as *beglerbegi* of Azerbaijan. Mirza Taqi [Shirazi] had been given the title of khan and had been appointed as *beglerbegi* of Fars. Hasan `Ali Khan (Hasan Alie Chan), the *mo`ayyer-bashi*, became governor of Isfahan and Iraq-e `Ajam (Erach). He also was expected to become grand vizier. The governor (*saheb-e ekhtiyar*) of Kerman, Mirza Reza (Miersa Resa) became vizier of Isfahan. The former *mostowfi*, Mirza Mohammad Hoseyn (Miersa Mhamed Hossein) became vizier of Fars and all lower lands. It was also reported that the treasurer, Mirza Mohammad (Miersa Mhamed) (then also khan) became Nader's steward or *nazer*. The well-known Miersa Keyas became *vaqaye`-nevis* (wakanevies). Mostafa Khan and Mohammad Latif Khan lost their posts and even were said to have run the risk of loosing their life, but for the intercession by Mohammad Taqi Khan Shirazi. Nader had allowed the latter to take Mohammad Latif Khan with him without employ. The new steward (*nazer*) was said to come ahead of Nader to clean the palaces. Nader also was said to have ordered 12,000 Afshar, and other northern (*bovenlandse*) families to come to Isfahan and settle around the city, because he could rely on them.[167]

On March 28, 1736 a courier (*chapar*) arrived from Chal Moghan with news that the *min-bashi* `Askar Beg (Askerbeeck) had been accused of mismanagement and had been dismissed from his new post of *zabet* or receiver of the royal revenues of Chahar Mahall (tjarmahaal). He had extorted 400 *tuman*s more than was usual from the subjects and had not recorded it in the ledgers and had used it for himself. He was said to have been strangled with a shawl. Van Leijpsigh feared that his letter to the treasurer, Mirza Mohammad, which he had sent with this *min-bashi*, would have been mislaid. After the coronation new silver `abbasis were struck in Nader's name. It was said that the *mo`ayyer-bashi* would not become grand vizier, but if Nader would appoint one then it would be him. It was also reported that Nader had sent a certain Mullah Mohammad Hoseyn (Molla Mhamed Hosseyn) to Tahmasp Mirza to inform him about Nader's election as shah, which he had not been able to refuse in the interest of the country and people's well-being and therefore he had assumed this heavy burden. Tahmasp Mirza was allowed to choose between Sabzavar, Qazvin or Cham [?] and that Nader would take care of his and his family's sustenance. Nader also had appointed a certain Sayyed Mirza Morteza (Seyit Miersa Mortusa), brother of the former Navab Mirza Moqim (Nabab Miersa Mockiem), as *ishik aghasi-bashi* of his harem and the well-known Hajji Kalb `Ali as chief (*rish safid* of the harem) of the eunuchs. Both of them had to take Nader's harem to Isfahan. Mirza Mehdi Kowkabi (Koukes) Astarabadi, "a rascal (*doortrapte gast*)," was made poet laureate, and, because he had written a history about the deeds of Mahmud and Ashraf he was ordered to write the heroic deeds of Nader. The new silver `abbasis were immediately struck in the Mint and the shoes were prepared in great haste, and it was ordered to bring them to Peria, because Vali Ne`mat (Welie Nahmed) would come via Hamadan to march against the Bakhtiyaris. Among the latter a leader called Shah Morad (sjah moeraad) had arisen, who had

---

167. VOC 2416, van Leijpsigh to Koenad (23/03/1735), f. 2401-06.

gone to Shushtar to exhort its population to join his cause. He had put the royal aigrette (*jiqeh*) on his head. The Shushtaris, however, offered him 6,000 *tuman*s to be left alone, because they still had not recuperated from the blow that Mohammad Khan Baluch had dealt them. However if he were able to defeat the enemy of the country (=Nader) then they would be ready to subject themselves to him wholeheartedly. Nader further was said to have decided to send his joker (*boufon*) Mirza Taqi to India as ambassador. He also reportedly had demanded the Russians to send him all Persians who had gone to Astrakhan. Nader had sent the ex-shah and his family to Sabzavar. He also had assigned 1,000 *tuman*s for their annual expenditures as well as allowed him 40 servants and two horses. However, the ex-shah was not allowed to go out riding, to walk around only inside his house, and to go to the bathhouse occasionally. Many Persians thought that Nader had already killed the ex-shah.[168]

NADER WANTS VOC AND EIC TO BE MORE HELPFUL

On April 6, 1736 Mohammad Taqi accompanied by Mohammad Latif Khan and Mir Mehr ʿAli Soltan arrived in Isfahan. Van Leijpsigh brought them a visit two days later. He was asked to read an order (*raqam*) from Nader for the directors of the VOC and EIC. In this order Nader had appointed Mohammad Taqi as his plenipotentiary to deal with both Companies, because he was too busy to wage war to deal with requests. Now that he had vanquished his enemies and there was peace with Turkey he hoped that the country would flourish. Mohammad Taqi was now the governor-general of all the lower lands and the Companies had to help him to take Bahrain as well as in other matters. If they failed to do so, or betrayed him, they would be held responsible. Van Leijpsigh interjected here that this applied to the English, but that the Dutch were tarred with the same brush. Mohammad Taqi would grant them privileges that the Companies would ask for, but that all requests had to be addressed to him. Later the dragoman was sent for and instructed not to divulge anything about the Bahrain plan because it was still a secret. Also, that he would send a special agent to Gamron to discuss this matter. When Mohammad Taqi made a contra-visit he asked van Leijpsigh whether he was satisfied that the merchant Zeyn al-ʿAbedin had been dismissed, because violent interference repelled them. He replied that it had calmed the merchants and now many more would come to trade at Gamron. Mohammad Taqi then asked why trade was so bad? Van Leijpsigh replied that the reason was because most merchants had been ruined, that there was a scarcity of money, and because trade was at such a low level that merchants could not even earn their overhead. This was clear from trade in Isfahan, based on his own observation. The other visitors confirmed this. Van Leijpsigh then raised the issue of road taxes. Mohammad Taqi replied that Fars ʿAli Beg had told him that he collected road taxes from all European merchants, and that he was now in an awkward situation how to deal with the Dutch in the future, for he had sent a request about the matter, but had not received a reply. Mohammad Taqi had told Fars ʿAli Beg to be satisfied with what he had collected, but in the future to allow exemption to the Dutch, for Vali Neʿmat (=Nader) had ordered to confirm their privileges. Mohammad Taqi treated the Banyans with much respect and gave them strongly worded orders (tallegas; *taʿliqeh*) addressed to his brother and son to return immediately all that had been taken from them. Mir Mehr ʿAli Soltan complained to the VOC dragoman about van Leijpsigh, because he had not wanted to lend him money the last time he had been in Isfahan. The EIC dragoman, Hermet,

---

168. VOC 2461, van Leijpsigh to Koenad (30/03/1736), f. 2409-2416.

received a sealed letter from Gamron that he forwarded unopened to the royal court. It was said that the Turk did not want to conclude peace. Therefore, Vali Ne'mat had demanded that Hoseyn Khan Qandahari send him 12,000 men. However, the latter made moves as if he were to attack the Persians. Nader therefore sent the *sardar* Tahmasp Qoli Khan and Pir Mohammad Soltan, the governor of Herat against him. On April 1, a Persian emigrant came from India, where he was in the service of the Mughal's grand vizier, with costly Indian articles with a value of 5,000 *tuman*s. He was a physician and came as an envoy of the grand vizier to the Persian court.[169]

Vali Ne'mat had been in Qazvin for some time, which had suffered much as a consequence. He was said to have marched to Hamadan. His envoys had been held up in Erzerum and so as to stimulate the Turk he had sent a small elephant to Ahmad Pasha. Furthermore, he demanded they send him some costly fabrics, apart from the rich presents that his envoys already had for the pasha. He also gave orders to read the names of Abu Bakr, 'Omar and 'Uthman in the *khotbeh* and to end it henceforth not any longer with the words "welie alie, but just with alie." There was a rumor that 15,000 of Nader's troops had rebelled, because of the change in religion, but the Dutch were convinced that it was only a rumor put about by ill-meaning people. It was not clear whether the Turks wanted peace or not. Hoseyn Khan Qandahari, who had both courage and might, had declared that he would take the Persian throne. However, Nader was already making preparations to attack him. In early June, Mirza Taqi, his buffoon, with some 20 of the oldest nobles, had ridden to Kerman to collect food supplies along the route to Seistan. Further, to clean out the old wells that had become stuck with dirt as well as to dig new ones. The ex-shah was in Sabzavar with 70 servants who had been hand-picked by Vali Ne'mat. The other servants were old slaves. The ex-shah allegedly had told them that it would be better to leave him and seek their fortune elsewhere. It was also reported that if peace would come that Nader would not go to Hamadan, but to the Alvand Mountain to take radix china as well as fresh air so as to be in better health. The Dutch were told that apart from normal food that Nader could not digest his food. He also would come there walking so as to enjoy peace and quiet of his labors in his old age (he was said to have passed 60), after so many tiring activities. Van Leijpsigh complained that you could not trust a Persian's word. In May 1736, Mirza Mohammad 'Ali (Miersa Mhamed Allie), the clerk of Fars 'Ali Beg, deputy-governor of Isfahan, showed van Leijpsigh in secret a letter from the governor, Hasan 'Ali Khan, to his deputy concerning the collection of imposts. It had been sealed on the back, as was usual. He copied the letter, and then raised the issue with Mohammad Taqi Khan. The latter replied that he had resolved the matter with the deputy-governor and there was a royal order (*raqam*) stating that no imposts should be taken from the Dutch. Fars 'Ali Beg wrote about this to the *mo'ayyer-bashi* who replied that this couldn't be true, because there was not such a royal order and Fars 'Ali Beg could collect imposts from the Dutch. If these would show a royal order exempting them then it had been obtained under false pretext. The road guards therefore came to the Dutch factory to demand 100 *mahmudi*s concerning imported goods, which the Dutch refused to pay. The Dutch lodged a complaint with Fars 'Ali Beg with reference to what Mohammad Taqi Khan had said and asked him to instruct the road guards accordingly. Fars 'Ali Beg replied that Mohammad Taqi Khan had told him to continue to serve Vali Ne'mat's interests and therefore to continue to collect road taxes and to stop doing so only when the Dutch director at Gamron would have given him satisfaction as to what Nader had

---

169. VOC 2416, van Leijpsigh to Koenad (30/03/1736 + appendix 11/04/1736), f. 2416-33.

demanded. Van Leijpsigh showed Fars 'Ali Beg the last royal order received from Vali Ne'mat in which he stated that he agreed to anything that Mohammad Taqi Khan would grant the Dutch. Fars 'Ali Beg said that the royal order was correct and he asked for a copy. He then would instruct the road guards not to bother the Dutch until he had written the governor. When he received the copy Fars 'Ali Beg told the Dutch that he had changed his mind. It would be better to pay something, because he impossibly could exempt the Dutch from payment of road taxes unless there was a clear-cut royal order. Moreover, Fars was under a different governor than Isfahan, who had no jurisdiction there. Fars 'Ali Beg told the Dutch to get a royal order addressed to the governor of Isfahan, which meant, so van Leijpsigh commented, that for each different governor a separate royal order would have to be obtained. The Dutch therefore informed Fars 'Ali Beg that the Isfahan factory was under the jurisdiction of the director in Gamron, and that they had a royal order granting total exemption of taxes. Therefore they asked for a delay until they had written about this matter to Mohammad Taqi Khan. Fars 'Ali Beg reacted that it would be better to pay something, because else last year's books could not be closed. The Dutch finally gave in and paid, while they also wrote to Mohammad Taqi Khan and his first clerk, Aqa Ja'far. The VOC Banyan who had traveled from Isfahan to Shiraz also had to pay 30 *mahmudi*s road taxes, despite the fact that under the terms of the VOC privileges he also enjoyed tax exemption. The Dutch had learnt that the total income of that tax had been fixed at 360,000 *tuman*s for the year 1736 and the two next years. The Banyan had protested and Mohammad Taqi Khan had allowed his tax exemption. The road guards had become so forward that they took two *mahmudi*s per person from the messengers, at each road guard station. The royal order had been written four days prior to Nader's election to shah and had not only granted exemption of road taxes (*rahdari*), but also from *malek al-tojjari*, *gushi* and others, because the Persian text stated *rahdari va gheyro* (radarie we geijre). Meanwhile, the plan to capture Bahrain was bruited all over town. The flight of the English and French from Gamron had led to their public mockery in Isfahan. Van Leijpsigh asked Gamron in case the Dutch would depart whether they also would have to pay 12½ % customs duties like the French. Joseph Jacob Hermet, the brother of the EIC dragoman, received and sent goods on account of the EIC claiming that he did not have to pay imposts. Some of the [Catholic] religious were not ashamed in agreeing with that young man. However, van Leijpsigh learnt that this so-called physician indeed had to pay duties. The Kermani Tovakkol Beg (Toackel Beeck) had arrived in Isfahan as tax collector (*mohassel*) with a pack of royal orders to confiscate the houses and some goods belonging to certain persons, just like already had happened to Mirza Mehdi Kowkabi (Miersa Megdie Koukes) and two others. The vizier of Isfahan, Mirza Reza, was shocked to see him, while other officials also were afraid and asked themselves what was in store for them. Rumors abounded, and the population suffered. There had been a general census of inhabited houses in Isfahan and it had been found that these numbered 8,000. In the time of Shah Soltan Hoseyn that number was 90,000 and during the reign of Ashraf, after he had constructed new walls and had destroyed many homes, the number had been 40,000. This number gave an indication of the level of ruination of Isfahan, which was depopulated and this oppressive government could not make this much better. The Bakhtiyaris (Bagtiarische Lorren) were active again at Gandaman (Genemoen), Peria and other locations where they plundered the villages and took its inhabitant as slaves into the mountains. Recently, pilgrims had returned from Mecca and were very angry about the treatment received from the Turks. They said that prior to Nader's proclamation to shah they had been treated well; this did not bode well for peace. It was also reported that the Russians wanted to go to war again with Vali Neʿmat. The empress was said to have returned the presents, and the *kholofa* to have had his ears, nose and lips cut off. Nader had the inhabitants of Qazvin pay for the cost of a new palace, total cost 5,000 *tumans* in addition to their normal taxes. Nader had said that the building was too beautiful for him and he would rather live in a tent. As far as he was concerned the Qazvinis could do with it what they liked. "Poor Isfahan, when he will come there" van Leijpsigh commented. His army consisted of 120,000 men. At the beginning of July he needed to have that amount ready in *tumans*, and if not there would be trouble. Also, it was rumored that Nader would send ʿAli Mardan Khan again as ambassador to India, but this had been contradicted, for he was said to have appointed Mostafa Khan Begdeli (Mostafa Chan Beegdeelie), the former ambassador of Hamadan as such.[170]

On July 17, 1736 the Dutch messengers returned to Isfahan, because the road guards did not let them pass without payment. They also disregarded the pass that the messenger had. Their chief, Mohammad ʿAli Beg, informed the Dutch that if he let them pass he would run a deficit and he would therefore write the deputy-governor about it. Van Leijpsigh wrote the *rahdar-bashi* to allow the messengers to pass, because it had not been customary to take road tax from messengers. Vali Neʿmat had marched from Qazvin to Hamadan. The road to Basra had been closed already for three months and during that period no couriers had come from there. Qazvin was said to have suffered much from Vali Neʿmat's stay there. He reportedly had sent 150 of its leading families to Khorasan. The remaining inhabitants had all been reduced to beggary. Furthermore, the Armenian families of which it had been said that they would be settled in the neighboring villages [around Isfahan?] had only reached Chamen Sawa [?], where they had been ordered to remain. They had suffered much misery and continued to do so. Later it appeared that Nader had ordered them taken to Khorasan as well. Many died like animals en route, because of their great misery, for they only received one *mann* of bad dry bread per day and one "boertje" (sic; probably a *yabu* or pony) to carry their rags [i.e., their clothes and bedding]. It was also rumored that Vali Neʿmat wanted to summon all *kadkhodas* from all over the country. The sending of an ambassador to India had been postponed again. It was also said that Vali Neʿmat had appointed 50, according to others 100, *min-bashis* to recruit men and garrison the towns with them. However, the men had to be able to maintain their own horse and servants and to come well-armed. They would received 10 *tumans* (Dfl. 425) per year and per person from the royal treasury. A certain ʿAli Khan came to Isfahan, while Tovakkol Beg left after having confiscated only the houses of those mentioned and then had returned to court. Meanwhile, many inhabitants left town to retire to the neighboring villages on the basis of the simple rumor that Vali Neʿmat would come to Isfahan. They wanted to be free of the army's harassment and also took their newest doors and windows with them so that these would not be burnt.[171]

---

170. VOC 2416, van Leijpsigh to Koenad (17/07/1736), f. 2447-2503.

171. VOC 2416, van Leijpsigh to Koenad (21/07/1736), f. 2505-11.

PREPARATIONS FOR QANDAHAR — SOLDIERS AND OFFICIALS ARE OPPRESSIVE

The *mo`ayyer-bashi* was greatly respected and everybody, big and small, came to pay their respects and give presents to be on his good side in view of his great influence with the shah. Van Leijpsigh also sent him a present on August 4, 1736 and visited him on August 19. Van Leijpsigh asked him not to expel VOC staff from their homes to quarter soldiers as had happened in other cases. Agha Mohammad, the treasurer, arrived on August 24 in Isfahan. The *kalantar* of Isfahan was Mirza Hoseyn (Miersa Hossein), and Mohammad `Ali Beg was the confidante of the *mo`ayyer-bashi*. They all asked for European spirits except for the deputy-governor. They now also were in the habit to have the women of the harem drink with them. Throughout the day one heard about carousals. They walked in public with their bottles of wine in their hands. Everywhere it was as the French say: *vive la joie*. The magnates, but also others, constantly bothered the Dutch asking them for spirits. They even came with money wanting to buy them as if the factory was a pub, but these were all sent away with kind words. The whole town was filled with soldiers and every night there was the sound of the drums, so that one's ears were ringing. Aqa Taher, the factor of Mohammad `Ali who had died at Divel, had received a commission from Vali Ne`mat together with four other persons to buy all the necessaries for the army. It concerned goods such as shoes, clothing, horse tack, etc. They were to sell this in the army for Nader's own benefit. He intended to march to Qandahar, but left on August 21, 1736 for Shiraz with the intention of visiting the coast. The Dutch first thought that the new Russian envoy was Petrus Joannits,[172] but it was Kalushkin, the ambassador's secretary. He was called *vaqaye`-nevis* by the Persians. He had come on August 17. His suite occupied the entire French house, from which he kicked out the French dragoman, Narcis. En route he had received defrayment of 120 *mahmudis* per day, but in Isfahan only 100 *mahmudis*. Van Leijpsigh brought Kalushkin on a visit on August 19. The Russians had only supported Nader with one iron mortar and 12 *mann* of gunpowder and then only at his request. Nader had received, however, barges with rice for his troops at Ganjeh. There also was a Russian consul with 300 men at Rasht to protect Russian merchants against Persian chicaneries. They also allegedly enjoyed exemption of customs duties. The son of the *nasaqchi-bashi* (nesjaagje basje) or grand provost, Abu'l-Hasan Beg, inhabited the EIC house, while there also were two gardeners who were paid by the English. It was said that Nader was held up in the Bakhtiyari Mountains, while others said that he was pursuing Morad Shah (Moeraad Sjah), who had pulled down the wooden bridge of Shushtar and had come hither. According to others he had marched to Hoveyzeh. The *vali* of Hoveyzeh was said to have sought refuge with his family with the Arabs in the desert. It was also said that preparations were being made at Isfahan for the campaign against Qandahar. Nader was said to march via Mashhad rather than Kerman. In Mashhad, *sardar* Tahmasp Qoli Khan had died a natural death before he could march on Qandahar. Because of this reason wells had been dug en route; the water samples that were sent to Nader all tasted bitter. Nader then summoned Mirza Taqi from Kerman telling him that he could not march via that route. There also were rumors that Herat had been taken, while the Lezgis also were making trouble again.[173]

There continued to be nuisance because of the soldiers, who all looked for alcohol. On October 9, 1736, Nader arrived in the Sa`adatabad garden and received many costly presents. On October 13, he entered the royal palace in Isfahan. He then whetted his greedy and

172. I have not been able to identify this person.

173. VOC 2416, van Leijpsigh to Koenad (13/09/1736), f. 2513-33.

murderous lust, for one day, people saw the corpses of executed people lying in front of the royal palace on the *meydan*, while the news was dominated by extortion and violence. He had been fighting the Bakhtiyari leader, Shah Morad. Nader caught up with him and cruelly killed him and 200 supporters. Another 200 families he sent to Khorasan. Nader was forced to leave another 5,000 of those robbers alone due to the severe cold in the mountains. During three nights an illumination was made in front of the royal palace, which pleasantry the Dutch had to attend twice at the behest of the royal treasurer. They watched from one of the upper rooms of the palace and remarked that the population no doubt had shed tears at the sight of the burning of so much wealth. When it was over there was a short instance of joy, which soon changed into a tragedy. For the annual tax burden was doubled. Isfahan had to pay 12,000 *tumans*, and other cities in proportion. "This shah is a consuming fire for this empire," the Dutch commented. His army of 200,000 soldiers, slaves, camp followers and animals was like a cloud of locusts for, *en passant,* it devoured everything. Nader had been busy inspecting his troops and sent 6,000 of them to Shirvan under the command of Sardar Khan (Serdaar Chan), a relative of his. It was said that this army had to tame the Lezgis who, led by Sorkhay Khan, had attacked Shirvan again. It was still unknown whether Nader would march via Kerman or Mashhad to Qandahar. A friend of van Leijpsigh opined that Nader would only march on Qandahar when there was peace with the Turks. Beyram `Ali Khan (Beyran Allie Chan), a well-known courageous man had been strangled by Nader, because he asked that unfortunate man during a wine-drinking get-together (*majles*) (Nader was said to drink deeply), what kind of children would be born to the women who had been loved by 10 soldiers. He then had answered: "One just like you, a *nader-e du-ru* [a rare two-faced (child),i.e., a bastard]. This Nero did not tolerate that." Nader further had done away with the Afshar cap and wore a turban mostly in the Arab fashion (not in the Afghan, Lur or *jehantazi* [?] fashion) with the aigrette (*jiqeh*) in the middle and not on the right side as was customary for the Safavids. He was addicted to alcohol as well as to women, whom he denied nothing, which cost him much. He also wanted to summon all governors to Chal Moghan. Van Leijpsigh in person had given Nader presents after his entry into Isfahan. He noted that the treasurer stood at his right side and the *mo`ayyer-bashi* on the left side, below Nader, who sat on the *talar* [gallery]. Van Leijpsigh approached till 60 paces separated them. Then he was quickly excused and taken away by the *ishik aghashi-bashi*. On October 10, 1736 Kalushkin was summoned by Nader in all haste.[174]

Because of the continuing requests for money and brandy in Isfahan, the council in Gamron unanimously decided that when the Isfahan office would be harassed because of a refusal to lend or give those items and unable to get redress, the staff would be permitted to leave Isfahan secretly with all that they could carry, especially the precious papers. In case a bond was demanded van Leijpsigh had to refuse and delay until the end. The dragoman, who would remain behind, would not be authorized to make any commitment on behalf of the VOC. He had to insist on VOC rights and refer them to Gamron and ask it for orders.[175]

---

174. VOC 2416, van Leijpsigh to Koenad (26/10/1736), f. 2534-64; VOC 2584, Beschrijvinge, f. 2022-23. This probably was not Naser `Ali Khan, who held the function of *ishik aghashi-bashi* in 1746. He was assisted by the *yasavol-bashi*, Shah Qoli Khan. VOC 2705, f. 371. The shah's treasurer at that time was Aqa Taher. VOC 2705 (31/07/1746), f. 98.

175. VOC 2417, Secret Resolution Gamron (12/09/1736), f. 3461-62.

MIRZA TAQI KHAN SUGGEST VOC TO GET CONFIRMATION
OF ITS PRIVILEGES

Mohammad Taqi Khan arrived on November 11, 1736 in Isfahan with costly presents for Nader, for which Shulgistan, Abadeh, Yazdekhvast, and Surmak had bled. The tyrant gave him a horse with a costly robe of honor, some minor presents, a piece of cloth, and a pocket watch. Mohammad Taqi Khan was well received despite the many cruel deeds he had committed in the lower lands on account of which he had feared for his life. According to his own minion, Aqa Ja`far, even he could not pluck anymore from those lands, because of the bottomless greed of that big beast, reason why he wanted to resign from his post. However, because of the presents, the reception of Nader, his harem and retainers in Yazdekhvast had pleased that despoiler so much, he abandoned that notion. Having escaped the noose and nothing to fear because of the destruction of the lower lands this money grubber stayed on. According to his secretary (monshi), Mirza Mohammad, 10,000 men had gone to Gamron for unknown reasons. Recently, Mohammad Taqi Khan summoned his agent (wackiel; *vakil*) from Gamron, the Banyan (*pythagorist*) Gesjaal Ketgoda Multani, who had told him all kinds of fanciful things about the two Companies, so that he might prepare his unreasonable demands with that information. Van Leijpsigh wrote: "it will cost you [Koenad] a good present when he will be there. We also gave him something to keep him in good spirits, because he delayed very much to try and get to talk to the shah about Company affairs." On September 19, Sahid the dragoman went to see him. Mohammad Taqi Khan reacted that he was so busy that he did not even have time to receive van Leijpsigh. Later he fell off the horse that Nader had given him and he hurt his left leg. Mirza Mohammad also had an accident after a merry evening. Nader ordered that both had to stay in the treasury (*sandoek chana*) of the royal palace until they had healed. Via the treasurer the Dutch were able to contact him to keep their relationship current. On November 17, 1736 Mohammad Taqi Khan said to the dragoman that he could not come to the factory to see van Leijpsigh, who had to wait till he was better, but that he would detail to the dragoman what he had to say about whatever the VOC wanted. Sahid said to him that Nader had delegated all VOC business to him and that without his approval no request could be submitted to Nader, in this case a new royal order. Mohammad Taqi Khan agreed with that. Sahid continued that the VOC wanted to request the confirmation of the royal orders that had been sealed by Tahmasp Mirza and Vali Ne`mat. Then the Dutch could send these royal orders to Batavia so that their great ones might see that one might do good business with the new shah. Mohammad Taqi Khan replied that without having seen these royal orders he could not do anything, but he assumed that there were copies in the factory and he asked Sahid to bring them to him. After this had been done, he read them from beginning to end and then kept them saying that he would discuss the matter with the shah. However, Mohammad Taqi Khan also complained and threatened much. He said, "what shall I reply when the shah asks me what to do, what have they done to enjoy such favors. For he himself had many complaints about the Dutch, which would anger the shah very much and make him angry with you. If he had been at Gamron then he would have clashed with you [Koenad] and he would have expelled the Company; yes, he would have taken the Comp. ships, because you had not been very helpful at all. … You traded many goods at Gamron without having to pay anything, while normally you would have to pay as much as 3,000 *tuman*s customs duties." He also accused the Dutch of landing goods at Gamron and then to forward them to Basra. Moreover, he had asked for fabrics for the shah, for which he had offered payment by the *shahbandar* and that had been flatly refused, with the excuse that the

VOC did not trade in these particular fabrics. Furthermore, that Koenad had refused to sell VOC ships at cost-price, and this at a time that Nader needed those to use against the Masqat Arabs, the Indians, etc. In short, the VOC had not done any service for the shah unlike the English who had supplied two ships and had been very obedient in all other things. Sahid pointed out that this was not true; the Dutch had transported two ambassadors to India at great cost and they had given support against the Arabs. As to tax-exempt trade, the Dutch had enjoyed that since the reign of Shah 'Abbas I and this had been very advantageous to the country. The forwarding of goods to Basra was a normal thing; merchants went where money was to be made, and right then there was no demand for them in Persia. In fact, if that was not possible the Dutch would have to leave. They almost had decided to do so already because of the road tax issue. As to the fabrics, Sahid pointed out that it was the truth the VOC did not trade in the fabrics asked for. As to the sale of ships he said that this was impossible without authorization from Batavia. Also, transporting troops to Masqat was out of the question, because the ships had been made to transport merchandise. Warships might be able to support the shah, but then he had to ask for them and spell out exactly what favors he would grant the Dutch, because sending warships was expensive. Naval assistance against the Turks or the Indians was out of the question, because the Dutch lived in peace with them. The English had received confirmation of all royal orders, according Aqa Ja'far, Mohammad Taqi's mignon, except for the royal order (*raqam*) that would grant them 1,000 *tuman*s of the customs revenues every year. Nader had said this is an old issue; let them now perform other services, in which case I will offer them ten times more. The English ships had belonged to private persons, and had been used in India and therefore could be easily missed. Also, Sahid could give him an accounting of all services rendered by the Dutch, but then he also had to take into account the services the English had rendered in Basra, referring to EIC naval support against Persian forces in 1734. Mohammad Taqi Khan reacted that during his period in office the Dutch had rendered no service, although he admitted that they had transported Mohammad 'Ali Khan. He finally promised to do what was possible. He hoped that the Dutch would not abandon Persia, for the collection of road taxes was not his fault, but that of Fars 'Ali Beg. For in his jurisdiction he had allowed free movement of Dutch goods. He told Sahid to come and see him again on November 18, 1736. Sahid also informed the treasurer about this discussion, who had high hopes that things would be alright. Thereafter, Mohammad Taqi Khan only had nice words for the Dutch, which, according to the treasurer, were all lies. For Mohammad Taqi Khan said that he had submitted the matter to the shah, which the treasurer said he had not done. On November 19, 1736 Mohammad Taqi Khan told Sahid that he would come that evening in the Dutch factory to visit van Leijpsigh. During that visit he said that he had talked with the shah about the matter that morning, who had ordered to give the documents to the writer of royal orders, Mirza Mohammad who had to examine the matter, after which he would confirm them. When Sahid came to collect the royal orders from Mirza Mohammad, the latter said that he had no time to verify them. Then he said he had to defend the shah's interests, or it was complicated because it concerned two powers. The Dutch always had excuses; the previous government had overlooked that, but this shah watched over his interests. He still could claim the supply of 'treaty goods' retro-actively or else demand payment of customs duties, which would amount to a considerable amount. Therefore, he had to study this matter carefully; else he would risk loosing his head. At the same time, he intimated that in the past these matters had been arranged with the payment of a few thousand *tuman*s. If the Dutch would give him something then he would do his best. According to Sahid, he wanted 3,000 ducats, in which case the Dutch would get the royal orders that would satisfy them. Van

Leijpsigh then promised to satisfy Mirza Mohammad properly if he would bring this matter to a satisfactory end, without committing himself as to the level of recompense. Mirza Mohammad was not pleased with this reply and wanted to know exactly how much he would get, or else he would put the documents aside. Van Leijpsigh then promised him 600 ducats, of each spice half a *mann*, three measures of coffee, five measures of loaf sugar, a chiming pocket watch, and one bag (*dabbe*)[176] of candied ginger. For his second, Hajji Mo'men (Hadji Moenien), he promised payment of 200 ducats, three chintzes, five *gaz* of cloth, but only after the reception of satisfactory royal orders. Sahid then had to travel to Aberquh, for Mirza Mohammad had gone there with the shah, who had left Isfahan on November 21, 1736 and the next day he had departed from a garden in Sa'adatabad to Isfahanak (Spahanak). During that time he had taken care of so many other things that the *raqam* writer could not deal with the matter. He therefore had told Sahid to travel with him for one stage, because then the royal orders would be ready and empowered with the royal seal. But this did not work out either. Because, when in Qomishah, Mirza Mohammad asked the shah how he wanted to formulate the orders for the Dutch he had replied to wait with that matter till Yazdekhvast and then to remind him of it. He had discussed the matter with Mohammad Taqi Khan who would give him further information. Van Leijpsigh therefore thought that Mohammad Taqi Khan had not truthfully presented the case to him or that the shah had forgotten about the matter and wanted to discuss it with him. Van Leijpsigh had sent a letter to Mirza Mehdi, the treasurer and Mohammad Taqi Khan. Elias Sahid, accompanied by his son Jacob, because of his old age, followed the royal caravan and returned in the evening of March 13, 1736. He reported that at Yazdekhvast, Mohammad Taqi Khan had been very disinterested to present the case to the shah. He therefore had appealed to a number of friends such as the *mo'ayyer-bashi*, the treasurer, Qasem Khan the first mace bearer, Mirza Reza, former vizier of Isfahan[177] and then inspector-general, the eunuch Hajji Kalb 'Ali, Aqa Ja'far, the first clerk of Mohammad Taqi Khan, and others to incite the obstructionist to bring the matter to a good end. Although at first Mohammad Taqi Khan was furious he then changed his tune and became very jovial and having been assured by the others that the Dutch had hardly any money anymore he then raised the issue one day before he would leave to his governate. But it happened only because the treasurer in the full royal council loudly said, so that Nader also heard it, "why do you not speak about the case of the Dutch?" He then gave an account to the shah, emphasized their importance to the kingdom, and requested the confirmation of the royal orders. Nader then said that he could not decide to do so, because he had not had one benefit from the Dutch, and therefore he did not care much whether the Dutch stayed or left. The treasurer pointed out the services that the Dutch had performed for Mohammad 'Ali Khan and others. Nader then said that he agreed to the confirmation. However, the two clerks, Mirza Mo'men and Mirza Hoseyn, then acted as if they represented the royal interest and said that the Europeans only traded in some rags, fruits and bark of trees without paying any taxes and exporting cash. The shah was about to embark on a difficult campaign and he needed all the money he could get to pay the army. Therefore, he could not afford to grant a tax exemption. They therefore intended to better inform the shah, to wit: (i) that he had to demand treaty goods from the Dutch; and (ii) that the Dutch had to pay customs duties just like they did at

---

176. See 'dubber' in Hobson-Johnson.

177. Other viziers of Isfahan were Fath 'Ali Khan (VOC 2477, f. 605, 636); Mirza Zeyn al-'Abedin (VOC 2477, f. 612), and Mirza Sa'id or Zeyd? (Miersa Sahid; Miersa Caid) (VOC 2584, f. 2432; VOC 2583 (25/03/1741), f. 1326). Mirza Eshaq was *mostowfi* of Isfahan in 1740 and 1741 (VOC 2583, f. 1326; VOC 2584, f. 2432).

Basra, for Nader was greater than the gonhaar [sic; *khondegar*, the Ottoman Soltan], and more of that kind of garbage. The Dutch therefore had to buy their silence with the promise of 300 ducats to be paid to their family in Isfahan, just like with the others, out of fear that the request would totally fail. Van Leijpsigh did not have money and therefore borrowed money by writing a draft on Gamron.[178]

NADER LEAVES FOR QANDAHAR

Nader had left Isfahan on November 21, 1736 and went to Sa`adatabad and from there to Isfahanak (Spahanek) on his way to Kerman. Nader's need for money was great at that time, but he did not know where to get sufficient amounts of it for his army. Therefore, he gave orders that henceforth the double copper *paisa*s were equal again to the single *paisa*, and its export forbidden. Every Banyan and financial agent (*sarraf*) was not allowed to have more than 50 *mahmudi*s of funds in his house or shop and in case of transgression a penalty of 12 *tuman*s had to be paid. Tovakkol Beg had been sent to Shirvan to arrange certain matters. Mohammad [?] Sayyed Beg (Maad Sayit beek) was harassed by a tax collector to pay 500 *tuman*s; he asked the Dutch for a loan of 200 *tuman*s, who refused. Mostafa Khan, the former governor of Lar, had become governor of Tehran-Veramin (Theroen Weramien), but then had fallen in disgrace and all his goods had been confiscated. Nader also strangled the *Sheikh al-Eslam* on his way to Aberquh, it was said because the latter was a rich man, who had sent presents to Tahmasp Mirza and also had ordered to send some of the latter's wives, who were kept in Nader's harem, to Sabzavar. Khan Jan was appointed as *sardar* to march against the Baluchis in Kich-Makran. He left Isfahan on December 12, 1736 to stay for two months in Shiraz to wait for orders from Pir Mohammad Soltan (Pier Mhamed Sulthoen). Together they would march against the Baluchis and await news from Kerman to determine which route to take, so as to attack them unexpectedly.[179]

On his departure Nader donned a new Afshar hat, the value of which was estimated at 40,000 *tuman*s. It was inlaid with costly stones and pearls set in gold. Nader did not leave anything behind in the royal palace and the arsenal; even the carpets had been taken away on camels. His army was an undisciplined lot, who committed all sorts of untoward acts and even stole the children of the peasants en route. Nader declared Aberquh free to these locusts, because, when he had wanted to stay there for two days, the population was not able or willing to provide him with more than half a day of food and fodder. As a result of the army's sacking of the town there was not a door or window left in the town. His army was estimated to number 200,000 men with 200,000 animals in addition to 20,000 women. Thus, it would be impossible to use the route via Kerman to Qandahar, for he would loose many men due to lack of water. The son of the Baluchi chief `Abdollah Khan, who resided at Kalat (Calaat) above Qandahar, came, accompanied by 12 men, to offer his help to Nader against Hoseyn Khan. It was said that the Afghans from Kabul also had offered their help and they reportedly numbered 150,000 men. They were very angry with Hoseyn Khan, because he had ravaged their country. The peace with the Turk was still uncertain, but the Persian embassy was on its way back accompanied by a Turkish ambassador. Kalushkin had first been given orders to follow Nader, but later he was told to stay home. Nader had passed his house and he had stood in front of it

---

178.   VOC 2417, van Leijpsigh to Koenad (26/12/1736), f. 3908-37.

179.   VOC 2417, van Leijpsigh to Koenad (26/12/1736), f. 3940-42.

to greet the shah. Nader then told him not to exert himself in making such a strenuous journey. It would be better to stay in Isfahan and advised him to learn Persian and Turkish thoroughly, so that on his return Kalushkin could speak directly to him. Kalushkin was very happy, for he was afraid that Nader would continue to drag him to the end of the world. Meanwhile, there was no news from the *kholofa* in Russia. Everybody hated the Russian envoy who did not keep order among his retainers, who caused much trouble in the bazaar. The Turkish ambassador, Qalich Aqa (Geliech Aga), arrived on December 26, 1736 with 50 men, while a larger embassy was on its way from Istanbul.[180]

SITUATION OF EX-SHAH AND ISSUES CONCERNING A NEW SILK CONTRACT

The ex-shah and his two sons were said to be at Sabzavar. They received too little for their expenses. The former shah therefore led a life of poverty. Van Leijpsigh hoped "that God returns the crown and scepter wrested [from Shah Tahmasp] for the well-being and tranquility of this almost moribund people and country." Some time ago a certain Emam Qoli Beg, a loyal slave and cup-bearer of Tahmasp Mirza, bought some fabrics for him and his family in public in the bazaar and then returned to him. From Mohammad Taqi's government in Fars the Dutch expected only misery, for he continued to fleece the population more to support the great devourer as well as to maintain himself despite the protests by Europeans and Indians and even from the natives themselves. In this manner everything had to go to pieces. If van Leijpsigh had to believe the Russian envoy it was Nader's purpose, as long as he lived, to ruin the people and the country by spending his days in sensual enjoyment, and that he could not care less how his descendents would fare after his death. He also hoped that Mohammad Taqi Khan would begin to behave better and would respect the privileges granted to the VOC after all the services it had rendered. Van Leijpsigh assured Koenad that if he had not recompensed Hasan ʿAli Khan, Mirza Mehdi, and Mirza Mohammad, the treasurer and others that the Dutch would never have obtained that much from Nader. The latter did not like it all that he had not been able to still his hunger as he wanted. "The presents that he had received in the past he had already forgotten as he had experienced, and still experiences every day, save the mark." Nader had finally realized that the presence of the VOC was beneficial to his kingdom and therefore he had decided to grant the VOC these favorable orders, van Leijpsigh commented. He only had requested confirmation of two previous royal orders, and had expected that the main royal order would be confirmed as is and that it would not drag on, but would be finalized in the village of Isfahanak (Spahanak) or in Isfahan. Van Leijpsigh had no idea at all that it had been Nader's intention to abolish the silk contract, otherwise he would have instructed the dragoman to oppose such a decision and to have it inserted into the new royal order. He considered it nevertheless doubtful if it would have made a difference. The shah after all had dictated the text to his secretary in the way he wanted it, and therefore nobody would have dared to change even one word, if they cherished their life. Moreover, the supply of silk by the court based on the condition of the old contract was not beneficial to the court anymore. For that reason Nader would not have inserted it into the new royal order. The next text did not state explicitly that the Dutch had to give treaty goods or that such a claim existed in exchange for the privileges. Unless the Persians started their chicanes again, saying "that no prince is in the habit of allowing foreigners to trade in his country for an amount of 20,000 *tumans* without

---

180. VOC 2416, van Leijpsigh to Koenad (26/12/1736), f. 3942-51.

reaping any benefit himself." The new royal order, or so van Leijpsigh believed, gave the Dutch the argument to say that they need not give anything. The five minor royal orders concerning the dragoman and private persons and the other royal order concerning all other VOC privileges still had not been approved yet. These five minor royal orders concerned the right of the drago-man to *dallali* or brokerage; exemption to pay capitation tax for the Banyans in VOC service; tax exemption for the landed property of the dragomans as well as of a large village called Daskasjan in the Peria district, that had not been listed with the others at van Leijpsigh's recommendation. He had told the dragoman to get a separate order, so that every time the native merchants had to show the royal order they did not offer an overview of all their properties, which might give the authorities ideas. The dragoman only obtained an order for seven instead of 17 persons exempted of capitation tax. An order with regards to their gardens and land had not been approved because Mohammad Taqi Khan had opposed this. No request had been made concerning an order of tax exemption for the descendants of François Sahid or of the village of Daskasjan, because the late Joseph Sahid had just been able to pay off the heavy taxes to which he had been subjected and had not wanted to let the royal fiscal authorities know about this property. Only David Sahid, dragoman at Gamron, and his brother Abraham knew about this property, which they wanted to cultivate again on behalf of their family. Also, they wanted to pay the usual taxes and imposts on it, for only then would they be able to get it back again. However, 20 other abandoned villages around there would be easy to obtain. Van Leijpsigh had recommended not to raise the issue with regards to the claim of 5,000 *tuman*s, because the shah needed money himself and claiming this amount of amount would have given rise to his ire, which might have caused him to refuse to grant the other order. Furthermore, an order had been obtained for the dragoman Elias Sahid regarding his debts to his son-in-law Auwannees at Shiraz in 1731 as well to other creditors stating that they should not be hard on him and allow him to pay them off in installments and without interest. Another request by van Leijpsigh on behalf of the VOC Banyans at Isfahan to instruct the governor of Shamakhi to assist them in collecting a debt from a pagan (i.e. a Banyan) named Tolsjieran resulted in the granting of an apostil (*ta'liqeh*); another one was granted with regard to the house at Gamron that belonged to the Banyans Wissendas and Heemraads, which allowed them to live there without molestation. Finally, Nader had granted a royal order that the authorities would leave the VOC Banyan servants in Isfahan in peace with regards to some houses that had been confiscated from Persians during the tyranny of Mahmud [Ghalzai]). Nader then had left for Seistan to march from there to Qandahar.[181]

NOT MUCH NEWS FROM QANDAHAR – RUSSIAN AGENT'S BEHAVIOR

It was very difficult to get news on the Qandahar operations in Isfahan, for all couriers (*chapar*s) coming from Nader were kept incommunicado by the governor of Kerman, Abu'l-Hasan Khan. Nader had given orders to prevent any news to leak out. At that time, it was said that the water level in the Helmand River was still too high, while on the other side the Afghans were waiting for him. Nader therefore had ordered strong heavy chains from Kerman to build a bridge, which they had to send him as soon as possible. According to van Leijpsigh, Nader would have a difficult task, because Hoseyn Khan had a good army and had already stored food supplies in the fortress of Qa-ndahar during the last seven years, and thus could easily sustain a long siege. "May God give that

---

181. VOC 2416, van Leijpsigh to Koenad (14/04/1737), f. 1264-81.

Iran will not fail, because else things will be ruined for years to come," he prayed. Many merchants had asked when would the VOC caravans come again, now that the Dutch had obtained exemption of taxes. "Because drunkenness and continuous repasts and baths, according to the country's custom, which were expressly organized for that purpose, have become so popular, that high and low, both secular and imagined religious persons, out of fear that they will be left out, collect grapes both ripe and unripe, yes even dried *kishmish* (a kind of grape), to make strong spirits, with a view to celebrate this permitted unbound appetite with full abundance." [f. 1296] Van Leijsigh gave Hasan 'Ali Khan, the *mo'ayyer-bashi* some presents, amongst which European liquor, the secret spirit of Nader, so that he was a friend of the VOC. "For Oriental friendship needs to be sustained with presents." Mohammad Sayyed Beg (Maad Saijit beecq) arrived in Isfahan to give an accounting of the revenues of Chahar Mahall, his district, to the governor Hatem Beg. Van Leijpsigh watched the activities of Kalushkin the Russian envoy closely, and reported that he allowed some of his staff to operate a bordello and a pub. He did not know whether Kalushkin had contacts with Kermani traders, but if that were the case he would take steps to torpedo such trade from developing. The vagrant and fortune-seeker La Porterie did not keep further contact with Kalushkin after having visited him four times. Kalushkin had some trouble with the local authorities about the rough-and-tumble life of his staff. Nothing was heard about the shah's ambassador to Russia, the *kholafa*. It appeared that he enjoyed himself there, and it was believed that he did not want to make haste to return. He had been one of the VOC baiters, and he did not like to be part of the royal court the way it then was. Nader had abolished the system of free merchants who would buy and sell goods for and to the army on his account. He preferred to have that money in his treasury, because he did not trust them.[182]

NO NEWS IS BAD NEWS — MORE TAXES

On January 3, 1737 the envoy from Ahmad Pasha and his small suite of only three persons had to be at the royal court. He therefore departed post-haste. He returned on February 2 and left for Baghdad on February 8, 1737. Otherwise there was nothing known about this mission. Nader was said to have ordered *sardar* Tahmasp Qoli Khan (who had been reported to be dead, but then seemed to be alive again) to march to Farah via Herat with his eldest son Reza Qoli Mirza and his Khorasani troops and to stay there until further notice. The latter was said to have also received orders to march with 6,000 horsemen to the Uzbek frontier to keep a close watch on them, for the Uzbeks of Orgenj were having internal troubles. Nader's army meanwhile was suffering from a dearth of food and high prices. The army was kept busy by enlarging and fortifying a large town in Seistan. He was said therefore to have given orders to have Khorasan pay its revenues in kind instead of cash. These had to be brought on the shoulders of the people if pack animals were lacking. In Isfahan prayers were said, at the orders of the governor Hatem Beg, to support the shah's victory. Since the additional 12,000 *tuman*s assigned to Isfahan in October 1736, the tax collectors were seen going about with sticks, swords, and hatchets to torment and beat people to get the money. Everybody was trying to sell his property (furniture, clothes and even bedding) on the royal square to be rid of the tax collectors. However, there were few buyers and thus the misery continued. Since Nader's departure the Dutch estimated that gradually 20,000 people had left Isfahan due to the dearness and the miserable conditions. The new city of Aq-su (Akzou) that had

---

182. VOC 2448, van Leijpsigh to Koenad (14/04/1737), f. 1281-1313.

been built five German miles south of Shamakhi had suffered the plague and 9,000 people had died. In Rasht, because of a large fire many houses and much merchandise had been burnt. "God's wrath reigns over this country and we pray with bent knees that he may withdraw his striking hand out of mercy," van Leijpsigh wrote.[183]

NADER EYES INDIA — ARRIVAL OF OTTOMAN AMBASSADOR

In May 1737, Van Leijpsigh was very happy to learn that two assistants (Brand and de Crane) would soon arrive at the Isfahan factory, because Elias Sahid who was 56 years old could then take it easier. Nader defeated Hoseyn Khan who withdrew that same night behind the walls of his well-supplied citadel. The siege was laid, while, at the same time, Nader started to make eyes at India, hence he was said to have sent a new embassy under Mirza Reza, his former do-all (*albeschik*) in Kerman, to the Moghul court. The embassy most certainly was a pretext to provide justification for Nader's unreasonable demands, after his ambassador did not get satisfaction, to get and fetch satisfaction himself.[184] His ambassador to the Porte, `Abdol-Baqi Khan, was about to return, for Hatem Beg was making preparations for the Turkish ambassador which accompanied him, by finding appropriate houses for him and his suite of 3,000, cleaning them and putting carpets in them. He was allotted an expense account of 4,000 *mahmudi*'s or Dfl. 1,700 excluding firewood of which he would need 2,000 *mann*. This certainly would not be to Vali Ne`mat's liking. Tahmasp Mirza was still alive. In early June 1737, Nader had ordered the treasurer, Mirza Abu'l-Hasan, to take Tahmasp Mirza's women who were still in Isfahan with their servants and eunuchs to Sabzavar to the ex-shah, while maintaining *qoruq* en route. Furthermore, to present Tahmasp Mirza with 12 pieces of heavy turbans, six *chahar gazi*s or waistbands, rich fabrics and other necessaries and 5,000 *tuman*s in cash for his expenses. The women were preparing themselves for their departure. Ebrahim Khan, Nader's brother, left Tabriz to the destroyed town of Shamakhi, allegedly to rebuild it. *Sardar* Tahmasp Qoli Khan together with Reza Qoli Mirza had taken a rich Uzbek location and was besieging Orgenj. The local authorities reproached Kalushkin from time to time, because of the irregular way of life of this people. He said that the shah would summon him to court. He wanted to watch the Turks and to encourage the split between the Persians and the Turks. Vali Ne`mat was said to have send orders to Darband to store large quantities of food supplies. It was believed that he also wanted to attack the Russians, because they were keeping his ambassador the *kholafa* at court. Khan Jan who had been summoned to court had complained about the violent deeds of Mohammad Taqi Khan. The shah allegedly had appointed commissionaires to ask him for an accounting. The *mo`ayyer-bashi* was about to return to Isfahan to check the account of the governors of Iraq to get money to be able to receive the Turkish ambassador properly, in which he was very experienced.[185]

Joris Brand and Johan de Crane arrived the evening of June 26, 1737.[186] On August 27 a small caravan with Jacob Hermet, the brother of the EIC dragoman arrived in Isfahan

---

183. VOC 2416, van Leijpsigh to Koenad (14/04/1737), f. 1314-17.

184. See Willem Floor, "New Facts on Nader Shah's Indian Campaign," in: Kambiz Eslami ed. *Iran and Iranian Studies. Essays in Honor of Iraj Afshar.* (Princeton: Zagros, 1998), pp. 198-219.

185. VOC 2416, van Leijpsigh to Koenad (11/06/1737), f. 1319, 1341-46.

186. The route that de Crane had followed was as follows: "Tsjah alie, Hoese-miel-radaer Ginauw (old dilapidated caravansera), at river Bieste tjaer (salt water, 8 feet wide and 1 foot deep), Dherdam

coming via Kerman with 40 cargas of garden seeds, old copperware, wine, etc. He had to pay road taxes, according to Mohammad `Ali Beg the *rahdar-bashi*,[187] although Hermet asserted that he had received tax exemption for the entire route. Traveling was very expensive; food prices and fodder were more than double than normal, and sometimes you had to take supplies for as many as four stages for both men and animals. Hoseyn Khan had allegedly asked Nader for free passage to India, which he had refused. The Dutch hoped that Nader would win soon, for the continuous outflow of cash towards Qandahar caused a great scarcity of money in Isfahan. Moreover, Hatem Beg, governor of Isfahan, had it made public towards the end of August 1737 that all money had to be accepted on the basis of its nominal and not its intrinsic value. The result was that the little good money that still was available totally disappeared, which was bad for trade. Mohammad Khan Turkman (Mhamed Chan Turkman) allegedly had been sent as ambassador to India with a suite of 500 persons. Mirza Reza, the sly fox, was his second. The purpose of the embassy was to claim the debt that emperor Homayun owed since 1530. Nader was also said to have demanded financial support from Persians who were in the service of the Moghul emperor. On June 29, 1737 Tahmasp Mirza's women left with a silent *qoruq* under supervision of Mirza Abu'l-Hasan, the *khazinehdar* to Sabzavar. Reza Qoli Mirza and *sardar* Tahmasp Qoli Khan had returned with a large booty to Mashhad. Mohammad Sayyed Beg (Maad Sayit beek) and a certain Mirza Nezan [?] (Miersa Nezoen), friends of the well-known *vaqaye`-nevis* Mirza Qiyas had been ordered by the shah to depart from the lower lands as commissionaires to keep an eye on Mohammad Taqi Khan during a period of three years. Further, that when Mohammad Taqi Khan wrote a request they also had to write at the same time so that the shah knew that these requests were credible. Mohammad Taqi would not like this. Mohammad Sayyed Beg, who was *zabet* (sobet) or administrator of the Chahar Mahall, had just returned from there and was about to leave for his new post. Mirza Nezan [?] was a military accountant (*lashkar-nevis*) and at court. There was no news regarding Kalushkin. Pirates, Russians and Cossacks, were making the Caspian Sea an insecure place. Van Leijpsigh intended to send the VOC caravan back via Bushehr, so that Schoonderwoerd might send the goods per tranki (an oared vessel) to Gamron. On July 31, 1737 the Turkish ambassador and `Abdol-Baqi Khan arrived in Isfahan. He was Mostafa Pasha, governor of Mosul, and his rank was *beglerbegi*. He had a suite of 700 men and two effendis or mullahs as advisors named Saleh and Osman. They daily received 36 *tuman*s (Dfl. 1,530) defrayment from the treasury in order not to burden the population much more. The *hammami* or bathhouse money was also paid out of the royal treasury by Hatem Beg; an amount of 1,000 *tuman*s. On July 22, when the Turk was at Gousaar [?], at about 20 German miles from Isfahan, a certain Hoster, a Swede

---

(nobody living here), Zeratoe, Gohera (still no people), river Abmaer, Rapaer, Galejouw, Doeradoe, Niera tammerbos [=date grove], Phoeseijgoen, Amierabaat (at 5 hours from Zirgoen), Ziergoen, Lutfie, Nedjassabaad, Bimid, Nasratabaad, Narakhoon, Hassaroe, Dhalabaad, Sjahtbabeecq, Khaleghero, Mahedabaad, Dhe hedje, Shehatie (radaer is mola Mhamed), Mhennetoe, Nherries, Abdul Mellik [f. 1561] (rahdaer basje of Yaes is Hadje Mhamed), Yeas with garden at 1 hour's distance with silkworms for local processing [f. 1562] Yeas was governed by vakiel of Nader named Mhamed Sjarief Beek, Harrestoen, Houssetaff, Madrachon (uninhabited), Noudousjaar (radaer), Gauhahoen, Gerepost, Warsena (radaer), Madrashoer, Golnabat and Ghauwer." [1563] VOC 2448, Journal of de Crane's journey to Isafahan (07/05-06/26/1737), f. 1543-68.

187. Mhamed Alie Beek was the brother of the *malek al-tojjar* (VOC 2477, f. 766). As of 1740 the function of *rahdar-bashi* of Mahyar (Majaar) and Urchini (Orsienie) was held by Mhamed Alie Beek and Safi Qoli Beg (Seffie Coelie Beek). VOC 2511, f. 906, 1404; VOC 2584, f. 2432.

and Roman Catholic, arrived in Isfahan. He was about 40 years of age, and claimed that he had been sent hither by the French ambassador at Istanbul, M. du Morpha.[188] The latter had recommended him to ʿAbdol-Baqi Khan so that he might travel in safety. Holster said that he had come to Persia to learn to speak, read and write Persian, Turkish, Arabic and Armenian. Of the latter three he already knew the principles. He had learnt to read Armenian and Arabic in France, while he had learnt to talk Turkish reasonably well in Istanbul, and he wanted to stay for two years with the Capuchin brothers. Trade was very bad. The Banyans had been forced to send drafts to their agents in Gamron, because Mohammad Taqi claimed a contribution there. They suffered therefore a loss of 30% in case of sale. They needed 4-6 months to sell the goods. On top of that Georgian merchants who were in trouble came from Basra to Isfahan and sold powdered sugar at 9.5 *mahmudi*s (Dfl. 4:12) per *mann-e shah*. There was hardly any sale for cash, because there was a dearth of money. The partners of the pagans in Gamron, Shiraz, Shirvan, Gilan and elsewhere drew drafts on them to be able to pay the royal treasury, which had to be done promptly. At the end of August 1737, they received drafts to the amount of 3,000 *tuman*s, which they had to pay immediately to two Qazvini gentlemen. The result was that trade came to a halt. From August 31 till September 6, 1737 the kettledrums were beaten, while during the last three days there also was an illumination in some of the bazaars that still were in a reasonable state, on account of the victory of Reza Qoli Mirza at Balkh and nearby places. The chief of the Uzbeks, ʿAbdol-Hasan, who was called 'king' in Isfahan had been made prisoner with many of his nobles and officers. The shah had pardoned them. The Turkish ambassador was still in Isfahan and was well treated, because the shah had ordered that the various authorities had to regale him in turns and to give him satisfaction. There also was a report of the outbreak of an infectious disease in Tabriz and Georgia.[189]

NOT MUCH PROGRESS IN QANDAHAR

The lack progress at Qandahar did not put Nader necessarily in a better mood. A Khorasani poet left for the court at Qandahar in search of a reward for the ode that he had made in honor of Nader. Having presented himself to the shah the poet declaimed his laudatory verses. Nader did not like them and ordered to have the poet offered for sale by having him taken around the army camp. However, nobody offered to buy the poet. Nader then asked him, "How did you get here?" The poet replied: "On a donkey." Nader then ordered the donkey to be put up for sale, for which immediately a good price was offered and accepted. Nader then ordered that this money be given to the court usher who had accompanied the poet through the army camp and then he chased the poet out of the camp as a point of ridicule to everyone.[190]

Nader, because he needed money above all, and also because of the high price of silk, collected cash instead of silk as payment of the total taxes in Rasht and Lahejan. Mohammad Taqi Khan reportedly had arrived sick in Shiraz, where he received orders from Nader to try once more and take Masqat. According to van Leijpsigh, this only would result in new troubles

---

188. There was no French ambassador of that name at the Ottoman court. For a list of all French ambassadors at the Porte see [http://mbarchives.blogspot.com/2005/12/liste-chronologique-des-ambassadeurs.html]. I have not been able to find any particular about M. Hoster either.

189. VOC 2416, van Leijpsigh to Koenad (31/08/1737 and appendix of 12/09/1737), f. 1319, 1341-46.

190. VOC 2584, Beschrijvinge, f. 2025-26.

for the VOC. Aqa Mohammad, Nader's do-all (*albeschik*), during a visit to the Dutch factory, related that Nader was very angry with the English because of their role in Basra [in 1734]. He intended to undertake action against them at a later date. The Turkish ambassador was still in Isfahan and was richly regaled. The bad times for trade persisted due to the continuous drain of money towards the army at Qandahar. The Swede Hoster paid a visit to the Dutch factory and presented a letter from the Dutch ambassador at Istanbul, Cornelis Calkoen.[191] The Dutch dragoman paid a visit to ʿAbdol-Baqi Khan, who asked the VOC to mediate between the EIC and the Persian court. The dragoman told ʿAbdol-Baqi that the Dutch had nothing to do with the matter. It was believed that he would be appointed grand vizier, because Nader liked him very much, the more so after the excellent reception of the Turkish ambassador. ʿAbdol-Baqi Khan was the son of the former grand vizier Shahqoli Khan (1707-1715). He had a penetrating intelligence and was of a pleasant disposition, but not less greedy than other Persians. On October 2, 1737 three couriers arrived in Isfahan from court. From them van Leijpsigh learnt that little justice was to be obtained from Nader. The magnates stood with open hands to receive money to resolve even trifling matters, and even then there was no guarantee that the matter would be decided in the donor's favor. The shah's steward (*nazer*) had taken Kalat, a location above Qandahar. It belonged to Hadje Agoe [?], uncle of Hoseyn Khan (Hossein Chenante). Seydal Khan (Seyitaal Chan), Hoseyn Khan's general and Hoseyn Khan's son and various officers had been taken prisoner. Also much treasury had been found. Nader had the eyes of Seydal Khan gouged and then sent him to his master to tell him the news. Hoseyn Khan then had everyone who was Persian killed out of revenge. Van Leijpsigh piously commented: "What else may one expect from such barbarians." According to Nader's do-all, it would take some time before Qandahar would be taken, because there were as many as 40,000 fighting men inside the citadel that was well supplied with food and ammunition. The defenders waited quietly till Nader would tire of the siege and go away. This would make or break Nader's reputation, for he could not afford to withdraw ignominiously. The Dutch hoped that the matter would be decided quickly, so that the drain of money would stop. In Qom reportedly 6,000 people had died due to a pestilential disease. Nader recently had sent for gunpowder and lead from Kerman and other towns. Isfahan had to supply 5,000 *mann-e shah* of powder. Hatem Beg therefore banned the sale of gunpowder. The shah also ordered the manufacture of 5,000 new muskets with barrels of two ells (*gaz*) long. According to news received at Isfahan, the Moghul emperor had given his Afghans (i.e., those of Kabul) permission to go and help their brethren in Qandahar. As to Khan Jan it was said that he had suffered a heavy defeat in a battle against Indian troops led by a certain Khodayar Khan Leti (Godja Jaarchan Lettie); he had lost 8,000 men. This Khodayar Khan Leti had been appointed *zamindar* by the Moghul emperor over a location situated between Moltan and Sind, towards the south and close to Qandahar, according to the Banyans. If this was true, this meant war with India, according to van Leijpsigh. Mirza Reza, who had been sent with the embassy to India, had arrived in Moltan and had died there. Nader was very sad about this, because the death of the wily old fox was a great loss. Lotf ʿAli Khan, the *sardar* for Hamadan and Kermanshah, one of Nader's brothers-in-law as well as ʿAli Mardan Khan, *vali* or prince of the Feyli Lors (Fijlische Lorren) had arrived in Isfahan on October 21, 1737 with 6,000 well-accoutered fighting men. It was said that they would march after 15 days to Fars and then march against the Baluchis in

---

191. On the Dutch ambassador see G. R. Bosscha Erdbrink. *At the Threshold of Felicity. Ottoman-Dutch Relations during the Embassy of Cornelis Calkoen at the Sublime Porte, 1726-1747* (Ankara, 1978).

Kich-Makran who were said to have revolted with a view to subjugate them. Later the Dutch learnt that Nader had sent him an royal order allowing him to stay 10 days in Isfahan, 5 days in Yazd, and 10 days in Kerman and other places. Then he had to march to Qandahar via the same route that Nader had taken. Nader then would take a decision as soon as possible whether he had to go to Kich-Makran or elsewhere. Reza Qoli Mirza reportedly would have gone to Badakhshan, where special rubies (robijn ballees)[192] are found, to take that place. Mirza Abu'l-Hasan, the royal treasurer, who had taken the ex-shah's women to Sabzavar, returned to Isfahan on September 25, 1737. Tahmasp was still spoken of as 'shah.' On October 5, 1737 the *kholofa*'s family received news that they should not count on it to see him back alive and that they should manage his affairs whereto he had sent them money. Van Leijpsigh believed that this would make Nader furious.[193]

It was expected that Qandahar would fall soon, for the Afghans had a great lack of firewood. Nader's troops had taken two forts in the mountains. According to information that had been received on December 16, 1737 Nader was said to have appointed his uncle, Morteza Mirza as grand vizier. Nader had also given orders to recruit 18,000 boys between the ages of 13 to 25 years. Isfahan and its villages had to supply 1,500 of them. These boys were taken by force from their parents; this caused so much misery that you had to close your ears so as not to hear the vilification of the author of that order, some of them even died of grief. The new soldiers received new clothes and 10 *mahmudi*s as pocket-money from the treasury. They had to train every day with new matchlocks of 2.75 ells (*gaz*) length, which they could hardly carry, let alone properly handle. They were quartered in caravanserais and *madraseh*s from which the mullahs had been expelled. Towards *Nowruz* the recruited boys were sent to Qandahar via Mashhad and Herat about which the inhabitants of Isfahan were very happy, since they committed all kinds of violence in the city and had respect for nobody. The inhabitants for the third consecutive year had to pay 12,000 *tumans*.[194]

CONQUEST OF MASQAT ORDERED — OPERATIONS AGAINST THE LEZGIS

Mohammad Taqi Khan had orders to conquer Masqat, and he was busy making preparations in Shiraz. He intended to leave from Gamron on November 1, 1737. He would leave his brother Mirza Esma`il as his deputy in Shiraz. His troops would be sent under the command of somebody else to Masqat, because he would remain in Gamron. According to van Leijpsigh, this would mean that the last inhabitant of Gamron now also would leave. It would be better for trade if Nader defeated his enemies, because in Isfahan trade was dead. Mohammad Hoseyn Beg (Mhamed Hossein Beek), the head (sarkeshiek; *sar-keshik*) of Nader's life-guard had become *sardar* of the troops at Qazvin, Tehran, Veramin, Qom, etc. Amir Aslan Soltan was at Tehran (Theroen); he was `Ali Mardan Khan's steward. He had died there of an infectious disease that had caused many deaths in Azerbaijan. In Erevan there was not a living soul any more. All the gates of the town stood open, but nobody dared to go inside to steal. In another location of the 800 inhabitants only one little boy survived. Qom was also almost empty of people, while there

---

192. For details see 'balass' in Hobson-Jobson.

193. VOC 2448, van Leijpsigh to Koenad (26/10/1737), f. 1392-1438.

194. VOC 2584, Beschrijvinge, f. 2027-28.

was fear that the disease had reached Golpeygan, because there also was a welling-up of water just like in Qom. A son of the Lezgi chief, Sorkhay Khan (Lasgie Sorgaal) was said to have marched from Daghestan with 50,000-60,000 men and had totally destroyed one place in Shirvan province. In Georgia one of the headmen (togas;i.e., *tawadi*) allegedly had rebelled. On November 5, 1737 'Ali Mardan Khan and Lotf 'Ali Khan marched to Kerman, where they were to await further orders. In stead of Khan Jan, Lotf 'Ali Khan was said to have been selected to fight the Baluchis of Kich-Makran. There also were rumors that Nader would send an army under four generals against India. Tovakkol Beg fearing to loose his head at the shah's orders had defected to the Afghans at Qandahar. Hatem Beg received orders to confiscate all his properties, which was done immediately.[195]

The presence of the Turkish embassy did not result in a flourishing of trade. There was hardly any demand for bulk goods, although precious stones were. There also was hardly any interest in textiles in Isfahan. *Salempouris* could only be sold at a loss and the same held for covers (*sprijen*), and *sjeklassen*. There had not been even a bid for nose tissues. Van Leijpsigh intended to hang one entire piece in a chintz maker's shop to promote interest in the fabric to be used as headgear. The road guards at Sagzi (Zagzie) were making problems. They obtained a written note from the VOC messenger and the cameleer that they would pay road taxes if they did not send an order than emanated directly from the shah or Hatem Beg. The road guard came to the VOC factory for such a royal order, because they did not accept any longer a simple road tax letter as before. Joris Brand, who was the second and bookkeeper of the Isfahan factory, died of pleurisy on November 19, 1737. On November 26, Tahmasp Beg, a former singer of Shah Tahmasp, came to see van Leijpsigh in the VOC factory. He had received a secret letter from the ex-shah in Sabzavar. He had asked for a new suit of European clothes to be obtained from the Dutch. Because of the danger involved van Leijpsigh said that he did not have any new clothes, for he had to order them. Tahmasp Beg then asked how long that would take, to which the reply was 14 months. Sardar Lotf 'Ali Khan and 'Ali Mardan Khan Feyli left with 7,000 men of November 5 to Kerman. Nader was still at Qandahar. The Afghans did not move and kept quiet. According to the Persians, it would be Ramadan in 25 days, when Nader would take Qandahar. The Afghans had a serious shortage of firewood. Persian troops reportedly had taken two Baluch forts near Qandahar. The Persian ambassador to India allegedly had been very well received. Hatem Khan received a robe of honor and royal order in November as confirmation of his appointment as governor and a raise in his salary of 100 *tumans* per year as recognition for services rendered. For apart from the normal revenues he had extorted for Nader an additional 500 *tumans* from the people in fines. About 9,000 inhabitant of the town had died. In Tabriz, 17,000 had died and from there the disease had gone to three other towns where every day 250 people were dying. The governor of Tabriz had left for Ardabil, which he had totally ruined, before the disease struck his town. The Lezgis were causing havoc in Shirvan province. The Turkish ambassador had drums beaten, shawms blown and fireworks launched during three consecutive evenings because he had received information from Istanbul that the Turks had defeated the Russians. On December 16, 1737 a courier came from court with a letter for the ambassador that he could come. He was said to leave after Ramadan in 35 days' time. 'Abdol-Baqi Khan, Mir 'Abdol-Qasem and his entire suite accompanied him. Hatem Beg had to accompany him till Yazd, the governor of Kerman from Yazd to Kerman, and so

---

195. VOC 2416, van Leijpsigh to Koenad (04/11/1737), f. 1441-47.

on.[196] Nader was still before Qandahar, but did not attack. He was said to be afraid that the enemies around him would attack him. He gave orders to recruit 18,000 young men. In Tabriz the infectious disease had run its course. In Qom some 9,000 people had died.[197]

ENVOYS TO OTTOMAN COURT — QANDAHAR'S CONQUEST IN SIGHT

Nader's *farrash-bashi*, Mohammad Qasem, came to Isfahan to get two tents for his master. One had to be 300 ells (*gaz*) long, made from heavy and light crimson, was destined for the guards. Also, 200 campaign chairs for the guards to sit on rather than on carpets. The news about the appointment of a grand vizier proved to be premature, because none was yet selected. As to complaints, van Leijpsigh advised that it were best to approach one of the leading courtiers rather than the shah directly. Jacob Hermet, the EIC dragoman, had a row with the road guards who wanted to collect road tax from him, because the royal order did not clearly state that no imposts might be collected from the EIC. The road guards therefore had already collected it from the EIC several times. It was not helpful for Hermet that the *rahdar-bashi* refused to budge. Because a merchant refused to honor a draft van Leijpsigh had appealed to the *darugheh* and *kalantar* of Jolfa to intervene and enforce payment. According to information that the Dutch had recently received, Shah Tahmasp sat three times per week with his women on a European chair while surrendering his soul to Bacchus. He also wore European clothes that he had received from Nader via the Russians. He was said to have secret correspondence with Nader, who recently had sent him 500 *tumans* and 8 beautiful horses. A few days ago two envoys arrived in Isfahan, who went to the Turkish court to try and mediate between the Turks and Russians. The envoys were Nazer `Ali (Nazer Alie) and Rahim Khan (Rahiem Chan) and they had left before New Year to Baghdad with a suite of 40 men. The Georgian Vali `Ali Qoli Beg (Welie Allie Coelie beek) and one of the tagaats [sic; *tawad*] or magnates had been summoned to court and from Tiflis passed through Isfahan with 200 men. Rostam Beg (Rustam beek), who had been *farrash-bashi* for some time, had been sent for by Nader from Qandahar to become governor of Georgia. All Uzbeks had banded together at Balkh and were now pressing and besieging Reza Qoli Mirza. Hatem Beg was reprimanded by Nader regarding the licentious behavior of Kalushkin's men with orders not to tolerate any longer that Moorish whores were taken into his house. If Kalushkin did not take action Hatem Beg had to put guards at his gate. Thereafter there was no more news about this irregular behavior. Hajji `Ali Mardan Khan, the former ambassador to India, arrived in Isfahan coming from the army at Qandahar with orders to kill an insect in the mountains and elsewhere, which was endangering the crops,[198] for which purpose he used 4,000 pressed peasants from the surrounding villages. The Afghans at Qandahar were eating their horses. Hoseyn Khan was a very greedy person and sold his food supplies at high prices to the other besieged.[199]

---

196. VOC 2416, van Leijpsigh to Koenad (29/12/1737), f. 1455-88.

197. VOC 2448, van Leijpsigh to Koenad (29/12/1737), f. 2512-13.

198. This was most likely a plague known as *senn, sun* or *sunneh* (hence now internationally known as *sunn* pest) caused by insects, the most important of which is the *Eurygaster integriceps*, which damaged the quality of grains. The other possibility is a swarm of locusts. On these agricultural plagues see Willem Floor, *Agriculture in Qajar Iran* (Washington, DC: Mage Publishers, 2003), pp. 231-36.

199. VOC 2448, van Leijpsigh to Koenad (20/03/1738), f. 2299-2300, 2304-38.

In early 1738, the Dutch received information that Nader was building a second new town opposite Qandahar. To populate the new town, called Naderabad, he had sent for Georgian and other families to settle there.[200] He also continuously sent detachments of 4,000 men into the direction of Kabul, often going as far as 12 *manzels* (halting stations) to get slaves and supplies. By that time Nader's appetite for India had been really roused due to the information he received on the differences between Mohammad Shah, the Moghul emperor, and Nezam al-Molk, the governor of Hyderabad. It was said that Nader had sent for his brother Ebrahim Khan in Azerbaijan in order to put him in charge of the Qandahar siege while Nader himself would move on to India. The fall of Qandahar was expected any moment, for the Afghans had been considerably weakened due to the plague, lack of firewood and salt. There had been a major battle between Reza Qoli Mirza and the prince of Bokhara and the former had won, and reportedly he was besieging Bokhara. From Shamakhi news was received that the *beglerbegi* had killed many Lezgis and many of their chiefs. Kalushkin men were still misbehaving despite the fact that he beat them, but that menagerie was accustomed to such treatment.[201]

The shah really was the Soltan Nader, i.e., the rare ruler, for he was difficult to find since he had no fixed dwelling. It was not even certain where he would sleep, for he kept this uncertain to prevent assassination attempts such as happened during the Qandahar siege when some royalists and Bakhtiyaris had made a plot to that effect, but they were betrayed.[202]

The Turkish ambassador wanted to stay in Isfahan; he was afflicted with small-pox, but against his will he had to leave to court within the next 20 days. Nader had abolished the custom of the *pa-bus* or foot-kiss and had introduced the European custom of taking of one's hat, which van Leijpsigh certainly thought would make Koenad laugh, [although he did not say why]. Nader reportedly had summoned Reza Qoli Mirza to court. Baba Khan Beg, a courageous soldier had died against the Uzbeks.[203]

FALL OF QANDAHAR

After one year the Qandaharis still did not want to surrender. Nader then finally gave orders to concentrate the attack on the bulwark called *Borj-e Zangi* (Zangie) and the other bulwarks situated on the mountain near the bulwark called *Borj-e Deda*. After Borj-e Zangi had been taken he had his cannons and mortars put there and ordered a shelling of the town without stopping for two weeks or till 3 Dhu'l-Hijja, 1150 (24 March 1738). On that day he ordered his soldiers to an all-out attack and to put the cannons and mortars on the *Deda* bulwark. The attack on that side had been entrusted to the Bakhtiyaris, who took that bulwark before any other group of the army. Nader sent Mohammad `Ali Beg, mace bearer of the royal council, as courier (*chapar*) to Hatem Beg in Isfahan with orders to pay him as courier's bonus (*chapari*) of 12,000 *tumans* cash and a robe of honor, which money the population did not have to pay for. The order also had to be sent to Hoveyzeh, Kuhgilu and all other towns near Isfahan. The order was written on 4 Dhu'l-Hijjah 1150 (March 25, 1738). In the margin had been written that a *cheraghani* or illumination was not

---

200. VOC 2584, Beschrijvinge, f. 2027.

201. VOC 2448, van Leijpsigh to Koenad- private letter (07/02/1738), f. 2346-48.

202. VOC 2584, Beschrijvinge, f. 2028-31.

203. VOC 2448, van Leijpsigh to Koenad (07/03/1738), f. 2351-54.

required, for it only contributed to the ruin and damage of the population and therefore only the striking of the kettledrums and the blowing of the clarions was required.[204]

The winter of 1738 had been severe and the factory in Isfahan had suffered major damage as a result. The interest rate was 2% per month, and Hatem Beg was still governor of Isfahan and Esma`il Khan was *darugheh*.[205] A certain Mr. Mesgens[206] [?] had arrived in Isfahan in the company of a Jesuit brother from Basra. They were lodged in the house of the Jesuits. Mirza Esma`il, deputy of the *beglerbegi* of Shiraz had sent them to Isfahan accompanied by a courier and had them defrayed en route. Mesgens had told Hatem Beg that he had a secret, but oral message from the emperor for Nader. He therefore asked to be sent to Qandahar. Hatem Beg asked him for his letters of credence, of which he said that these would come later. Hatem Beg then told Mesgens that he could not go to the shah. Nader had spared the lives of Hoseyn Khan and leading Qandahari families at the intercession of the former's sister. Some were sent with their families to Khorasan; Hoseyn Khan was sent to Mazandaran. Nader declared the city a free-for-all to his troops for a three-day period. The troops were led by the Bakhtiyaris who also had led the final assault and thus now also got the best part of the plunder. A treasury of 300,000 *tuman*s in cash and jewels, as well as food and war supplies fell into Nader's hand. Nader also had given order to raze Qandahar. An envoy from the Moghul emperor (sjah of Hindoestan) had brought a present of 20 lakhs of rupees or one million *tuman*s so as to be left alone. The shah sent six months of food supplies from Herat with a view to march against the Uzbeks and subjugate them. Everybody was curious to know how the Turkish ambassador would be received. If the shah did not get his way he would declare war on Turkey again. It was reported that Lotf `Ali Khan had been appointed *beglerbegi* of Qandahar. Ebrahim Khan, the shah's brother and Amir Aslan Khan the *sardar* of Iraq [-e `Ajam] had been summoned to court. A certain Mohammad `Ali Beg (Mhamed Alie Beek) had arrived at Tehran as *sardar*.[207]

`ALI MARDAN KHAN SENT TO OTTOMAN COURT WITH DEMANDS

Mr. Mesgens (alias Megam) boasted much of his mission, but he had no letters of credence, and without these Hatem Beg did not allow him to go to court. La Porterie was still looking for employment as engineer or cannon-caster in royal service. There was a rumor that the shah intended *sardar* Amir Aslan Khan or Sardar Khan to march with 100,000 men via Isfahan to Fars to assist Mohammad Taqi Khan. On July 22, 1738 those who had remained behind of the Turkish ambassador's suite had left to Qazvin to find him there. `Ali Mardan Khan, prince of the Feyli Lors,

---

204. VOC 2584, Beschrijvinge, f. 2031-36; VOC 2448, van Leijpsigh to Koenad (20/04/1738), f. 2342 (reported that 28 days ago Nader took Qandahar; the kettledrums were struck; with Dutch translation of the royal letter).

205. Ismael Chan, *schout* of Isfahan (VOC 2477, f. 774; VOC 2510, f. 667; VOC 2860, f. 115) was replaced Ebrahim Beg as *darugheh* and was described as "the darling of the governor." (VOC 2510, f. 661). As of 1740 Hoseyn Beg (Hossein beek; Hassan beq) was *darugheh* of Isfahan. VOC 2511, f. 906, 1404; VOC 2583, f. 1326; VOC 2584, f. 2432. Other law enforcement officials in 1740-41 included Aqa Hadi (Aga Hadje), who was the police official or *ahdath* (agtaas). The castellan or *kutval* in 1739 was Aqa Baqer (Aga Backer). VOC 2477, f. 461.

206. I have not been able to identify this person.

207. VOC 2476, van Leijpsigh to Koenad (18/05/1738), f. 876-89; VOC 2584, Beschrijvinge, f. 2036-37.

accompanied him and had been sent as ambassador to Istanbul with them with the task to get agreement on:

◊ All Persians taken from Persia by the Turks had to be returned or failing that an appropriate amount of blood money would have to be paid.

◊ Repayment of revenues enjoyed by Turks in Persia to the amount of Dfl. 15 million.

◊ Ceding of one–fourth of the revenues of Mecca.

◊ Henceforth no Turkish caravan leader had to be sent to guide Persian pilgrims to Mecca, for Nader would appoint one himself. Moreover, a separate prayer place had to be allotted for the Persians in Mecca so that they might pray in peace.

◊ The cities that had been Persian in the days of Shah ʿAbbas, viz. Erzerum, Baghdad, Basra, Diyarbekr and Mosul had to be returned to Persia; if not the war would be resumed.

Nader was said to have ordered his brother, Ebrahim Khan, not to permit any ship, boat, or vessel belonging to the Russians or to whomever to drop anchor on the roads of Darband. All these had to be sent to the ports of Mazandaran where they could load or unload their merchandise. Nader monopolized the silk trade for himself, because the best quality could only be sent to Ebrahim Beg. This caused much trouble for the merchants. News had been received that little ʿAbbas Mirza had died of natural causes in Sabzavar.[208]

TRADE IS BAD — OPERATIONS AGAINST THE LEZGIS

Van Leijpsigh hoped that finally trade would get better, because if the violent activities continued the little trade that was left would also founder. The cost of a heavy silver-cloth robe of honor was 2,140 *mahmudis* (Dfl. 909:10). Van Leipsigh also hoped that the news that Nader had appointed his brother regent with power to appoint and dismiss governors, as he liked, was not true, for Ebrahim Khan was one of the most greedy persons, who even would press money from a totally destitute person in a harsh and tyrannical manner. Kalushkin had received 9 donkey loads of Persian silver money, with which he had not done anything yet. He apparently had orders to shine brighter at this court than others. It was rumored in Isfahan that Mohammad Taqi Khan had been taken in irons to court from Kong; also that he had poisoned himself, and that Abuʾl-Hasan Khan had received orders to confiscate his properties. Further, although not confirmed, that Mohammad Taqi Khan, the former admiral, had been appointed in his place as *beglerbegi*. It was also expected that Emamverdi Soltan would be appointed governor of Lar and Gamron. Everybody expected that Mohammad Taqi Khan would finally get his deserts. The Masqat Arabs still prevailed, and Sheikh Jabbara had defected to the Arabs. Nader had instructed the officials at Isfahan in secret not to have any contact with Kalushkin. On 27 September, 1738 the latter had fired cannons at his house and had made there an illumination because of a victory over the Turks.

---

208. VOC 2476, van Leijpsigh to Koenad (?/07/1738), f. 915-22. In 1739 Nader had farmed out the silk trade to Hajji Mohammad ʿAli. VOC 2477, f. 778. In 1741, the royal merchant (*kipje bassi* from the Russian *kuptshin* or merchant and the Turkish suffix *–bashi* or chief, head) was ʿAli Akbar (Alie Ekber). VOC 2583 (23/05/1741), f. 1335.

The *kholofa* had been allowed to return from Russia and was expected to arrive soon. The only information with regards to Nader was that he was above Kabul. Ebrahim Khan was recruiting troops in Tabriz to march on the Lezgis. The fortune-seeker de la Porterie had been hired in royal service and would depart to Kerman in a few days with a few cannons that had to be used against the Baluchis of Kich-Makran.[209]

NADER MARCHES TO INDIA — REZA QOLI MIRZA AS VICEROY

The presents that van Leijpsigh had given to the officials in Isfahan had made them friendlier to the Dutch. The brother of the chief-bird of prey, Ebrahim Khan, had been killed in Daghestan. The Lezgis were said to have been supported by the Russians. The Uzbeks had raided Reijebaax[210] in Khorasan. Therefore rumors circulated that the deposed shah would be taken to Isfahan out of fear that he would be removed from there. Nader was at Jalalabad. He allegedly wanted peace with the Moghul, so much so that he had sent his treasurer, Mirza Mohammad, as ambassador to the Moghul court. It was also rumored that Nader would send his eldest son as viceroy to Isfahan. Mohammad `Ali Khan had been appointed *sardar* of Iraq (-e `Ajam); he came in Isfahan on November 17, 1738 with 600 wild mountaineers and left on December 1. He went to Golpeygan and Khvonsar to await the shah's orders. It was believed that he would go to Tabriz where his help was expected, but also that he would go to Fars. Because he was related to Nader the young gad-fly (*horzelkop*) behaved very proudly, brazenly, and greedy and the town officials, out of fear for his incivility and anger, continuously brought him presents. This did not help much, for during his short stay he gave offense to many people. The officials feared for their lives and thanked God when he left. On December 18, 1738 Abu'l-Hasan Khan arrived to become the new governor. People were not pleased with that, for he also was known as a greedy and proud person. Nobody dared to come close to his house out of fear for his pitiless behavior and his quick handing out of the bastinado. Everybody hoped for the return of Hatem Beg, who, however, had been summoned to court, but later received orders to stay in Isfahan until *Nowruz* awaiting further orders. Kalushkin had given Mohammad `Ali Khan a present of 100 *tuman*s and had himself addressed as ambassador. Mohammad `Ali Khan felt that the VOC had not properly treated him, because it had not complimented him appropriately. He wanted to take revenge, but the *nabab* inter-vened, and he gave one day of delay. Van Leijpsigh then gave him a present of Dfl. 1,668 as well as presents to his second, Mirza `Abdol-Motaleb and his steward `Abdol-Hoseyn. Van Leijpsigh considered them all mischief-makers. Mohammad `Ali Khan promised friendship for the VOC. From 12 to 14 November, 1738 Kalushkin fired his 14 borrowed small cannons again, because of a Russian victory against the Turks, who lost 60,000 men. Recently, there was news that the shah had sent a royal order (*raqam*) to the governor of Yazd to demand 10,000 *tuman*s from the Rus-sian, because Russian merchants had been engaged in smuggling for some time with Armenians, Georgians and others by passing off their goods as being Russian. These had been allowed to pass without paying customs duties. Van Leijpsigh was happy with that, for he really wished that something happened to that half-barbaric nation. On December 5, 1738 a French doctor named

---

209. VOC 2476, van Leijpsigh to Koenad (09/10/1738), f. 925-36. Mirza Kafi, the *kholofa*, "recently" returned, the Dutch reported, "together with Mhamed Taggie Chan, the son of the well-known wakanevies of Sulthan Hossein." VOC 2564 (31/10/1742), f. 1178-vs-79r.

210. I have not been able to identify this location.

Galib[211] arrived from Basra. He had become a merchant and had beautiful Venetian mirrors with him as well as some French cloth and boxes for opium. On December 26, 1736 at 11.00 a.m. the kettledrums were beaten on arrival of a royal order forwarded by Reza Qoli Mirza from Herat (where he would stay there for two months), addressed to Mohammad `Ali Khan, *sardar* of Iraq instructing him to depart from Khvonsar to join Abu'l-Hasan Khan. Furthermore, that Nader had appointed Reza Qoli Mirza viceroy of the country, with the exception of Azerbaijan, of which was his brother Ebrahim Khan was in charge. It was rumored that the tyrant Mohammad Taqi Khan had been killed by Baluch robbers near Kerman, who had taken his treasury that contained 50,000 *tumans*.[212]

On the night of January 3, 1739 the rescript (*raqam*) announcing Nader's victory at Peshawar was received in Isfahan.[213] In April 1739, van Leijpsigh reported that there was almost no news in Isfahan about Nader's fate. This was due to the fact that all *chapar* houses had been broken down and the soldiers in it withdrawn, for Nader needed them for his battles. This was true for the Kerman route as well the route between Mashhad and Naderabad. Communications with Reza Qoli Mirza, the viceroy, were maintained via Ghani Khan in Naderabad, where there was a large garrison. This was the reason that there was hardly any news in Isfahan from or about Nader. Persians therefore asked the Dutch whether they had news from India or whether they could ask for it via Surat. Van Leijpsigh denied having such news, for he wanted to avoid unsolicited consequences and acted as if he knew nothing. People believed that Nader's first successes had been due to a ruse in order to draw him deep into Moghul territory and then to cut him off and down to size. Indeed, once he had crossed the river [Attock] the Afghans attacked him in the rear and were defeated with a loss of 20,000 men. Nader was said to be afraid and looking for peace, but that the Indians were acting as if they were deaf. People considered it a miracle if Nader would get out unscathed. People also had doubts about the viceroy, who meant well and was expected to bring order to the country after he had dealt with the Lezgis and Uzbeks. His father having emaciated the country everybody expected Reza Qoli Mirza, being totally bare [of funds], to make his try and get money to pay for his court. Van Leijpsigh feared that the Dutch would not remain unscathed. The same held for the government officials, who also would demand money, the more so because the Russian envoy was the bitter enemy of the Dutch. It was not a major problem, but van Leijpsigh opined that if he did not do anything the Russian might win terrain. He had started to pester the Dutch as the English had done in the past, and he aimed to expel the Dutch from Persia, if possible. Van Leijpsigh needed therefore some presents for the viceroy and his mignons. Ebrahim Khan had been succeeded by his 24-year old son, who was just another tyrant, van Leijpsigh commented. Two envoys had returned having achieved nothing in trying to mediate between the Turks and the Russians. The road between the Persian Gulf coast and Shiraz had become unsafe due to marauding by a nomadic family of the Loulouwie [?] caste.[214] On April 12, 1739 at 13.30

---

211. I have not been able to identify this person.

212. VOC 2476, van Leijpsigh to Koenad (26/12/1738 with appendix of 28/12/1738), f. 964-84; VOC 2511, Resolution Gamron (18/04/1740), f. 438; VOC 2477, f. 468.

213. VOC 2476, van Leijpsigh to Koenad (04/01/1739), f. 986.

214. VOC 2477, Van Leijpsigh to Koenad (12/04/1739), f. 456-96; Ibid., idem to idem (29/04/1739), f. 446 (`Ali Mardan Khan Feyli, ambassador to Turkey, was said to have died at Diyarbekr). I have not been able to identify the Loulouwie tribe.

hours the kettledrums were beaten at Isfahan, because via a copy of a royal order from the vice-roy the officials had been informed that Nader had taken Lahore and was marching to Shah Jahanabad, and that he had coined money everywhere en route.[215] From Bushehr, Schoonder-woerd reported that it was rumored that Tahmasp II had appeared again and was said to have given orders to the *na'eb* of Shiraz that all tax revenues of Fars had to be paid to him as the lawful shah rather than to Nader Shah. It also was perceived that the situation in Central Persia was totally topsy-turvy, for all news coming from there was kept secret.[216]

DUTCH-RUSSIAN DIPLOMATIC INCIDENT

Kalushkin (Kalutski), the Russian agent, publicly and on purpose offended van Leijpsigh in the bazaar on January 4, 1739. He behaved worse than the English had ever done and wanted to expel the Dutch from Persia, according to van Leijpsigh. In the afternoon of January 4, with a suite of 70 armed Russians and Georgians and other rascals in the Nimavard (Niema) bazaar, he offended van Leijpsigh, who was returning from a visit to the Carmelite padre Tomaso di Aquino at the Meydan-e Mir (Meidoen Mier). His small number of *shater*s or grooms was beaten with sticks and long whips by the Russians as were van Leijpsigh and assistant de Crane. Van Leijpsigh asked satisfaction from the governor, who on January 19, 1739 summoned both van Leijpsigh and Kalushkin at Nabab Mirza Ebrahim's house.[217] The latter had been charged to mediate in this matter and he had invited the Dutchman and the Russian to a sumptuous meal. The *nabab*, or *sadr*, who normally only rose for the shah and some of the most important state counselors, rose to welcome van Leijpsigh. He also seated van Leijpsigh higher than Kalushkin, at only two paces on his left hand side. The Russian behaved so obstinately and impertinently that he was not ready to accept this, because he wanted the Dutch to ask for pardon and thus he could not stomach this. The governor was in a bind, for in the absence of the shah and the court he could not do any-thing, because Kalushkin was an ambassador (he was referred to as *ilchi beg*, but more popularly as *vaqaye`-nevis* [which latter term in this context meant report-writer]) and the incident might be used as a pretext for war, for the Russians were in agreement with the rebellious Lezgis. Van Leijp-sigh nevertheless insisted and asked for permission to depart for Gamron, for the Dutch could not remain in a country where a newly arrived stranger can shame long-time friends of the shah, and thus hurt the shah and the VOC Directors. The governor then promised that he would admonish Kalushkin and tell him to further not to repeat such actions, for else he would be forced to take other measures. Kalushkin by spending money tried to blame the Dutch, and even incited the *mehmandar-bashi* to proceed against them on account of a head wound and to demand a penalty of 1,000 *tuman*s. The Dutch then took action against this, and spent Dfl. 3,855 to prevent things to get worse. Kalushkin had intimated that now that the EIC had gone he also could get rid of the Dutch. He tried to influence the court to expel Europeans, or, at least to have them tolerated,

---

215. VOC 2477, Van Leijpsigh to Koenad (12/04/1739), f. 499.

216. VOC 2477, Schoonderwoerd (Bushehr) to Koenad (21/04/1739), f. 514.

217. Mirza Ebrahim was described as the chief of all olama in Iran. VOC 2511, Resolution Gamron (18/04/1740), f. 438. He had many people in his employ such as Mohammad `Ali Beg, his first mace bearer. VOC 2477, f. 582. His all-do (*albeschik*) was Aqa Sayyed (Agha Sayit), who at the same time was *ghassal-bashi* (kassel bassie), the "visitator of the wounded and the dead. VOC 2477, f. 747. Mirza Ahmad (Miersa Ahmet) was his physician. The latter's brother, Mirza Sadeq (Miersa Sadigh), was physician to Nader. Another brother, Mirza Taher (Miersa Taher), was physician to Hatem Beg, governor of Isfahan. Mirza Ashraf (Miersa Escheraf) was physician to Abu'l-Hasan Khan. VOC 2511, f. 893.

at best. "He must have orders to do so else he would not expose himself so much," van Leijpsigh commented. "His predecessor, Semen Avramov had been a subtle enemy who acted against the Dutch covertly. Kalushkin used violence seeing that the Persian did not act," and maybe, van Leijpsigh opined, the English were also involved in this. The *kalantar* of Isfahan, Mirza Mohammad Hoseyn, was a friend of Kalushkin and supported him, and so did the *jarchi* or the public herald, who had been appointed by the shah. Van Leijpsigh entertained the idea to hire armed men and take action himself to countervail the Russian offenses until the shah or viceroy had set things aright. The alternative was for the Dutch to stay inside their house, which would make them the laughing stock of everybody and encourage the Russian to do more of the same. As a second best solution and to bolster Dutch reputation he had put armed guards at the houses of the VOC's interpreter and Banyans. This was better than looking for trouble, which would cost money; the other option was to temporarily depart from Isfahan.[218]

Van Leijpsigh reported that Kalushkin was said to have been confined in his house, with guards at his doors, and that he was not allowed to send messengers. He did not know what the truth of the matter was, though he knew something was going on. For if Kalushkin knew about these rumors he would have to be riding about town to put to shame the rumor-mongers, which he had not done, as he remained in his house. He had sent messengers to Russia, who had been brought back in chains. Kalushkin then made it known he wanted to go to Mashhad to see the viceroy and asked the *kalantar*, Mirza Mohammad Hoseyn (Miersa Mhamed Hossen), permission to depart. Van Leijpsigh further observed that, "Kalushkin does not like Europeans and causes discord. He insists on the expulsion of all Roman Catholic priests from Persia. He thinks that the time is favorable for such an event, for the Armenian bishops also want that, because of the occasional conversion of an Armenian to Catholicism."[219]

NEWS FROM INDIA AND THE VICE-ROY

On March 25, 1739 the Dutch received information that Nader had been killed with his troops in India.[220] On April 12, 1739 at 13.30 hours the kettledrums were beaten because a decree (*raqam*) had been received from the viceroy announcing Nader's victory at Lahore on January 25, 1739 (14 Shavval 1151). Reza Qoli Mirza sent Abu'l-Hasan Khan Afshar a *raqam* announcing his own victory over the Uzbeks and ordered him to beat the kettledrums. At the time of writing he was in Herat. He had learnt that `Abbas, *Vali* of Orgenj, intended to invade Khorasan with 30,000 men, because he believed it to be unprotected. His troops had already advanced as far as Chezek (Chessek) and Tejen (Tesem; [a continuation of the Hari Rud]). The viceroy personally had led his troops and had ridden to Sarakhs (Sarges) and detailed part of his troops towards the Chezek mountains. Out of precaution he had sent a second party behind enemy lines. The Persian troops met with an advance scouting party of Uzbeks; the battle was engaged which was brought to the notice of the viceroy who hastened to assist his troops.

---

218. VOC 2477, van Leijpsigh to Koenad (12/04/1739), f. 448, 477-88; VOC 2477. "Relaas van een onverwagd geval … on 04/01/1739", f. 573-671.

219. VOC 2510, van Leijpsigh to Koenad (18/08/1739), f. 672-73. Mirza Mohammad Hoseyn (who is also referred to simply as Miersa Hossen) was still in office in 1746. VOC 2583, f. 1326; VOC 2584, f. 2432; VOC 2705 (31/07/1746), f. 96 (Mhamet Hossein beecq).

220. VOC 2510, Koenad to Batavia (25/12/1739), f. 97.

Having arrived in Chezek, the viceroy learnt that ʿAbbas had retreated in disorder to his own country. On May 16, 1739 at 8.00 hours a *chapar* arrived from the viceroy in Mashhad with the news of his victory, after which the kettledrums were beaten. This was also done in Qom and Qazvin and elsewhere. The viceroy also had received information from Shahinshahabad that the Moghul had been defeated. Ironically at the same time the Lezgis were making the Shamakhi area unsafe. They were said to have taken the town and massacred and enslaved its population. The whole area was in confused state and that was the reason why the viceroy had gone there. On June 23, 1739 the kettledrums were beaten in Isfahan after a courier had arrived. Kalushkin stayed in his house; van Leijpsigh did not know whether this was his choice or whether had been forced to. The town was also illuminated, in which the Russians preceded the population, while the Dutch stayed their hand. To set Abu'l-Hasan Khan's mind at ease, as well of everybody else, van Leijpsigh told him that the news of Nader's victory had been confirmed from Surat. To underline the truthfulness of this news, the Dutch fired salutes during the whole day, which pleased the governor very much, and he sent a report about it to the viceroy. At that time rumors also circulated that Shah Tahmasp had fled, though it was not known whereto. Later it was learnt that the viceroy had killed Shah Tahmasp and all his family, and that his killer was Mohammad Hoseyn Qajar.[221] On June 16, 1739 the Dutch reported a rumor that circulated in Isfahan that the former shah, all his wives and children had been killed and that their bodies had been thrown into a well. The next day this rumor was confirmed and it was further reported that the former shah had been warned by a certain Mirza Mohsen (Miersa Mohsem) from Mashhad what was about to happen. He then fled with 12 servants from Sabzavar, but at 20 German miles distance from that town he was arrested and killed.[222]

Khan Jan, son of Mohammad ʿAli Khan the late ambassador was said to have intended, with the help of the Uzbeks, to put Tahmasp II on the throne again. But he first had to dislodge the viceroy, who was with 40,000-50,000 men at Mashhad. He also hoped for help from the Russians. But it all came to nought. The Lezgis, who had overran Persian positions at Shamakhi, had massacred the population, plundered the town and made many slaves, also had defeated and killed Khan Jan and captured his artillery and baggage train. It was said that Shah Tahmasp II's murderer, Mohammad Hoseyn Khan Qajar had been sent there with 4,000 horsemen, while the viceroy was raising an army of 60,000 men.[223]

On June 20, 1739 Nader Shah from Kabul ordered to have 30,000 camels send to him to transport his Indian booty. He had medals of 100 *tuman*s struck with one one side his name and on the other side *Gharib-navaz* (Gerieb newaas). His troops could not use them as currency and when he accepted them into his treasury he only paid 90 *tuman*s for them. In the royal mosque of Isfahan three royal decrees were read in public on June 23, one of which announced the granting of three-years of taxes. It was rumored on June 23 that the viceroy had beheaded

---

221. VOC 2477, Van Leijpsigh to Koenad (12/04/1739), f. 499; VOC 2510, idem to idem (18/05/1739), f. 610; Ibid., idem to idem (30/06/1739), 640-43; VOC 2510 (18/08/1739), f. 676; VOC 2477, Ragem Resa Coelie Miersa to Abol Hasan Chan (14 Shawwal 1151-25/01/1739), f. 738-41; VOC 2510, Ragem Resa Coelie Miersa to Abol Hasan Chan Afsjar (24 Dhu'l-Hijja 1151/April 4, 1739), f. 1253-55.

222. VOC 2455, Extract Spahans Dagverhaal (14/07/1739), f. 286-287.

223. VOC 2510, Koenad to Batavia (25/11/1739), f. 97-98; VOC 2510, van Leijpsigh to Koenad (30/06/1739), f. 643; VOC 2510, idem to idem (18/08/1739), f. 676; VOC 2510, Auwannees to Koenad (18/07/1739), f. 1332 (rumor that ex shah had been killed); VOC 2510, idem to idem (18/08/1739), f. 674 (ex-shah murdered with all his childen), 676.

the governor of Sabzavar, its *Sheikh al-Islam* and 150 of their retainers. On June 26 and 27 the pressing of horses into the viceroy's service started, while it was further rumored that the former shah had sent the little 'Abbas III to the Lezgis some five months earlier.[224]

VICEROY'S OPERATIONS IN KHORASAN

By summertime 1739, the viceroy was said to have pitched his tents outside Mashhad to move to Herat. "He is greedy and bloodthirsty, and is worse than his father, who kills people for trifling things. He sent tax collectors here to extort as much money as possible from the few wealthy people that have remained. Although they oppress the people very much even the governor does not dare to say anything." The viceroy was said to have raised an army of 60,000 men. Mirza Hadi, son of Mohammad Taqi Khan, arrived in Isfahan on August 11, 1739, coming from Shiraz with 300 horsemen to join the viceroy. He had first to go to Tehran to see the *sardar* Mohammad 'Ali Khan, who summoned him on August 14. On the same day a courier arrived from the viceroy for Abu'l-Hasan Khan with instructions to 'borrow' 7,000 *tuman*s from the merchants of Isfahan to buy cloth, sugar, spices, and fine fabrics and to send these as quickly as possible. The governor had no money, the taxes had been granted for a period of three years, while the sale of royal grain was forbidden. He therefore demanded 3,000 *tuman*s from the Armenian merchants, 2,000 *tuman*s from the Banyans, and 2,000 *tuman*s from the Moslem merchants, or to give him the equivalent in goods. Van Leijpsigh commented that these merchants would never see a penny of it. Protests did not help much although the governor reduced the amounts as follows: Armenians 2,000 *tuman*s; Banyans 1,000 *tuman*s and Moslem merchants 4,000 *tuman*s. Meanwhile, soldiers forced the warehouses open belonging to the Banyans, from which they took 700 *tuman*s in sugar, spices and piece-goods. The governor then had fixed the prices of these goods. The VOC dragoman was summoned on August 14, 1739 by the *darugheh* of Jolfa, Vali Beg (Welie Beek), at the governor's instruction. He referred to the viceroy's orders and asked for goods for which he would pay in cash and urged the Dutch to be accommodating. The dragoman replied that the Dutch only had received Java cardamon for which there had been no buyers so far, and there the matter rested.[225]

Vali Beg's father, who was in Bushehr, had been ordered to move to Mashhad with his troops.[226] It was difficult to find food en route to Mashhad via the Kerman route. Sometimes there was no food for five day's journeys.[227] In Mashhad itself the situation was not better. The Dutch surgeon Hezelman, who had been sent to the viceroy at his request, only received board and no money from the viceroy and suffered. He asked to be allowed to return to Gamron, because the viceroy did not take his medicines anyway. Food and drinks were bad, while he could not have [European] clothes made and there was little for sale, while the cold season was approaching. He expected to have a rough life there and asked Koenad, the VOC director at Gamron, to send him clothes, amongst which a padded coat made of broadcloth. Also, writing materials and food such as conserved fish, fresh butter, cheese and some smoked meat,

---

224. VOC 2455, Extract Spahans Dagverhaal (14/07/1739), f. 287vs-288 (the *kalantar* of Isfahan was Mirza Mohammad Hoseyn, f. 286 vs).

225. VOC 2510 (18/08/1739), f. 675-80.

226. VOC 2510, Schoonderwoerd to Koenad (16/11/1739), f. 941; Ibid., idem to idem (29/11/1739), f. 950.

227. VOC 2510, Hezelman (Mashhad) to Koenad (18/05/1739), f. 982.

which were unobtainable in Mashhad. Hezelman felt entirely uncomfortable. His 'servants' were Baluchis; he did not know their language, and they behaved rudely, drank alcohol to great excess and held bacchanals with prostitutes in the room next to his.[228]

The viceroy had left Mashhad on August 30, 1739 but he was back again in early October. In the evening of October 5, 1739 the viceroy sent for the Dutch physician Hezelman and apologized for having neglected him and not having taken his medicines, but he had been too busy. He would have to stay for six months in Mashhad to wait for his father and promised that he would start right away with the medicines. The viceroy ordered Mirza Rahim to give Hezelman all that he required, but the latter commented that whenever he asked for something he could not get it.[229] The viceroy ruled in a strict and bloodthirsty way, according the Hezelman. People who deserved some minor punishment had their heads cut off; he was very much his father's son. He also was very avaricious and suspicious. He had his medicines tasted by those who had a similar malady. The viceroy left Mashhad again on August 30, 1739. Hezelman died in Mashhad at the end of 1739, where he was buried according to Christian ritual by the Armenians at orders of the viceroy's vizier, Mirza Rahim (Miersa Rahiem).[230]

Hezelman was not the only Dutchman who died that year in Persia. For van Leijp-sigh, who had been in Persia since 1713, died on November 12, 1739 after a long illness and was buried with much pomp that same evening. He was provisionally succeeded by Aalmis who reported on December 12, 1739 that there was again some news about Nader's exploits, about whom nothing had been heard for a long time. That same day a courier (*chapar*) arrived, coming from Peshavar in 27 days, with orders for Abu'l-Hasan Khan to prepare in eight days 20,000 pieces of clothes, from head to feet, for stable-grooms and 280,000 complete uniforms for Nader's army. These had to be within one month at Herat where Nader would arrive short-ly. Nader had given rich presents to the viceroy, jewels to the value of 20,000 *tuman*s, to the latter's son 15,000 *tuman*s, to his own youngest son 10,000 *tuman*s and to his nephew, whom he renamed Ebrahim Khan, 10,000 *tuman*s, whom he also appointed to the governorship of Azerbaijan. It was said that Nader had ordered the viceroy to leave Mashhad and proceed to Tehran and to inspect the lower lands. He, as well as all governors, was expected there in a fortnight to give an account of their financial administration. People concluded from this piece of news that Nader wanted to divide India and Persia into three parts and make each of his three sons a king of one part. According to others the viceroy had left Mashhad, because he had run out of supplies in view of the presence of his father's big army there. The Russian resident claimed to have received a royal order from Lahore in which the shah stated that he wanted to give a present to the empress of Russia of 70,000 *tuman*s, viz., three elephants and their accouterments that were studded with diamonds and pearls as well as fine textiles. Al-though he had nothing received as yet, he was very pleased with this news. On November 30, 1739 Abu'l-Hasan Khan paid a visit to the Russian, who paid him a return-visit two days later. He was not received, however, as an ambassador and did not ride out any more with as much

---

228. VOC 2510, Hezelman (Mashhad) to Koenad (27/08/1739), f. 985-991. Prices in Mashhad were very high in mid-1739. For example, bread per *mann* of 6 lbs cost: 5 *mahmudi*s; butter: 25 *mahmudi*s; rice 8 *mahmudi*s and meat: 8 *mahmudi*s. Prices of other necessities were accordingly high. VOC 2517, f. 2219.

229. VOC 2510, Hezelman (Mashhad) to Koenad (19/09/1739), f. 994; Ibid (27/10/1739), f. 998-99.

230. VOC 2510, Koenad to Batavia (25/12/1739), f. 104-05, 108; VOC 2511, (08/02/1740 received) f. 1286-87; also f. 1319-22.

pomp as before.[231] Shah Tahmasp and his whole family had been killed by Reza Qoli Mirza, and had been buried in the shrine of Emam Reza, people told Hezelman, the Dutch physician staying at the *vali`ahd*'s court. Nader on his return was angry about the murder of Shah Tahmasp and his family and deposed his eldest son and appointed his second son Nasrollah Mirza as *vali`ahd* or crown-prince.[232]

NADER RETURNS FROM INDIA

Nader was said to have used 2,000 elephants to carry his booty from India, according to couriers (*chapar*s) who arrived from Kerman. Others said 1,700 elephants and 700 lions plus 30,000 camels. He had ordered to build a bridge across the Indus near Kabul with a fortress on both sides. Nader further had married an aunt, and the viceroy, a sister of Mohammad Shah. Nader also had taken a Moghul prince with him to teach him the military arts. Nader was said to have returned to Persia under the name of Badas Khan (Badas Chan), referring to the governor of the rich Uzbek city, Badakhshan. Although Nader took much treasure with him this did not mean that he was less demanding. When his troops were crossing the Indus, Nader was seated on a chair on the other side of the river, reviewing them. He had them appear before him one by one, where they had to take their clothes off and he then took everything from them. All their possessions were recorded, but so far he only had returned 30 *tuman*s, the rest he kept, though he would return another 70 *tuman*s to each of them.[233]

On January 11, 1740 Abu'l-Hasan Khan left for Tehran with his officials. Nader had sent additional orders for another batch of 10,000 uniforms. As deputy-governor, the viceroy had appointed Mohammad Rahim Beg, the *jabbehdar-bashi*. On February 2, 1740 Nader's do-all (*albeschik*), Aqa Mohammad (Aga Mhamed), son of Hajji Rahim, arrived in Isfahan coming from Kabul.[234] The *mo`ayyer-bashi* had written to the *nabab* that he hoped to see him shortly in Herat. The *mofti* and *Sheikh al-eslam* also have to go to Herat. Nader was said to wish to make his son shah. He himself would wage war with the Turks. His other son would be king of India. Meanwhile, Hatem Beg, the ex-governor, came to Isfahan with a decree from the viceroy to collect 11,000 *tuman*s, which were the governor's arrears in payment of the royal revenues.[235]

It was said that Nader had dismissed Reza Qoli Mirza as viceroy and that he had taken everything from him. Nader appointed him as chief of the skirmishers (tjarg gatsi bassie; *charkhchi-bashi*) of the army. The viceroy's councilors Mirza Baqi (Miersa Baggie) and Mirza Rahim (Miersa Rahiem) had been roughly treated, but had not been killed. Hatem Beg, gover-

---

231. VOC 2511, Aalmis to Koenad (12/12/1739), f. 842, 854-55. Abu'l-Hasan Khan's staff included Mirza Mohsen, his first clerk (VOC 2511, f. 1404; VOC 2584, f. 2432); his *na'eb*, a function held by his nephew (VOC 2584, f. 2432); Aghasi Beg (Agasie Becq), his first mace bearer (VOC 2584, f. 2432); Mirza Qasem (Cazum), and his steward or *nazer* (VOC 2584, f. 2432).

232. VOC 2511, Resolution Gamron (08/03/1741), f. 298-302.

233. VOC 2510, Koenad to Batavia (25/12/1739), f. 99-100, 102-03.

234. VOC 2511, Aalmis to Koenad (27/03/1740), f. 865, 875, 898; VOC 2583, f. 1326 (Mhamed Rahiem Beek); VOC 2584, f. 2432 (Maad Rahiem beecq); VOC 2477, f. 612. The nephew of Abu'l-Hasan was `Ali Jan Beg (Allie Jan Beek). In 1740 Nader's all-do (*nazer*) was Mohammad Qasem Beg. VOC 2546 (31/03/1740), f. 52.

235. VOC 2511, Aalmis to Koenad (21/04/1740), f. 914-15. The *naqib* was Mirza Mohammad Taqi. VOC 2477, f. 769.

nor of Isfahan, had been renamed Hatem Khan and appointed governor of Fars. He was highly regarded by Nader, although he was an enemy of Mohammad Taqi Khan, and he was expected to search for some of the latter's dirty linnen to cause him problems. Mohammad Taqi Khan had been appointed *mirza-bashi* (?) (Niersa basje) and the shah took 25,000 *tumans* from him. The ex-*nazer* Emamverdi Khan was appointed *sardar* of the lower lands and was subordinate to Hatem Khan, who had to pay his troops.[236]

GAMRON WANTS TO CLOSE ISFAHAN OFFICE

On March 8, 1740 the VOC council at Gamron decided to close down the factory in Isfahan, because it only yielded a loss. Moreover, it was felt that if Nader would die en route in India the Isfahan factory would be exposed to extortion. Also, van Leijpsigh had died and the council did not have much faith in Aalmis's qualities. The few products that the Isfahan factory purchased for export (dried almonds and seeds) could also be obtained by other means and elsewhere. Aalmis was ordered to take the whole administration with him as well as the two brokers and their books. Non-movables had to be left behind in the care of the dragoman who could stay on with the pay of a clerk. He would have to act as a caretaker and wait for better times. The Dutch had the EIC example in mind when taking this decision, for they considered that EIC abandonment of Isfahan in 1735 had worked out very well for them. Aalmis submitted that he would not be able to carry out the order because he believed that he would not get permission to leave. And without a pass he could not leave. Moreover, even if the governor would give leave, he would have to appoint financially sound guarantors as had happened previously when two VOC servants (Pruymelaar and de Crane) had wanted to leave Isfahan. If that happened it would create talk in town, and all VOC creditors would come and claim their money. For example, Nader's agent (*vakil*) had been to the factory as well as the surgeons who had treated van Leijpsigh, but Aalmis had no money, not even to prepare the caravan. The same held for the VOC brokers, who had no money either. If the brokers also would have to leave the problem would become even bigger, for it would hurt the VOC's reputation. He therefore asked for a delay and for money (including for the caravan) and advice what he had to do about van Leijpsigh's creditors.[237] [What the council had feared happened. Aalmis was continuously bothered about presents, and he freely gave them. The council was exasperated and in 1746 sent a two-man's committee to investigate the activities by Aalmis. Although the council was not very pleased with the speed of the action taken by the committee it at least returned with Aalmis and his staff leaving the dragoman behind to take care of the factory and with strict orders to give no more presents.[238] A similar decision had taken with regard to the Kerman office in 1740, which also was closed down.]

---

236. VOC 2546, Aalmis to Koenad (18/08/1740, f. 1208-10.

237. VOC 2511, Aalmis to Koenad (27/03/1740), f. 894-96. Aalmis received his money and the VOC caravan left Isfahan. Pruymelaar was in charge of the caravan and wrote from Shiraz, where he had visited Esma`il Khan, the *na'eb* of the *beglerbegi*. Mirza Reza, the road guard, refused to accept the VOC caravan pass, pretending that a permit was required from the governor. After much trouble Pruymelaar received the permit. VOC 2511, Pruymelaar to Koenad (28/06/1740), f. 953.

238. VOC 2705, van der Welle to Batavia (31/07/1746), f. 104-21.

THE TURKESTAN CAMPAIGN

In April 1740, Nader marched into Uzbekistan and was able to take it by November 1740. On 20 Sha`ban 1153 (November 10, 1740), he sent a victory decree to Reza Qoli Mirza from Orgenj. According to its text, they had parted company on 24 Rajab 1153 (October 15, 1740) at Chahar Ju (Tjehaar Joe). On 28 Rajab 1153 (October 19, 1740), to take Khvarezm, Nader marched *manzel* after *manzel* along the Amurya until Thursday 13 Sha`ban 1153 (November 3, 1740) when he arrived in Dereh Boyun (Diwiboenie), which was the frontier town of Khvarezm. Its governor, Albars Khan (Albars Chan) had withdrawn into the citadel with his Uzbek en Turkman troops. Nader waited two days for Albars Khan to come and fight. This did not happen, and, because he had nothing to fear, he therefore left his heavy baggage there. Nader continued his march on 16 Sha`ban until he arrived at one mile from the citadel Hazar Asp (Hazaar asb), whose governor wanted to remain behind its walls. On 17 Sha`ban 1153 (November 7, 1740), Nader's army moved another half mile towards the citadel, to entice the governor to sally forth. But he did not come, for it was a strong citadel surrounded by water, like a lake. Nader therefore decided to attack Yengi Orgenj (Gieli and Orgenj), the capital situated at 10 German miles from Hazar Asp, to induce its Khan to fight. After one day's journey Nader learnt that all Yamut Tekkes and Turkman troops had left the citadel to oppose him. He immediately rode fast towards them and defeated them; part of them were killed, part of them fled. The Khan then fled into citadel of Khanga (Gangah), being one of the five citadels of Khvarezm, situated between Hazar Asp and Khiva. Nader remained there during the night; on the following day he went to Khangah, where he arrived when nine hours of the day had passed. The Khan had readied his artillery, which he had captured from Bekovich Cherkasski (Gadergerai), the Russian general, as well as many match-lock men, Uzbek cavalry and Turkmans, to fight the invaders. Nader immediately attacked and defeated them; many were killed and enslaved. The rest fled, but were overtaken and killed. Many leaders were captured alive. The Khan moved his court into the citadel and Nader laid a siege. The Uzbeks had made a round wall around the citadel to shelter their horses, sheep and other possessions, which Nader's infantry immediately conquered with all its tents and artillery. Nader took some soldiers and civilians and the first low outer wall of the citadel. After having shelled the citadel for three days and nights his army stormed and took the citadel and on 25 Sha`ban (November 15, 1740) the Khan surrendered. Nader appointed a new Khan and pressed the young Khvarezmi men into his service and returned to Persia.[239]

NADER HENCEFORTH SHAHENSHAH — INVADES TURKESTAN

On December 20, 1740 (Ramazan 10, 1153) Nader issued a *raqam* ordering that henceforth in reading the *khotbah* and in writing requests to him he should not be addressed as *Vali Ne`mat* any more, but as King of Kings of the world, Nader of this period, Command giver of Persia, Throne giver of Hindustan and Khvarezm, land of the Uzbeks.[240] By that time, Nader had returned in Mashhad on December 21, 1740. It was believed that he intended to attack Turkey, a belief re-

239. VOC 2584, Beschrijvinge, f. 2083-87.

240. VOC 2584, Beschrijvinge, f. 2091. In July 1740, Koenad reported that Nader wanted to have a meeting of the royal council in Herat and that he now called himself *shahenshah*. VOC 2511, Koenad to Batavia (31/07/1740), f. 142.

inforced by the rumors about an understanding reached with Ahmad Pasha of Baghdad, whom he was said to have asked in June 1740 to strike water wells from Baghdad to Mecca at each days journey's halting place as well as to prepare 80,000 leather water bags, because Nader intended to make the pilgrimage. Others, however, maintained that Nader intended to attack the Lezgis.[241]

Nader had sent orders that he sealed with his own hands to the *nabab* to take his wife, Maryam Begum, sister of Shah Tahmasp II, to Sabzavar and informed the *nabab* that he would be in Mashhad in 50 days. The *nabab* further told Aalmis that he also had instructions to take Mir Sayyed Mohammad (Mier Seyd Mahamed) with his wife, whose mother was a Safavid princess, with him, so that the entire Safavid family would be together and he might console them because of Tahmasp II's death. He further had to give them robes of honor and assure them of Nader's favor. Then he had to bring them all to Mashhad, where Nasrollah Mirza would marry Tahmasp II's daughter and be proclaimed king of Iraq. The *nabab* believed that on his return to Isfahan the young couple would take up residence in the royal palace and that he would be Nasrollah Mirza's teacher, who was only 15-16 years old. Nader also had heard that the tsarina of Russia had a beautiful niece, whom he wanted to marry. After the Russian agent had said that this was not possible, Nader sent a special ambassador Sardar Khan (Sardaar Chan) to Russia with large presents to the value of more than 200,000 *tuman*s for the niece, who was quickly married off by the tsarina. Nader, informed by his ambassador about this marriage, became very bitter towards the tsarina and Russia, though he did not show it. Sardar Khan died en route and was replaced by Hoseyn Khan (Hossein Chan).[242]

When Nader had arrived at the river Chahar Ju (Jhoen) in Turkestan he had sent Mohammad Taqi Khan back to Mashhad to audit the *daftarkhaneh*s (defterchonas) or accounting departments and to examine some other matters.[243] It was clear that Mohammad Taqi Khan had once again obtained the shah's trust and had been given great authority. At the end of 1740, he was the first royal counselor in the kingdom and the shah's great mignon. He presided over his peers while seated on an elevated very costly seat which the shah had given him as appreciation for his services rendered in the lower lands (Garmsirat). Apparently, the shah did not want to hear any complaints about Mohammad Taqi Khan. The English, for example, who had complained about him in 1738, through an official letter from Bombay, were informed to take the matter up with the viceroy and there the matter rested. Mohammad Taqi Khan was also said to have influenced the shah to pardon those Arab mutineers (of Nader's navy) who would subject themselves again. It was rumored on January 10, 1740 that the ships, which Sheikh Rahma had taken would be returned to Emamverdi Khan. If that would be true then the ships sent for by the English from Bombay would come too late to retake these ships.[244]

When he was back in Mashhad, where he arrived on Friday, 12 Ramazan 1152 (13 December 1739), Mohammad Taqi Khan wrote to Koenad that he had received the latter's message. He promised Koenad support and if the *daryabegi* did not behave himself well regarding the Dutch, Koenad had only to write (via his brother Mirza Esma'il in Shiraz) and action would be taken. Mohammad Taqi Khan also informed Koenad that Nader had taken

241. VOC 2584, Beschrijvinge, f. 2089.

242. VOC 2546, Aalmis to Koenad (08/12/1740), f. 1233-36.

243. VOC 2546, Mohammad Taqi Khan to Koenad (27/12/1740 received), f. 1778-82.

244. VOC 2546, Koenad to Batavia (31/03/1741), f. 49-50.

Turkestan.[245] Because two VOC messengers stayed in Mashhad from January 7 till April 9, 1741 there was correspondence between Mohammad Taqi Khan in Mashhad and Koenad in Gamron. Koenad had sent them to present some requests (for submission to the shah) to the *mostowfi al-mamalek*, Mirza Taqi Khan,[246] who received and defrayed the VOC messengers well. This was very fortunate, for they reported that bread was very expensive in Mashhad due to the presence of the shah, the court and his army, which they estimated at 500,000. Both the troops, who had much money and jewelry, and Nader and his court, spent much money. They further related that shah had taken Timur's tombstone, which changed color every hour and measured 5 x 2 to 3 feet. When the royal kettledrums were beaten the elephants, cows, sheep and monkeys, which Nader had brought with him, danced. Daily the shah 'liberated' 8-10 persons from hunger, thirst and dearness by having them strangled. His son, Reza Qoli Mirza, rode through the army accompanied by only one *shater*, from which they concluded that he still enjoyed his father's favor.

The *mo'ayyer-bashi* would already have been dead if the *mostowfi al-mamalek*, Mohammad Taqi Khan, had not forbidden [sic!] it.[247] The latter behaved very free in the shah's presence and has been accorded a seat by him. However, he behaved as if he almost would die when he took that seat. This was, of course, because he feared that he would enjoy the same fate as the shah's brother-in-law, who had to loose his head because he sold some food supplies at too high prices. The shah did everything himself and trusted nobody in maintaining justice. The soldiers were paid in cash (rupees). When big daddy (*baba bozorg*; i.e., the shah) leaves his camp he declares gorog [*qoruq*] so that all doors and windows have to be closed, and those who are about or are seen, loose their lives.

The VOC *shater-bashi*, Hasan Rabi' (Hassan Rabie), who had seen Nader many times in Isfahan, had spied on him (in spite of the *qoruq*) and reported that "the shah rides with 36 runners in front, of which 24 big fellows and 12 boys." The messengers further reported that an ambassador on behalf of Mohammad Shah had arrived with a suite of 100-120 men and costly presents. When the messengers left in early April they learnt that the shah would leave for Tehran to first fight the Lezgis and then the Turks. Mohammad Taqi Khan gave both messengers a surcoat (*qaba*) and 100 *mann* of grains and told them that Koenad had to make a

---

245. VOC 2546, Mohammad Taqi Khan to Koenad (27/12/1740 received), f. 1778-82.

246. Mirza Taqi had been appointed *mostowfi al-mamalek* on September 25, 1740 (5 Rajab). VOC 2546 (04/12/1740), f. 1920-25; VOC 2583 (24/04/1741), f. 1287. His deputy was Miersa Maad Alie. VOC 2583 (02/1741 received), f. 1788, 1927-29. Prior to his appointment the function was held by Mirza Esma`il who also was *mostowfi-ye khasseh*. VOC 2253, f. 660. In 1742, Miersa Asherra (Mirza `Askari?) was *mostowfi al-mamalek* and he became *monshi al-mamalek* one year later. VOC 2860, Resolution Gamron (30/11/1743) unfoliated; VOC 2680, Resolution Gamron (14/04/1744). In 1744, Mirza Abu'l-Hasan was *mostowfi al-mamalek*. VOC 2680, Resolution Gamron (14/04/1744), unfoliated. In 1746, Mirza Mehdi was temporary *monshi al-mamalek*; he was also referred to as *raqam-nevis* (regam newies), i.e., writer of royal orders or as the first *regam newies*. He had much clout at court. His *vakil* was Aqa `Ali. VOC 2705, f. 371; VOC 2860, f. 116, 147; VOC 2705 (31/07/1746), f. 95.

247. This did not mean that the two men were friends, for, according to the Dutch, they were old and bitter enemies. A few months after this intercession they had a serious conflict. VOC 2583 (18/07/1741), f. 1338.

public illumination (sjeraghoen,i.e., *cheraghani*). The road back was deadly, because there was nothing to eat. They even had to burn their shirts to get some fire for their water pipe.[248]

NADER PREPARES FOR DAGHESTAN CAMPAIGN

Meanwhile, the situation in N.W. Iran was deteriorating. The Lezgis had invaded northern Azerbaijan, in particular Shirvan. They had plundered many villages and had taken the new town of Aq-Su (Aksoe; New Shamakhi), whence they were ousted by *sardar* Farah Khan (?) (Fara Chan). Abu'l Hasan Khan, governor of Isfahan, was ordered to come with all officials and the Russian resident to Tehran by *Nowruz* 1741, for which purpose was unknown. Nader was not expected to stay long in Tehran. It was rumored that he intended to attack Turkey. This did not mean that he had forgotten the Lezgis for the Afghan general Ghani Khan (Gani Chan) and three Persian generals were ordered with 30,000 men to march against the Lezgis, who had fled into their inaccessible mountains with their jungles and ravines, where they lived in houses made of reed and brushwood. They had to kill them and destroy their land. Large quantities of military supplies were sent from Isfahan to Tehran, where the four generals had arrived. Sobhanverdi Khan, governor of Kurdistan came to visit his family in Isfahan who were held hostage there for his good behavior. He was received with much pomp by the officials and was ordered by the shah to remain in Isfahan.[249]

The Russian resident had thrown a party on the occasion of the succession of the tsarina by her nephew. In February 19, 1741 he left for the royal court, though it was unknown why. It was expected that he would return to Russia for his house was empty. The shah, however, according to a passing *chapar*, had ordered the resident to return to Isfahan. He received 170 *mahmudi*s per day as defrayment. Nader Shah was at that time near Tehran, where he had summoned the governors to join him. It was believed that he would shortly march against the Turks or the Russians.[250] Sobhan Verdi Khan (Sepan Werdie Chan) performed the foot-kiss on 20 Safar 1154 (May 7, 1741). The shah showed him much honor and invited him several times to talk to him and paid him favors. On the last day of Safar (Tuesday, May 17, 1741), when Nader arrived in Firuzkuh, he sent for Sobhan Verdi Khan, Mohammad Hoseyn Khan (Mhamet Hossein Chan) and Hajji Safi al-Din Khan (Hadje Seffiedien Chan) and honored them with the title of Rokn al-Dowleh-ye Naderiyeh. Their task was to bring to the shah's at-

248. VOC 2540. Verslag Comps. Lopers Hassan Rabie and Hassan Noeroes on the trip to Mashhad from January 3 till April 9, 1741. f. 1698-1701. Bread remained very expensive in Mashhad in the first quarter of 1741, viz. 5 *mahmudi*s per *mann* of 6 lbs. as were other life necessities such as butter (25 *mahmudi*s), rice (8 *mahmudi*s) and meat (8 *mahmudi*s). VOC 2546, (15/04/1741), f. 2219; see also f. 1698.

249. VOC 2546, Aalmis to Koenad (15/01/1741), f. 1245-49; VOC 2584, Coenraad to Schoonderwoerd (19/04/1741), f. 1431.

250. VOC 2583 (24/04/1741), f. 1274, 1299-1301; VOC 2584, Aalmis to Schoonderwoerd (17/04/1741), f. 1496. It was, however, later reported that he would march against the Lezgis. VOC 2583 (23/05/1741), f. 1310.

tention anything that would contribute to the shah's, the law's and the kingdom's advantage and welfare.[251]

ASSASSINATION ATTEMPT

From Tehran, Nader went to Gesini[252] en route to Mazandaran. At Pol-e Safid (Poul Sefiet) he was shot and hit in his right side. The bullet went through his waist belt (*kamarband*) and hit his horse, which died. The shah's thumb became dislocated. It was rumored that the royal *shater*s, who normally rode at two musket shots' distance before and behind him, had ridden at him with drawn swords with the intention to kill him. The shah defended himself and the attackers then fled into the woods. Nader had all his men checked out, but he did not find any trace of the attackers. Nader had sworn that if the attacker would give himself up himself he would forgive him, because of his courage, and reward him with 50 *tuman*s. Nader also summoned all royal counselors whom he examined closely and asked them: "what have I done to you that you seek to kill me? Do you want another shah?" He also ordered to find the would-be assassin. It was believed that it was no common soldier, but someone from high-up.[253]

CLASH BETWEEN HATEM KHAN AND MOHAMMAD TAQI KHAN

Hatem Khan complained to Nader Shah about Mohammad Taqi Khan, who, and his family, were the cause that the population of Fars (i.e. the *kadkhoda*s and leading men of Shiraz and the province) had accused Hatem Khan of being too demanding and having left them impoverished and unable to pay. Hatem Khan also alleged that Mohammad Taqi was the cause of the rebellion of the sailors on the fleet. The leaders of Fars informed the shah that Mohammad Taqi Khan was a rich man, who advanced them the money, which was due to the shah, and allowed them to pay him in installments. However, Hatem Khan was a poor man, who could not do the same, and, therefore, the whole province had become ruined because of the violence which he used to collect what he needed. They therefore requested the shah to appoint Abu'l-Hasan Khan, Mohammad Taqi Khan's brother or one of his sons in Hatem Khan's place. Nader Shah, who liked Hatem Khan very much, was upset by this request, and said: "Rascals, what evil has this poor man done to you that you dare to complain about him. Prior to this, you complained about Mohammad Taqi Khan that he had extorted 18,000 *tuman*s more than the legal revenues. So who has ruined the country, Mohammad Taqi Khan or Hatem Khan, who has only been there for three months?" The *kadkhoda*s replied that at the time that they had complained about Mohammad Taqi Khan the shah had ordered the deaths of the *kalantar* of Shiraz, Mohammad Taqi Khan's brother-in-law, the *kalantar* of Neyriz (Neris), also one of his relatives, and Sait Matjeep [?] of Shiraz. Nader, moreover, had wanted to kill more than 40 people who had also signed the complaint. Their lives

---

251. VOC 2584, Sepan Werdie Chan, former duke of Ardaloen to his brother Ibrahim beecq (08/04/1741 arrived in Isfahan), f. 2214-15; VOC 2583, Aalmis to Gamron (24/03/1741), f. 1290 (Sobhan Verdi Khan was lodged in the house next to the VOC factory). In 1743, the son of the governor of Kurdistan, Mohammad Mo'men Beg (Mahmed Moemien Beecq) was brother-in-law of Mohammad Taqi Khan Shirazi and guardian of the royal jewels. VOC 2680, f. 199.

252. I have not been able to identify this location.

253. VOC 2583, Aalmis to Gamron (12/07/1741), f. 1338-41. In another letter, VOC 2583, Gamron to Batavia (31/12/1741), f. 46-47 it is reported that Nader had been shot through his cummerbund and that he saved himself by acting as if he were dead.

were spared, however, due to the intercession by Mohammad Taqi Khan, who swore that they were guiltless and had only been incited by the three killed ones. There was a rumor that the shah had ordered Mirza Esma`il, the sons, wife and Mohammad Taqi Khan's entire family to leave Fars and come to Isfahan as their place of banishment. It was even rumored that their properties had already been confiscated and that they had been ordered to make the ruined villages flourish again with their own money. It was said in public that the shah had confiscated those goods that Mohammad Taqi Khan had with him, and that he almost had lost his life. It was only by swearing on the Koran that he had no hand in the complaint and had no knowledge of it that he had been saved. The Dutch concluded that Mohammad Taqi Khan's power had come to an end, and that he still might loose his life, because the matter had not ended yet.[254]

On August 25, 1741 Mirza Esma`il indeed arrived with Mohammad Taqi Khan's entire family in Isfahan to stay there, but they continued to the court on September 16, where they had been summoned. However, when they arrived at Tehran a *chapar* from the shah ordered them to return. He further brought orders to claim 35,000 *tumans* from the governor of Isfahan, to be paid by the royal treasury, as well as to collect all royal male and female slaves and to provide them with supplies and animals until further notice. Mohammad Taqi Khan, meanwhile, had written to Mirza Esma`il that the shah intended to march on 10 Rajab 1154 (September 21, 1741) from Daghestan to Persia and that this year no war with Turkey would take place. The border areas, however, would be reinforced and `Ali Mardan Khan, governor of Hoveyzeh, had been ordered to have his troops ready till the shah arrived at Hamadan. On October 1, 1741 Mohammad Rahim Beg (Mhamet Rahiem Beek) arrived from court and confirmed that information. He added that six months ago the Arabs at Basra and Baghdad had sent an ambassador to Nader Shah to make an agreement with him, which news was also confirmed from other sources. Nader Shah also was said to have good relations with Ahmad Pasha. The Lezgis of Saag Hophaar [?] were said to have voluntarily subjected themselves.[255]

VOC ASKS AND RECEIVES CONFIRMATION OF ITS PRIVILEGES

In June 1741, Aalmis sent a request to Nader Shah in which he asked for an extension of Dutch privileges. For in towns like Rasht the governor prevented VOC agents to buy silk. He therefore asked for a *raqam* to order the governor and officials of the province of Rasht to stop their interference with VOC agents from buying silk at market rates as agreed with merchants. The shah's reply was that the *shahbandar* and other officials in Gilan and the entire kingdom should not interfere with VOC agents, for the coming and going of merchants was in the national interest.[256]

---

254. VOC 2583, Aalmis to Gamron (24/06/1741), f. 1352-56; VOC 2546, Koenad to Batavia (31/03/1740), f. 47 (confirms Mirza Taqi Khan's foreknowledge about the mutiny).

255. VOC 2583, Aalmis to Koenad (02/10/1741), f. 1383, 1392-94; Ibid, idem to idem (06/11/1741), f. 1416 (information about the Arabs was said to be a rumor, not necessarily true). I have not been able to identify the name Saag Hophaar.

256. VOC 2584, request Aalmis to Nader Shah (09 Dhu'l-Hijjah 1153 or 24/02/1741). The copy is from Rabi' al-Avval 1153 or April 1741. He sent the result on 06/06/1741 to Gamron. It was sealed by qadi Miersa Abol Hussein, Ibid., f. 2209-11.

THE FAILED OPERATION AGAINST THE LEZGIS

By August 1741, for more than two months no *chapar*s had come to Isfahan, so that the news changed all the time and could not be relied upon. One piece of news was that the shah had sent his ambassador to the Porte and that the Turk in reply had sent an ambassador with 5,000 soldiers. The shah was in August at Berba [?] (between Tabriz and Gilan) which had good pasture for the horses, where he intended to stay three months.[257]

On 24 August 1741, David Sahid arrived in Tabriz. He had thought that Nader would stay for two months in Gantjaman (Ganjabad ?), but he did not stay at any fixed place, and had left *chapar*wise to Laogistan (Lakestan?). Sahid wanted to travel to the royal court, which was at one- month travel from Tabriz, but friends and merchants counseled against this. They said the shah had left Barda` (Barda) and had left the throne and the *ordu-bazar* in Ganjeh and Barda`. He had left instructions that nobody from court was allowed to come there. Sahid further reported that en route it was not possible to buy anything, for you had take your own food with you. Many people who wanted to see the shah therefore remained in Tabriz. Meanwhile, in Tabriz life necessities were being collected so that Sahid could not get any barley for his horse. He had to send some people to the outlying villages to get a small quantity, and he wondered how the situation en route would be in comparison. It was also rumored that the shah would come to Tabriz and stay there for 25 days after which he would march to Hamadan. From Tabriz many cannons, mortars, bombs, bullets, powder and other war equipment was sent to Hamadan. Sahid felt therefore that he had to stay in Tabriz and await the shah's arrival. Because this was expected to last another two months he feared for the cost of his stay, also because it was very difficult to get things on credit in Tabriz. He had only 15 *tuman*s with him, and did not know how long he had to remain in Tabriz. Sahid asked for instructions what to do. He furthermore informed Aalmis that the latest news was that Nader had gone to Ghorrouwdagh [?] in a castle built by the Sorkhay (Sorghab), which was situated on the top of a mountain into which he had withdrawn with many people and provisions. The castle was built in such a way that it seemed as if it covered the entire mountain and was hewn from it. To get in one had to pass through a narrow passageway and it was said to be difficult to take. Also, snowfall was high there, some 3 to 4 *gaz* (ells).[258] Aalmis reacted by sending a letter to Gamron in which he bemoaned the fact that Sahid had remained in Tabriz, for in this way many opportunities at court had been lost to the VOC. However, he had not instructed Sahid to go anyway, but had only sent him a draft for 16 *tuman*s.[259] Sahid informed Aalmis that Nader had been able to take Sorkhay (Sorghab), the Usmi (Ismien), and the Shamkhal (Chamghal), but the latter's sons had rebelled and remained free. They had withdrawn into a fortress in the mountains, which Nader after many attacks had not been able to take. Having lost 12,000 men and suffering from cold and heavy snow Nader returned to Darband where he decided to stay for the winter until he had finished with Daghestan, after which he would march to Turkey. Bread cost 40 *mahmudi*s per *mann-e shah* and en route there was hardly anything to get, and then only at very high cost. He also did not dare to go there, because a *chapar* from court had arrived

---

257. VOC 2583, Aalmis to Koenad (15/08/1741), f. 1376-78.

258. VOC 2584, David Sahid (Tabriz) to Aalmis (09/08/1741 received 06/11/1741), f. 2221-27.

259. VOC 2584, Aalmis to Gamron (09/12/1741), f. 2737-40.

three days before in Tabriz with news that the shah had arrived in Darband and intended to stay there. The journey to Darband would take 25 days and would cost more money than he had and nobody would give him a money draft. For example, Aqa Mohammad son of Hajji Rahim (Agha Mehmet son of Hadje Rahiem) was in Tabriz, but despite their acquaintance did not want to give him anything. On 7 November 1741 some clerks would travel to court and Sahid would join their caravan to reduce cost. He had bought three mules to transport food. Allahverdi Khan (Alla Werdie Chan), the EIC interpreter, Jacob Jan Hermet's agent, also was in Tabriz. He offered to get Sahid some money, and he had been able to get him 49 *tuman*s. Sahid gave him an IOU, stating that if Hermet would not get the money in Isfahan, he, Sahid, would pay 20% interest.[260]

Sahid had delayed too long in coming to court and raise the issue of the silk trade. Mohammad Taqi Khan had promised that he would make a written request to the shah. He was irritated, however, with Sahid and, at first, refused to see him for three days. Also, because he had left court Sahid would have to hasten to bring the VOC interests to his attention. Mohammad Taqi Khan and his brother arrived on January 13, 1742 in Isfahan and Kalb ʿAli Khan on January 26, 1742. The former had already left on January 16, 1742 for Shiraz. Clement did not believe Sahid's story, because, according to information he had received, various merchants in Tabriz as well as Mohammad Taqi Khan's *nazer* had offered him as much money per draft as he had wanted. The *nasaqchi-bashi*, Mohammad Hoseyn Beg, had even offered to take him to court at the shah's expense and to have his requests brought to the shah's attention. However, Sahid had refused because of illness, or rather laziness. Clement therefore ordered him to come to Gamron to give an accounting of his mission, if not, he was fired. The result was that the VOC complaint about Emamverdi Khan had no effect, which was contrary to expectations, for on November 18, 1741 it had been sent in secret to Isfahan with orders to forward it. On December 6, 1741 Clement had once again urged Aalmis to forward it quickly. The first time Aalmis had written that Sahid was still at Tabriz and that Elias was too old to go. Finally, Clement had ordered Aalmis to send the Persian clerk, Mirza Mohammad Reza, to go to court. As a result, he left on December 26, 1741. When Mohammad Taqi Khan arrived in Isfahan they did not talk to him about it, because they wanted to carry out this complaint in secret, so as not to make mistakes. On February 5, 1742 Clement had copies sent of his complaint to Mohammad Taqi Khan for his advice. The latter gave a rather non-committal reply: "wait with the complaint till I am in Gamron." He then would send personally a messenger to court with orders through whom to give the complaint to Nader Shah. By that time the Lezgis were said to have contained the shah in Darband, while the Turks were rumored to intend to attack Persia at Hamadan and Erevan, to which end two armies of 300.000 European janissaries had been raised. On March 16, 1742, the council decided that if this were true it would be better to recall their Persian clerk en route for court, for the shah would have neither time nor patience to listen to VOC complaints. Aalmis had already recalled the clerk, however, because he had the same information, for which action the council reprimanded him.[261]

It was clear to the Dutch that the entire operation against the Lezgis was Nader's reaction to his brother's death. He wanted to whet his anger on the Lezgis, and, by December 1741, he reportedly held the whole of Daghestan, in particular the town of Tarkhu (Tarkem).

---

260. VOC 2584, David Sahid (Tabriz) to Aalmis (04/11/1741, received 29/11/1741), f. 2745-50.

261. VOC 2584, (31/10/1742), f. 1717vs-1726 vs.

This town, however, did not remain loyal and rebelled. He then marched against the Lezgis with 60,000 men, according to a courier who arrived from the royal court in Gamron on December 17, 1741, having traversed the distance in 23 days. Nader had left the management of the country to Mohammad Taqi Khan, the *mostowfi al-mamalek*. In addition to the latest news, the *chapar* brought a *raqam* in which the shah asked the Dutch to send him three carpenters and supplies to build ships (the same request also had been sent to the English and French). Sheikh Sa`dun of Bushehr, meanwhile, was causing trouble for the Arabs at Basra, allegedly at the shah's orders.[262]

NADER'S ATTEMPTS AT RELIGIOUS REFORM

In early 1742, Nader had given orders to abolish the Shi`ite faith and that the population had to embrace Sunni Islam. This had no effect and the Dutch did not believe that as long there was a Persian alive that this would happen. This was also confirmed by the blood of many olama who had opposed this order. Clement wrote that: "The difference between the Sunnis and Shi`as has already led to many bloody wars. The hatred goes so far that one of the [Sunni] prophets [he meant the second caliph `Omar] is burnt every year. We do not believe Aalmis, who writes [on May 5, 1742] that the Porte has granted Nader's request to make room for the Persians at one of the four prayer sites at Mecca. Baghdad and Basra have refused and the Turks would rather give up one of these towns that give such an important privilege to the Persians. The Turks have reinforced their border with 60,000 men."[263]

[This abandoning of the Shi`a faith was but a logical consequence of earlier steps that Nader had taken to question the state of religious affairs. In 1734, he had already forbidden the *ta`ziyeh* commemoration, or passion play, of the death of the Shi`a Imams Hoseyn and Hasan. Then, after Nader's return from India, he once again gave evidence of his unorthodox approach to religion.]

The Dutch reported that, one day, when somebody had died in the royal camp, "Nader ordered a mullah to bury the corpse, which the mullah did in the Persian fashion by asking the corpse how their prophet was faring, whether he had been a good believer and whether he really had died. He then gave the corpse a Koran and wanted to bury it. Nader asked the mullah whether the dead really could answer the questions that he had asked. The mullah answered in the affirmative. Nader then ordered to fill the corpse's mouth with flour and had it thus buried. After a few days Nader ordered the corpse to be exhumed and seeing that the man was still in the same condition as before he told the mullah that he was dabbling in lies and deceived people with his tricks. While cursing the mullah, Nader ordered him killed and the corpse buried again."

The next episode occurred on June 7, 1740 when Abu'l-Hasan Afshar, the governor of Isfahan, received an order from Nader in which he was informed that Nader had instructed Mirza Mohammad Mehdi (Miersa Mhamed Megdie) to translate the New Testament (*Injil*) and Psalms of David into Persian, for which the governor had to pay the Mirza 12 *tumans* from the royal treasury. If the Mirza needed help the governor had to provide it. Moreover,

---

262. VOC 2583, Koenad to Batavia (31/12/1741), f. 47-51.

263. VOC 2584, (31/10/1742), f. 1775 vs- 1777 vs. On the symbolic burning of `Omar see Willem Floor, *The History of Theater in Iran* (Washington, DC: Mage Publishers, 2006) pp. 203–12.

Tahmurath Mirza of Kakhet (Tamoeras Mirsa of Kagt), and the *khalifeh* or Katholikos of Uch Keliseh had to be sent for. If the Mirza needed 20 people or more [to help him] the governor had to make them available.[264]

THE NEVER-ENDING OPERATION AGAINST THE LEZGIS

The religious issue was but a marginal affair to what was going on in the Caucasus. The shah was said to be still at Darband fighting the Lezgis, who, according to some, had pinned him down. Others said that he had left his nephew, `Ali Qoli Khan (Alie Coelie Chan), there with a large army and he himself had invaded Tartary to attack the Lezgis from that side, without having received or asked for permission from the Crimea Tartars. On January 17, 1742 Aalmis reported that Nader was said to have lost 80,000 men against the Lezgis and to have only 50,000 able men left with whom he had withdrawn into Darband. Because of lack of food supplies the Persian troops had been forced to eat horse and donkey meat. It would have gone bad for Nader if the Russian empress had not sent him some ships with supplies via the Volga and the Caspian. The chief of the Lezgis, Jahan Shah (Jehoen Sjah), was said to have send Nader a mocking letter with the following contents: "Your Majesty, why do you take so much trouble to command your victorious army against a bunch of ignorant, inexperienced, unarmed mountaineers. If you win, what fame will it bring you? Nothing, for people will say that the Lezgis are a stupid, defenseless people. But if we are so lucky and defeat you, what harm will this bring you? The victor of India was chased by a bunch of loutish mountaineers! Therefore, go home, leave us in peace." Nader was so angry about this letter that he was unable to contain himself. He had sworn that whatever the cost to the kingdom or life he would punish the Lezgis and not return to Iran before had extirpated that entire nation.[265]

David Sahid was once again sent to Nader Shah's army camp in 1743 to discuss the silk treaty. Before he left, he discussed the situation with his bishop Philippe, who had just returned from Nader Shah's camp. Sahid arrived in Tabriz on August 24, 1743. The shah had given orders that nobody was to come to court and thus he was sent back. Travel on the roads was bad and food was hard to get. On October 31, 1743 Sahid learnt that the shah was in Darband, and that traders and sutlers were allowed to go there. He also wanted to go, but had too little money, and therefore borrowed some money and departed on November 15, 1743. On December 10, he arrived at Qobbeh (Goba) at 12 German miles from Darband where he met Mohammad Taqi Khan, who just had left court and was en route to Gamron. He said to Sahid: "you should have been there three days ago; I would have taken care of everything, but my friends at court will help you." Mohammad Taqi Khan could not do anything right then for he was traveling post-haste to return to the Persian Gulf. He assigned a *min-bashi* (Mir Ja`far Beg; Mier Jaffer beek) to accompany Sahid to Shamakhi where he arrived on December 16, 1743.[266]

---

264. VOC 2584, Beschrijvinge, f. 2078-81; for the Dutch translation of the royal order see also VOC 2511, f. 1317-18.

265. VOC 2584, (31/10/1742), f. 1173-75 vs.

266. VOC 2680, Resolution Gamron (22/03/1744), unfoliated. The price of barley had risen in Isfahan in June 1743 from 2 *mahmudi*s (Dfl. 0:13) to 5 *mahmudi*s (Dfl. 2:3:8) and straw from 2/5 to *mahmudi*s. VOC 2680, Resolution Gamron (29/06/1743), f. 199.

[There are no documents (at least I have been able to find them), which report on the outcome of this last mission. We know that it did not lead to anything. This report is also the last report from Isfahan, which is worthwhile publishing here, although there are not many for the 1744-46 period.]

LAST REPORTS FROM ISFAHAN

The situation in Isfahan remained very bad. Aalmis had made many unauthorized expenditures and was considered to have been a bad manager reason why Gamron had finally decided to dismiss his servants, the interpreter Buffkens and the four messengers, because the cost of maintaining the Isfahan factory was too high. It was decided to leave only one person as a listening post. Aalmis, assistant van de Wall and the commission, which had been sent to carry out this decision, returned to Gamron by July 1746.[267] The remaining persons in the factory (Buffkens and Elias Sahid) still passed on news and correspondence. The most important item concerns the news that Nader had arrived in Isfahan between November 14 and December 26, 1746 with the intention to eradicate the rebel Fath ʿAli Khan. He sent a *raqam*, as did his *molla-bashi*, or chaplain, to the VOC servants in Isfahan asking for a physician and surgeon. The chief surgeon in Gamron, Jan Goosman, said he was not healthy enough to undertake the trip. The *molla-bashi* asked that, if need be, to have a physician come from Batavia. Gamron instructed Isfahan to say neither yes nor no.[268]

[Although I have not found any document with the formal decision to divest the Isfahan factory, it is likely that with the death of Nader Shah and the uncertain times that followed as well as the decision by Batavia to concentrate Dutch activities on Khark and Gamron that the ownership of the Isfahan factory was just written off as a loss as the other claims on the Persian government and other Persian debtors were.]

---

267. VOC 2705, van der Welle to Batavia (31/07/1746), f. 92-97, 104-121; VOC 2680, van der Welle to Batavia (10/08/1745), f. 130-44. Aalmis had also been rather liberal in giving presents such as to the *molla-bashi*, Naser ʿAli Khan, the chief mace bearer, Mehdi Khan, the interim *monshi al-mamalek* and to Shah Qoli Khan the *yasavol-bashi* (jassaoel basje). VOC 2705, f. 370-71. The commission consisted of junior-merchant Jan George Schemming and bookkeeper van Nes. Initially Frans Canter had been selected, but he protested, because he also was a junior-merchant. They were accompanied by an interpreter, because the commission members did not know Persian. VOC 2680, Resolution Gamron (07/09/1744), unfoliated. Schemming died on August 18, 1745 and he was replaced as (pro tem) secretary of the policy council by bookkeeper H. van Post. VOC 2705, f. 122-23.

268. VOC 2705, van der Welle to Batavia (28/02/1747), f. 538-40, for the text of the *raqam* see f. 716-7, for the letter of Mierza Alie Ekber, the *molla-bashi* Ibid., f. 718.

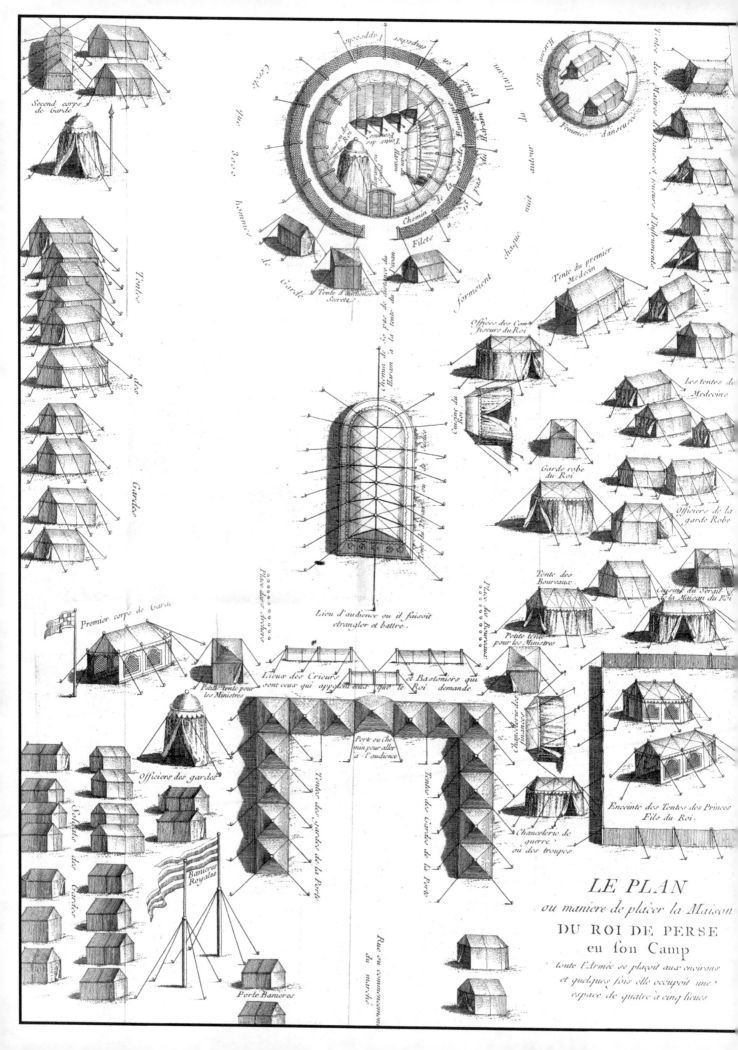

Second corps de Garde

Tentes des

Gardes

Premier corps de Garde

Petite tente pour les Ministres

Officiers des gardes

Soldats des Gardes

Banieres Royales

Porte Banieres

l'appréhendes que les chapelets

C'est

3. a 3.2

hommes

de

Garde

Chemin

Filets

Tente d'audience Secrete

Harem

formoient

chaque

nuit autour

de la

Place des Archers

Lieu d'audience ou il faisoit etrangler et battre

Lieux des Crieurs sont ceux qui appellent ceux que le Roi demande et Bastoniers qui

Porte ou Chemin pour aller a l'audience

Tentes des gardes de la Porte

Tentes des gardes de la Porte

Rue ou commencement du march.

Femmes danseuses

Tente du premier Medecin

Offices des Confiseurs du Roi

Les tentes des Medecins

Garde robe du Roi

Officiers de la garde Robe

Tente des Boureaux

Concours du Serail de la Maison du Roi

Place des Boureaux

Petite tente pour les Ministres

Chancelerie des finances

Enceinte des Tentes des Princes Fils du Roi.

Chancelerie de guerre ou des troupes

LE PLAN
ou maniere de placer la Maison

DU ROI DE PERSE
en son Camp

toute l'Armée se plaçoit aux environs
et quelques fois elle occupoit une
espace de quatre a cinq lieues

CHAPTER TWO

THE SITUATION AS SEEN FROM GAMRON (1730-1745)

LAST DAYS OF AFGHAN RULE

Leendert de Cleen, the new VOC director in Persia arrived on September 5, 1729 in Gamron and soon was confronted with the problems of the demise of the Afghan rule. Trouble for the Afghans started at that time and rumors of war were rife. The council in Gamron, therefore decided to strengthen the Dutch factory. It had suffered damage as a result of shelling by the Afghans during their engagement in February 1729. The repairs and construction work were delayed because of intermittent alarms of the approaching enemy, which led to the flight of the laborers.[1]

On October 23, 1729 Neda Khan, governor of Lar, informed de Cleen that ʿAbdol-Jabbar Khan (Abdoel Sjabaar Chan) had been sent for by Shah Ashraf. He had ordered Neda Khan to totally destroy Mohammad Zaman of Sulgar (?) (Mhamed Zamoen of Sulgaar), who hailed from Sulgar a village in the district of Lar. He had attacked with his Afghan match-lock men and had been opposed at the village of Gheyst (?), which he took after a battle. The defenders had fled behind four walls, which did not deserve the name of a citadel. But he could not batter them down with his cannon, for his smiths were unable to make balls of the required caliber. He therefore sent Mohammad Khan as his courier (*chapar*) to ask for 100 balls of 1.25 *mann-e Tabriz* (7.5 lb) weight as well as good gunners. The Dutch were requested to send these by sea to the *Sheikh al-Shoyukh* Sanad ibn Rahma (sjeeg of the sjeegs Saned son of Rama) who would take care of their further transport. De Cleen replied that he could not comply with the request.[2]

---

1. VOC 3168, de Cleen to Batavia (06/05/1730), f. 17, 41-44. Batavia had approved the plan. In particular, two wooden doors at the posterior gate on the landside could easily be blown away by artillery, if positioned in nearby houses, which the Dutch could not prevent. This had almost happened during the last siege. Ibid., f. 44.

2. VOC 3168, Nedda Chan (governor Lar) to de Cleen (Received 23/10/1729), f. 463-4; Ibid., de Cleen to Nedda Chan (24/10/1729), f. 523.

On November 24, 1729 the Dutch decided to remain neutral during the coming battles. On that same day a letter from Ashraf arrived announcing that he had departed with his army to destroy Shah Tahmasp, while at the same time Delaver Beg, *na'eb* of Shiraz, reported that the *beglerbegi* had arrived with his army in that town. The outcome of the major battle was made known to the Dutch three weeks later when Mir Mehr-e 'Ali, *kalantar* of Tezerg Ahmadi, informed de Cleen from Ghinaw that *chapars* had reached him with the news that Shah Tahmasp II had defeated his enemies. The shah had sent him a decree (*raqam*) ordering him to consult with friends of the shah such as the Dutch and to destroy the enemy. He also had to inform the vizier of Jahrom about this news who had to appoint a *na'eb* and formally had to take possession of Gamron. Mir Mehr-e 'Ali had arrived with his men in Ghinaw and asked for De Cleen's advice what he had to do.[3] The vizier of Jahrom, Mohammad Reza (Mhemet Resa) informed de Cleen of the fact that the shah had appointed him *vakil* of Gamron and Lar on 7 Jomadi al-Avval 1142 (November 28, 1729), and he asked de Cleen to destroy all the Shah's enemies and to confiscate their property for the shah.[4]

De Cleen gave a neutral reply with reference to what had happened between him and the Dutch in the past. Mir Mehr-e 'Ali replied that at that moment it was not the time to raise old problems. He had received a decree from the shah and orders from Nader to destroy as many enemies as possible. He therefore had advanced towards 'Essin and wanted to know whether the Dutch would support him, when he would attack. De Cleen replied that he only had doubtful and unreliable information so that he could not tell Mir Mehr-e 'Ali anything definite. He expressed the hope that the kingdom soon would be peaceful and flourishing again.[5]

Despite this reply Mir Mehr-e 'Ali moved towards Gamron where he arrived early in the morning of December 16. He took up lodgings at the house of Sheikh 'Ali Bin and from there urgently asked for advice and support from the Dutch.[6] De Cleen did not reply to this letter. Mir Mehr-e 'Ali then acted alone and attacked the citadel which he surrounded as well as Baru Khan's house. He wrote again to de Cleen asking him to aim the Dutch cannons at the citadel and blast that damned nation out of there, for his men then could easily deal with them.[7] De Cleen replied that in these dangerous times he could not afford to give a written answer, he therefore told the messenger that he wished his master the best of luck. Between the Afghans and the Persians a fight ensued, while the population tried to find refuge under

3. VOC 3168, Mhier Mheer Alie, calanthaar of Thesirk Ahmaddie from Ghinauw to de Cleen. (13/12/1729), f. 469. Nader had sent a *ta'liqeh* to Mhamed Alie Sulthan Bamie, governor of Abraha and Mir Mehr 'Ali in which the two were ordered not to allow the enemy, who was hiding in the mountains and fortresses, to escape. Mir Mehr 'Ali had to take counsel with the captains of the Europeans [Companies], the *yuzbashi*s of Hormuz and the *kalantar*s of Minab and other townships and other friends of the shah, or else they would incur his disfavor and anger. 24 Rabi' al-Thani (November 16, 1728). On the back was the seal of the grand vizier (E'temad al-Dowleh) and the note "written under the eyes of the shah." VOC 3168 (Received 12/12/1729), f. 470-72.

4. VOC 3168, Mhemet Resa, second of Jahrom to the Dutch (Received 14/12/1729), f. 473.

5. VOC 3168, de Cleen to Mir Mehr 'Ali in 'Essin (15/12/1729), f. 527-28; Ibid., Mir Mehr 'Ali to de Cleen (Received 15/12/1729), f. 475-76.

6. VOC 3168, Mir Mehr 'Ali to de Cleen, at 08.00 hours west from Gamron (16/12/1729), f. 177.

7. VOC 3168, Mir Mehr 'Alie to de Cleen, evening at sunset, West of Gamron (Received 16/12/1729), f. 178.

the walls of the Dutch and English factories. The center of the town became the domain of the warring parties. The best houses were pillaged and set fire to. In the afternoon of December 20, 1729 the son of Mir Mehr-e 'Ali came to see de Cleen. He said that his father was very much surprised to see that the Dutch remained neutral, for if they both would attack the Afghans certainly would be defeated. De Cleen told the son to tell his father that the Dutch indeed were neutral and would remain so.[8]

The leading officials or *yuzbashi*s of Hormuz had contacted the Dutch in early December 1729, after having received Nader's decree through their good offices. De Cleen had replied that if they would write him that they were under VOC orders he then would comply with their request and tell them what to do. Despite their uncertainty about the Dutch position the Hormuzians decided to act. On December 21, towards noon, *yuzbashi* Kalb 'Ali Beg arrived with six vessels under the English flag with 100 men to assist Mir Mehr-e 'Ali. At sunset de Cleen again was asked for his advice to which he gave a non-committal reply.[9]

The next day (December 22, 1729) one of the *yuzbashi*s of Hormuz, Mohammad Amir Aqa (Maet Amier Aga), came to see de Cleen, while in the afternoon two envoys from Mir Mehr-e 'Ali and the Hormuzians, accompanied by four leading Banyans, came to see de Cleen to repeat the request for support against the Afghans. Only one of the envoys, a customs official, was allowed inside the factory to guarantee secrecy and to show Dutch neutrality. After consultation with his council, de Cleen told the envoy that his advice was that the Persians should better coordinate their efforts and keep their troops together rather than permit them to roam through the town in groups of 20 to 30 men. For in case of an Afghan sortie they surely would be destroyed. He further advised them to enter the old 'Portuguese' factory with the two cannons brought from Hormuz and from there fire upon the Afghans in the citadel, which might force them to surrender.[10]

On December 23, 1729 some Afghans arrived from Masqat to support Baru Khan. Four days later at 17.00 hours the Hormuzians returned to their island, while during the night Baru Khan received more relief troops, whence and how many the Dutch did not know. This made Mir Mehr-e 'Ali decide to retreat, pursued by the Afghans who killed some of his men. The whole town was in ruins and the population had suffered considerable damage. De Cleen believed that the population, which had sought refuge under Dutch walls, would be killed. Through his intercession Baru Khan calmed down and did not undertake further action against the population.

On January 9, 1730 Baru Khan summoned the VOC dragoman, whom he gave the keys of the citadel. Baru Khan told him that he would leave the castellan (*kutval*) and some men behind. He himself would go to Lar. When the dragoman delivered this message Baru Khan with all his troops, including the *kutval*, left Gamron. An Afghan horseman in haste passed the VOC factory to tell the doorman that the citadel was open for the Dutch. The council unanimously decided to take possession of the citadel to which end junior-merchant Gutchi was sent to see whether there were any Persians, Afghans or English there, in which

---

8. VOC 3168, de Cleen to Batavia (06/05/1730), f. 109-112.

9. VOC 3168, Ormusians to de Cleen (17/12/1729), f. 179; Ibid. de Cleen's reply dated same day. f. 529

10. VOC 3168, de Cleen to Batavia (06/05/1730), f. 112-14.

case he had to do nothing, if not he had to give signal that Dutch soldiers could be sent. Since the citadel was empty the Dutch took it and decided the next day to keep it, as well as the old 'Portuguese' factory, because it commanded the Dutch factory as they had found out during the Afghan attack in February 1729. The council therefore decided to demolish that old factory as well as two houses near the Dutch factory to prevent these being used by hostile parties as artillery posts against the Dutch.[11]

Because of Dutch neutrality the coastal petty chiefs were uncertain about the reliability of the news that Ashraf had been defeated. The qadi of Hormuz, Pir Mohammad (Pier Mhammed), wrote de Cleen on January 4, 1730 that he was puzzled by the Dutch attitude. For when the Safavids were helpless the Dutch had assisted them; all those who helped them would be rewarded. Now when the news was that the enemies had been destroyed the Dutch did nothing. He expressed the hope that the Dutch would do more than they had done before to defeat the enemies. On the same day a letter from Ra'is Jahangir, *kalantar* of Sindirk (Cindirk)[12] was received by the Dutch. Mir Mehr-e `Ali had written to the chief *yuzbashi* of Hormuz, Morteza Qoli Beg, that Ashraf had been defeated and sent him the copy of the Shah Tahmasp's *raqam*. Morteza Qoli Beg had also passed a copy to Ra'is Jahangir who wanted to come to Gamron, since the *raqam* had asked for assistance. He, however, wanted to have de Cleen's advice on this matter before doing anything. A similar query reached the Dutch from Sheikh `Abdol-Safi, *kalantar* of Minab, who wanted to know what was true of all the information which reached him. Would not the Dutch as old friends advise him what to do?[13]

De Cleen replied to `Abdol-Safi that he also only received conflicting information which he did not want to pass on to him. The qadi got a rather sour reply referring to past relations, further saying that only madmen told what their intentions were. Nevertheless, he assured the qadi that in time everything would be all right.[14] On January 11, 1730 Kalb `Ali Beg wrote to de Cleen stating that the new governor of Gamron had appointed him *vakil* (agent) of the town. When Mir Mehr-e `Ali had attacked the Afghans he, therefore, had landed with some troops counting on Dutch support. However, through the soldiers' lack of understanding everything had become confused. Since then Mir Mehr-e `Ali had fled, while Baru Khan had vacated the citadel which the Dutch had occupied for the shah. He offered to be friends like in former times in which case he would come to Gamron with some troops to take care of the town until the governor himself would come. De Cleen replied that since he had received orders he should know best what to do; the town was empty and nobody was in charge of it, so if he would come de Cleen would tell him what needed to be done. Kalb `Ali Beg thanked de Cleen for his friendly reply, but complained that de Cleen had neither said that he should come to Gamron as had been ordered, nor anything about Dutch support. He asked for clear

---

11. VOC 3168, de Cleen to Batavia (06/05/1730), f. 109-116 plus a note on English intentions regarding the fortress, Ibid., f. 117; Ibid., Instruction to Gutchi how to guard the fortress (16/01/1730), f. 591. See also Gamronsch Dagregister. The name of Portuguese factory is a misnomer, because the building had been constructed by the Safavids near the site of the old Portuguese fort, which had been destroyed in 1614. For details see Willem Floor, *The Persian Gulf* (Washington DC: Mage Publishers, 2006), chapter five.

12. On Sindirk see Alfons Gabriel, *Weites Wildes Iran* (Stuttgart, 1940), p. 38.

13. VOC 3168, Mier Mhamed to de Cleen, f. 480-1; Ibid., Reis Jehoengier to de Cleen (received 04/01/1730), f. 482-3; Ibid., Sjeeg Abdul Seffie to de Cleen (received 04/01/1730), f. 483.

14. VOC 3168, de Cleen's reply, f. 530-31.

replies to these matters so that he could act accordingly and not be later reprimanded for having neglected his task. De Cleen again replied that Kalb `Ali Beg had to act according to his own lights.[15]

After his defeat at Morchehkhvort, Ashraf fled in southerly direction to Baluchistan or, according to others, to Qandahar. When the news of his defeat and flight became known in Shiraz the population rose in revolt. At that time the city was governed by Ja`far Khan. However, the revolt was badly planned and implemented. The Afghans knew about it and did not hesitate to make use of this information by suppressing the revolt. They murdered and imprisoned so many that the remaining Persians were no threat to them. After this massacre of the population the city was pillaged, burnt, and sacked for three consecutive days and nights and again a great number of people were murdered. One of the victims was junior-merchant Jelmer Laan, who had been staying for one month in Shiraz on his way back to Isfahan. He was staying at the VOC wine-maker's house and had been ill. He was taken with the other people staying in that house to another place, after having been beaten and having his golden buttons ripped off his shirt. He then was again asked for money and taken outside. Later he was found killed lying in his underpants on the road.[16]

In Kerman the infamous `Abdollah Khan was said to have intended to kill the population of the city prior to his flight. On the approach of the new *beglerbegi* Taleb Khan he had exploded the powder-house and then `Abdollah Khan had fled from the citadel towards Shiraz.[17] [Whether out bravura or out of the belief that the situation had not yet been lost is not known,] but Neda Khan, governor of Lar, wrote from Morbagh to de Cleen (a letter received on February 2, 1730) that he had arrived there some days ago to discuss matters with Sheikh Ahmad Madani. Because Baru Khan had left Gamron and had left the town in the charge of de Cleen he asked him to secure the town against all enemies. He believed that a certain Sheikh Mohammad Majid (sjeeg Mamed Madjed) had been appointed to the governorship and *shahbandari* of the town, which was the reason why Baru Khan had become angry. Neda Khan announced that he would come to Gamron within a few days with many troops, both his own and those supplied by Sheikh Ahmad Madani and `Abdol-Jabbar Khan (Abdul Sjalar Chan) to destroy the enemy. He also asked the Dutch to keep him daily informed about developments.[18]

Neda Khan did not come, however, for Persian troops were close on the heels of the Afghans. A fortnight later Hajji Ghani Khan, vizier of Jahrom, wrote to de Cleen that Nader had arrived with his troops at Khord-e Marvdasht (Chord-o-merdest), 8 day's journey from Shiraz on January 19, 1730 (Rajab 1142) and had sent a letter to the Dutch which he passed on. In this letter Nader informed de Cleen of Ashraf's defeat who thereafter had fled from one place to the other. He had received information that Baru Khan and Ashraf's brother and his women and children as well as all his goods had been sent to the coast to escape. He therefore had ordered Mir Mehr-e `Ali to destroy the enemy. He demanded that de Cleen assist Mir

---

15. VOC 3168, Kalb `Ali to de Cleen, f. 485-6; Ibid, de Cleen's reply (14/01/1730), f. 532; Ibid., Kalb `Ali to de Cleen (13/03/1730), f. 487; Ibid., de Cleen's reply (13/03/1730), f. 533.

16. VOC 3168, Report by Amier Chan, Armenian servant of Jelmer Laan. f. 560-64.

17. VOC 3168, de Cleen to Batavia (06/05/1730), f. 129-30.

18. VOC 3168, Nedda Chan to de Cleen (now in Morbaaq on the Arab side) (received 05/02/1730), f. 488-89.

Mehr-e ʿAli and to order all his ships, vessels and *gurab*s not to transport any goods belonging to Ashraf on pain of severe punishment.[19]

Two weeks later this letter was followed by another one from Nader in which he informed de Cleen that the *yuzbashi*s of Hormuz and others had reported to him that the Dutch had not assisted Mir Mehr-e ʿAli, but Baru Khan. He did not believe this slander, because of the ties of friendship and the behavior of the Dutch in Isfahan. He also had understood that Baru Khan had fled and that the Dutch had taken possession of the citadel, which they had not reported to him, however. He assumed that the Dutch had had no time to do so. He had ordered Mir Mehr-e ʿAli to proceed at once to Gamron to hold the citadel together with the Dutch. He further ordered de Cleen not to assist those Afghans who had fled into the direction of Lar, amongst whom the women and children of Mahmud Khan and Ashraf Khan, nor to give them vessels but to arrest them.[20]

De Cleen in reply to these letters congratulated the shah and Nader with their victory and expressed his pleasure of having been asked to assist Mir Mehr-e ʿAli. The latter, however, had left Gamron without having done anything useful out of sheer stupidity and bad intentions of his soldiers. He also had heard that people had spread slander about the Dutch, but he assured Nader that the Dutch were still friends of the Crown. He had tried to entrap Baru Khan, but the latter had been forewarned and then hastily fled. On that same day the Dutch had taken the citadel to keep it till a trustworthy person from the shah would arrive, otherwise it would become a refuge for robbers. He therefore had ordered the demolition of the so-called Portuguese factory, so that in case of the return of the Afghans they could not bother people from there. This information he already had sent to Isfahan on January 12 to inform both the shah and Nader himself.[21]

The EIC and others circulated slander about the VOC as reported inter alia by the VOC winemaker in Shiraz and Mirza Mohammad Taqi, who commented that Nader did not believe these stories in view of their old friendship and Schorer's behavior. He also said that the Dutch had done the right thing by occupying the citadel and added that others had told Nader that the Dutch had done much for shah's cause.[22]

[Despite the traditional bickering and competition between the Dutch and the English] De Cleen made an oral agreement with the EIC in September 1730 to return deserters to each other, because the level of desertions was so high that both Companies suffered from it. The English insisted that deserters on being returned would not be punished, to which de

---

19. VOC 3168, f. 493-94; Ibid., Atumadoula Tamas Coelie from Chorde-e-Merdest to de Cleen (Rajab 1142/January 1730/received February 13, 1730), f. 491-93.

20. VOC 3168, Tamas Coelie Chan to the Dutch (Rajab 1142/February 1730/received February 7, 1730), f. 499-501 plus note by Miersa Mhamed Taki to the Dutch. Ibid., f. 502-03. The shah and Nader had been informed by Schorer, who had not told them that the Dutch had destroyed the fortress. VOC 2168, Schorer to de Cleen (30/03/1730), f. 205. Other local residents had spread the rumor that the Dutch had set a trap for Baru Khan, who therefore had fled. Although it was not true, the story was well liked by the authorities, reason why the Dutch considered it diplomatic to take credit for it, although it was a fabrication. VOC 3168, de Cleen to Batavia (06/05/1730), f. 123.

21. VOC 3168, f. 536-39.

22. VOC 3168, VOC wine-maker to de Cleen, f. 495-98; Ibid., Mohammad Taqi to de Cleen, f. 502-03.

Cleen grudgingly agreed.[23] On March 3, 1730 de Cleen congratulated Nader with his victory over the Afghans, after Mohammad Reza Beg, the new governor of Lar, had informed the population of Gamron that Nader had victoriously arrived in Ghafier-o-Tahadon [?]. To add to the joy he had ordered salutes to be fired from the citadel and the Dutch factory. He informed Nader that he had two ships on the roadstead which he would use if the enemy would come to Gamron. About the slander put about he remarked that in time the slanderers would not escape their just punishment.[24]

Meanwhile Ashraf and his men had fled towards Orsu (Orsoe). Mir Mehr-e `Ali immediately went there with his men to cut off Ashraf's retreat at Tang-e Mardunu (Tanga Moerdon). He also sent men to ask the authorities in Rudbar and the governor of Kerman to take similar measures until Nader would catch up. Mir Mehr-e `Ali encountered the flying Afghans at Orsu and a fight ensued, he claimed to have killed many Afghans and that Ashraf himself had been hit by four bullets, and had been forced to fly.[25] Finally, Schorer reported from Isfahan that he had news that when Ashraf had reached the province of Gereshk (Sjerisk) near Qandahar he had been beheaded by Hasan Khan, brother of Mahmud Khan. The latter was said to have sent Ashraf's head and two Safavid princesses, whom he had taken with him on his flight, to Isfahan and had already arrived in Kerman and were expected any moment in Isfahan.[26] However, later van Leijpsigh reported, that the Baluch chief `Abdollah Khan had informed the shah that he had fought with and killed Ashraf and had taken all his goods. He was said to have asked the shah for troops in order to take Qandahar for the shah.[27] Van Leijpsigh's version probably is the more reliable one, since it was confirmed by Mohammad Neshan Khan who had accompanied Ashraf, but had been able to escape and reach Basra.[28] Armenians who had recently arrived from Basra in Isfahan told van Leijpsigh that many Afghans, amongst whom Mohammad Neshan (Mhamed Nessjoen), were begging in the streets, while half of them with their women and children had gone to Baghdad to see whether they would be able to find better times there.[29]

In reaction to Nader's orders to jointly keep the citadel of Gamron with the Dutch Mir Mehr-e `Ali sent six men to de Cleen, because he himself was pursuing Ashraf at that time. The Dutch refused to hand over the citadel to these vagrants, as de Cleen called them, the

---

23. VOC 3168, de Cleen to Batavia (06/05/1730), f. 62; some of the deserters had taken service with Sheikh Jabbara. Ibid., f. 133. The agreement was broken on April 14, 1744 after the EIC denied that it had taken in Dutch deserters. The Dutch then ordered the EIC staff not to come near the VOC factory. In reply Widwell, the EIC chief, said that he henceforth would accept all deserters so that the Dutch would not have anybody anymore shortly. VOC 2680, Resolution Gamron (14/04/1744), unfoliated. The result was that both Companies accepted deserters from each other. The Dutch, for example, received nine English deserters between August 5-16, 1744, VOC2680, Resolution Gamron (20/08/1744), unfoliated.

24. VOC 3168, de Cleen to Nader (30/03/1730), f. 544-47. Ghafier-o-Tahadon, may be Khafr va Tahuneh, both villages in the Jahrom district.

25. VOC 3168, Mir Mehr `Ali from Tezerg-Ahmadi, f. 506-07; Ibid, from Nabban, f. 508-10 (received 10/03/1730).

26. VOC 2253, Schorer to de Cleen (01/07/1730), f. 860-2; VOC 2255, van Leijpsigh to de Cleen (28/01/1731), f. 2294-5.

27. Ibid., f. 2294-5.

28. VOC 2253, Basra Diary (17/09/1730), f. 482-3.

29. VOC 2255, van Leijpsigh to de Cleen (28/01/1731), f. 2296.

more so since they could not show the royal *raqam* (decree) and the strength and quality of the Persian delegation was considered not to be commensurate with the respect which was due to the VOC. Another reason to hold on to the citadel was the fact that the English were putting about rumors that they also held the citadel for the shah. On March 18, 1730 Mir Mehr-e `Ali himself came to Gamron believing that the citadel would be handed over to him. However, he made little effort to induce the Dutch to do so.[30]

Probably as a result of Nader's activities in Kuglihu province things also started moving in Khuzestan. For the VOC Basra office reported on February 3, 1730 that the prince of Hoveyzeh, later called the Pasha of Hoveyzeh, was expected there. On hearing the news of Shah Tahmasp's victory the people had declared themselves for him and wanted to kill the prince, who was a creature of the Turks. On June 1, 1730 the Turks counteracted, for at the orders of Ahmad Pasha, Sheikh Mohammad b. Mane` (sjeeg Mamet bin Manna) and his Arabs had to go to Hoveyzeh and join forces there with Sjeeg bin Nilaam [?] to retake that town. On June 9, some 9,000 men left for Hoveyzeh commanded by Sheikh Mohammad b. Mane`'s son and his brother's son. Sheikh Mohammad b. Mane`'s troops did not go to Hoveyzeh, but pirated vessels with grain and sheep at Qorna. In the beginning of 1731 the situation in Khuzestan had still not become normal. From Kuhgilu information was received that the Arabs were fighting amongst themselves and killed each other as dogs. For one side wanted to support the *vali* appointed by Nader, whilst the other side preferred another candidate.[31]

`ALI MARDAN KHAN'S EMBASSY TO INDIA

On April 22, 1730 `Ali Mardan Khan's equerry asked de Cleen for two ships to transport his master to India. De Cleen replied that this was impossible.[32] On learning that `Ali Mardan Khan would come to Gamron nobody dared to come to the town anymore for as long as he stayed there, which was very bad for trade the Dutch commented.[33] `Ali Mardan Khan himself arrived in Gamron on May 25, 1730. Despite the salutes, which the Dutch fired he treated them coolly [f.5]. The ambassador's suite was a rascally lot, for already after their first day in town they started to fight amongst themselves which led to bloodshed. Part of the servants therefore fled pursued by Mir Mehr-e `Ali [f.7]. On April 1730, he came to see de Cleen and

---

30. Mir Mehr-e `Ali wrote that he had been ordered by the shah's *vakil*, Tahmasp Qoli Khan, who had been renamed by the shah Dhu'l-Feqar Khan (Zulphecaar Chan) to occupy the citadel. He had sent two *yuzbashi*s, Mohammad Qasem Beg (Mhamed Casem Becq) and Mohammad Hoseyn Beg (Mhamed Hosenbec), and Qurchi Mohammad Mohsen (Cortsie Mhamed Mohossen), with some soldiers. VOC 3168, f. 507, 509; Ibid., de Cleen to Mir Mehr `Ali (13/03/1730), f. 551; Ibid., de Cleen to E`temad al-Dowleh (13/03/1730), f. 555-56 (only *yuzbasi* Mohammad Qasem Beg with five men had arrived); Ibid., de Cleen to E`temad al-Dowleh in Shiraz (01/04/1730), f. 558 (Mir Mehr-e `Ali arrived with some badly armed soldiers on Saturday, 28 Sha`ban 1142); Ibid., de Cleen to Batavia (06/05/1730), f. 126-28.

31. VOC 2254, Extract Basra Diary, f. 453, 456 (19/02/1730), 462, 465 (29/06/1730); VOC 2255, van Leijpsigh to de Cleen (28/01/1731), f. 2294.

32. VOC 2254, Gamronsch Dagregister, f. 1-2; VOC 2168, `Ali Mardan Khan b. Safi Qoli Khan Shamlu to de Cleen (received 29/03/1730), f. 513 he asked for two ships to transport him and 300 soldiers, 200 horses and baggage to India; Ibid., de Cleen's reply, f. 559-60, because the monsoon has passed it is impossible to sail to India; Ibid. `Ali Mardan Khan to de Cleen, f. 542, the shah has ordered me to live in harmony with you.

33. VOC 3168, de Cleen to Batavia (06/05/1730), f. 135.

asked for transport for `Ali Mardan Khan to Divil-Sind. He asserted the English were quite willing to do that service, but unfortunately they had no ship on the roadstead. Not only would Shah Tahmasp grant the Dutch many favors for this service, but the Dutch would help lighten the burden on the poor town of Gamron which had to pay 11 *tumans* per day for the ambassador's upkeep. The Dutch after deliberation replied that in view of the monsoon it was impossible for the ships to sail to India, but their sloop would be able to call at Divil-Sind. `Ali Mardan Khan accepted this offer, for he wanted to make use of four local vessels as well as of those which had been sent from Basidu [f.8-10].

On May 18, 1730 the ambassadorial suite and 13 horses had been taken in the *Maria Laurentia* followed by the ambassador himself under the firing of salutes. On May 20 the sloop sailed away [f. 38]. On June 10, the *Maria Laurentia* returned to Gamron. Due to storm and thunder it had been forced to call at Masqat, where `Ali Mardan Khan had been ill ashore for six days. The government of Masqat had shown him no respect whatsoever. Feeling mortally ill, `Ali Mardan Khan had come aboard again and had given orders to return to Gamron [f. 56].

NEW *SHAHBANDAR* OPPRESSES MERCHANTS

Since their arrival on April 27, 1730 the *shahbandar* Mirza Mohammad and the *ham-qalam* Mohammad `Ali Beg had already illegally collected 500 *tumans* from Moslem and Banyan merchants.[34] The leading citizens therefore had met and decided to write to court to lodge a complaint. But the local merchants were not the only ones having problems with the *shahbandar*. The latter casually remarked to the VOC dragoman that the Dutch acted as if they were friends, but nevertheless they had returned the ambassador against his will. In Gamron, people had learnt to fife to the Dutch dance, but now they would be punished as an example to others. For it was intolerable for true believers to be ruled by unbelievers [f. 58-60].De Cleen became very angry about this and demanded that the *shahbandar* show proof for his accusations, if not, he himself would be branded as the source of this piece of slander. He wanted to be friends, but would stand for no nonsense. The *shahbandar* lamely replied that so far he had not harvested yet one fruit of this friendship. If the Dutch wanted friendship they had to seek it, he from his side was prepared to give it. He ominously added that he knew more than the Dutch would believe [f. 61-63]. The dragoman was sent to `Ali Mardan Khan on June 20, 1731 to ask him to write a letter to Shah Tahmasp and Tahmasp Qoli Khan that the Dutch had served him well and that he himself had ordered them to return to Gamron. `Ali Mardan Khan refused this, for he asserted that he had been taken back against his will. Moreover, he had been exposed to all kinds of incivilities from the crew. He accused the Dutch that they never had had the intention to transport him to Divil-Sind and he would report the events to court [f. 64-66].

In a discussion with the *shahbandar* the latter showed himself even more anti-Dutch, for he said that they were the worst enemies in the world, who had neither respect for king nor law and who behaved in Gamron as if they were its masters. He was prepared to shed his last drop of blood for the shah and told the dragoman to go away [f. 68]. The next day (June

---

34. The Dutch observed an innovation, to wit, that whereas formerly the function was sold to the highest bidder now all net revenues were remitted to the royal treasury. The *shahbandar* only received a salary. VOC 3168, f. 135. This was a return to the practice that had existed until about 1668.

21, 1730) de Cleen asked the ambassador whether he wanted to speak with somebody of the VOC council, but `Ali Mardan Khan replied that he did not talk to the enemies of the shah. De Cleen thereupon wrote the ambassador a letter stating that his reply had been unreasonable and uncivil and would he be so kind as to state his reasons for such accusations. `Ali Mardan Khan did not bother to reply and left on June 30 to Tezerg-Ahmadi to enjoy the better climate there [f. 69, 70, 74].

The *shahbandar* meanwhile had been summoned by Nader to return and he wanted to take a present of 500 *tumans* with him. He therefore sent for all important merchants and ordered them to give him that amount within a few days. On July 13, 1730 the *shahbandar* threatened the Banyans with the bastinado, who then gave him 120 *tumans* and remained scot-free. At the same time, the *shahbandar*, with the help of the EIC dragoman and clerk (molla), was busy drawing up a statement accusing the Dutch of all sorts of crimes and offenses. Mir Mehr-e `Ali promised the Dutch to provide them with a copy [f. 77-82].

On July 24, 1730 messengers arrived with orders from Nader to transfer the citadel to Mir Mehr-e `Ali.[35] This order was in reply to de Cleen's letter of March 13, 1730 asking him to send a *raqam* authorizing a person of sufficient standing to return the citadel to [f. 84]. Although Nader was reported to have opened the Dutch letters with his own hands and had his reply drawn up in his presence, but not in the case of the EIC letters, his reply nevertheless was disappointing for the Dutch. For Nader's reply was simply to hand over the citadel to Mir Mehr-e `Ali and to deal henceforth with him.[36] On July 25, 1730 the Dutch officially handed the citadel over to Mir Mehr-e `Ali in the presence of the *vakil* of the deputy-governor of Gamron, and the qadi of Gamron and Minab, Mohammad Ja`far (Mhamet Jaffer). The latter also witnessed the official documents that were proof that the Dutch had returned all the artillery, ammunition and goods that had been in the citadel at the moment of its capture.[37]

The *shahbandar* continued to look for trouble. He had the VOC broker arrested and vilified the VOC servants. He demanded 1,000 *tumans* from the broker, if not, he would get the bastinado and his eyes would be taken out. Haverman at first sent the dragoman to *shahbandar*, who sent him away. The dragoman was then sent to Mir Mehr-e `Ali and Haverman held 29 grenadiers ready to set the broker free, but this was not necessary for the *soltan* sent the broker back. On August 17, 1730 Haverman sent the dragoman to the *shahbandar* to learn why he acted so obnoxiously, but the latter gave no clear answer. The next day, however, he ordered guards, whom he had especially hired for that purpose, to levy imposts on water and firewood that was brought into town. The *shahbandar* continued to collect the imposts and to recruit more rascals. On August 26, 1730 he left to `Essin with the intention to leave for Isfahan. The *kalantar* of `Essin, Mirza Mohsen, came to see de Cleen that day and handed him the statement which the *shahbandar* had drawn up against the Dutch, which was of the following nature [f. 99-103]:

---

35. VOC 2253, Tamas coelie Chan to de Cleen (Sha`ban 1154/received 23/05/1730); Tamas Coelie Chan to de Cleen (Dhu'l-Hijjah 1142/received 23/07/1730), f. 542-43.

36. VOC 2253, Schorer to de Cleen (01/07/1730), f. 856-59.

37. VOC 2254, Gamronsch Dagregister, f. 85; VOC 3168, de Cleen to Nader (13/03/1730), f. 555-56; for the receipt of the transfer see VOC 2253 (Moharram 1154 – 29/07/1730), f. 543.

"Report by Qanber 'Ali (Camber Alie) on what he heard at the house of Mir Mehr 'Ali. The two new *shahbandar*s had drawn up a statement aimed as an accusation against all Europeans; in particular the VOC and the VOC broker Issourdas. They demanded that the soltan and the most important *kadkhoda*s seal it and send it to court. These refused to do so. The two [*shahbandar*s] then threatened to behead the inhabitants so that they signed out of fear [f. 104, 106-11]. The most important points were:

◊ The keeping of horses has never been permitted to Europeans nor to have burning torches with them as they do now;

◊ They have never kept vessels on the roadstead as they do now;

◊ They have introduced many activities to their own liking, which were not customary;

◊ They consider themselves to be so important that they do not show respect for officials;

◊ They sometimes talked to Moslem women and sometimes kept them in their houses as if they were their wives;

◊ The Moslems enslaved by the Afghans and sold to Europeans had been forced to convert to the Christian religion;

◊ They had helped the Afghans in various ways;

◊ They had fortified factories in such a way that these were stronger than the royal citadel;

◊ Formerly it had been customary that, if they had to request something from the shah or the E'temad al-Dowleh, they used to consult the *janeshin* (deputy governor), and after his permission presented their request to the shah. Now they did not do this and acted to their own liking;

◊ It had always been customary that native servants in case of unlawful acts were handed over for punishment, now they did it themselves;

◊ It also had been customary that at night they stayed in their house, now they walked drunken in the streets and the bazaars and caused trouble for the inhabitants;

◊ If the shah and the E'temad al-Dowleh will do nothing the Hormuz situation, as it existed under the Portuguese, might be restored;

◊ The Dutch director had not welcomed the ambassador 'Ali Mardan Khan.

With regards to the Dutch:

◊ In their factory the Dutch had made a bulwark, which previously was not there;

◊ The Dutch had taken goods from the citadel and only returned the worst ones;

◊ They had demolished the old 'Portuguese' fort, which had always been a refuge for the population in dangerous times;

◊ Close to that site they had built a bulwark equipped with heavy cannon.

With regards to Issourdas, the VOC broker:

◊   It was customary that the shah ordered Dutch goods from him and only paid after delivery;

◊   The *shahbandar* had done that, [i.e.,] ordered goods and received none;

◊   Mirza Zahed ʿAli had given him [Issourdas] goods prior to his departure;

◊   Issourdas had taken the inheritance of Kimsjant unlawfully.

Two originals of this document were made, one for the shah and one for Nader. Thirty-two inhabitants had sealed it. The report was also sealed by the *kalantar* of ʿEssin, Mirza Mohsen (Mosum).[38]

Mir Mehr ʿAli offered his good services to mediate to which de Cleen replied that all would be forgotten if the *shahbandar* would give satisfaction for his uncivil behavior. The *shahbandar* replied on August 31, that he wanted to be friends, but would de Cleen mind and pay him the first visit else he would lose face. De Cleen answered that this was too vague a response, he first wanted to have the false statement, which, on September 2, the *kalantar* of ʿEssin brought to de Cleen. After preliminary talks with the dragoman the dispute was settled on September 4. Later de Cleen complained to his EIC colleague about the role of the EIC dragoman's role in the entire affair, which, of course, was denied [f. 109-112, 117, 122, 141-43].

Meanwhile, ʿAli Mardan Khan had written from Bouchon [?] to the English for a ship to transport him to Surat, to which they replied the next day (August 2) that they would be pleased to be of service to him. On September 22, 1730 ʿAli Mardan Khan returned to Gamron and left per the *Britannia Galley* seven days later [f. 101, 125-26].

CHANGE OF *SHAHBANDAR* AND GOVERNOR AT BANDAR ʿABBAS

The new *shahbandar*, Mohammad ʿAli Beg, who arrived at the end of September 1730, also carried a royal order for the Dutch in which Shah Tahmasp ordered him to pay the Dutch 5,000 *tumans* out of the revenues of Gamron, confirming herewith a previous *raqam* issued by his father. The *shahbandar* said that he could not pay, however. In the first place, because he needed an order from his immediate superior, Mohammad ʿAli Khan, governor of Shiraz to the same effect; and in the second place, even then he could not pay, because his predecessor had not only cleaned out the cash-box, but had taken 150 *tumans* more than he had been allowed to [f. 129-30].

On January 3, 1731 a new *shahbandar*, Mirza Esmaʿil, arrived in Gamron who refused to pay one cent to the Dutch let alone 5,000 *tumans* [f. 183]. On July 23, 1731 he received a new order from the shah ordering him to repair the town walls as much as possible and to complete its construction, to pay the debt to the Europeans, and only deal with mercantile affairs [f. 955]. On April 20, 1731 Mir Mehr ʿAli was appointed as governor of Gamron and his son arrived in town, to take charge on his father's behalf, on April 25. However, on May 1 the appointment of the governor of Lar, Hajj ʿAli Qoli Khan, as governor of Gamron was made public. As a result Mir Mehr ʿAli left the town on May 4, 1731.[39]

---

38. VOC 2253, f. 551-59.

39. VOC 2254, f. 232, 238, 915, 917. On October 27, 1730 the *shahbandar*, Mohammad ʿAli Beg, was dismissed after, *inter alia*, complaints from the Dutch. The shah himself had selected his successor,

Towards the end of October 1731, a beginning had been made to circumvallate the whole town, although the VOC factory, with some houses, remained outside the wall. De Cleen inspected the wall on November 1, 1731 and concluded that it was a worthless construction. The builders did not know their job, while only clay and stones had been used. Moreover, the manner in which the construction of the wall had been organized called for such slovenly work. Each citizen had been assigned a certain part of the wall in relation to the level of his income. They either had to erect their part of the wall or to pay somebody else to do it for them, in which case the deputy governor received 50 *mahmudi*s [f. 982, 986].

On November 17, 1731 it became known that the shah had dismissed Mirza Esma`il as *shahbandar*.[40] The governor of Shiraz had been charged with that function, who in turn had appointed the deputy-governor of Gamron, Mirza Mohammad, in conjunction with the *daftar-nevis*, Mirza Zeyn al-`Abedin,[41] as his agents. The latter also had to demand an accounting from the previous *shahbandar*s. The new *shahbandar* told de Cleen that he was unable to pay the royal debt of 5,000 *tuman*s to the Dutch; in fact, he had been given explicit orders by Mohammad `Ali Khan not to do so. De Cleen therefore wrote to the latter, drawing his attention to the royal decree and asked the governor to instruct his agent to pay [f. 1002-03]. Hajji `Ali Qoli Khan left Gamron on November 29, 1731 to recuperate at Tezerg-Ahmadi, for he was ill [f. 1008]. On January 9, 1732 Mir Heydar came from Tezerg with a letter from Hajji `Ali Qoli from Jevem that Mir Heydar had been appointed acting deputy-governor, in which function he was formally confirmed on March 3, 1732 [f.1027, 1046]. On January 20, 1732 the powder-house of the fortress of Hormuz exploded [f. 1029]. On February 5, 1732 de Cleen received an order from Mohammad `Ali Khan in which he instructed the acting-*shahbandar* to pay the 5,000 *tuman*s to the Dutch. His agent however said that he still had no orders from the *beglerbegi* [f. 1036]. On March 3, 1732 Mir Heydar, the deputy-governor arrived in town with 350-400 horsemen and cattle stolen from the surrounding villages [f. 1054]. On April 9, 1732 Mirza Esma`il Zamindavari informed the Dutch that the *beglerbegi* had reappointed him as *shahbandar*. He arrived in Gamron on May 5, 1732. He received a salary of only 150 *tuman*s per year, which was less than his predecessor.[42]

---

namely the *mostowfi-ye khasseh*, Mirza Esma`il, who, according to the Dutch, "was an upright and pleasant person, who was civil and not greedy, which is a miracle in the case of Persians." However, he immediately asked van Leijpsigh for a loan, which he refused. Mirza Esma`il, accompanied by Hajj Qoli Khan, the new governor of Lar, left Isfahan on November 19, 1730. Van Leijpsigh to Koenad (28/01/1731), f. 2348-51, 2275.

40. The shah had replied to the list of complaints drawn up by the Zamindavari *shahbandar* that an order should be issued that he should not bother the Dutch, nor give them cause for displeasure and to repay the 5,000 *tuman*s. VOC 2255 (03/111731), f. 1846.

41. On November 25, 1730 Hajji Zeyn al-`Abedin (Hadje Zijnalebed-dien) had visited the Dutch factory in Isfahan and had told van Leijpsigh that the shah had chosen him as second *shahbandar* of Gamron as well as registrar of all royal revenues and chief merchant with the task of purchasing, for the shah's account, all the best merchandise that arrived at Gamron. VOC 2255, Van Leijpsigh to Koenad (28/01/1731), f. 2278-79.

42. VOC 2254, f. 1052, 1067. The events from April 22, 1730 till May 15, 1732 are all based on VOC 2254, Gamronsch Dagregister, unless otherwise indicated. For easy reference the relevant folio numbers have been inserted in the text between brackets. Mohammad Khan Baluch wrote a letter to the Dutch informing them that Mirza Esma`il was a relative of his. VOC 2254, f. 1254-54 (dated 27/04/1732 but received on 18/05/1732); VOC 2322, de Cleen (30/09/1733 + appendix 30/11/1733), f. 130 vs.

On November 13, 1732 the VOC council at Gamron decided to put *de Winthont* at the disposal of Mohammad 'Ali Khan, the ambassador to India, at the request of Nader to oblige him to the VOC. Mohammad 'Ali Khan arrived in Gamron on December 18, 1732. The directors of both Companies did not welcome him, because information from Isfahan had it that Nader wanted to arrest both of them. The behavior of the ambassador's servants, who were trying to collect information on the daily habits and residence of de Cleen, confirmed Dutch suspicions, although they had no proof whatsoever that such a plan really existed.[43]

On August 7, 1732 Mir Mehr 'Ali visited de Cleen and told him that he had been appointed governor of Lar and Gamron and that he was going to Nader as he had been ordered. Mir Mehr 'Ali, however, did not make his appointment public as was customary.[44]

'ALI MARDAN KHAN AND WAKHTANG MIRZA IN BANDAR 'ABBAS

On December 8, 1732 'Ali Mardan Khan returned from India with a Moslem vessel, while that same day Wakhtang Mirza also arrived, who had been appointed tax collector by Nader and to discuss with both the VOC and EIC various outstanding problems. The Dutch made use of this opportunity to discuss their problems not only with Wakhtang Mirza, but also with the arriving and departing ambassadors and the three *shahbandar*s (the two outgoing and the newly appointed one), Mirza Mohammad and Mohammad 'Ali Beg, who had arrived with Wakhtang Mirza. On January 10, 1733 the VOC council decided to give these gentlemen some presents to help them make up their minds. Mohammad 'Ali Khan, in particular, needed money, for he was very busy extorting it from the local population. He had arrested all leading merchants in Gamron and demanded 900 *tuman*s from them to obtain their release. The Banyans were told separately to pay 600 *tuman*s. His suite was a rough and undisciplined lot, who committed all kinds of untoward activities such as the rape of women and girls, the stealing of cattle and extortion of food.[45] The gentlemen especially appreciated the horses given to them, which they needed badly. As a result of these activities all recipients sent a favorable report to Nader, stressing that the Dutch version about the problems was the right one, and that the welfare of Gamron totally depended on the Dutch.[46] The letter by Wakhtang Mirza in particular was flattering for the Dutch. He wrote that Gamron lacked fortresses, walls and ammunition; in short everything required to defend a town. Only on the seaside there was a small fortress, which deserved the name of 'defensive installation'. All inhabitants were without exception totally destitute and poor. Their income was mainly derived from serving the European Companies as porters, water carriers, peddlers and sailors on their vessels. All food had to be brought from afar, even the water, and it was all sold at high prices. Even the leading citizens were poor and lacked servants and other domestics. The only surety these people had was the presence of the European factories, for in case of danger they sought

---

43. VOC 2269, Extract Gamronsch Daghregister (17/11/1732), f. 6604; VOC 2322, de Cleen to Batavia (30/09/1733 and appendix 30/11/1733), f. 35-36. The purpose of Mohammad 'Ali Khan's embassy was to ask for an indemnification of 500,000 *tuman*s for the services rendered by the Safavid state to emperor Homayun in 1540.

44. VOC 2269, Gamronsch Dagregister, f. 6604.

45. VOC 2269, Gamronsch Dagregister (04/01/1733 and 10/011733) f. 6604 vs; .VOC 2232, de Cleen to Batavia (30/09/1733), f. 36vs-38r.

46. VOC 2322, de Cleen to Batavia (30/09/1733), f. 38-40; Ibid., Mohammad 'Ali to Nader (Thamas Coelie Chan) (23/01/1733), f. 507-08 vs.

refuge under their walls. Especially the Dutch had exerted themselves to assist Persia, both where its citizens were concerned as well as by putting a vessel at the disposal of Mohammad `Ali Khan to sail to Sind, despite the fact that the Dutch had already suffered great losses because of the country's condition and the fact that trade had diminished to one-tenth of its former volume.[47]

On January 20, 1733 `Ali Mardan Khan left Gamron, while Mohammad `Ali Khan sailed on January 24 to Lahori Bandar where he arrived on 28 Sha`ban 1143 (March 8, 1731).[48] The crew of *de Winthont* after having delivered Mohammad `Ali Khan to Sind mutinied and even had intended to sell the ship to the governor for Dfl. 20,000.[49] However, the crew decided to start a career as pirates and even tried to take a Dutch ship on March 4, 1733. The affair ended badly for the mutineers; they were unsuccessful in their piratical exploits and in mid-June went ashore in Makran. There a part of the crew decided to return with their ship to Gamron where they arrived on June 19, 1733. The other part of the mutineers were arrested by another Dutch ship and punished by the council in Gamron.[50] Nader thanked the Dutch for the assistance given to Mohammad `Ali Khan. He informed them that he had troops and vessels gathered at Basra to punish all those who had been so foolhardy to oppose the interests of the kingdom. For the same reason he wanted to conquer Masqat. Nader therefore asked the Dutch to make available as many ships as possible to ferry troops across, so that the troops that were already en route would not experience any trouble on arrival. Because he also had heard that merchants who arrived with Dutch ships did not pay customs duties on the goods that they brought with him Nader asked the VOC director to see to it that this did not happen, as required by treaty.[51]

Mir Mehr `Ali who had been appointed governor of Lar and Gamron on October 12, 1732 with a salary of only 150 *tuman*s, left for Tehran as ordered on February 5, 1733. As his deputy he appointed Mirza Baqer, a shopkeeper of bad repute. Wakhtang Mirza was still in Gamron and acted as if he were the governor and demanded an accounting of each of the officials in the area such as of Hormuz, Larek and Qeshm, while on July 15, 1733 he went to Minab, where he still was at the end of September. Although Mirza Baqer, the *na'eb* and Mirza Esma`il, the *shahbandar* were very weak officials having hardly any force at their disposal they nevertheless were strong enough to extort money and goods from merchants and the population. Mirza Baqer sequestered a lot of money, rice and butter, which he liked very much. The *shahbandar* used all kinds of tricks to get what he wanted. Although the whole area was in uproar due to the marauding of the Baluch and the uprising of Sheikh Ahmad Madani the town officials in no way assisted the poor population. This situation continued throughout the

---

47. VOC 2322, Wagtan Miersa to Thamas Coelie Chan (04/02/1733), f. 509-14.

48. VOC 2322, Mohammad `Ali Khan to de Cleen (received 19/06/1733), f. 460-vs; Ibid., de Cleen to Batavia (30/09/1733 + appendix 30/11/1733), f. 38vs.

49. VOC 2269, f. 6537 vs.

50. VOC 2322, de Cleen to Batavia (30/09/1733), f. 13-21. For a discussion of the mutiny see D.L.M. Weijers, "Dappere waterleeuwen versus schelmen: een muiterij in Perzische wateren, 1733," in J.R. Bruijn and E.S. van Eyck van Heslinga eds. *Muiterij. Oproer en berechting op schepen van de VOC* (Haarlem, 1980), pp. 44-57.

51. VOC 2322, Thamas Coelie Chan to de Cleen (received 03/05/1733), f. 457vs-58vs.

year 1733[52] as well as part of 1734. Its aftermath also dominated much of the remainder of the year 1734.[53]

REQUEST TO SUPPLY SHIPS FOR IRANIAN NAVY

On July 18, 1734 Mohammad Latif Khan unexpectedly returned to Gamron and sent the Dutch a thank-you letter on July 21. On July 25 he left for Bushehr with two vessels, which he had taken from Sheikh Rashid. He invited the Dutch to come and trade in Bushehr, for he intended to build a new town and citadel there. However, the Dutch gave a non-committal reply and they hoped that he would not raise the issue again, for it would mean the end of all trade there, they believed, if he stayed in that village.[54] Nader did not approve of Mirza Taqi Khan's plan to farm the customs revenues of Gamron to Sheikh Jabbara and Sheikh Rashid for an amount of 20,500 *tumans* over a period of 2 ½ years. As a result, Mirza Esma`il was reappointed and Sheikh Rashid left for Basidu in early November 1734. The *sardar* of the lower lands, Tahmasp Khan (Tamas Chan) imposed a contribution of 4,000 *tumans* (Dfl. 170,000) on its inhabitants. The local VOC servants, such as the Banyan brokers, also had to pay, viz. 300 *tumans* (Dfl. 12,750), which they paid with an IOU at two months' sight. As these servants were not supposed to pay such contribution, as per royal decree, the Dutch protested and send the *sardar* a letter.[55]

On December 16, 1734 Mohammad Latif Khan arrived in Gamron. He did not come totally unexpected, since Dames Hey, the VOC director, had received information from Isfahan that somebody would come to discuss matters of importance with him. Van Leijpsigh had been ordered by Hasan `Ali Khan, the master of the assay (*mo`ayyer-bashi*) and governor of Isfahan, to come to his house on the evening of October 27, 1734 to get a decree from Nader. The English had received the same order. When the Europeans arrived at the governor's house they also found Tahmasp Qoli Khan Jalayer to be there. They were very politely received. Hasan `Ali Khan handed van Leijpsigh and Geekie the decree and said that it was an order to send a qualified person to Gamron in the company of Tahmasp Qoli Khan who would leave in five days for Shiraz. This qualified person had to inform the directors of both Companies in Gamron that they had to prepare a few ships with war supplies and keep these ready for Tahmasp Qoli Khan. Van Leijpsigh and Geekey had to write to their directors that these should

---

52. VOC 2322 (30/09/1733), f. 130 vs- 134 vs. In particular in the months of February, March and October 1733 the Baluch attacked Gamron, but were repulsed by the Dutch and English. They destroyed the EIC garden at `Essin in October. The government officials did not do anything to help the inhabitants of the town. The *shahbandar* asked for the protection of the Europeans. Ibid., f. 132 vs-133 vs, 145, 151.

53. As indicated above the years 1733 and 1734 were dominated by the rebellion of Sheikh Ahmad Madani. There is extensive material on this rebellion in the VOC archives, which has been previously published, see Willem Floor, "The Revolt of Shaikh Ahmad Madani in Laristan", *Studia Iranica* 8 (1983), pp. 63-93 and which article has been reprinted here as chapter four.

54. VOC 2323, Hey to Batavia (22/09/1734), f. 206. Mohammad Qasem Beg, *farrash-bashi* came from Shiraz to Gamron on March 20, 1734 as did Mohammad Hoseyn Beg, the chief of the governor's life-guard. VOC 2356, Resolution Gamron (30/09/1734), f. 58-59. In November 1734, Baqer Khan, the inspector-general of fortresses paid a visit to the Dutch at Gamron. The council then decided to henceforth pay visits again to Persian officials and thus annul the decision of 18/12/1732 not to do so, when there was fear that VOC officials might be taken prisoner. VOC 2356, Resolution Gamron (04/11/1734), f. 82.

55. VOC 2356, Hey to Batavia (09/11/1734), f. 35-38. On the affair with Sheikh Rashid see Floor, "The Revolt".

not refuse this royal order. Tahmas Qoli Khan observed that former Persian kings had been powerful and had had ships made in Surat. However, since the arrival of the Europeans they had these entrusted with the task of maintaining security in the Persian Gulf, because they were loyal and trusted friends. He stressed that as a result of their services they would get even better privileges than they had at that time. He added that if it would be impossible for the Companies to render the service they had to write how much wood had to be brought from Mazanderan to build enough ships to expel all enemies from the Persian Gulf. Van Leijpsigh replied that the Dutch had always been prepared to assist the shah, but he expected that at that moment there would not be any ships on the roadstead. It was very exceptional for ships to remain on the roadstead for a long time, which only happened in case of an Arab rebellion. He promised, however, to inform his director and said that he would send his dragoman to Gamron with Tahmasp Qoli Khan. Geekie replied in the same vein and wanted to go himself. Hasan ʿAli Khan refused this and said he had to stay, although Tahmasp Qoli Khan remarked that it was totally unimportant. Van Leijpsigh reported that according to rumors the requested ships were to be used against Masqat, but more likely against Basra. Tahmasp Qoli Khan had also intimated that he was willing to buy ships to which van Leijpsigh had replied that if he intended to use these against Hindustan, Turkey or Masqat he would never get them from the Dutch. The dragoman left Isfahan on November 1, 1734.

Mohammad Latif Khan had received oral instructions from Tahmasp Qoli Khan in Shiraz and left for Gamron in the company of the Dutch dragoman. During his discussions with Koenad (who after Hey's death on December 20, 1734 had been appointed by the council as his *pro tem* successor) Mohammad Latif Khan promised better privileges if ships were put at the Shah's disposal to transport 3,000 men. Koenad replied that the Dutch were willing to be of assistance whenever this was possible, for they would not lend ships for actions against states with which they had friendly relations. Mohammad Latif Khan said that the proposed action was only aimed at rebellious Arabs. He also promised to take measures that the bad treatment of VOC servants in Gamron would not occur again and would report the interfering officials to the shah. Koenad was very prudent with Mohammad Latif Khan, whom he not only considered to be one of the most influential men in Persia at that time, but whose ingenuity he also respected. Mohammad Latif Khan had lived in Istanbul, where he "had become too acquainted with the European way of life." The English had told Koenad that when Mohammad Latif Khan had visited one of their ships that he had shown more curiosity and intelligence than they had credited him with when discussing shipbuilding and navigation.[56]

With the agreement of the council Koenad informed Tahmasp Qoli Khan about his discussion with Mohammad Latif Khan. He promised that the Dutch would be willing to lend ships for the area where Nader had jurisdiction, i.e., the seaports and the islands. However, if he wanted to take action against Basra, India or Masqat Koenad impossibly could commit Dutch ships without the explicit authority from his masters. The Dutch would also be willing to destroy pirates in the Persian Gulf. At the same time Koenad asked for a decree ordering all officials in the Garmsirat to respect Dutch privileges and to exempt all VOC servants from all kinds of imposts and duties so that these could peacefully be engaged in trading activities.

---

56. VOC 2357, Koenad to Batavia (24/08/1735), f. 232. The *shahbandar* Mirza Esmaʿil died on January 6, 1735. Ibid., f. 577.

Mohammad Latif Khan was pleased with the discussion and letter and left for Bushehr on January 7, 1735.[57]

Mohammad Latif Khan had intimated that the Dutch would be welcome to trade in Bushehr as well. Whether this had to do with his orders to attack Basra has not been reported. At any rate the matter was not pursued any further neither by Mohammad Latif Khan nor by Mohammad Taqi Khan, who on February 19, 1735 asked the Dutch to put ships at his disposal to fetch the property of Mohammad ʿAli Khan, Nader's ambassador to India, who had died in Thatta. He sent his brother Mirza Esmaʿil to Gamron who raised the old issue of the treaty goods and the tax exemption of VOC servants. This was just an excuse to put the Dutch under pressure, for he said that he would take care that all Dutch privileges would be respected if only the Dutch would lend him a ship. Because of the disadvantageous consequences and because of the value of the estimated goods in Thatta, viz. 60,000 *tumans* (Dfl. 2.5 million), the Dutch promised a ship on the following conditions. The ship would be ready to sail within seven days; Mohammad Taqi Khan had to see to it, and give guarantees to that effect, that the goods would be shipped immediately. If not he would have to agree to pay the costs of 700 *tumans* (Dfl. 29,750). He also would have to indemnify the Dutch if anything happened to the ship. Finally, he had to promise to induce Nader to allow the Dutch to collect their claim on the Gamron customs revenues. Mirza Esmaʿil, however, said that this would be very difficult, since he himself had come to Gamron to collect money for Nader, but he showed himself very cooperative by issuing orders to all local authorities not to demand any taxes or imposts from VOC servants.

On May 16, 1735 the Dutch received a letter from Mohammad Taqi Khan in which he informed them that Nader had sent two of his servants to fetch Mohammad ʿAli Khan's property in Thatta. These were Safi Khan Beg and Mohammad Saʿid Beg Tharwerdi (?), the brother of the governor of Lar, Mostafa Khan. The Dutch replied to this request that it was too late in the season to make such a trip and supplied him with a statement to that effect. Although the Persian officials were not very satisfied with this answer they accepted the logic of the argument and recalled the two envoys stating that they would return at the end of the year.[58]

Meanwhile the Dutch had refused to supply a ship for the third time already that year, for Mohammad Latif Khan had asked on April 11, 1735 to escort a Persian vessel to Surat. This voyage was made at the express order of Nader. The cargo of the vessel, asafetida, had to be sold in Surat, the proceeds of which had to be converted into ships, masts, planks and other woodworks for the fleet. The Dutch were also asked to have their Surat office arrange for the sale and purchase of the various goods and to keep the accounts thereof. To show how much honor was bestowed upon the Dutch he told them that he had orders not to do anything with-

---

57. VOC 2357, Koenad to Batavia (24/08/1735), f. 231-39; VOC 2357, Resolution Gamron (20/12/1734), f. 449; VOC 2357, Resolution Gamron (27/12/1734), f. 445-57 (text request Mohammad Latif Khan to Thamas Coelie Chan and apostil to this letter dated 20 Jomadi I, 1147-15/10/1734); VOC 2357, text order Thamas Chan to Serdaar Thamas Coelie Chan, f. 459-62; VOC 2357, Koenad to serdaar Thamas Coelie Chan (27/12/1734), f. 462-64.

58. VOC 2357, Koenad to Batavia (24/08/1735), f. 247-60.

out consulting the Dutch in Surat. Despite this nice gesture the Dutch informed Mohammad Latif Khan on June 8, 1735 that they were unable to comply with his request.[59]

FAILED ATTACK ON BASRA

At that time Mohammad Latif Khan had other problems, for his attack against Basra had been repulsed through English naval intervention. Mohammad Latif Khan's force consisted of two gurabs, one brigantine and about 40 various smaller vessels filled to the brim with soldiers. Toward the end of May 1735 the expeditionary force had approached Basra at a distance of six German miles, viz. at the island of Haffar.[60] According to the Dutch, the Persian attack would have succeeded if the English had not supported the Turkish force. These, 14 galleys under the command of the *qaputan-pasha*, were totally demoralized as the result of a disastrous defeat against rebellious Arabs earlier that year. The pasha of Basra, therefore, forced the English, with two ships, which they had at Basra at that time, to attack the Persian force. Under the threat of violence and the sequestration of their property the English gave in and took Turkish troops and military equipment aboard their ships and defeated Mohammad Latif Khan. The latter withdraw, because on June 3, 1735 the Turks and the Arabs had concluded a peace agreement, which would make it very difficult for the Persian forces to sail up the Shatt al-Arab a second time. On July 27, 1735 both the VOC and the EIC received a confidential letter from Mohammad Taqi Khan in which he reported that Mohammad Latif Khan had written him that Dutch and English ships had collaborated with the Turks and had attacked him. Mohammad Taqi Khan could not believe this; he threatened, however, that if it were really true that the Europeans had rewarded friendship with enmity, they could be assured that proper measures would be taken against them. The Dutch replied that they had not been involved in this affair and that he should address himself to the English. Mohammad Taqi Khan at the same time ordered the European Companies to see to it that no more goods would be shipped to Basra by their ships. He added that it was useless anyway, since the Persians counted on conquering that town in two months time. Finally he advised the Europeans to have their servants contribute to the present that had to be offered to Nader at the occasion of his victory over the Turks. For the Europeans, he stated, were keeping a lot of servants in their houses, who were not real servants but merchants; if Nader would learn about this it would have disadvantageous consequences for them, so he urged the Companies to mend their ways in their own interest.[61]

The English meanwhile were feeling very insecure about possible Persian punitive actions because of their involvement in the defense of Basra. On September 8, 1735 the English suddenly left in a hurry, putting their goods in two English vessels and a hired French one and

---

59. VOC 2357, Mohammad Latif Khan (Bushehr) to Koenad (received 11/04/1735), f. 879-80; VOC 2356, Resolution Gamron (08/06/1735), f. 682 (letter Koenad to Mohammad Latif Khan).

60. According to Lorimer, J. G. *Gazetteer of the Persian Gulf, Oman and Central Arabia* (Calcutta, 1915 [London, 1971]) pp. 598-99 is "a tract on the right bank of the Karun river, beginning about 7 miles above Muhammareh Town and ending about 1 mile above the point of divergence of the Karun and Bahmanshir."

61. VOC 2357, Resolution Gamron (08/06/1735), f. 683; VOC 2357, Mirza Taqi Khan to both Companies (for your eyes only; was first handed to Koenad; received 27/07/1735), f. 916-17; VOC 2357, Gutchi (Basra) to Koenad (13/06/1735), f. 1237-44.

left during the night of September 14. Only Geekie and their dragoman remained behind together with Doctor Smith, their gunner and the old Italian count Cherubini.[62]

Mohammad Latif Khan told van Leijpsigh that he would have been victorious despite the English, if only Mohammad Khan Turkman, governor of Shushtar, had assisted him with troops, supplies and ammunition as he had promised. Mohammad Latif Khan, who was mad at the governor, left Isfahan on August 11, 1735 to go to court and expected to return with full powers to Gamron to take revenge on the English. However, on August 24 he returned with Mohammad Taqi Khan whom he had met in Qom and to whom he had to give an accounting of himself for a second time at Shiraz. The Carmelite padre Placidio told that Mohammad Latif Khan, after his debacle at Basra, on his return voyage met with a vessel with wine belonging to the English. He took the vessel to Bushehr and arrested its captain.[63]

NEW DEMANDS FOR SHIPS AND TAXES

On September 8, 1735 the Dutch also had received a letter from Nader in which he had expressed his appreciation for their willingness to transport his envoys to Sind as well as to transport troops to the other side of the Persian Gulf. To this letter Koenad replied that he indeed was willing to transport the envoys to Sind. When these arrived in Gamron, however, the Dutch had no ship ready but the English had. The Dutch therefore offered to hire big vessels from Basidu and Kong, which was accepted. Geekie meanwhile was welcoming the envoys richly and induced them to accept the English ship, which they did. To show that they had taken a real interest in the voyage, the Dutch offered a present to both envoys.[64]

Despite the rumors that Mohammad Taqi Khan would come with 4,000 troops to Gamron, for which everybody was afraid, he did not come. Finally on October 10 his *vakil* or representative, the *daryabegi*, Mohammad Zaman Beg, arrived in Gamron. His master was still in Bushehr at that time. On October 19 the *daryabegi* presented a letter from Nader and two letters from Mohammad Taqi Khan for both Companies with the request to help with the purchase of ships or (which according to the Dutch was the real objective) to lend ships to the government of Persia. The last letter was to raise the issue of the payment of customs duties up to 1,000 *tuman*s, to which the Dutch replied that the whole issue was contradictory to their privileges and that without authorization from Batavia they could not do anything about it. The Dutch were also a bit surprised that this matter was brought up, and they assumed that at court no distinction was being made between the European Companies. They bluntly asked the *daryabegi* why their offer for rendering services to the Crown, such as the hiring of three vessels for the envoys to Sind, were not appreciated. The latter assured them that Nader

---

62. VOC 2416, Resolution Gamron (21/09/1735), f. 490-99; VOC 2416, Resolution Gamron aboard de Valckenisse (21/09/1735), f. 654.

63. VOC 2416, van Leijpsigh to Koenad (30/08/1735), f. 2188-89, 2219. The Carmelite monk was Placid of St. Nicolas, see Anonymous, *A Chronicle*, vol. 2, pp. 993-94.

64. VOC 2416, Resolution Gamron (21/09/1735), f. 486-87 (Dutch text of letter from Thamas Chan, wakiel douleth to Koenad, dated Rabi` I 1148/July 1735; received 05/09/1735), f. 489-92 (text reply Koenad); VOC 2416, Resolution Gamron (30/09/1735), f. 515-19.

had greatly appreciated the offer indeed, and presented therewith gifts from Mohammad Taqi Khan as proof of the latter's continued affection for the Dutch.[65]

Towards the end of November 1735 it became known that Nader had ordered to collect an extraordinary contribution from the Garmsirat of 3,000 *tumans* or Dfl. 212,500 to buy pearls and two ships. The *shahbandar* had been ordered to collect the money. The latter was the only ranking Persian official who was still in Gamron, for all the others had left to participate in the big national council that Nader had convened for early 1736. The money was being extorted by force, as a result of which a few people died. The VOC brokers were demanded to pay 250 *tumans* as their share of the total contribution by the Banyans. The Dutch protested about this to the *daryabegi*, *shahbandar* end the *na'eb*, who replied that they were not better than others and were obliged to lend the money to Nader for which they could get an IOU with the promise of repayment. Koenad pointed out that it was contrary to the VOC privileges, but the official pointed out that an order had been given to collect 3,000 *tumans* without any buts. Moreover, why worry the *daryabegi* said, for the money would be paid back. The VOC brokers paid 52 *tumans* to be rid of the business, but the *shahbandar* continued to bother them.

On November 22, 1735 the VOC dragoman was sent for by the *shahbandar* who told him that he had orders from Mohammad Taqi Khan to buy two ships. If his funds were not sufficient he had been ordered to borrow the money from the merchants with the help of the European Companies. The *daryabegi* meanwhile had been unable to collect the full quota, and was forced to demand 500 *tumans* each as a loan from the Companies in lieu of which he would give them an assignation on the customs revenues. The *shahbandar* requested the Dutch to cooperate, or else he would be forced to use violence, though against his wishes. For if he did not do it, he would lose his head and Koenad risked the displeasure of Mohammad Taqi Khan. The Dutch said they were unable to accommodate the *shahbandar*; moreover, the proposition was contrary to their privileges and their own orders. The *shahbandar* replied that he knew that, but he could not help it either and could only implement his orders. The local merchants and the English had already paid their part, he said and the next day at the latest he had to send news about his actions to court.[66]

Although it was against their orders the Dutch, to avoid further problems, offered to lend 300 *tumans*. The *shahbandar* said, because they were friends, he would try and see whether he could settle the matter now, provided the Dutch paid 50 *tumans* in cash and the rest with a draft on Sheikh Rashid. The Dutch accommodated the *shahbandar* because had treated them more civil than anybody else. A slightly positive event was the return of the envoys to Thatta, who in a letter to Nader expressed their satisfaction about the cooperation of the Dutch, without which they would have had big problems. This letter was very much appreciated by the Dutch because there was a danger of Arab attacks, which they feared would be blamed on the Europeans in general instead of on the English. It was also for this reason that they accepted to transport the money that the *shahbandar* sent to Sheikh Rashid in Basidu for the sale of two ships.[67]

---

65. VOC 2416, Resolution Gamron (23/10/1735), f. 526-34.

66. VOC 2416, Resolution Gamron (23/11/1735), f. 665-72. The EIC had offered Mohammad Taqi two capital ships with crew and equipment for 8,000 *tumans* of Dfl. 340,000 if he agreed to their request. VOC 2368, Koenad to Batavia (19/03/1736), f. 23.

67. VOC 2416, Resolution Gamron (23/11/1735), f. 673-80; VOC 2416, Resolution Gamron

From January 18 to March 30 Mohammad Taqi Khan's brother and son stayed in Gamron which led to a decline in trade. The English spent a lot of money on the two representatives and the Dutch therefore felt obliged to give them something as well. The Dutch did not report what these two were doing in Gamron, but their activities may have had something to do with the preparations for the conquest of Bahrain to which end a fleet with about 8,000 to 12,000 men had been concentrated in Bushehr. The recently acquired ship, the *Tavakkol* also had to go to Bushehr, but due to a recent storm it lacked certain equipment. The *shahbandar* asked the Dutch for an anchor cable, tar and other supplies which they refused. The *shahbandar* persisted however, and even threatened to inform Nader about their unwillingness to assist him, so the Dutch gave in.[68]

REQUEST FOR VOC NAVAL ASSISTANCE AGAINST THE HULAS

Meanwhile, Nader had proclaimed himself shah; he informed the Dutch about it in a decree, which they received on April 8, 1736. In this decree he also announced that Mohammad Taqi Khan had been appointed *beglerbegi* of Fars and the other parts of S. Persia. The latter moreover had been ordered to retake Bahrain to which end he would come soon to Gamron. Nader ordered the Dutch to assist him in which case they would be showered with privileges and favors. In case of refusal, however, they would be considered traitors and be punished. Mohammad Taqi Khan further had orders to deal directly with the Dutch about their privileges, and whatever he would propose Nader would agree to. The Dutch were not very happy about these developments, since this meant that ships would be demanded for the transportation of troops as well as interference with trade, which would suffer. They also were angry with the English who caused considerable damage to trade by their disproportionate presents, the offer of the sale of ships and by their attitude in general. Cockill had already promised a ship for the Bahrain operation, and another one had just arrived which also would be used for the Bahrain expedition. This would make it very difficult for the Dutch to refuse the loan of one of their ships. On May 1, 1736 Mohammad Taqi Khan wrote Koenad from Bushehr stating that the expeditionary force had arrived in good shape in Shiraz and that it would leave for Bushehr. Mohammad Latif Khan had orders to embark all troops on May 26 and to sail to Bahrain. Because Mir Mehr-e 'Ali also had been ordered to come with troops from Gamron Mohammad Taqi Khan renewed his request for the loan of a ship. Koenad gave an indirectly reply to that letter hoping to delay matters. The council in majority decided to send the Dutch ships to Batavia to get orders about the lending of ships to the Persian government as well as orders about what should be done to acknowledge Nader as the new shah.[69]

Mohammad Taqi Khan had not liked Koenad's reply, although he considered the points he had made about the dispatch of the royal decrees reasonable. He replied that he would discuss the matter with Koenad when he would be in Gamron. Mohammad Taqi Khan was less satisfied with the non-compliance of his request for the loan of a ship. As far as he was

---

(30/11/1735), f. 689; VOC 2416, Resolution Gamron (22/12/1735), f. 715-39.

68. VOC 2416, Resolution Gamron (28/02/1736), f. 840-43; VOC 2416, Resolution Gamron (14/03/1736), f. 865-70; VOC 2416, Resolution Gamron (05/04/1736), f. 937-39; VOC 2416, Resolution Gamron (13/04/1736), f. 982-84.

69. VOC 2416, Resolution Gamron (06/05/1736), f. 988-996; VOC 2416, Resolution Gamron (01/06/1736), f. 1033-70 (also contains the Dutch text of various letters such as Koenad to Nader Shah; Koenad to Mohammad Taqi Khan).

concerned it had been totally unnecessary to send the ships to Batavia to inform the governor-general about Nader's *raqam* (decree) and all what it entailed. However, since Bahrain had been conquered already it was not necessary any longer to have a Dutch ship. He only asked the Dutch to assist him in assuring the Hula Arabs, who had become frightened by the Persian action against Bahrain and had fled from their normal habitations to the islands. Mohammad Taqi Khan had already written them not to have fear and that they could return to their villages in peace. But, he informed Koenad, if the Hulas did not execute his orders, he would be forced to make them return to which end he would send troops to Gamron. He therefore asked Koenad to detain the Dutch ships for some time more, in case he might need them. If not they would be allowed to leave.[70]

It was only on October 4, 1736 that Koenad was asked to assist Mohammad Latif Khan with ships and other kinds of support. The latter had undertaken action against the Hulas of Charak, but had been defeated. The 200-vessels strong Hulas were even pursuing him with his five ships and other smaller vessels. At the same time the Hulas were also infesting the islands near Gamron, interfering with the collection of firewood and water, while they also had set fire to large parts of Qeshm on October 12. Mir Mehr-e ʿAli and the *shahbandar* Hajji Mohammad had asked for assistance against the Hulas. Because of Dutch interest in water and firewood Koenad promised to do what he could, but he would only undertake action from Minab as far as Basidu and other places from which water and firewood were collected. To that end one ship was made available for the period of one month. Koenad also used the occasion to ask for the repayment of the money which the town officials had borrowed from the VOC.[71] The VOC ship *De Rithem* left on October 19 accompanied by a vessel prepared by Mir Mehr-e ʿAli with Persian soldiers to act as pilot and as guide to tell the Dutch who was the enemy and who not.[72] *De Rithem* returned on November 16 without having been able to catch any Hulas. It had patrolled the area around Qeshm and only had taken two vessels, which later appeared to be ordinary fishers from Jolfar who were released. The *shahbandar* of Basidu told the Dutch on October 30 that the Hulas had already left two days earlier. Koenad decided to keep the ship on the roadstead for the time being in case the Hulas might consider attacking Gamron as well as to act as a reminder of Dutch power in case the Persians were going to use violence.[73]

The Hulas meanwhile had taken notice of the Dutch patrolling action. Sheikh Rahma b. Faysal Charaki (Sjeeg Rama bein Fasal Tjareeki) informed both the English and the Dutch that the seizure of Dutch and English vessels had been a mistake due to ignorance. He apologized and returned the goods that had been stolen and expressed the hope for a continued friendship. Because further action by the Hulas was not excluded the Dutch council ordered *De Rithem* to be ready to sail immediately.[74]

---

70. VOC 2416, Resolution Gamron (30/06/1736), f. 1175-80.

71. VOC 2416, Resolution Gamron (13/10/1736), f. 1390-92.

72. VOC 2416, Resolution Gamron (30/06/1736), f. 1444-47f (also includes the text of the instruction for the captain of *de Rithem*).

73. VOC 2416, Resolution Gamron (08/11/1736), f. 1476-83; VOC 2416, Koenad to Batavia (10/12/1736), f. 336-37.

74. VOC 2416, Resolution Gamron (15/11/1736), f. 1506-08 (also contains the Dutch text of Sheikh Rahma's letter).

Further trouble caused by the Persians had led to an increase of the Arab rebellion. Sheikh Rashid had died in October 1736 and Mir Mehr-e `Ali, the *shahbandar* and the *ham-qalam* wanted to appropriate his property. Mir Heydar, Mir Mehr-e `Ali's son, had gone with 40 soldiers to Basidu to arrest Sheikh Rashid's widow. However, Mir Heydar was beaten off, before he was able to set feet ashore. The widow and her supporters then left Basidu, which, at Mohammad Taqi Khan's orders (who had been the instigator of the action), was attacked by Mohammad Latif Khan. He sacked Basidu and tried to seize as much property as was possible. However, his force was too weak to beat off an attack by the Arabs and he therefore withdrew pursued by 200 Arab vessels bent on revenge.[75]

The Hulas meanwhile again had seized a Dutch vessel in the beginning of January 1737. Koenad immediately sent *De Stadswijk* to Basidu to try and get the vessel back. On January 25 Sheikh Rahma b. Feysal Charaki sent Koenad the flag of the vessel that had been plundered in October 1736. He assured Koenad that he had no knowledge of this action, the two perpetrators of which he had ordered killed. He asked for the continuation of the friendly relations and promised that all that which had been stolen would be returned. His envoy was received in the Dutch factory and was told that the Dutch hoped that henceforth they would not be bothered anymore by the Hulas. On February 11, 1737 Koenad received a letter from Mohammad Taqi Khan asking him to keep the Dutch ship on the roadstead until his arrival in Gamron where he hoped to arrive in 22 days. The council therefore decided to keep *De Rithem* in Gamron, because else they would be confronted with new difficulties. The more so, since Nader at the insistence of Mohammad Taqi Khan had renewed all but two of the Dutch privileges.[76]

SHIPS, DEBTS AND BUSHEHR

On February 24 Mohammad Taqi Khan arrived in Gamron with about 10,000 men, both horse and foot. Koenad hoped to get a renewal of the two remaining old privileges, though he did not expect to bring this about without new presents. For the English gave Mohammad Taqi Khan and his retainers the red carpet treatment. They addressed the least of their servants who swept the floor as *agha sarkar* (Your Excellency), while the EIC dragoman was dabbling in medicine to curry their favor. Because the monsoon was coming to an end *De Rithem* was ordered to sail to Batavia.[77]

On March 9 and 13, 1737 the Dutch dragoman held discussions with Mohammad Taqi Khan about the two privileges, which had not yet been renewed. Mohammad Taqi Khan told the dragoman that he would be willing to petition Nader to agree to the renewal, while he also promised to confirm himself all renewed privileges as Koenad had asked. However, after having received the decrees, Mohammad Taqi Khan did nothing. Koenad also had been informed that Mohammad Taqi Khan intended to demand 3,500 *tumans* from each of the

---

75. VOC 2416, Koenad to Batavia (10/12/1736), f. 331-332; VOC 2417, Resolution Gamron (21/01/1737), f. 3423-24; VOC 2417, Resolution Gamron (19/10/1736), f. 3235-39.

76. VOC 2417, Resolution Gamron (12/02/1737), f. 3745-56.

77. VOC 2417, Resolution Gamron (08/01/1737), f. 3677-83; VOC 2417, Resolution Gamron (12/01.1737), f. 2710-3716 (contains the text of the new privileges granted); VOC 2417, Resolution Gamron (304/04/1737), f. 3666.

European Companies. To prevent this from happening and to get the decrees back the Dutch decided not to wait any longer and give Mohammad Taqi Khan and his advisors the expected presents. This had the desired result. Mohammad Taqi Khan, though pleased with the Dutch presents, at the same time asked for all kinds of supplies, viz. a new tent, powder, balls, planks, tar, cotton, ropes, anchor cables, anchors, tarpaulin and many other things. The English had already given a considerable number of similar goods, so the Dutch were forced to give something as well.[78] On March 15 Mohammad Latif Khan arrived at Gamron with five ships, one *gurab* and a number of smaller vessels. The Dutch gave him a present in order to avoid that demands would be for the use of *De Rithem*, which was still on the roadstead. The vice-admiral of the Persian fleet was the English captain Cook. On March 20 Mohammad Latif Khan spoke with the Dutch dragoman about his earlier proposal to the Dutch to come and trade in Bushehr. He offered to make room for the Dutch in the citadel, or if they wanted they would be allowed to build their own factory. Cook told the dragoman that it was a good proposal since Bushehr was a safer place to live than Basra, because of the uncertainty about the peace with the Arabs there. As a result of these discussions, on May 21, 1737 (20 Moharram 1150) Mohammad Taqi Khan gave a decree (*ta`liqeh*) granting the VOC the privilege of free trade at Bushehr. The VOC was allowed to build a house at Bushehr and to keep servants and a residency, at any place between the town and Fort Naderiyeh. The council deliberated the matter and wondered whether they should accept the offer in view of the decreasing profits of Basra and the extortions to which VOC personnel was exposed there. It was decided to send a ship with goods to see how trade fared there; when having gained a foothold there the Basra office could be transferred in case the situation deteriorated there.[79]

The dragoman also had discussed the Persian debt owed to the VOC with Mohammad Taqi Khan and his confidantes. Mohammad Taqi Khan was willing to support the Dutch claims, because he believed there was a chance of success, if they would be willing to give substantial presents and promised to deliver a ship. The VOC might also consider sending an ambassador, Koenad commented, but that would also be expensive. He estimated that the presents for such an embassy would amount to at least 2,500 *tumans*, while it would not be certain that the money would be a good investment. He, therefore, counseled caution and circumspection and to act only on explicit instructions from Batavia on this matter, to which the council agreed.[80] In the night of March 27, *De Anthonia* and *tHuys Foreest* arrived on the roadstead. Mohammad Taqi Khan immediately asked for the loan of one ship to transport troops to Jolfar, which was agreed to.[81]

The *beglerbegi* were constantly asking for all kinds of goods amongst which the loan of two mortars and 300 lbs. of gunpowder. On May 4, 1737 he asked the Dutch to transport 100 horses to Jolfar, which Mohammad Latif Khan had recently taken. He stated that this would be the last time that he would ask a favor. The English who had offered voluntarily to transport the horses and other goods, had assisted him during the preparation of the campaign

---

78. VOC 2417, Resolution Gamron (09/03/1737), f. 3792-96.

79. VOC 2417, Resolution Gamron (23/03/1737), f. 3814-25.

80. VOC 2417, Resolution Gamron (26/03/1737), f. 3828-30.

81. VOC 2417, Resolution Gamron (28/03/1737), f. 3831; VOC 2417, Resolution Gamron (31/03/1737), f. 3860-61; VOC 2448, Resolution Gamron (10/04/1737), f. 255.

and had recently regaled him munificently at `Essin, Mohammad Taqi Khan said. However, he did not trust them and declined their offer. In fact he demanded 1,000 *tuman*s from them and notwithstanding their protests and offer to pay 300 *tuman*s they had to pay the full amount. Because he continued to treat the Dutch with much respect and asked them politely for the use of their ship Koenad complied with this request. To this end *tHuys Foreest* was prepared which left accompanied by the dispenser's vessel and returned on May 24 with a letter of gratitude from Mohammad Latif Khan.[82]

At this time, Mohammad Taqi Shirazi also gave Koenad a *ta`liqeh* to start trading in Bushehr to which end he had already invited the Dutch a few times just like Mohammad Latif Khan[83] The presence of large number of troops around Gamron had a dampening effect on trade; the merchants stayed away from the town out of fear for oppressive activities. On June 7, 1737 Koenad received an order from Mohammad Taqi Khan in which he informed the former that he had been ordered to conquer Masqat and to destroy the unbelievers of Bu'l-`Arab (Bol Arab). Because the Dutch had rendered him so many services he granted exemption of all normal and extra-ordinary taxes to 60 persons working for the VOC. With satisfaction the Dutch noted that the English got a similar degree but only 20 of their personnel were granted tax exemption. They concluded that apparently Nader had granted full powers to Mohammad Taqi Khan, who moreover preferred the Dutch to the English. The reverse of the coin was that he continued to bother them with all kinds of requests for anchors and ropes. He also asked for help in repairing ships as well as transport facilities for war supplies. All these requests were however turned down. On June 6 the *shahbandar* called on Koenad to assure him that such a service would be really appreciated by the shah; it was then daily repeated. After three times the Dutch wondered whether he would not conclude that, since the royal ship could not sail, he had better ask for the loan of a Dutch ship. They therefore consulted the captains of their ships who might be willing to supply Mohammad Taqi Khan with a topmast who was very pleased with it.[84]

On July 19, 1737 the Dutch received a *raqam* from Nader Shah in which he *inter alia* thanked them for all the vessels they had prepared for the supply of Jolfar. This showed they were real friends, and he ordered them to be prepared to do more of such services in consultation with Mohammad Taqi Khan. Because the shah ended by stating that the Dutch could be assured of his favor Koenad wanted to sound out Mohammad Taqi Khan whether the shah would be willing to pay back the royal debt of 17,000 *tuman*s and do something about the Minab debt of 600 *tuman*s. However, due to the general confusion and fatigue among the Persian officials the time was not right. However, when in August the Dutch were asked to supply planks, Koenad asked for an order about the Minab debt, which he received on August 6, 1737. Another opportunity to discuss the royal debt offered itself when Mohammad Taqi Khan returned to Shiraz. The English wanted to regale him in their garden, but Mohammad

---

82. VOC 2448, Resolution Gamron (30/04/1737), f. 303-320; VOC 2448, Resolution Gamron (26/05/1737), f. 386.

83. VOC 2448, Resolution Gamron (26/05/1737), f. 369-73.

84. VOC 2448, Resolution Gamron (13/06/1737), f. 402, 416-25 (Mohammad Taqi Khan also asked whether his friend, Duke Aga Chan might stay for a while in the old Dutch garden at Neyband to recuperate from an illness. The Dutch agreed, but had to defray the cost of the governor's stay there, of course).

Taqi Khan preferred to be received by the Dutch, who despite the cost grabbed this chance to get him to promise to speak the shah about the debt.[85]

The so-called Minab debt had come into being as follows. From June 10-16 Koenad had been bothered by various officials to grant them a loan of 700 *tumans*, which they needed to assist local merchants and the population in general. They promised payment after two to three months. On June 11, 1736 Koenad received a letter signed by Soltan Mir Mehr 'Ali (Sultoen Amhier Mheer Alie), the *shahbandar* Mirza Mohammad, and the *ham-qalam* Sheikh Hadi, which was brought by the vizier of the former, named Sheikh 'Ali Reza and had the following contents. The town of Gamron and its dependencies had to pay a contribution of 3,000 *tumans* of which 700 *tumans* were still lacking. The tax collector (*mohassel*) Hasan 'Ali Beg had 10 days in which he had to collect the shortfall and he was putting pressure on the local officials. Because the land only produced dates, which would become ripe only three months later, the landowners, tenants and the population at large would suffer a loss of 50 per cent if they would sell the crops in June, the more so since so far nobody had offered to buy the harvest. Also, because all officials of Minab such as Sayyed 'Abdol-Reza *kalantar* (or *shahryari*) (Seijet Abdul Resa calanthoer or sariari) and further all notables of Jahrom were still at Gamron they were not able to execute the order with regards the contribution and collect the money. They were very embarrassed by this and because the Dutch had always been helpful to the Crown and the population they requested on behalf of everybody concerned a loan of 700 *tumans* silver money in cash or merchandise. They promised repayment in three months' time in silver or black money with 25 per cent agio. To that end all the notables of Jahrom and Minab, including its *kalantar*, would sign an IOU to that end. The English had received a similar request, but for 2,000 *tumans*, but their condition to do so was unacceptable to the officials. The Dutch were not enthusiastic about the request as they knew well that signing an IOU is one thing, paying it another, for "ere payment would take place the world would have perished." On the other hand not granting the loan would result in much local resentment. Also, the tax collector as well as the local officials would give a favorable report about the Dutch role to Nader and Mohammad Taqi Khan. Moreover, if the harvest and lands of Jahrom were demanded as security for the loan then the borrowers might be able to pay as the annual proceeds of these lands was 55,883 *tumans*. Besides, a refusal would mean that the Dutch would be exposed to much trouble concerning the lending of ships, sale of ships and the like, while the pressure on the merchants would be increased who then would depart which was not good for Dutch trade, and therefore the council decided on June 16, 1736 to lend 400 to 600 *tumans* for a period of two months.[86]

Mohammad Latif Khan had gained much influence with Nader Shah after his successful operation in Masqat and Bahrain and was believed to have been earmarked as Mohammad Taqi Khan's successor as *beglerbegi* of Fars. When he asked for carpenters for some days the Dutch send him one of these artisans for one week to prevent that he would ask the English. Koenad wanted the local authorities to be in a pro-Dutch mood when Mohammad Taqi Khan would return after a few weeks, when they wished to discuss the matter of the royal debt.[87]

---

85. VOC 2448, Resolution Gamron (30/07/1737), f. 589; VOC 2448, Resolution Gamron (08/08/1737), f. 613-21.

86. VOC 2448, Resolution Gamron (16/06/1736), f. 1111-19.

87. VOC 2448, Resolution Gamron (08/11/1737), f. 789-92.

On December 18, 1737 Mohammad Taqi Khan returned to Gamron with many troops and much pomp accompanied amongst others by Sheikh Jabbara, the powerful Hula chief, Mohammad Latif Khan, and Mehr-e `Ali Khan, governor of Lar.[88] Mohammad Taqi Khan friendly raised the question of equipment for the royal ships, and the loan of vessels for transportation to Jolfar. His assistant, Aqa Ja`far, told the Dutch that both the shah and his master really appreciated them very much. He told them to have some patience with regard to the Minab and royal debt, for the shah was busy besieging Qandahar and Mohammad Taqi Khan had to go to Jolfar. He assured the Dutch that these matters would be easily dealt with after the conquest of Qandahar and Masqat. Because Koenad believed that Mohammad Taqi Khan would gain even more influence after the conquest of Masqat he made *De Anthonia* available for a journey to Jolfar.[89]

[The end of December 1737 and the beginning of January 1738 were no pleasure for the Dutch or for many others.] There had been a heavy earthquake as well as heavy rains causing much damage to houses, many of which had been swept away. The roads between Gamron and Shiraz were hardly passable due to the swollen rivers. Even the well-constructed Dutch factory had suffered damage from the heavy rains. However, what shocked them most was the fact that on January 8, 1738 they learnt that their privileges, which he had granted only in 1737 in return for services rendered had been revoked.[90]

PRESSURE ON VOC TO ASSIST MASQAT OPERATION

Having returned Mohammad Taqi Khan found that the EIC was still ready to render services, but not the VOC, which therefore had lost the right to their privileges, or so he argued. Mohammad Taqi Khan therefore ordered that customs duties and imposts be levied from the Dutch and their servants when the inhabitants had to pay a contribution. Mohammad Taqi Khan would have punished the Dutch director for this negligence, but he had no time at that moment since the shah had ordered him to proceed to Masqat. He therefore had deferred the exemplary punishment until his return. If the Dutch captain, however, wanted to leave in the meantime he would be allowed to depart, if he wanted to. The dragoman then went to the *major domus* who told him that his master was furious with Koenad, but he did not know its reason. The dragoman asked how it was possible that 130 years of having been treated with respect the VOC now was looked down upon, and this after everything the Dutch had done for Mohammad Taqi Khan. The major domus agreed with him, but he could not offer an explanation, only advice. He advised Koenad to give 300 *tuman*s in cash to Mohammad Taqi Khan and the major domus would try and see whether that would make him more amenable. However, the next day early in the morning Mohammad Taqi Khan had already left to Jolfar with the *Fathi- Shahi*. The *ham-qalam* was prepared to give a copy of Mohammad Taqi Khan's order, but neither he nor the *shahbandar* were prepared to seal it saying that he was a fickle person who might not like this being done without

---

88. VOC 2448, Koenad to Batavia (31/12/1737), f. 74. There had been a fast turn-around of governors at Lar. Koenad reported in the beginning of 1737 that Mostafa Khan had been dismissed as governor of Lar and was replaced by Abu Taleb Khan. VOC 2368, Koenad to Batavia (19/03/1736), f. 21. The VOC horses were grazed at Shamil until April 24, 1737 under the supervision of the *kalantar* of Shamil, Casje Mhosen. VOC 2448, f. 376.

89. VOC 2448, Resolution Gamron (10/12/1737), f. 885-89.

90. VOC 2448, Resolution Gamron (20/01/1738), f. 906-22.

his permission. The dragoman then refused to take the copy. He therefore was sent to Mirza Abu'l-Hasan, Mohammad Taqi Khan's brother and representative, to ask for the reasons for his brother's anger. Mirza Abu'l-Hasan at first questioned whether the VOC had rendered services, but the dragoman asked how he dared raise such a question since he had been there when Dutch ships had plied between Gamron and Jolfar. He pointed out that the Dutch were invited friends, any honor bestowed on them would reflect on the giver. He asked him to take action now that Mohammad Taqi Khan was still nearby. Abu'l-Hasan promised that he would inform his brother and see to it that everything would be set aright. On January 13, 1738 he sent a courier (*chapar*) to his brother and all local officials were convinced that everything would be as in former times pretty soon. Nevertheless, the *ham-qalam* or deputy-governor on January 16 asked for the payment of customs duties when a merchant had come to collect his purchases. He would give the money or IOU's back when Mohammad Taqi Khan would revoke his order. The Dutch council however unanimously decided not to pay customs in any form, and, as long as the officials acted contrary to their privileges, no goods would be delivered, which decision caused much regret amongst the merchants. The relations with the local officials remained good, however. Koenad was even invited for dinner at the occasion of `eyd al-fetr at the end of Ramazan, but he refused in view of the dispute. The Persian officials insisted, however, that he come, or else Abu'l-Hasan Khan would be very despondent, but Koenad persisted in his refusal. However, the *shahbandar* pointed out to the dragoman that despite the possibility to demand money from the VOC personnel no official had done so. Moreover, the shah had not revoked the royal commands (*raqam*s), so that the offense only rebounded on Mohammad Taqi Khan himself. The very fact that his own brother and the other officials invited Koenad for `eyd al-fetr was a sign of respect for the VOC. Accepting the invitation would be a show of the persistence of the good relations between Persia and the VOC. The council discussed these arguments and decided that Koenad might accept the invitation. The more so, since Abu'l-Hasan had already twice asked for VOC vessels for royal services to fetch water and firewood, for which a great scarcity existed ashore. *De Anthonia* was send to Qeshm to get both, the more so since he might ask the English.[91]

Mohammad Taqi Khan sent back the *chapar*, whom his brother had sent, with the following reply:

> He had always shown friendship to the Dutch and had rewarded them for the royal services which they had rendered. However, now they had acted ungrateful and refused to do royal service. He had been unable to punish them properly, because he had to leave soon. He would inform HM about it, so that HM would punish them and make their house a ruin. He had ordered the *shahbandar* and *ham-qalam* to collect customs duties from them. Therefore urge them to do this. If I hear it has not happened I will send someone to take their heads.

The *chapar* also had an oral message for his brother, viz. if the Dutch would give him 1,000 *tuman* white money (or 12,000 *tuman* black money or Dfl 51,000) he then would be willing to accept the offer of *De Anthonia* and restore their rights and show them his friendship as before. If they were not prepared to do so he need not bother about the Dutch anymore. The council was in a quandary. Mohammad Taqi Khan had full powers and could do what he liked. He still had

---

91. VOC 2448, Report concerning the discussion between Mohammad Taqi Khan and David Sahid, interpreter (04/01/1738), f. 923-27; VOC 2448, Resolution Gamron (20/01/1738), f. 949-55.

troops near Gamron against whom they could do very little, the more so since they also lacked water and firewood. He moreover would complain to the shah, and might have all officials sign the document, stating that the Dutch were in league with the Arabs. This would lead to punitive action by the shah against the offices at Kerman and Isfahan. It would be better, therefore, to give in to "this second Nero" rather than allow the dispute to grow out of proportions which would lead to war. The council therefore decided to lodge a complaint to the shah at once and further to suffer quietly as the English did and to inform the other branch offices. Further to continue to trade and, like the English, to give presents, for else only the English would remain in the Persian Gulf. Finally, they also could ask the shah to be allowed to leave the country, because the profits had not been sufficient to cover the expenses for quite a number of years already.

Abu'l-Hasan Khan publicly declared that he would not be able to accept less than his brother had demanded, so they would have to give him also 1,000 *tumans*. At that time, the officials were already taking VOC vessels from the beach in front of the VOC factory, porters were bothered, which in themselves were reasons to fight. The council therefore unanimously decided to wait and see for the time being. Later that month Koenad asked the council to reconsider its decision. For Mohammad Taqi Khan had given no sign of weakening his position, while all friends of the VOC were pessimistic about the outcome. The *shahbandar* had told Koenad that he had tried to reason with him but to no avail; he did not know what to do anymore and pointed out that he would have to obey him. If force would be used, he assured Koenad, he would inform the shah secretly about the whole affair. The Dutch decided to offer 100 *tumans*. Abu'l-Hasan Khan, however, said that the Dutch would not be served well with the offense that would be given to him if he did not execute his brother's orders. He added that his brother had a strange nature and that he was afraid of him. Because the only alternative was war, which would also backfire on the staff in Isfahan, Kerman and Bushehr the Dutch decided to give in, "before the brook turned into a river." For if Mohammad Taqi Khan would be defeated by the Arabs he undoubtedly would put the blame on the Dutch whom he would accuse of being in cahoots with the Arabs. The council therefore decided to offer 600 *tumans* (Dfl. 25,500) to Mohammad Taqi Khan and 72 *tumans* to his brother for his trouble. The payment was made on January 31, 1738. Mohammad Taqi Khan wrote to Koenad in reply that he had been angry, but all had been forgotten now. He also had thanked his brother for his good offices and ordered him to revoke the order given to the *shahbandar* to levy customs and imposts on the Dutch and their servants.[92] *De Anthonia*, which meanwhile had transported troops and supplies to Jolfar, was also thanked for its trouble. The Dutch dispenser's vessels also had made nine trips to and fro Jolfar.[93]

MASQAT OPERATION TURNS BAD

On April 18, 1738 the Dutch received a letter from Mohammad Taqi Khan in which he reported the conquest of the towns of Bahila (Bahela) and Nizwa (Nosua). Koenad congratulated him and received his son on one of the VOC ships. On April 27 and 28, Abu'l-Hasan Khan pestered the

---

92.   VOC 2448, Resolution Gamron (28/01/1738), f. 957-75; VOC 2448, Resolution Gamron (31/01/1738), f. 977-85; VOC 2448, Koenad to Batavia (30/04/1738+ appendix 04/06/1738), f. 1840-41.

93.   VOC 2448, Resolution Gamron (03/03/1738), f. 1998.

Dutch for 500 balls for the royal fleet, for he feared an attack by the Arabs with their ships. The royal fleet had no balls at all; since he first had asked the English, who had given him 300 balls, the Dutch *nolens volens* also had to give him something. The reasoning was that if the Arabs would attack the tottering, rotting royal fleet and would win they would be blamed, and so the Dutch gave 100 balls of four lbs. each.[94]

By June 1738 things had gone very bad for Mohammad Taqi Khan in Masqat and he had to withdraw in shame to Jolfar, where he was totally surrounded, both at land and at sea. The royal fleet, under cover of the English *Galley Roos*, ran to Jolfar. Both the fleet and the infantry ashore lacked sufficient amounts of ammunition. Mohammad Taqi Khan therefore asked the English to assist him to take money and other supplies to Jolfar, which they did. They even sent a vessel with a gunner and some men to escort the ship about which Mohammad Taqi Khan was very pleased. He also tried to get a Dutch ship about which he showed himself totally unreasonable. The Arabs, in the presence of the English ship, attacked the Persian troops, who lacked the leadership of Mohammad Latif Khan and the English captain Cook, who both had died. The Persians, when they were defeated, fled with a galley and with the help of the VOC dispenser's vessel to Kong. The Arabs then boarded the English ship, which had been borrowed to transport supplies, and arrested its captain and two sailors. The vessel, which had not helped the Persians, had been released by the Arabs and then returned to Gamron. The Arabs had warned the English if they returned then they would set fire to their fortress. It was expected that the governor of Gamron, on his return, would blame both Companies for the disaster, whether they had assisted him or not, viz., the English who had deserted him during the battle and the Dutch who had not assisted him. He said as much in his letters and was said to have given his brother instructions to act against the Europeans, who were very worried about these rumors. Meanwhile Jolfar and the royal fleet were contained by the Masqat Arabs; some ships of the royal fleet had to be beached after having lost the sea battle, amongst which the *Fatti Sjahi*. However, the Dutch regretfully remarked that the Masqat Arabs were not "anymore like in 1718, we wish that they were still like that, for in that case they would have destroyed the Persian fleet already a long time ago." Now, however, they were divided by internal dissent, which blunted their power. The Arabs had already arrived in Basidu, Bahrein and Kong, which they were said to have set fire to. The Dutch informed the factories in Basra and Bushehr to be careful and like the Gamron factory to take defensive measures. The *Adriana*, at Basra, had to leave for Bushehr if this was feasible without incurring commercial loss.[95] Abu'l-Hasan Khan, having arrived at Kong in August 1738, asked for 3,000 lbs. of gunpowder for the besieged Mohammad Taqi Khan in Jolfar, which the Dutch felt they could not refuse given the circumstances and the possible consequences and they therefore gave 250 lbs of powder.[96] Despite this assistance, Abu'l-Hasan Khan commandeered without asking for permission, a Dutch supply vessel to be used in the attack of Masqat. The crew was beaten to remain on board and they made 12 trips to Jolfar. Meanwhile, after the plague of locusts foods

---

94. VOC 2448, Koenad to Batavia (30/04/1738+ appendix 04/06/1738), f. 1838; VOC 2448, Resolution Gamron (06/05/1738), f. 2090-91.

95. VOC 2476, Resolution Gamron (08/08/1738), f. 182-86; VOC 2476, Koenad to Batavia (25/02/1739), f. 87-88.

96. VOC 2476, Resolution Gamron (12/08/1738), f. 190-95

had become very expensive in Gamron. The price of dates had risen from 5 *mahmudi*s to 30 *mahmudi*s per pack.[97]

CONTINUED DEMAND FOR MARITIME SUPPORT

Meanwhile, on July 7, 1738 Mohammad Taqi Khan had sent a letter to Koenad informing him that he was quite aware of the Dutch lack of enthusiasm to assist him with vessels. However, fortunately, he had almost completed his business at Jolfar and he did not any vessels anymore. If Imam Seyf might still oppose him he, nevertheless he had 7-8 ships in the roads plus the EIC ship and 100 small and big vessels belonging to Arabs and other of the shah's subjects. Imam Seyf only had two rotten and dilapidated ships, which the royal fleet could handle. He had only asked for a ship to stop rumors put about by maligning people who had said that the Dutch were in league with the Arabs and did not do any service for the shah. Since September 14, 1738 Abu'l-Hasan Khan and his *na'eb*, Mirza Mohammad, had been putting daily pressure on the Dutch to lend his brother 40,000 *tuman*s (Dfl. 1.7 million) for three months.[98] Because the Dutch had written that their ship was under repair, Mohammad Taqi Khan urged them to support him nevertheless with boats and vessels, for they owed that to the shah, due to the large annual profits they made due to their exemption of payment of customs. If they would have to pay these it would cost them 10,000-15,000 *tuman*s per year. This royal favor the Dutch did not acknowledge by their behavior, for they were secretly in contact with the Arabs. Also, they had their ship put in dry dock at Laft for repairs when he needed it. In short, the Dutch were not acting like true friends of the shah, who, he hastened to add, did not need their assistance of course against a handful of Arabs.[99]

The news of the turn of the tide also led to actions elsewhere in the Persian Gulf. On June 14, 1738 Schoonderwoerd reported from Bushehr that the Arabs in his part of the Persian Gulf, the Hulas, were already becoming restive and had robbed vessels with grain of Sheikh Madhkur of Bushehr destined for the army. On July 23, 1738 the Dutch who were on Qeshm to repair *de Antonia* reported rumors that the Masqat Arabs had come to Basidu in 25 big vessels and had invaded the town. All inhabitants had fled, and the Arabs were expected to come also their way. They warned Koenad to be on his guard and to put himself in state of defense. The Masqat Arabs took not only Basidu and Laft, but also the surrounding villages. Most of the inhabitants had fled and the few remaining ones told the Dutch on *de Antonia* that it was only due to their presence that the Masqat Arabs had withdrawn, for else they certainly would have taken the citadel as well. From Kong orders arrived for the officials in Qeshm to press all available men to serve as sailors for the ships to transport supplies. On August 12, 1738 the Persians were said to have concluded a peace with the Arabs. On September 1, 1738 the Dutch learnt that four royal ships and some vessels with supplies had left Bushehr for Jolfar to combat

---

97. VOC 2476, Resolution Gamron (29/09/1738), f. 244-49.

98. VOC 2476, Resolution Gamron (10/03/1738), f. 255-58 (the letter was dated last of Rabi`a al-Avval 1151 or July 17, 1738).

99. VOC 2476, Mohammad Taqi Khan to Koenad (14/09/1738 received), f. 259-61. *De Anthonia*, which was at Laft for repairs, complained in July and August that the governor of Laft, Seyfollah Beg (Sevola Beecq), did not supply them with laborers as he had promised. Koenad therefore sent men from Gamron to scrape this ship's bottom. VOC 2476, f. 184-86.

the Arabs and that they already had seized some *tranki*s. Furthermore, cavalry troops had arrived at Kong to renew the war with the Arabs.[100]

The *na'eb* of Dashtestan asked Schoonderwoerd, the VOC agent at Bushehr, to transport grain supplies for the army with VOC vessels for the sea was unsafe for Persian vessels, which were taken everywhere. Schoonderwoerd gave a non-committal reply, which seemed to satisfy him. Meanwhile the Masqat Arabs had totally ruined and pillaged Bahrain, but were said to have left it again by mid August 1738. The outbreak of robberies on the beaches had come to a stop due to orders given by Sheikh Jabbara to the rebel Hulas to keep quiet. Mohammad Taqi also wrote a flattery letter to Sheikh Madhkur in the beginning of August, which, according to Schoonderwoerd, only served to sweeten his demand for 4,000 men for his fleet. Recruitment had started immediately.[101]

The Masqat Arabs continued their depredations and took a *gurab* and a *gallivat* (both small sailing vessels) of the royal fleet at Bandar Taheri. Another had exploded by its own powder. From Qeshm various rumors were reported, viz. that four ships of the royal fleet with supplies had gone from Bushehr to Jolfar to look for the Masqat fleet and were said to have taken some *tranki*s. Further, that new troops had arrived at Kong to reopen the war with Masqat.[102]

Although Mohammad Taqi Khan had been summoned by Nader Shah he remained at Kong. From there he put pressure on the English in particular. They had to pay as much as Dfl. 50,000 or 1,200 *tuman*s. After September 14, 1738 Abu'l-Hasan Khan especially became a pest by his constant demands for all kinds of goods. Mohammad Taqi Khan had not been satisfied with the English present, for, in September 1738, he wanted to have a loan of 40,000 *tuman*s for three months. Abu'l-Hasan Khan told the Dutch that he would try and have it reduced to a few thousand *tuman*s only and do a good word for the Dutch. The Dutch decided to wait and see what happened, hoping that Mohammad Taqi Khan would not come to Gamron. From Qeshm it was reported that he would not move from Kong until he had settled the war with the Masqat Arabs. He was expecting ships from Jamael [?] and then would leave for Gamron. He wrote in July 1738 that he did not need any vessels anymore in Jolfar. In a follow-up letter Mohammad Taqi Khan reacted to Koenad's excuse for not lending ships, because they were undergoing repairs. He questioned whether this prevented the Dutch from helping the shah at sea with small vessels and *gurabs*. After all, the Dutch made large profits every year due to the exemption of customs duties, which if they would have had to pay them would amount to 10,000 up to 15,000 *tuman*s per year. They did not return the shah's favor by their attitude he wrote, for the Dutch had contacts with the Arabs, and had their ships drawn on dry land to repair them, while he needed them. The Dutch were clearly lacking in friendship for the shah, although he assured Koenad that he, of course, did not need the Dutch vessels to wage war on a handful of Arabs. He also had asked about the repairs being done to *de Antonia*, what size the ship was, and whether the Dutch were sabotaging the repair works or not.[103]

---

100. VOC 2476, f. 1130 (04/08/1738), 1134 (06/08/1738), 1140-41 (14/08/1738), 1146 (02/09/1738).

101. VOC 2476, Schoonderwoerd to Koenad (17/08/1738), f. 1064-67.

102. VOC 2476, Schoonderwoerd to Koenad (16/09/1738), f. 1077.

103. VOC 2476, Resolution Gamron (03/10/1738), f. 255-58 (contains letter Mohammad Taqi Khan to Koenad received 14/09/1738, f. 260-61); VOC 2476, Koenad to Batavia (25/02/1739), f. 90-91; VOC 2476, 1156 (10/10/1738).

On September 29, 1738 Seyfollah Beg (Sevola Beecq) even came to inspect the work being done.[104] Mid-night of October 19, Mohammad Taqi Khan with a few men only arrived in Gamron and would leave within a few days to Nader Shah. The Dutch decided to foster his friendship, for he still had great influence with the shah. Moreover, he was still very angry with the English about the naval affaire, when he was attacked and the English vessel had not assisted him. The Dutch therefore gave Mohammad Taqi Khan a present and a letter for Nader Shah. Mohammad Taqi Khan gave them an order (ta`liqeh) for the collection of outstanding debts.[105]

MASQAT ARABS ATTACK IRANIAN POSITIONS AND SHIPS

On Qeshm it was rumored in December 1738 that the Masqat Arabs, with two ships and 600 small vessels, had attacked Jolfar and had tried to dislodge the Persian troops from there. A land attack had been mounted at the same time by 6,000 troops. Because *de Antonia* had arrived from Basra on November 6, 1738 and finally returned from New Laft on January 9, 1739 the Dutch felt safe again due to the continued danger of a naval attack by Masqat Arabs and Sanganian pirates.[106]

On January 17, 1739 Abu'l-Hasan Khan learnt about the lack of supplies for Mirza Reza, Mohammad Taqi Khan's son, who was still in Kong. That same night he asked the Dutch to transport 30,000 men to Kong to which they willy-nilly consented, because *De Antonia* had not to do anything anyway. They used this occasion to ask Abu'l-Hasan Khan to make haste with collecting the Minab debt.[107] Towards the end of the month, Abu'l-Hasan Khan again asked three times for ships to go to Jolfar where the Persian troops were facing hunger. For, although Kong was being supplied by small vessels, there were no ships to transport it to Jolfar, because the entire royal fleet had gone to Masqat.[108] At that time, it was also rumored that Bahrain was being besieged again. Sheikh Jabbara had arrived at Qatif it was said, possibly to conquer Bahrain, where the entire royal fleet had gathered to its relief. The new *vakil* of Bahrain, Mohammad Amin Khan, who was in Bushehr, could not even go there.[109]

---

104. VOC 2476, f. 1127 (04/08/1738), 1157 (10/10/1738).

105. VOC 2476, Koenad to Batavia (25/02/1739), f. 92-96; VOC 2476, Resolution Gamron (19/10/1738), f. 273-76 (the council discussed whether anybody should leave the factory to welcome Mohammad Taqi Khan as he had shown himself to be an untrustworthy friend, while van Leijpsigh had reported that horsemen had been sent to arrest the English director. The council decided that only Koenad and van de Crane would welcome him to avoid resentment); VOC 2476, Resolution Gamron (20/10/1738), f. 279-84; VOC 2476, Resolution Gamron (05/11/1738), f. 330-33 (text letter Koenad to Nader Shah and text of the ta`liqeh).

106. VOC 2476, Resolution Gamron (13/01/1739), f. 443; VOC 2476, Resolution Gamron (06/11/1738), f. 341; VOC 2476, Resolution Gamron (10/01/1739), f. 419, 430.

107. Heydar Qoli Beg (Heyder Coelie Beek) was *kalantar* of Minab and Kalb `Ali Beg (Calb Alie Beek) was castallan (*kutval*) of its citadel. VOC 2546 (29/08/1741), f. 1819; VOC 2546 (24/11/1740), f. 1969 (here Heydar Qoli Beg is called *shahriyar* of Minab).

108. VOC 2476, Resolution Gamron (20/01/1739), f. 470-71; VOC 2476, Resolution Gamron (29/01/1739), f. 495-99.

109. VOC 2476, Schoonderwoerd to Koenad (12/11/1738), f. 1079; VOC 2476, Schoonderword to Koenad (12/01/1739), f. 1106.

The Masqat fleet had been attacked by the Persian fleet in January 1739 near Qassab. One of the big Masqat ships, the *Malek*, sank with about 700 men due to a fire they had caused themselves. Because of heavy thunder, both sides were forced to seek a safe harbor. Around February 20, 1739 six ships were sighted of which it was reported that they would take in water and then return to Qassab again. At the same time it was said that Imam Bu'l-'Arab, with 20,000 soldiers, had induced the Persian troops in Jolfar to engage him in battle. Although their commander Assur [?] Soltan (Assour Solthan) was in Kong the Persian defeated the Arabs. Assur Soltan *min-bashi*, who had been collecting supplies, immediately returned to Jolfar.[110] The situation in Gamron, however, was even worse, for the poor had no food anymore. They were forced to eat grass and wherever one went in town they were found lying dying or dead in the streets. Their fellow Moslems, however, did not bother about them and did not even bury them. This situation had been caused by locusts, which had eaten the entire date harvest.[111]

FORCED LOAN OF SHIPS

On March 16, 1739, Mohammad Taqi Khan returned to Gamron. He told the Dutch that Nader Shah would be prepared to pay the 17,000 *tuman*s royal debt in annual installments of 1,000 *tuman*s on the condition that the Dutch would deliver one fully equipped ship against cash payment, as well as equipment and supplies for the other ships of the royal fleet, for which Mohammad Taqi Khan would send a separate order list. The Dutch told him that the sale of a ship was impossible, but Mohammad Taqi Khan was not prepared to listen to any arguments. He just repeated: "the shah has ordered it, and it is the condition for the repayment of the royal debt." This list was presented shortly to the Dutch and when they stalled doing anything about it Mohammad Taqi Khan sent the *ham-qalam*, Sheikh Hadi, to ask for it.[112] He threatened that if his request would be refused he would take the supplies himself from the Dutch ships and would deal harshly with the Dutch, whether on land or at sea. He gave them respite till the night of March 28, 1739 to choose between enmity and peace with Persia. Refusing to give in would lead to hostilities, which would be disadvantageous to the VOC. The council, therefore, decided to see what might be supplied by the ships to satisfy Mohammad Taqi Khan. If, however, the bloodhound would find that unacceptable they would not give more and, if need be, defend Dutch interests by force. Van Leijpsigh reported that he had learnt that Mohammad Taqi Khan had carte blanche to willy-nilly commandeer all ships to whomever they belonged, to mount his attack on Masqat.[113]

---

110. VOC 2476, Koenad to Batavia (25/02/1739), f. 132-33; VOC 2476, Schoonderwoerd to Koenad (12/01/1739), f. 1106 (it was rumored that the Masqat Soltan Seyf had arrived at Jolfar with three large ships and some smaller vessels and that the Persian troops had already withdrawn from there).

111. VOC 2476, Koenad to van Leijpsigh (31/01/1739), f. 616.

112. To put the Dutch in the right frame of mind, the *ham-qalam* of Gamron, who knew Nader personally, told Koenad that the shah was so avaricious that for a small sum of 50 *mahmudi*s (Dfl. 21:5) he would have people travel 100 German miles, or send them tax collectors at their cost. Mohammad Taqi Khan was not much better, who had ruined him, and with him at least another 1,000 persons. VOC 2477, Koenad to Batavia (12/05/1739), f. 100.

113. VOC 2510, Resolution Gamron (14/05/1739), f. 177-79; VOC 2477, Resolution Gamron (20/03/1739), f, 205-08; VOC 2477 (24/04/1739), f. 214-15; VOC 2417 (28/03/1739), f. 235-38; VOC 2477, van Leijpsigh (12/04/1739), f. 462; VOC 2477, f. 812-15; VOC 2477, Mohammad Taqi Khan to Batavia (01/05/1739), f. 844-45; VOC 2477, Koenad to Batavia (14/05/1739), f. 33 (with a marginal note [by the Batavia council ?] not to send an ambassador when Tahmasp Qoli Khan ascends the throne) 84, 89.

The only consolation which the Dutch had from this event, apart from the fact that Mohammad Taqi Khan accepted their offer, was the fact that he seemed to have had less respect for the English whom, according to the Dutch, he just had told what to deliver and order from Bombay, while he, at least, had asked them. Moreover, the English had even supplied Mohammad Taqi Khan with a brand-new ship, without having been asked for it, while they also gave him many presents. On May 1, 1739 Mohammad Taqi Khan returned to Shiraz. With the conquest of India, Nader also wanted to strengthen his grip on the Gulf area. It is within this strategic context that his action in Makran, Bahrain and Masqat-Oman must be seen. His failure to ensure the loyalty of the coastal Arabs proved to be a debilitating affair. His commanders therefore once again demanded the services of the Europeans.[114]

On July 14, 1739 Koenad received a letter from Mohammad Baqer Beg stating that, at the orders of Mohammad Taqi Khan, he had to get a ship to send supplies to the relief of Jolfar. He literally begged for help, after the Dutch had declined to help him on July 16, 1739, because the Dutch vessels had to be repaired and resupplied. Moreover, the crews were weak due to illness and death, amongst whom the two carpenters, so that they also could not help Mohammad Baqer Beg with his request for artisans. The latter replied on the next day, that he would have his *hammals* (porters) fetch water and firewood for the Dutch, until their ship would be back; could they please help him. Because he continued to press the Dutch finally gave in. On August 6, 1739 *'t Hof niet altijd Somer* left with grains to Jolfar which was unloaded there on August 19. Assur Soltan the Persian commander thanked them and the ship was back on September 5, 1739.[115]

The Dutch suffered because of these loans of the vessels. The dispenser complained that one of the vessels had become totally worthless and was only good enough to be used as firewood. He had to pay the crews out of his own pocket to avoid that things became worse, because it was date harvest time. The crews normally would be on land in their date-groves, but to ensure the steady supply of water and firewood to the Dutch factory he had to pay them double rates. He had sent the VOC interpreter and clerk to Mohammad Taqi Khan for payment, who refused each time. *Nakhoda* Kamal (Nacha Camaal) received for the May 16-June 6 trip to Jolfar 490 *mahmudis*, *nakhoda* Mohammad for the June 18-23 trip to Jolfar 150 *mahmudis*, and for the June 24-July 23 double trip to Jolfar 300 *mahmudis*. To sail to Laft, the *nakhodas* received 75 *mahmudis* for a two-day trip and 150 *mahmudis* for a one-week trip.[116]

MOHAMMAD TAQI KHAN'S POWER AND NEW OPERATIONS

The power of Mohammad Taqi Khan seemed to grow rather to diminish. He prevailed against the viceroy, Reza Qoli Mirza, as to the counterorder for the fiscal exemption of three years. He was set over many *beglerbegis*, e.g., the one of Kuhgilu, Dhu'l-Feqar Khan (Sulphagoen Chan), whom he received while seated, and acknowledged their bows. Recently one of his sons, Mirza

---

114. VOC 2417 (06/05/1739), f. 303; VOC 2477, Koenad to Batavia (12/05/1739), f. 109-111. See also Floor, "Navy", and Ibid., "New Facts."

115. VOC 2510, Mohammad Baqer Beg to Koenad (14/07/1739), f. 1247-9; Ibid. (17/07/1739), f.1250-52.

116. VOC 2510, resolution Gamron (29/09/1739), f. 278-80.

Hadi, had been appointed as governor of Lar by his own decision.[117] He also seemed to have done well, financially and politically, with the Masqat affair. For he had made peace with the Masqat Arabs; probably in exchange for a 50,000 *tuman*s tribute per year for Nader, 10,000 for himself, and 5,000 *tuman*s for Assur Sultan (Asjoer Sulthan) and the possession of Jolfar. To ensure Persian power on the Arab littoral, Sheikh Rahma b. Matar, the same who had made eyes at Hormuz in 1728, had been invested with the hereditary rule of Jolfar and its dependencies. In addition, the Imam's brother, Seyf, would come to Nader's court with other hostages. At that time, Mohammad Taqi Khan commanded a navy and a land army, consisting of 25,000 foot and horse; 7 large and small ships of 2-3 masts and several hundred of various kinds of small vessels. Food supplies for these troops and their cattle had been continuously brought in abundance to Gamron since August 1739, so that there was not enough storage capacity. Troops, supplies and money were also demanded from the *beglerbegi* of Kerman. Nevertheless, the governor of Kerman still owed him 1,805 loads of supplies, as well as, 500 *tuman*s in cash and 500 *tuman*s in kind. To make the whole operation work smoothly everybody and anything, be it human being, animal or vessel on both sides of the Persian Gulf were pressed to do royal service. On December 17, Mohammad Taqi Khan was joined by his son Reza who boarded the Dutch ship with 85 men. From Delhi, Nader had sent a governor for Bahrain, Mohammad Qoli Khan (Mhamet Coelie Chan), so that Mohammad Taqi Khan had yet another governor under him. Koenad opined that, "One cannot anymore doubt that there is a secret agreement between Nader and Mohammad Taqi Khan, which they reached during the coronation in the Moghan steppe in 1736, but this is unconfirmed."[118]

Meanwhile, people were expecting Mohammad Taqi Khan to mount the expected attacks on Qatif and Hasa. This report was believed to be true since the Sheikh of Hasa had sent 10 horses to Shiraz at the end of July with the request to be left alone. However, others maintained, that he had come to organize the attack on Masqat, for in Bushehr orders had been given to bring 80,000 *mann* of grain to Jolfar with *trankis*. In Gamron actions to help out Jolfar also were continued. Mohammad Baqer Beg commandeered all vessels he could lay his hands on, willy-nilly, and even seized the vessels of the Dutch dispenser, which were forced to make five trips to Jolfar and two to Laft. Mohammad Baqer Beg said he had to use force, for the Persian troops in Jolfar would die if help were not forthcoming. The royal navy was in Bushehr (probably commanded by the provisional admiral Mohammad Qasem Beg). Protests did not help much, sometimes he returned the vessels, when they came back with water and firewood, and sometimes he would take them again, for the troops were in need.[119]

---

117. Hadi Khan had just been appointed when he arrived in Gamron. VOC 2511 (01/03/1740), f. 1248, 1261. His precedecesor was Mohammad Khan. VOC 2546 (31/03/1740), f. 52. In 1741, the deputy-governor (*na'eb*) of Lar was Mirza Abu Taleb. VOC 2546 (04/02/1741), f. 1783, 1956-57. In 1743, he is mentioned as being the vizier of Lar and Hadi Khan was still governor of Lar. VOC 2680, f. 199.

118. VOC 2510, Koenad to Batavia (25/12/1739), f. 103-116; Ibid. Schoonderwoerd (16/11/1739), f. 941 (the tribute was only 3,000 *tuman*s); one third of the country was under Mohammad Taqi Khan. VOC 2417 (28/03/1739), f. 239. Mirza Mohammad `Ali (Miersa Mhamed Alie) was Mohammad Taqi Khan's keeper of the seal (*mohrdar*) and his all-do (*albeschik*). VOC 2511 (05/01/1740), f. 1235, 1253, 1260-61.

119. VOC 2510. Schoonderwoerd to Koenad (03/08/1739), f. 895; Ibid. (16/09/1739), f. 897; Ibid., (31/09/1739), f. 910-19.

On September 17, 1739 Mohammad Taqi Khan arrived in Bushehr with 12,000 men. He took up lodgings in Fort Naderiyeh. Schoonderwoerd warned Gamron to see whether they might send the VOC ships away to avoid having to put these at his disposal. During his stay in Bushehr, the qadi of Masqat had visited Mohammad Taqi, who had departed from there with the intention to go to Baluchistan (via Gamron at the end of September). On November 4, 1739 Mohammad Taqi Khan entered Gamron coming from Shiraz. A week later he asked the Dutch for a ship to transport supplies and troops to Divil-Sind. Whatever argument they used to make him change his mind it was of no use and so the Dutch decided to use *tHof niet altijd Somer* for this trip. Mohammad Taqi Khan publicly promised to land the troops at Gaischk (?) near Jask. The Dutch had given in because his power appeared to have grown.[120]

The subsequent, not so successful, campaign in Makran hardly had any effect on Mohammad Taqi Khan's career. He was appointed *mostowfi al-mamalek*, but dismissed as *beglerbegi* of Fars in which place Nader appointed Emam Verdi Khan with the same powers. He also dismissed the *daryabegi* Mehr-`Ali Khan Turkman (Mier Alie Chan Turkomani) and replaced him by Mohammad Taqi Khan Masidie [?], former *beglerbegi* of Kerman, and later, commander in the service of the *vali `ahd*.[121] They all had orders to mobilize a large army and the *daryabegi* had to sail the fleet to Bushehr. It was rumored that Nader wanted to attack Masqat. Of the latter it was said that it wanted to attack Jolfar with the assistance of the Sanganian pirates, with seven ships and some large native vessels, and, after having taken it, to attack the royal fleet at Gamron and both destroy the fleet and the town. This news caused much fear in that town during the entire month.[122] Nader had decided to attack Masqat and had ordered Emamverdi Khan to form a large army in two months' time in Shiraz. Those Europeans who would help might expect the most favor, and, contrariwise, the most vexations. Dutch fears were allayed a bit when a letter from Nader was sent to Masqat on July 13, 1740, which they hoped meant that there would not be war. Meanwhile Mehr `Ali Khan, the new *daryabegi*, through Aqa Baqer continuously asked equipment for his ships and after June 5, 1740 almost daily, so that the Dutch finally gave him some things. On August 5, 1740 it became known that the royal fleet would sail to Bushehr, where the new *daryabegi* would take over. It was rumored that an attack was contemplated on al-Hasa or Basra.[123]

---

120. VOC 2510, Koenad to Batavia (25/12/1739), f. 119-125; VOC 2510, Resolutions Gamron (10/11/1739), f. 411 and (13/11/1739), f. 414-6. VOC 2510, f. 1256-60, various thank you notes from Mohammad Taqi Khan and Assour Coelie Chan.

121. Mohammad Taqi Khan wrote Koenad that he had been appointed admiral (*daryabegi*), governor (*begler-begi*) of Dashtestan and commander plenipotentiary (*volmacht*) of all the ports from Persia to India. VOC 2511 (01/09/1740 received), f. 1708-10; VOC 2546, f. 1164-70. Mehr `Ali Khan Turkman's brother was the royal *farrash-bashi*. VOC 2511 (31/07/1740), f. 148.

122. VOC 2511, Koenad to Batavia (31/07/1740), f. 156. The Sanganian pirates had their home-base in the coastal region of Kathiawar and Cutch.

123. VOC 2511, Koenad to Batavia (31/07/1740), f. 156-67; VOC 2511, Koenad to Batavia (11/08/1740), f. 206.

MUTINY OF THE ROYAL FLEET AND COMMANDEERING OF VOC SHIPS

However there were heavy storms from August 12 to 16, 1740, which caused damage to all ships in the area. The Persian ships started drifting and gave distress signals and on August 14, *the Captain* (a ship sold by the English supercargo Mr. Placock) was about to shipwreck. Only the *Fatti Sjahi* kept well during the storm; the rest of the fleet was roaming pell-mell and miserably about. The English gave the Persians three small anchors, but the Dutch refused to give any when the *daryabegi* came to ask for them. They said their ships had only four anchors of which they had already lost two so that they could not risk these, for they did not know how long the storm would last. They advised him to go to the English who had sold *the Captain* to them; they were responsible for its upkeep and maintenance. They added that even the shah would consider them mad to endanger their own ships. The Persians persisted, however, and when the Dutch learnt that *de Cronenburgh* had fished up one of its lost anchors on August 20, they lent one anchor, for which Mullah `Ali Shah, the *vakil* of the royal fleet and `Abdollah, the mate of *the Captain* had to sign a bond that they would return it, which was done on August 20, 1740 (Jomadi al-Avval 1153). The Dutch in fact only had given in because the Persians threatened to write to Nader that the disaster of *the Captain* was their fault, which disaster was prevented by a change of the weather so that the ship drifted to deeper water. Emamverdi Khan, the *sardar* of Fars, Lar, Bahrain, Masqat, Sind, Kich-Makran and Gamron, ordered that the royal fleet had to remain in the roadstead until the arrival of the new *daryabegi*, Mohammad Taqi Khan. Only then the anchor would be returned.[124]

In the evening of September 6, 1740 it was learnt that Mehr `Ali Khan, the *daryabegi* had been murdered together with 170 Persian soldiers by the Arab crews of the fleet. The other soldiers had jumped overboard and fled. The news was confirmed by the shah's *na'eb*, Mohammad Taher Beg, to Koenad that same day. Mehr `Ali Khan had orders to take the fleet to Bushehr, but the mutiny intervened. The mutineers were led by Sheikh Rahma (sjeeg Rama), Sheikh `Abdol-Sheikh (sjeeg Abdul Sjeeg) and Sheikh `Abdol Khur (sjeeg Abdul Khoer) and it all had happened on August 26. Sheikh Madhkur (Sjeeg Maskoer) had also been murdered and his nephew had been taken prisoner. This news caused panic among the authorities ashore throughout the Persian Gulf down to the Euphrates. Since the *na'eb* of Gamron, Aqa Baqer, had no force to oppose an attack by the mutineers, he asked the Dutch for help to protect the remaining vessels of the fleet and the town. The Dutch declined the honor saying their ships were in too bad a state due to the heavy storm to defend the city and fleet. The rebels meanwhile had split up. Sheikh Rahma had gone to Kong with the *Fatti Sjahi*, two smaller ships and most of the best smaller vessels. `Abdol-Sheikh had fled with two small ships and 10 *tranki*s and had hidden somewhere near Qeshm. The mutineers had plans to take the remaining ships as well, viz. a one master and a two-mast vessel, whose crews had refused to rebel. At the same time they were believed to pillage the coast area as well *en passant*. The *na'eb* of Gamron, Aqa Baqer, came to the Dutch factory to ask for naval assistance. The mutineers had neither ammunition nor food supplies and had to resupply themselves. If that were to happen the mutiny would spread and they would ravage the Persian Gulf and take all the Arab areas then under Persian control. Such a situation was bad for the shah as well as Dutch trade. The mutineers would jump overboard the moment they would see the Dutch ship and it would

---

124. VOC 2546, Koenad to Batavia (31/03/1740), f. 30-32; Ibid., Resolution Gamron (25/08/1740), f. 164-74.

earn the Dutch the shah's favor. The Dutch only had to take his men on board and sail for Laft to overtake the mutineers. If they were not there then they had to sail to Kong, which was one of their bases. Clement, the deputy-director received Aqa Baqer and told him that he would write to Koenad who was in the village of Ormund-Ghinaw at 3.5 German miles.[125] He added, however, that *de Cronenburg* was unable to sail, because its rigging was entirely down, it had insufficient ballast and it would take a few days to make it sea-worthy. By that time the Arabs would have come to their senses. Moreover, the crew of the *Middenrak* was tired. Aqa Baqer insisted on immediate help, but Clement told him that a ship was not a horse that only required a saddle to be ready for use. Aqa Baqer swore by the head of the prophet, the shah and the Koran that this service and all previous ones would not be forgotten. Because writing to Koenad would take too much time Aqa Baqer would ride to Ghinaw and kiss his feet, and not leave until he had promised his assistance. Koenad told the representative of the council, Willem Slaars, that he could not order them, being not in the factory and taking the waters for his old, sick and plagued body, he would agree with whatever the council decided. The council did not like this and under pressure of the pleas by Aqa Baqer, the fear of being accused of help-ing the rebels and the real need, the Dutch on September 6 decided to permit *De Cronenburgh* and *De Middenrak* to provide the requested assistance. An additional reason was that the shah might give the Dutch more privileges and repay the royal debt; moreover, if the Arabs became stronger at sea the navigation between Bushehr and Basra might be endangered as well as the supply lines between the Dutch factory and Qeshm. However, the ships were only allowed to sail to Laft and Kong and not farther. On both ships an interpreter was stationed (assistant Slaars and a Persian who spoke Dutch). Slaars was also charged, at the request of Aqa Baqer, to hail the Arab mutineers and to promise them that if they surrendered no punitive steps would be taken against them. The Dutch demanded a written and sealed pardon for the mutineers, or else they would not perform that service, which document they received. Both ships left on September 8, 1740.[126]

The dispenser, Jacob Carelsz., complained about the damage done to the supply ves-sels, because of the regular ferrying of supplies to Kong, Jolfar, Basidu, Laft and Bahrain. These supplies included heavy canon, camels, and horses. Two of the vessels could not be used any-more, so that he had them publicly cut up as firewood. In addition, there was the cost of the *nakhoda*s or ships' captains, who had been pressed to transport the heavy cannon. Total cost had been 2,436 mahmudis (Dfl. 1,060:16). The *daryabegi* also had been appointed as governor of the Dashistan and informed the newly appointed castellan of Fort Naderiyeh, Hoseyn Khan Beg (Hossein Chan Beek), of his new function.[127]

On September 7, 1740 the ships *Tavakkol, the Captain* and *de Pol* with Sheikh ʿAbdol-Sheikh's family who had embarked as well sailed to Basidu followed by the two Dutch ships.

---

125. The mountain village of Ghinaw is situated at 18 miles from Gamron. The prefix Ormond probably an incorrect rendering of the name of one of the seven springs at the village, in this case may be the Imam spring. Sadid al-Saltaneh, *Bandar ʿAbbas va Khalij-e Fars* ed. Ahmad Eqtedari (Tehran, 1342/1963), pp. 18-19.

126. VOC 2546, Resolution Gamron (06/09/1740), f. 234-72; VOC 2546. Koenad to Batavia (31/03/1740), f. 33-37; VOC 2546, secret instruction for Slaars (07/09/1740), f. 1664-68.

127. VOC 2546, Resolution Gamron (25/09/1740), f. 213-20, 314 (Mohammad Taqi *daryabegi* was also *beglerbegi* of Dashtestan. His messenger (*chapar*) was Hoseyn Khan Beg, who was the newly appointed castellan of Fort Naderiyeh).

On September 11 they sighted the two ships with seven smaller vessels. *De Cronenburgh* by that time was closing the gap with *de Middenrak* and both of them attacked. Sheikh `Abdol-Sheikh fled, however, in which he was successful, for the Dutch could not get him within gun range. *De Pol* aimed for shore. The galley accompanying the Dutch was ordered to remain close behind *the Tavakkol* and stick to it and try to do it as much damage as possible. However, after two shots and hitting nothing the galley turned away. From there the squadron sailed to Kong, which, like all other ports had rebelled, to take in water and firewood. The Dutch ships there-fore, against the wishes of Mohammad Baqer Beg returned to take two two-masters and 20 smaller vessels (*tarrad*s, *tranki*s), which were lying ashore at Laft. Mohammad Baqer Beg had wanted to return to Kong but the Dutch captains refused, for the rebel Arabs had plundered the town and were still surrounding it and not allowing anybody ashore. On September 23, after having taken some animals at Qeshm belonging to `Abdol-Sheikh, the squadron returned to Gamron.[128]

The new *daryabegi*, Mohammad Taqi Khan Masjeddie[129] [?], a relative of the shah, with great insistence and persistence, demanded that the Dutch lend him ships to attack the rebels and get the 19 royal ships back from them. Koenad replied that the Dutch ships had just returned from assisting the government and he first needed time to assess their condition. The *daryabegi* said on September 26, 1740 that he needed a decision that day. He reminded them of the fact that the *mostowfi al-mamalek* had ordered (by a letter arrived on the previous day) that each time convoying ships had to be made available for the supply ships going to Jolfar or elsewhere, by both the VOC and the EIC. He would not insist on it, for else the Dutch were in trouble. He promised that as soon as he would get the *Fatti Sjahi* he would let the Dutch ships return, and would not bother about the *mostowfi al-mamalek*'s orders which he admitted were obnoxious. Widwell, the EIC agent, had offered his assistance as soon as the English would get a ship on the roads, and that he personally would command them against the Arabs. At the *daryabegi*'s request he also had sent threatening letters to Sheikh `Abdol-Sheikh. If he would re-turn *the Tavakkol* and *De Paal* and the 10 to 12 lesser vessels and anchor them on the roadstead in front of the English factory he would be forgiven. He would be, moreover, granted a robe of honor and get back the *kalantar*ship of Qeshm. If he would not comply with this demand Widwell promised that he had sworn to pursue him to the end of the world. He also, to make his verbal support more credible, undertook to equip two barquetines which the Dutch had brought from Qeysh, on September 23, 1740 with ammunition, supplies, crews, lead, powder and guns and to make them sea-worthy again. The barquetines would fly the English colors when they would accompany the Dutch ships he had decided. The Dutch finally decided to agree to the Persian request on the following conditions: [i] in case of damage to the Dutch ships the Persian government would be pay for the repairs; [ii] in case ships of the royal fleet were damaged the Dutch would not be responsible; [iii] no Persian troops would board Dutch ships; [iv] in case of attack the Dutch were in charge, and the Persians would not interfere with Dutch command of the ships; [v] the Persian admiral would supply the ships with sufficient water and firewood; and [vi] after having accomplished their tasks at Bahrain, Nakhilu or

128. VOC 2546, Middenrak to Gamron (10/09/1740), f. 1407; VOC 2546, idem to idem (18/09/1740), f. 1408-10; VOC 2546, Dagregister Middenrak, f. 1415; VOC 2546, Koenad to Emamverdi Khan (25/09/1740), f. 1871-74.

129. I have not been able to identify this person. The term 'Masjeddie' or variation thereof may be Majidi or Masjedi.

Bushehr the ships would be allowed to return immediately. To reinforce the military capability of the ships the Dutch put a squad of soldiers on each ship.[130]

Meanwhile, Emam Verdi Khan was also taking measures to collect forces at Bushehr. He sent an instruction (ta`liqeh) to Mohammad Baqer Beg and Mohammad Qasem Beg in which "this Nero" gave orders to take the VOC two-master *de Valk* which was lying on the roadstead of Bushehr and all other vessels they could lay their hands on. These had to be charged with supplies sufficient for one month and to be manned with 300 soldiers all of which had to be obtained from Sheikh Madhkur of Bushehr. They had to board these vessels and sail to Nakhilu where he himself would arrive on 22 Rajab 1153 or October 10, 1740. Any ships met en route had to be pressed into the royal service as well. He also informed the Dutch agent in Bushehr, Schoonderwoerd, about his orders, although he added that, he had asked Gamron to give their agreement. Although Schoonderwoerd replied that *de Valk* had to be repaired and had no military equipment, it was of no avail. Due to the heavy pressure Schoonderwoerd gave in on October 5, 1740 to transport some troops to Nakhilu. Mohammad Qasem Beg boarded the ship on October 7 and he arrived on November 2, 1740 in Gamron.[131] Emamverdi Khan had left Hallohosier [?] and had gone to Nakhilu. At that time it was reported that the rebel fleet was near Henderabi [?] (Injiwa), an island near Kong where all the Hulas and their families had fled.[132] Sheikh Madhkur was summoned to Shiraz on November 28, 1740 to discuss measures to induce the Hulas to return the ships, which he was ordered to try to bring about.[133] The English agent made good his promise; he put his small salute cannon on aboard, some Indian soldiers under a European corporal, and hoisted the English flag. This development; put the Dutch into an awkward position and they therefore decided to lend their ships as well in order not to loose Nader's favor. On October 3, 1740 Mohammad Taqi Khan, the *daryabegi* boarded *de Middenrak* and `Ali Soltan *de Cronenburgh*; the *Royal Galley* was commanded by the EIC constable. It was first decided that course would be set to Khor Fakkan (where the *Tavakkol* and *de Paal* were), but later the *daryabegi* had second thoughts and preferred to go to Qeysh where the big ships were (Fatti Sjahi, Capitaine, Fat Rahmaniyeh). They then sailed to

130. VOC 2546, Resolution Gamron (26/09/1740), f. 275-305; VOC 2546. Koenad to Batavia (31/03/1740), f. 38; VOC 2546, Koenad to Emamverdi Khan (27/09/1740), f. 1875; VOC 2546, Koenad to Emamverdi Khan (01/10/1740), f. 1879 (on their return from Laft, the two Dutch ships were out of firewood and drinking water, which was being seen to day-and-night right then, so that they only would be able to depart on October 3).

131. VOC 2546, Schoonderwoerd to Koenad (08/10/1740), f. 1346-47; VOC 2546, Emamverdi Khan to Koenad (28/10/1740 received), f. 1756-58' VOC 2546, Tallega from Emamverdi Khan for Mohammad Baqer Beg and Mohammad Qasem Beg (24/10/1740 received from Bushir), f. 1849–51; VOC 2546, Emamverdi Khan to Schoonderwoerd (24/10/1740 received copy), f. 1153-54 (Arabs have mutinied, the Dutch have to help. On 9 Rajab I arrived in Fale Assur and learnt that Dutch two-master was at Naderiyeh; keep it there and await further orders); VOC 2546, Emamverdi Khan to Schoonderword (26/11/1740), f. 1855-56 (both you and received letter Koenad approving the lending of Dutch ship; ready it for use), for this letter see VOC 2546, Koenad to Emamverdi Khan (01/10/1740), f. 1880 (agreed to the lending of the ship, if it was not fully loaded); VOC 2546, Schoonderword to Emamverdi Khan (24/10/1740), f. 1843 (*de Valk* has to be repaired; it has no war supplies and thus can be of little service); VOC 2546, Resolution Gamron (27/11/1740), f. 498, 517.

132. VOC 2546, Schoonderwoerd to Koenad (11/10/1740), f. 1355. *De Valk* called on Halileh to take Mier Asmeddin on board at Emamverdi Khan's orders. VOC 2546, Schoonderwoerd to Koenad (09/11/1740), f. 1158.

133. VOC 2546, Schoonderwoerd to Koenad (31/01/1741), f. 1391.

Kong to have talks with Emamverdi Khan, the *sardar*, but en route the latter ordered them to go to Nakhilu where he had already arrived. He had learnt from two prisoners that all cannons of the ships were ashore, and that the sails of *the Captain* were unrigged. Around the island the Arabs had built artillery platforms and during the night not more than 50 men per ship guarded the ships. But since the enemy was in sight the *daryabegi* wrote the *sardar* that taking council was useless. On October 15, 1740 the fleet saw 15 vessels fleeing from Qeysh where, having arrived there, they sighted 60 to 70 vessels. Willem Slaars, the Dutch deputy, suggested to the *daryabegi* to take this attractive booty but he declined. When `Ali Soltan also urged him to do so he sent a boat with six men ashore. At 23.00 hours, four of them returned without the envoy, who had been killed on the beach without having been heard. The next day anchors were raised and the fleet sailed past Qeysh and saw 14 vessels. These were hunted and some cannon balls were shot at the houses of the enemy with good effect. Because the enemy vessels sailed close to the reef the Galley and some other small vessels pursued them. At 09.00 one of the enemy vessels was taken, the other three beached. At 15.00 hours the fleet saw three vessels at Sho`eyb (Sjab) engaged the enemy, who was coming towards the fleet. *De Cronenburgh*, which was in a bad state and had orders to keep out of cannon range, if possible, was engaged by a two-master and many small vessels followed by *the Captain* and 60 smaller vessels. The *Fatti Sjahi* attacked *de Middenrak* and the battle would have gone bad for this small Dutch ship if at 10.00 hours *de Cronenburgh* had not come to its assistance. They then together gave full blast at the *Fatti Sjahi* until 13.00 hours. The Persian *tranki*s, which had accompanied the Dutch ships, had fled as soon as the shooting started, while the Arabs had still many *tranki*s lying ashore. The *Fatti Sjahi* responded in kind and gave the Dutch a good return. It was supported by two ships and 110 well armed and well manned *tranki*s. At 13.00 hours the Dutch found that they had depleted their balls and powder considerably while they had suffered one dead and eight wounded (*Cronenburgh*) and two dead and two wounded (*Middenrak*). Moreover, the big mast of *de Cronenburgh* was damaged, its sails sieved and many ropes shot to pieces; it had become almost helpless due to the heavy fire from the *Fatti Sjahi*. At 16.00 hours, the two Dutch captains held council and decided that in view of their instructions, the fact that *de Cronenburgh* mast would break in a storm and the ship had received 50 direct hits they had to withdraw. For although they had kept their ground they would be unable to defeat the enemy. Slaars informed the *daryabegi* about this, who agreed to it. He said that he was very pleased with their performance, for he had never seen anything like it before and would publicly report it to the shah and the *sardar*. The Dutch did not know the damage which the enemy had suffered, but they were sure the outcome would have been different if the Arabs had not had so many *tranki*s with such good crews, while their own 19 Persian *tranki*s had been less well supplied and their crew lacked both the courage and skills of the Arabs.[134]

---

134. VOC 2546, Resolution brede scheepsraad (01/11/1740), f. 403-09, 411-12 (list of wounded), 413-14 (how much powder and how many balls had been shot); Ibid., report on rigging and sails lost-damaged and ammunition used, f. 416-26. The local gunpowder cost 7.5 *mahmudis* per 6 lbs.; VOC 2546, Koenad to Batavia (31/03/1740), f. 39. VOC 2546, Dagregister on event near (Qeysh) Keyts and Sho`eyb (Sjab), f. 1423-37; VOC 2546, Koenad to Emamverdi Khan (Nakhilu) (24/10/1740), f. 1889-90 (*daryabegi* and your *nazer*, Mohammad Beg Soltan, the *soltan* of Dashtestan returned here on 23/10/1740; gives details about the fierce battle; the enemy had 300-400 *tarrads* and smaller vessels; Dutch casualties; damage to ships). Koenad also wrote to Nader informing him about the battle and the assistance provided by the Dutch. He further pointed out that he impossibly could continuously keep a ship on the roadstead as Nader had instructed. VOC 2546, Koenad to Wali Nahmed Sjahinsjah in Khorasan (04/12/1740), f. 1912-15.

Although the *daryabegi* publicly showed his satisfaction about Dutch support, the *sardar* had different ideas, and wrote them that he was not satisfied. The Dutch wrote about this to the *daryabegi*, who replied that this was due to the *sardar*'s lack of experience, and that he would inform him properly. It would, of course, also help if the Dutch escorted supply vessel to and from Jolfar and Kong and would try to induce the rebels to come to an agreement with the shah he suggested. The Dutch therefore sent Slaars, a man well versed in Arabic and Persian, who, moreover, had a winning way with the speakers of both languages. He was well received by Emamverdi Khan in Kong in front of his troops. He publicly praised the Dutch and denigrated the English, who promised much, but only gave honeyed words. Although he promised to help the Dutch in getting a decree on the silk trade and other matters his main contribution was to order the *na'eb* of Gamron to help them collect outstanding debts. Slaars on his departure received a robe of honor from Emamverdi Khan, who, in front of his troops read the letter, which he would send to Nader listing the services the Dutch had rendered to the state and how well they had fought against the rebels.[135]

Koenad informed Emamverdi Khan about the return of the *daryabegi* and his *nazer*, Mohammad Beg, the *soltan* of Dashtestan, on October 23, 1740 and gave a report of their activities, the sea battle and the extent of the casualties suffered. A few days later he wrote to Emamverdi Khan that the latter's request to send ships to Kong to transport troops could not be complied with in view of the state of the ships, which needed repairs badly. Emamverdi Khan who was en route from Nakhilu to Kong replied that he did not understand why the Dutch ships, supported by Persian *trankis*, could not defeat and take the Arabs. He was not happy about the result and assured Koenad that it would do the Dutch name no good. He therefore asked him to keep the ships ready and send them to Kong, for after the arrival of *de Valk* from Bushehr he intended to attack the Arabs himself and to tell the Dutch crews to be courageous.[136]

After Koenad's reply Emamverdi Khan sang a different tune and he assured Koenad that "his face was white." He did not understand why the Dutch ships had been unable to get the Arab mutineers, but after repair of the ships he would attack them himself. Emamverdi Khan had written to the *daryabegi* at Ganaveh [?] (Ghinoe) and had ordered him to take in supplies and sail his fleet to Kong from where he had to go to Jolfar. The Dutch ships also would be needed for royal service and Koenad had to give his ships the same instructions. For the Arabs from Mangoese and Ghinoese[137] Arabs at the island (*jazirat*) of Qeysh (Jiszerit Qeish) had decided to subject themselves, which would be speeded up when they saw the big Dutch ships. He later assured the Dutch that he had appreciated all their services so far and that he would favorably report to Nader about it.[138]

---

135. VOC 2546, Resolution Gamron (26/11/1740), f. 507, 508-09 (Slaars asked Emamverdi Khan for an order to obtain payment of the Minab debt. The debtors included Kalb`Ali Beg, the *kalantar*, and Morteza Qoli Beg and other leading men of Minab); VOC 2546, Koenad to Batavia (31/03/1740), f. 40-44. The *sardar* did not want to assign these debts on the customs revenues because Mohammad Taqi Khan had already collected them entirely, without the shah knowing it. Slaars died on January 18, 1741 and the VOC lost a very able and eloquent defender of its interests.

136. VOC 2546, Emamverdi Khan (Nakhilu) to Koenad (28/10/1740 received), f. 1756-58.

137. Probably the Arabs from Moghu and Ganaveh, both Persian Gulf coastal settlements, are meant here. See Floor, "A Description."

138. VOC 2546, Emamverdi Khan (Kong) to Koenad (Sha`ban 1153; 30/10/1740 received), f. 1759-

Meanwhile, piracy at sea had increased enormously between September 8 and December 1, 1740 and Emamverdi Khan even feared an attack on Kong. The shah's troops lacked all kinds of supplies, both food and military. In Gamron everybody was on his guard as well. The Dutch had their ships well supplied and prepared in case of an attack, while their biggest cannons and a big mortar aimed at sea. Two 12-pounders on the SW bulwark also were aimed at sea.[139] This led again to urgent and repeated demands for the use of their ships to escort vessels with supplies to Jolfar. The Dutch finally gave in on December 3, 1740 in view of the dire straits the Persian troops there were in. However, a few days later Koenad reported that the *gallivat* commanded by Mhamed Beg, which had come from Jolfar had seen no sign of Arabs rebels, so that the escort was no longer needed.[140]

CONTINUED PRESSURE TO LEND SHIPS

The Persian officials continued to press the Dutch to transport ammunition, powder, balls, and food to Jolfar for the Persian invasion force. This pressure increased when the *daryabegi* returned from Jolfar on November 29, 1740 en route to Emamverdi Khan in Kong. He wanted to urge the latter to send a relief force as soon as possible. Emamverdi Khan's servants also came to see Koenad to discuss a new voyage of Dutch ships to Kong. Koenad informed Emamverdi Khan in writing that this was impossible due to the damage the ships had suffered and in particular their rigging that had been totally ruined. Already the next day Emamverdi Khan asked the Dutch to provide naval assistance not to Kong, but to do convoy duty to Jolfar. Koenad repeated once again that his crews were repairing the ships day-and-night, a work that had not finished yet. Also, the wounded had to convalesce; while he pointed out that the Dutch were not in Bandar `Abbbas to wage war, but to trade. On November 29, 1740, the *sardar* told Slaars in Kong that he preferred to wait the return of the *Galley*, which had left for Jolfar on November 25, 1740 to learn the latest news about the enemy. The latter had only ill intentions and attacked anybody at sea. The *Galley* returned on December 1, 1740 without having seen the enemy, though the Jolfar garrison complained about the lack of food. Therefore, that same night the Dutch were pestered to provide convoy for the boats that transported the supplies. The *sardar* wanted an immediate reply, because he had to answer the Imam's letter of November 15 and 29, 1740 and to appease him through the relief of Jolfar. The Dutch wrote back that there was no trace of the enemy, so there was no need to protect the supply boats; this task could be taken care of by the *Galley*. The *daryabegi*'s letter to the *sardar* contained the following information: An Arab sailor who had fled to his family in Jolfar had said that the mutineers were in Qeysh (Kiets) and Sho`eyb (Sjahab). The *daryabegi*'s guards patrolling the coast confirmed this information. The *soltan* of Jolfar, Mohammed Beg [?] (Mahmed Boca) reported that he suffered from lack of supplies, which discouraged his troops, while it incited the enemy. He therefore had ordered Sheikh Naser to send 30,000 *mann* (240,000 lbs.) of food supplies and 3,000-4,000 *mann* of powder and lead (2,400-3,200 lbs.) under Dutch protection to Jolfar as soon as possible. Because the risk was too high to have these supplies fall into the hands of the Arabs the Dutch decided to help with three ships. At that time

60; VOC 2546, idem to idem (11/11/1740 received), f. 1765.

139. For an exact inventory of the caliber and localization of all cannons in the Dutch factory. VOC 2477, f. 202.

140. VOC 2546, Koenad to Emamverdi Khan (06/12/1740), f. 1930-34; VOC 2546, Koenad to Batavia (31/03/1740), f. 45-57.

it was assumed that `Abdol-Sheikh was at Jolfar-Khor (Jolph a ghoor) [a creek behind the strip of land on which Jolfar was situated], while the other Arabs were near Qeysh and Sho`eyb, and therefore the ships had to look out for them.[141] On December 5, 1740 Emamverdi Khan wanted to know why there had not arrived any Dutch ships at Gamron as was usually the case at that time of the year. He especially sent one of his decurions (*deh-bashi*s), Sheikh `Ali, to learn more about this matter. Apparently he still had plans to attack the Arabs, although this visit produced no further development.[142]

Despite the military actions undertaken against them, there was some willingness on the Arab side to return to the Persian fold. Mirza Taqi Khan, *mostawfi al-mamalek* and Nader's confidante, had been able to induce the shah to promise a pardon to those Arab mutineers who would return the ships that they had taken. Two sheikhs wrote to Koenad from Qeshm that the shah had ordered to return the ships that they had taken to Gamron, where they would be given a receipt, which would be sent to the shah as proof of their loyalty. However, they were cautious and wrote that they had taken the ships to Qeshm to return them, under protection of some of their own vessels. If the shah could use them he was welcome to them, if not they would take them back. The Dutch did not reply to avoid being accused of being in league with the mutineers, so that the two sheikhs wrote that they still had not received a reply to their previous letter. They therefore did not know whether they were considered to be friends or not, which indicates that the Dutch were supposed to provide protection for them. The two sheikhs further reported that some Hulas that were with them had mistakenly taken two large Dutch supply vessels and three smaller ones at Laft, which they would return.[143] The Arabs also had taken English, French and other supply vessels, which "bound our hands," wrote Koenad. He further reported that the Arabs with much audacity burnt, plundered and destroyed the homes of the population of Qeshm right in front of the Persian officials. The latter did not do anything to help the poor populace not even transport 2,000 soldiers from Gamron which the vessels that were available there.[144]

`Abdol Sheikh sent a reply to a letter sent by Widwell, the English director in which he wrote that on hearing the rumor that Mehr `Ali Khan had died he had summoned his foot soldiers and had gone to Laft. He also had informed Miersa Mahmet Momim that he had mustered his men. The latter had replied that he had had been the cause of the incident and that it was therefore unnecessary to send soldiers, which `Abdol-Sheikh had intended to use to stop ships passing by. Seeing how things stood and that the men were in a killing mood and were already enslaving women and children he decided that it was in his best interest to flee. He did his best to go to Basidu or elsewhere to get ships so that he might sent news to Widwell. Near Basidu the Company ships had come so close to him that `Abdol-Sheikh

---

141. VOC 2546, Koenad to Emamverdi Khan (Kong) (29/10/1740), f. 1894-95; VOC 2546, Koenad to Emamverdi Khan (Kong) (01/11/1740), f. 1896-1900 (the Dutch also fired their cannon to celebrate Nader's victory in Turkestan); VOC 2546, Resolution Gamron (03/12/1740), f. 522-29.

142. VOC 2546, Emamverdi Khan to Koenad (received 09/12/1740).

143. VOC 2546, Sjeeg Shajin and Sjeeg Rama from Jazirat Daraz (09/04/1741 received), f. 1814; VOC 2546, idem to idem (09/04/1741 received), f. 1815; VOC 2546, idem to idem (09/04/1741 received), f. 1816-17. Koenad replied that only one letter had arrived via the English; there also had been a problem with translation as Slaars, who knew Arabic had died. He advised the sheikhs to return the vessels. VOC 2546, Koenad to Sjeeg Shahin and Sjeeg Rahma on the Long Island (10/04/1741), f. 1961-63.

144. VOC 2546, Koenad to Batavia (15/04/1741), f. 142-43.

had wanted to send a letter or a message by someone, but he was greeted with gunfire and he therefore fled. `Abdol-Sheikh did not dare to return, because he did not expect anything good from it, although he had brought together a lot of Arabs with him in peace. However, he could not stay because of all the violence that was being committed. When `Abdol Latif Khan (sic; properly Mohammad Latif Khan) was admiral `Abdol-Sheikh had fled with all Arabs. Then a royal decree had promised the restitution of all the goods taken from him if he would return. He believed and trusted the royal decree, but he did not even get one *dinar*, neither his cattle nor his vessels. `Abdol-Sheikh then wanted to stay on without his property, but they had not allowed that either. He barely had arrived in Masqat when tax collectors (*mohassel*) arrived to take the few animals that he had there. In view of that experience why should he now return and have trust, `Abdol-Sheikh asked.[145]

On April 3, 1741 a letter arrived from Emamverdi Khan in Kong for the *daryabegi* in Gamron in which he reported that his men (who patrolled the coast between Kong and Charak [Tjareek]) had spotted the Hulas with the *Fatti Sjahi*, one other ship, and 30 to 40 *tarrad*s and other smaller vessels anchored at Shinas[146] on Wednesday 11 Moharram 1154 (20/03/1741). Later these ships had sailed past Kong at night, whilst ship movements had also been observed in the direction of Basidu. He assumed that the *daryabegi* of course had sent the two master *tarrad*s and other royal vessels to get the ordered vessels from Sind, which were sent by Shah Qoli Khan, its governor. Only if they were still within reach he had to send the *galwat* after them to alert them. He therefore ordered the *daryabegi* to find out where the Hulas were and what their intentions were, for he was worried that they would sail towards Sind to intercept the new ships. He also instructed him to ask the Dutch to send their four ships via Khor (?)[147] (Ghoor) to Kong. He then would embark and sail to Jazireh-ye Qeysh (Jessierigh Keyts) and Sho`eyb (Sjaheb) to destroy the Hulas. The Dutch, however, refused to lend their ships for this purpose; two ships (*Slot te Cronenburg* and *Middenrak*) were ready to make the return voyage to Batavia. *De Ketel* had not even been unloaded, while there was the chance of an attack by the Hulas on Gamron, as they had done on the other side of the Gulf. The *daryabegi* was vexed by this reaction and sent the Dutch a letter on April 4, 1741 saying that now a unique opportunity offered itself. They had the ships; the Hulas were concentrated at Shinas and would just surrender on the sight of the Dutch. He therefore was not pleased with this totally unexpected answer. However, the Dutch persisted in their refusal and the Persian generals did not make any further trouble.[148] The Dutch were unable to unload *de Ketel*, because all porters had fled into mountains after the town officials had demanded 800 *mahmudi*s in so-called *hammali* fees from them, and also because they were afraid to be killed. After the Dutch lent the porters 600 *mahmudi*s they returned and started to work. Due to the delay, it was by then June 1740, *de Ketel* could not leave anymore, due to the changed monsoon.[149]

---

145. VOC 2546, Abdul Sjeeg in reply to Widwell (12/10/1740 secretly received from the *na'eb*), f. 1752-55; VOC 2546, f. 1725 (Rhama son of Sjahin Naghiloehi wrote that after the mutiny he had fled with his ships to Sjahi and Bandar Hoela). The Dutch believed that Sheikh Rahma had returned the ships that he had taken. VOC 2546, Koenad to Batavia (31/03/1741), f. 50.

146. A small village near Kong.

147. I do not know to which Khor or inlet the text is referring to.

148. VOC 2583, Resolution Gamron (15/04/1741), f. 179-188; VOC 2584, Koenad to Welie Nhamet now Sjahinsjah (18/11/1741).

149. VOC 2583, Resolution Gamron (19/04/1741), f.202; Ibid. (07/06/1741), f. 322-24, 326-32.

Koenad, who later wrote to Nader Shah about these events reported that the Dutch had advised against this action, because the Hulas had much and better maritime experience and that without 10 big ships and 150 smaller vessels, all well equipped and crewed with experienced men, nothing effective could be done anymore. For such an operation would only result in the strengthening of the enemy, while the Dutch ships were exposed to danger, although they had only been sent to Persia to serve the interests of the VOC,i.e., to carry on trade and not tarry long in the Persian Gulf. Koenad also drew the shah's attention to the fact that the local authorities pressed half laden vessels into their service as well as porters, which they even took from the Dutch factory, although the royal decrees forbade such activities.[150]

It was only on June 17, 1741 that Mohammad Baqer Beg and `Ali Soltan of Dashtestan, on behalf of Emamverdi Khan, again asked the Dutch for the use of *de Ketel* to sail with another Dutch ship and English vessels against the Hulas. At Kong, Persian troops would board the proposed flotilla. The Dutch refused, however, for *de Ketel* was undermanned and had a crew suffering from illness. It moreover had to return to Batavia very soon. Koenad also sent instructions to Bushehr to order Schoonderwoerd to refuse the use of *de Valk* based on the same arguments.[151] On August 10, 1741 the same officials again called on Koenad to inform him about the dispersal of the Hulas. The strongest group intended to go to Masqat, and the remainder would seek refuge elsewhere they reported. They had been ordered to contain the Hulas with their own vessels, but they also had to ask the Dutch for one ship to make sure that they would be successful. Koenad again refused, but Mohammad Baqer Beg told him not to make life difficult for all those concerned. If only he would sail to Qeshm, to fetch water and firewood, and stay there for a week he would do them a service while the VOC would suffer no harm at all. He implied that in this way the suggestion that the Dutch were having contacts with the Hulas, as had been inferred by Emamverdi Khan, would be proven wrong. He agreed that the Dutch arguments were reasonable, and he was willing to report these to Emamverdi Khan, but he did not want to so before warning Koenad about the possible disadvantageous consequences of such action. Under this veiled threat, and the easy way out given to them, the Dutch agreed to what Mohammad Baqer Beg had proposed and send *de Ketel* to Qeshm.[152] As a result, the Dutch at Gamron had no vessels themselves and they therefore felt rather helpless, because they could not expect assistance from anybody. The native sailors and carpenters were still hiding in the date plantations out of fear for the violence that they would be exposed to when transporting 300 cannons, which they were expected to do. Nevertheless, Koenad still hoped that *de Ketel* might return to Batavia on September 26, 1741.[153]

However, events took a different turn. On August 27, 1741, the Dutch received a letter from Emamverdi Khan that he would leave Kazerun [?] (Canderoen) on 18 Jomadi al-Thani (August 31, 1741) at the orders of Nader Shah and that he expected to arrive after one week in Gamron. He asked Koenad to detain all Dutch ships, and if these had left already to send a vessel after them to have them return. If the Dutch would not comply with this request

---

150. VOC 2584, Koenad to Welie Nhamet now Sjahinsjah (18/11/1741), f. 2568-71.

151. VOC 2584, Koenad to Schoonderwoerd (18/06/1741), f. 1446-49.

152. VOC 2583, Resolution Gamron (15/08/1741), f. 395-400; VOC 2584, Tallega by Mohammad Baqer Beg, deputy governor of Gamron (21/08/1741) to Amir Heydar Beg, *kutval* or castellan of Qeshm to help the Dutch vessel that would come to fetch water.

153. VOC 2583, Resolution Gamron (13/09/1741), f. 474-75.

they would incur the shah's disfavor and would feel his displeasure. Soon after his arrival he asked for the loan of *de Ketel*, which was at anchor at Qeshm. He had information that something had gone wrong in Hengam, and was afraid that the Arabs had taken his vessels lying there. He would send `Ali Soltan with 25 men as an auxiliary force aboard. The Dutch were willing to make this trip, but refused to take Persian soldiers aboard. Mohammad Baqer, however, advised them to give in, for Emamverdi Khan already had a low opinion about the Dutch attitude towards Persian interest due to slander. He, moreover, intimated that if the Dutch gave in on this point they would certainly not be asked to lend a ship for the transportation of Mozaffar `Ali Khan who was about to arrive with 800 horses and 1,200 men to make a journey to Divil-Sind. To forgo the doubtful pleasure the Dutch finally acquiesced. The captain of *de Ketel* was instructed that if he faced a force of one ship and eight vessels he had to try to chase them away. If that would fail he had to return immediately to Gamron. He moreover had to use as few balls as was necessary and not to endanger his ship. The next day the Dutch learnt that Emamverdi Khan had ulterior motives. For he was convinced that prior to VOC director Gutchi's death he had promised Mohammad Taqi Khan Shirazi that he would sell one of the VOC ships to the Persian government. Now that Gutchi had died Emamverdi Khan was afraid that the Dutch would retract this promise. Koenad informed the *sardar* that he was mistaken and that Gutchi never could have made such a promise, since nobody had the authority to sell a ship without the express wish instructions from Batavia. Emamverdi Khan became very angry on receiving this news and remarked that the Dutch did not want to help Nader Shah, the conqueror of India and of half of Turkey. However, they assisted his enemies with supplies and food, especially Sheikh Rahma. He realized that they did not want the shah to have a fleet, but they need not worry. The shah would put things aright. Formerly the VOC paid each year so-called treaty goods to the value of 1,000 *tuman*s, the total arrears of which amounted to 20,000 *tuman*s, which was sufficient to buy six ships. He then walked away in anger, but after having calmed down a bit, he very pleasantly told Wissendas, the VOC broker, that he had a perfect solution. Koenad had to sell *de Ketel* to him, which he for appearances sake would take by force and then pay for it. One of his principal servants would leave with Koenad to Batavia as ambassador on the other ship, and would explain his master's action and that he had paid for the ship. For the property of the shah and VOC were one and the same to him where care and consideration was concerned. In this way Koenad would have to fear nothing from his masters.[154]

IRANIANS TAKE CONTROL OF TWO VOC SHIPS

That same evening *de Ketel* returned from its trip. The next day the Persians refused to disembark their soldiers from the ship, for they needed the *sardar*'s permission to do so. They then asked permission for the *daryabegi* and Mohammad Baqer Beg, quinturion (*panj bashi*), to go aboard *de Ketel*. The Dutch refused this as long as the soldiers were still aboard, for they did not trust Persian intentions. They instructed the captain secretly on September 15, 1741 to put the arms all in one place where he could always remain master of them and to be on his guard. Just when they wanted to dispatch these instructions the second mate of *de Ketel* arrived relating that during

---

154. VOC 2584, Emamverdi Khan to Koenad (from Canderoen; received 27/08/1741), f. 2105; VOC 2583, Resolution Gamron (21/09/1741), f. 493-503. For the Dutch text of the letter that Emamverdi Khan wrote to the governor-general see VOC 2584 (18/10/1741 received), f. 2111-15 and for the Dutch text of the contract that he proposed for their use see or VOC 2584 (Rajab 1154/received 08/12/1741), f. 2117-19.

that morning the vice-admiral `Ali Soltan had arrived at *de Ketel* with 25 soldiers pretending to relieve the squad aboard. However, he deceived them and had left the new squad aboard. The Dutch sent their instructions anyway and ordered *de Ridderkerk* to ready its sails and take up a position as close as possible to *de Ketel* and on a signal from that ship to come immediately to its assistance. Koenad, who was at that time in Ghinaw taking the waters, was asked to return in view of the danger to his own person there. The Dutch sent a protest to Emamverdi Khan about `Ali Soltan's behavior and warned him if this would be repeated that all vessels would be fired upon which came to the Dutch ships without a written pass from the council. Emamverdi Khan replied that this was alright with him and that the two officers would not come. However, he insisted on having *de Ketel*, because of Gutchi's promise in reply to the written request by Mohammad Taqi Khan.[155]

Shortly thereafter the Dutch observed that the cannons of the citadel were closely trained on the Dutch factory and were being loaded with balls. They therefore also had their cannons loaded and girded themselves for battle, and armed all inmates of the factory.[156] At 18.00 hours the *sardar* informed the Dutch that he would send `Ali Soltan and Mohammad Baqer Beg to the factory at 20.00 hours. The Dutch accepted this provided they came with no bigger group than six persons. If they would come in larger number the gate would remain closed and they would be considered to be enemies. The delegation arrived on time and asked why the Dutch had refused the visit of the two officers to *de Ketel*, for they were friends not enemies. To this the Dutch replied that the Persians had put 25 soldiers aboard *de Ketel* without their foreknowledge and permission, which was an indication of ill-intentions. They, therefore, had been obliged to take precautionary measures, as was their duty. They again repeated that any unauthorized ship would be fired upon if these approached the Dutch ships. They also requested to withdraw the soldiers from the ship, for they could not guarantee that fights between the crew and the soldiers would not occur. The delegation remarked that surely the Dutch did not consider them to be enemies. The *sardar* only asked to be allowed to buy *de Ketel*. He was prepared to pay 1,500 *tuman*s more than its value, although he personally held the opinion that the Dutch should have made the shah a present of one in view of the long time that the VOC had enjoyed its privileged position in Persia. Because Koenad was so much in fear of his masters, the *sardar* had offered to send one of his servants to Batavia with a letter that he had taken *de Ketel* by force. Koenad replied that this would be not acceptable and that any such action would be opposed by force. He asked them to induce the *sardar* to forget about his demands and if not to give his sufficient time to recall his staff in Isfahan, Bushehr and Kerman for the Dutch then would abandon Persia altogether. He stressed that this would be no sacrifice for them, since no profits were made, while the vexations could not be tolerated any longer. Moreover, if the *sardar* did not want to recall his soldiers he would be forced to take his own measures. `Ali Soltan then asked whether he intended to kill them and

---

155. VOC 2583, Resolution Gamron (21/09/1741), f. 504-12.

156. This event was immediately reported by Emamverdi Khan to Hatem Khan, the governor of Fars who wrote to Koenad that he had heard that the Dutch refused to carry on trade and had closed the gate of their factory. This was not wise, and he therefore gave a friendly warning, because it was harmful to the shah as well as to the VOC and if the shah would hear about it he would not be pleased. Hatem Khan therefore urged Koenad to start trading again so that merchants would be able to make profits; he further wrote that he intended to come to Gamron shortly. VOC 2584, Hatem Khan to Koenad (received 14/1//1741), f. 2137-38.

heave them overboard. For in that case his men would not stand by idle, but use their arms. Koenad, however, assured him that he hoped it would never come to that, but if need be the Dutch knew how to deal with that situation as well, he added. The Persian delegates then asked what reply they had to take back to the *sardar*, for to report what had been said so far his reply would result in the immediate orders to start firing. They suggested that the Dutch asked for a delay till they would have consulted with Koenad. The council thanked the delegates for their suggestion and told them that Emamverdi Khan had better not start shooting, for in that case they would shoot back.[157]

The next day (September 16, 1741) the *sardar* sent for the VOC broker and told him that he requested that Mohammad Baqer Beg, `Ali Soltan, his secretary Mirza Hoseyn, and his private secretary, Mirza Morteza, be allowed to pay a visit to *de Ketel*. To show their good-will the council sent the necessary pass. However, the party did not come with a small vessel but with a large one, which had not been permitted. When they did not respond to the warning *de Ketel* fired one ball before and one behind the vessel. It then stopped and the party was fetched by a boat from *de Ketel*. During their visit they saw that the Dutch were ready for all eventualities for all guns were ready with burning fuses, as if expecting an enemy attack. After their return the *sardar* again requested that his mace bearer and three other unarmed men might visit *de Ketel* the next day, which was allowed.[158]

In the morning of September 17, 1741 Koenad returned from Ghinaw. It was only in the morning of September 20 that Emamverdi Khan, the *sardar* undertook new action by asking for the loan of the two Dutch ships for 25 days to recapture the *Fatti Sjahi*. Koenad replied that this was impossible, as he well knew. The Persian envoys replied that the *sardar* had strict orders to destroy the pirates and he hardly could refuse to carry them out. Koenad drew their attention to all the services the Dutch had already rendered, and how many times they already had lent their ships without authorization. He feared to be punished, for the Dutch ships came here to trade and not to wage war. In the past this had only been done at the request of the shah or the E`temad al-Dowleh. The Persian envoys said that the Dutch had better think it over, the *sardar* was desperate and if he decided to use force the Dutch were only few in number. They asked what reply should they give him, for he was a stubborn man and probably would start firing immediately. Koenad said that he had not changed his mind, but would they return in the afternoon, for the council would discuss the matter further. He added that may be the *sardar* had orders to make war on the VOC, but that he did not have similar orders to make clear where the blame was lying.[159]

In the afternoon, the Dutch sent answer that first the 50 soldiers had to disembark, to which Emamverdi Khan, the *sardar* responded immediately by having them return ashore that same day. He then informed the Dutch that they would have to perform the following royal services, viz. to transport Mozaffar `Ali Khan to Thatta and to assist him with ships against the Hulas. We believed that the transport to Thatta would be difficult for the Dutch, and he could have Mozaffar `Ali Khan travel overland. However, the attack on the Hulas was an easy task

---

157. VOC 2583, Resolution Gamron (21/09/1741), f. 512-21; VOC 2584, Koenad to Welie Nhamet now Sjahinsjah (18/11/1741), f. 2573-77.

158. VOC 2583, Resolution Gamron (21/09/1741), f. 521-24.

159. VOC 2583, Resolution Gamron (21/09/1741), f. 524-31.

that could be done within 25 days. If the Dutch would agree to do it right away they would win the shah's and his favor. When no reply was forthcoming the *sardar* sent Mohammad Baqer Beg to Koenad for an answer. He himself had gone to `Essin where the English regaled him in their garden. Koenad asked whether he could buy off the lending of the ship with a present, but Mohammad Baqer Beg told him that this was impossible. After deliberation the council decided to offer *de Ridderkerk* for the voyage to Thatta, for *de Ketel* had to return to Batavia. The Dutch feared that a flat refusal would have led to hostilities and they were too weak to defend themselves, while the interests of the VOC were in trade and not with war. If attacked they would have to fire back and that would lead to total disaster for VOC staff and goods, the council's majority ruled. A small minority, however, wanted to call the *sardar*'s bluff, for they expected that there would be no end to the vexations and the *sardar* would not give up asking for *de Ketel* as well. Although overruled, they proved to be right.[160]

VOC AGAIN SUPPLIES SHIPS UNDER THREAT

On October 3, 1741 Mozaffar `Ali Khan arrived in Gamron and Emamverdi Khan asked the Dutch to prepare for his transportation to Thatta. The dragoman told the *sardar* that this would be impossible since the ship was too small to take all of Mozaffar `Ali Khan's suite. The *sardar* said Mozaffar `Ali Khan had 800 horses and mules, and the VOC would have to transport at least 300 men, horses and supplies. He would worry about the transportation of the rest. He added that, because had Koenad refused to assist him to fight the Hulas, he had to assume that he was in league with them, as had been reported to him. The dragoman denied this, for the event the *sardar* was referring to had occurred in broad daylight when an Arab had returned a vessel taken by the Hulas from the Dutch. If the Persian officials had reason to suspect that Arab why then had not they arrested him? The *sardar* refused to listen, however, and said that he was certain about the talks between Koenad and the Hulas, which he was prepared to forget, if Koenad complied with his wishes. He then would write to Batavia that Koenad had refused several times. He further ordered that by Saturday the Dutch had to transport Mozaffar `Ali Khan and his 300 men to Thatta. Koenad sent reply that he would try and see what he could do, but the ship had first to be unloaded so he probably would be unable to be ready on time. He added that he hoped that the *sardar* would desist asking for *de Ketel*, for he needed Batavia's authorization to lend him the ship for that purpose. As for being friends of the Arabs he reminded the *sardar* of their sea battle and other actions in 1740 against the Hulas and the fact that their two biggest cannons were aimed towards the seaside to be used in case of an attack from that side.[161]

Emamverdi Khan, the *sardar* did not give up, however. He continued to remind the Dutch to be ready on time, while other officials told the dragoman that it was clear for everybody that the ship was too small to take in Mozaffar `Ali Khan's suite. The *sardar* was ready to forget about the voyage to Thatta if only they would assist him with a ship to attack the Hulas. The dragoman replied that the VOC had never defaulted on his debts, while the reverse was not the case. They replied that if Koenad gave in the *sardar* would see to it that the outstanding debts would be collected immediately. Koenad, however, sent the dragoman with the message

160.   VOC 2583, Resolution Gamron (21/09/1741), f. 523-45; VOC 2584, Koenad to Welie Nhamet now Sjahinsjah (18/11/1741), f. 2581-88.

161.   VOC 2583, Resolution Gamron (07/10/1741), f. 558-74.

that *de Ridderkerk* would go to Thatta and that *de Ketel* would go to Batavia and that this was his final word. Emamverdi Khan became furious and yelled that he had been made a fool of by sweet talk during one month. He ordered the dragoman to tell Koenad that he would destroy the factory and would cause damage to the VOC wherever he could, unless his request was complied with that evening. However, that same evening he still did not have his reply and he therefore vilified the VOC. The next morning Mohammad Aqa Baqer and `Ali Soltan visited the Dutch factory and asked for two ships, to attack the Hulas or to make the trip to Thatta. The *sardar* did not brook any further delay. Begging for ships was too much; he could not execute the shah's orders, who might have his life for that. He therefore, humbly, and for the last time requested the ships for a period of 25 days; he wanted a clear and definite answer, right away. Koenad wanted to persist in his previous reply but the Persian officials said that this would lead to the dissolution of a long friendship. Koenad said that he already had lent *de Ketel* four times. All these ships loans were too big a burden for the VOC, which had better leave Persia altogether. The profits were not much to speak of and he asked them to go to the English or others. The Persian officials asked Koenad whether this small matter was worth a break with Persia, apart from the fact that the *sardar* would not allow them to leave Persia peacefully. Koenad then asked them whether the *sardar* had orders to make war on the Dutch. They countered by asking Koenad whether he had orders to break the relations with Persia and to start a war because of the lending of one ship, to which he said that he had no such orders. The officials did not dare to return with such an answer and asked Koenad to give in. For else disaster would strike, the *sardar* had already given orders to allow no water and firewood to be taken to the Dutch factory as of the next day. He would allow nobody to go in out of the Dutch factory and would starve its inmates, for he would rather die than not execute the shah's orders. Koenad said that he would discuss the matter once again with the council and asked them to return in the afternoon.[162]

Because of the threat of a siege, having only water for three days and a small garrison, and thus unable to man the walls and aim all cannons, an outbreak of hostilities would lead to total ruin for the VOC. The *sardar* then also would claim that they had joined the Hulas. It therefore was better to give in, for already three months had been wasted without any benefit for the VOC while an attack on the Hulas would make navigation in the Persian Gulf safer which also was in the interest of the VOC. Only three members of the council were against giving in, but the rest agreed, on the condition that Emamverdi Khan would sign a contract in which he stated that: he would return the two ships after one month and that he would indemnify the VOC for all damages that the ships would suffer during the action.[163] To Nader Shah Koenad wrote that during the last 100 years the VOC had never before been treated thus in Persia.[164]

---

162. VOC 2583, Resolution Gamron (07/10/1741), f. 575-94; VOC 2584, Koenad to Welie Nhamet now Sjahinsjah (18/11/1741), f. 2589-95.

163. VOC 2583, Resolution Gamron (07/10/1741), f. 595-619. For the Dutch text of the contract with Emamverdi Khan concerning the loan of the ships, Ibid., f. 620-22; VOC 2584, Tallega by Emamverdi Khan to Koenad (Rajab 1154-10/1741), f. 2108 (orders `Abd `Ali Beg, chief of the Long Island to allow its bearer to buy straw, hay, etc. and not to molest him or his vessels); VOC 2584, Tallega Emamverdi Khan (13/10/1741), f. 2123-24 (orders the tax collector or *mohassel* or whoever is in charge of Shamil to allow the Dutch to take as much like as they want without molesting or opposing them).

164. VOC 2584, Koenad to Welie Nhamet now Sjahinsjah (18/11/1741), f. 2596.

Koenad and some council members went personally to the ships to break the news to the crews, who were not in favor of having Persian troops aboard. Emamverdi Khan promised to pay the crew a bonus on the safe return, while he would take care to treat the crew properly. He also gave an order to the local officials to provide the VOC with carpenters and masons to help them repair their boats and the factory. Koenad had the crew line up mid-decks to encourage them and tell them about the bonus. However, he and his council were beset by mutinous sailors who told them that they did not want to go on this trip. They jeered and mocked the council in front of Emamverdi Khan and other Persian officials who also were aboard. They even threatened to keep the council aboard and three times untied the side-rope that fastened their sloop to the ship. The council considered their objections and asked Emamverdi Khan to reduce the number of his men aboard, which he refused. Emamverdi Khan then threatened to take matters into his own hands and ordered some of his soldiers to light their muskets and surrounded the council. The sailors threatened to blow up the ship, but after discussion with the council they were promised good terms and accepted to sail.[165]

However, all troubles were not over. `Ali Soltan and his men acted high-handedly and put the captain and the mate of out of their own cabins and made a kitchen where the captain would not allow it. Emamverdi Khan ordered that `Ali Soltan would not further molest any of the crew of both *de Ketel* and *de Ridderkerk* and to return the cabin to the captain. He further ordered that three cabins had to be prepared for him aboard *de Ketel* and that the kitchen should be prepared at the location indicated by the capitan.[166] When he came aboard, however, new problems arose. Koenad had asked that no more than 30 to 40 Persians be taken aboard. For during battle these would be in the way, due to their lack of seamanship and language difficulties, which could lead to dangerous situations. However, even more soldiers came aboard, despite previous protests, which were ignored. The majority of the crew then jumped overboard and swam ashore claiming that they wanted to be with their captain who had been arrested at the orders of the council, because of his crew's and his own behavior. Emamverdi Khan after having tried via the dragoman to have them stay aboard allowed them to leave, for some hotheads had even been ready to blow up the ship. Only 12 Europeans and two Moslem sailors remained aboard *de Ketel*. `Ali Soltan had the same problem on *de Ridderkerk*, for after its captain had left on October 12, the crew had abandoned ship the night of October 13 and had gone to Gamron. Emamverdi Khan asked Koenad to inform him whether one of his men had offended the sailors, for he then would punish them. If they had left without cause he asked Koenad to punish the crews. He promised chief-mate Jan Zion that he would return *de Ketel*; the 12 remaining European and two Moslem sailors were well treated, while Zion remained in command of the ship.[167]

165. VOC 2583, Resolution Gamron (12/10/1741), f. 651-66; VOC 2584, Koenad to Batavia (22/01/1742), f. 2205.

166. VOC 2584, Koenad to Emamverdi Khan (08/10/1741), f. 2291-2300 (complains about `Ali Soltan and the huts and informs him that the latter cannot board yet, because there is not enough ballast); VOC 2584, Tallega Emamverdi Khan at Koenad's request and letter send to `Ali Soltan aboard de Ketel (Rajab 1154/October 1741), f. 2120-22.

167. VOC 2583, Resolution Gamron (12/10/1741), f. 666-77; VOV 2584, Emamverdi Khan to Koenad (14/10/1741), f. 2125-29; VOC 2584, Zion to Koenad (12/10/1741), f. 2677-68; VOC 2584, Koenad to Welie Nhamet now Sjahinsjah (18/11/1741), f. 2597-2601.

The council at Gamron replied Zion that it was clear from his letter that the crew had left freely and on its own accord and that they might return if they wanted to. It further informed him that Sahid the interpreter would inform Emamverdi Khan that they wanted to have the ships returned to them as soon as possible. The council also wrote that the crew would remain in Gamron to prevent further trouble between them and the Persians, which would only endanger the ship. The crew would gladly return and sail against the Arabs, on condition that Emamverdi Khan would disembark his soldiers. The council ordered Zion to be on his guard, look after the Company's property as well as gather the crews' chests that had been remained behind and, if need be, to seal them.[168] On October 13, 1741 Emamverdi Khan asked Zion to give him the inventory of ammunition aboard his vessel as well as a list of what he needed. After he had done so, Emamverdi Khan politely asked Zion to write Koenad to send 40-50 European sailors, a request that Zion supported. Meanwhile, he was doing the best he could and so far there had been no problems.[169] The council replied that to send the crews back was not possible. The crew had asked that only 30-40 Persians would be put on *de Ridderkerk*, but this was not respected. Seyfollah Beg (Saffoela beek) had refused this at Emamverdi Khan's orders. This was made known to the council at that time and shortly thereafter more armed Persian soldiers had come aboard, so that the crew became even angrier leading to more trouble. They also insisted that more men were needed to sail beyond the roadstead and therefore asked the captains of both ships to send a list with VOC servants and native sailors on board.[170] In a separate letter to Emamverdi Khan Koenad expressed his satisfaction about his good treatment of the Dutch crew, but that he would not send the men he had asked for. He reminded Emamverdi Khan that he had asked him to send no more than 30-40 men to *de Ketel* and 20-30 to *de Ridderkerk*, because during battle the Persians would be in the way. Moreover, the Dutch crew did not speak Persian; all of these factors would result in confusion and danger. The crew had swum ashore, because the men believed that they would be unable to do their duty when they had to do battle under these circumstances. Koenad repeated that he had told this to Emamverdi Khan and others several times. He therefore asked him to do as asked, or else his people could not do their job. If he did not do so the letter would serve as proof in case something went wrong. Finally, Koenad once again informed him that the crews refused to return unless the maximum number of Persians was aboard and both ships returned to Gamron to allow them to embark.[171]

The Dutch were very much upset about Emamverdi Khan's behavior and on October 11, 1741 Koenad had a meeting with Widwell, his English counterpart. He asked Widwell to make a record of the taking of the Dutch ships and the flight of most its crew, so that he might later use it as proof when he would complain about it at court. Widwell counseled calm; he said that "our business in Gamron was done, our honor and credit is battered to-day; now it

---

168. VOC 2585, secret letter from the Council at Gamron to Zion, Somers, Willemse and Sahid (13/10/1741), f. 2643-47.

169. VOC 2584, Zion to Koenad (13/10/1741), f. 2679-81. In a separate letter Zion asked Koenad to send him additional crew, voluntarily or not. He added his crew was not molested by the Persians; on the contrary they were very polite. VOC 2584, Zion to Koenad (13/10/1741), f. 2682.

170. VOC 2584, secret letter from the Council at Gamron to Zion and Deeldekaas (15/10/1741), f. 4648-51.

171. VOC 2584, Koenad to Emamverdi Khan (15/10/1751), f. 2304-11; VOC 2584, Koenad to Welie Nhamet now Sjahinsjah (18/11/1741), f. 2602.

is you, and tomorrow it will be us." He further related that Emamverdi Khan had told him that the shah had ordered him given 200 lashes with the sticks for burning Kabul without permission. The latter then had said that he might get 100 lashes for burning the Dutch factory. Widwell therefore advised not to be hasty and put off thoughts of revenge for a while and to demand satisfaction from the shah.[172]

FAILED ATTEMPT TO CAPTURE THE MUTINEERS

On October 17, 1741 the fleet saw 14 Arab vessels under the island of Henjam (Hingam), which it chased for a while, but then it continued to Kong, where the fleet arrived on October 19, 1741. Emamverdi Khan, who was very satisfied, went ashore, but ordered the crews to stay aboard and guard the ships. He further ordered the Persians on board to obey the Dutch crew and Zion reported that all was well so far, but he once again asked Koenad to send him more sailors.[173] The reason why Zion continued to ask for more men is clear from the letter sent by Deeldekaaas, the captain of *de Ridderkerk*. He reported from Kong that

> The weighing of the anchor or something else causes complete disorder, for these so-called native sailors are not used to this work, and also because of the yelling of the Persian soldiers, so that they do not hear what I order and also because of the lack of a good interpreter, so that they do it wrong. If the weather gets bad I fear for the ship, also in case of an attack, for there is no carpenter to make repairs or to close hits under the waterline. We are like slaves, deserted by everybody except for my God on whom my only hope is fixed.[174]

The ships stayed for six days at Kong. Emamverdi Khan sent 200 matchlock men aboard together with five cannon and 500 *mann* of gun-powder despite Dutch protests. He embarked 1,500 men and 200 horses on the accompanying *trankis*. The squadron left Kong on October 24, 1741 (13 Sha`ban 1154) and arrived the next day at Qeysh. Before he departed for Kong, Emamverdi Khan had sent the Arab rebels a peace proposal. If they did not accept it he threatened to kill them all and enslave all their women and children and destroy their islands. The Arabs replied that they preferred to wait for the worst and would shed their last drop of blood before making peace with the Persians. A messenger reported that the Arabs were reinforcing the beaches of Qeysh with many men, where many trankis and *Fatti Sjahi* had gathered. On October 25, 1741 the two Dutch ships, two gallivats and 40 other vessels sailed from Kong to Qeysh, where the flotilla arrived on October 27 at 16.00 hours. Here they received information that the *Fatti Sjahi* with 50 large vessels had left to Bahrain. The other ships and vessels of the Hulas were lying under Qeysh, the beaches of which had been reinforced with a great number of defenders. On that same day the battle was engaged, where the Hulas had the advantage because of their greater seamanship and experience. One Persian soldier in his ignorance even killed three and wounded nine of his fellow-soldiers because he was not careful with his fuse. They spotted the *Captain* with 20 other

---

172. VOC 2584, Notes of a conference with the English (11/10/1741), f. 2763-64.

173. VOC 2584, Zion (Kong) to Koenad (20/10/1741), f. 2683-84.

174. VOC 2584, Deeldekaas (Kong) to Koenad (20/10/1741), f. 2686-87.

vessels at which *de Ridderkerk* fired two balls and received a reply in kind without suffering or causing any damage. That same evening Emamverdi Khan send some vessels with soldiers ashore who returned the next morning saying that they had been unable to land, because everywhere they were opposed by armed Hulas. Emamverdi Khan immediately cut off the left ear of two of the commanding officers and sent them back to try once more. On October 26, 1741 the two sides fought again after Emamverdi Khan had held council with his officers and had exhorted them to fight better. The plan was that he would attack with the Dutch ships while they had to put the infantry ashore. The Dutch ships bombarded the shore to support the landing party, which unsuccessfully tried to beach with five vessels, for the Arabs after a fierce fight forced them to withdraw leaving many dead and wounded behind. The Dutch then sailed towards the Arab ships and engaged them at 14.00 hours in the afternoon. However, *de Ketel* could not come close, because the depth was only seven fathoms, so little or no damage was done. The Hulas responded by shooting back and at 16.00 hours Emamverdi Khan came into the well-deck to encourage the gunners. He also directed some pieces himself, during which one six-pounder burst causing the death of 6 and wounding 10. This came about because of the inexperience of the gunners who put two cartridges in one cannon. During the landing *de Ketel* bombarded the Arab positions and Emamverdi Khan came on deck to encourage his gunner. In his frenzy to score a victory Emamverdi Khan wanted to train himself a cannon on a *tranki*. The cannon was too heavily loaded and burst. He was wounded and died three hours later, with him 10 other Persians died. The Dutch ships continued to bombard the Hulas till sunset without suffering any damage and then sailed to deeper waters. After this mishap the battle stopped immediately and the *daryabegi* came aboard. The next day (October 29) the *daryabegi* was appointed acting *sardar* by the council of war. The latter wrote to Koenad that by heavy shelling they had forced the Hula fleet, consisting of the *Captain* and 100 *trankis* to withdraw. He ordered the corpse of Emamverdi Khan to be taken to Kong at once, and then held a council of war. The council decided to sail to Charak to take in water and firewood and then to sail to Bahrain. The Dutch, however, opposed this, for their contracted period had expired, and told the *daryabegi* that if he persisted in their plan they would all leave. Faced with this ultimatum and the fact that all his gunners had died as well as their horses the *daryabegi* changed his mind and decided to go to Kong.[175]

On October 30, 1741 the flotilla sailed to Batana a village N.N.E. off Qeysh to take in water and new soldiers. On November 7, the fleet anchored at 03.00 a.m. near Moghu, 4 German miles west of Kong near the hook of Shanas to take in water, but only brackish water was found. He also wanted to get new soldiers, for Emamverdi Khan's men did not want to fight anymore as he was dead. If they would be able to get new soldiers the *daryabegi* wanted to sail to Bahrain, which was the reason why the Persians wanted to evade the enemy who was to be seen every day. "This piece of stupidity causes us misery" for the two Dutch captains did not want to sail there with an inexperienced crew. Moreover, after Emamverdi Khan's death

---

175. VOC 2584, Ibrahim Sahid (Congo) to Coenad (18/11/1741), f. 2229-34; VOC 2584, Zion and Deeldekaas to Koenad (11/11/1741), f. 2692-96; VOC 2584, Mohammad Taqi *daryabegi* to Koenad (11/11/1741 received), f. 2134-35; VOC 2584, secret letter Koenad to Zion and Deeldekaas (06/11/1741), f. 2655 (this morning we learnt that the *sardar* died; we hope you return, if the *daryabegi* wants to prevent this show him the contract, of which a copy goes herewith), f. 2655; VOC 2584, secret letter Koenad to Zion and Deeldekaas (15/11/1741), f. 2657-58 (received the *daryabegi*'s letter on November 11. He wrote that the ships would return; that there was a maximum 50 Persians on board. Remind him of the terms of the contract, whose duration has expired and tell him we never had gunners here).

the ships were neglected. Formally the two captains were in command, but only of their own crew. On November 9, 1741 Mohammad Taqi Khan the *daryabegi* convened a council. The Dutch captains told the dragoman to inform the *daryabegi* that the contracted period had expired and that they wanted to return. The *daryabegi* asked them to have patience and that he had written to Koenad about the new situation. He gave the ships, however, permission to sail to Kong to await further orders, where they arrived two days later. The captains wanted to go home, for now with Emamverdi Khan dead there was no hope for a speedy end to the affair. The Persians were afraid of the Hulas, they commented, for they were looking for them where they were not. It was their belief that if Emamverdi Khan was still alive that the war at Qeysh would have been over by then and they at Gamron with good prize money. However, now they were stuck with stupid, innocent, senseless, lazy, beastly people whom it was impossible to work with. "There is no authority among Persian and Arab sailors anymore and they do not want to fight anymore either." The captains asked Koenad for order what they should do or to send a sloop with a Dutch crew to Kong so that they could sail to Gamron.[176]

Near Qeysh the fleet encountered some Arab vessels but no action was undertaken by either side. To get fresh water it was decided to return to Kong. It was still uncertain what would happen next. According to rumor, the fleet would either sail to Bahrain or to Gamron. If it was not Gamron, the two captains assured the council at Gamron that they would neither interfere with nor take any responsibility for any of the ships' operations, because they did not dare to sail with the inexperienced crew. They also criticized the council, which had highly recommended `Ali Soltan. However, they had experienced him to be a stupid and arrogant man, who continuously demanded things from Deeldekaas as to the operation of the ship, "as if he wants to sail without wind against the current. If I say, 'it is impossible' he vilifies me. In view of this I am not surprised they have lost their ships, due to the bad treatment of their crew, who complain daily about hunger and thirst so that they had to rebel."[177]

The *daryabegi* told the Dutch that the ships would be returned when Hatem Khan, *saheb-ekhtiyar* of Fars, would have arrived there.[178] In similar terms he also wrote to Koenad whose help he asked to send him 10 to 15 gunners. He also had reported to the shah about the obnoxious behavior of Emamverdi Khan towards the Dutch, who got all the blame. Meanwhile, Mozaffar `Ali Khan wrote to the *daryabegi* to return the Dutch ships to Gamron, because he needed them for his voyage to Thatta; he received the same reply, viz., that the ships had to wait until the arrival of Hatem Khan. Since all the chief officials feared the shah's displeasure about the past events Sahid advised Koenad that now was a good moment to write Hatem Khan about what had happened, the more so, since he would decide whether to return the ships or not. Sahid further listed the names of the officials who were the cause of all the troubles that the VOC had suffered. These were: Aqa Baqer, Seyfollah Beg (Sieefal Beq), Mirza Zahed Ahmad [?] (Miersa Zeyt Ahmet) and Mirza Morteza.[179]

---

176. VOC 2584, Zion and Deeldekaas to Koenad (11/11/1741), f. 2697-2701; VOC 2584, Koenad to Welie Nhamet now Sjahinsjah (18/11/1741), f. 2603-04.

177. VOC 2584, Deeldekaas to Koand (11/11/1741), f. 2689-91.

178. Hatem Khan had been appointed *saheb-ekhtiyar* of Fars and all the lower lands (Garmsirat) in mid-1740. VOC 2546 (23/08/1740), f. 1162-63. The royal *vakil* for Fars was Mirza Mohammad `Ali and the deputy-governor (*na'eb*) was Mirza Ja`far. VOC 2546 (31/03/1740), f. 52.

179. VOC 2584, Ibrahim Sahid (Congo) to Coenad (18/11/1741), f. 2334-39 (Emamverdi Khan had

The situation remained unclear. On November 13, 1741 Deeldekaas wrote that there were only 90-100 Persians on board, who had replaced `Ali Soltan who had gone ashore with all his men and baggage. The situation did not change for one week later he wrote that the ships had been ordered to wait for the arrival of Hatem Khan. Daily soldiers came and left the ships. `Ali Soltan was a bully and a bad man; moreover, there were 60-70 Persian soldiers aboard, so the Dutch felt they were like slaves.[180]

Mohammad Taqi Khan *daryabegi* had written to Koenad that he had asked Hatem Khan to come (who had been friendly to the Dutch in the past). He asked Koenad to make gunners available (although he had written earlier that there were none at Gamron) and for each ship 20 sailors and promised that he would return both ships as soon as Hatem Khan had arrived in Kong. In view of the fact that there were now so many pirates at sea there was a real need to get the ships back. Due to lack of water and food supplies he had been forced to abandon the pursuit of the enemy who had fled to the neighborhood of Qeysh. Meanwhile, a messenger had brought news that Hatem Khan had left Shiraz six days ago.[181] Because Koenad replied that he could not comply with the request Mohammad Taqi Khan wrote that when he received Koenad's letter on 10 Ramazan (19/11/1741) he had written several times to Hatem Khan asking him to move with greater speed. In fact, he even had sent Allahverdi Beg *panjsad-bashi* to urge him to do so, while he once again assured Koenad that he would return the ships as promised.[182]

On November 21, 1741 the two captains had written in exasperation that despite Mohammad Taqi Khan's promise that the number of Persian soldiers would be reduced to a maximum of 50, reality was different. *De Ketel* had 180 soldiers and the smaller *de Ridderkerk* likewise proportionally. Both captains twice raised the question of the return of the ships to Gamron with Mohammad Taqi, but he always said there was a delay. If they would have their own full crew aboard they would have returned already, but although they had asked for them several times the council had not sent them and the current crew of 14 could not do anything by force. On November 20 the two captains, accompanied by Sahid the interpreter, met Mohammad Taqi Khan in his tent and in the presence of Allahverdi Khan gave Koenad's letter in Persian to the *daryabegi*. After having read it Sahid said that the ships had to return to Gamron, but Mohammad Taqi Khan said that they had to wait until the next day, when there would be a meeting. The next day a two-hours meeting took place with Mohammad Taqi Khan who told the two captains and Sahid that they still had to wait another three days until the arrival of Hatem Khan. Alternatively, the council would have to send their crews to Kong. If the crew would be unwilling he asked that Koenad would send regular [i.e. non-maritime]

---

wanted to behead Sjeeg Golamalie, the captain of the *Fathi Jengi*, but he only was bastinadoed due to intercession (Ibid., f. 2338). Mozaffar `Ali Khan arrived at Kong on November 25. 1741 and wanted to leave with the Dutch ships immediately. Mohammad Taqi Khan said that this was impossible; the ships' departure had to wait until the arrival of Hatem Khan and then the ships would be returned to their captains and not to Mozaffar `Ali Khan. The latter said that he had already permission to take them, but Sahid told him that this was not the case as only the council at Gamron could decide that. VOC 2584, Ibrahim Sahid (Congo) to Coenad (28/11/1741), f. 2250-51.

180. VOC 2584, Deeldekaas to Koenad (13/11/1741), f. 2704-06; VOC 2584, idem to idem (20/11/1741), f. 2707-09.

181. VOC 2584, Emamverdi Khan (Kong) to Koenad (received 18/11/1741), f. 2139-40.

182. VOC 2584, Mohammad Taqi Khan *daryabegi* to Koenad (received 24/11/1741), f. 2145-46.

VOC servants with the supply vessel. The captains finally asked the council whether it wanted to have the ships back right away, because then they would sail away, although this would mean the loss of the anchors.[183]

Because no orders were given to return the two ships, they remained at Kong. On November 27, 1741 the two captains wrote that they had received the council's letters of November 19 and 25, but they were still at Kong and would remain there. On November 26 they had gone ashore to give Mohammad Taqi Khan Koenad's letter. Mohammad Taqi Khan's reaction was one of surprise that Koenad had written sio many times to ask for the return of the ships, because he had already written a few times that he would do so as soon as Hatem Khan arrived at Kong. The captains complained about the delays, while the Persian soldiers and sailors complained about hunger. The two Dutch captains were at their wit's end. Requests were useless and they were too few to use force, but if the council ordered to do so they would give it a try. The ships were being neglected, while they had already lost 40 fathoms of their daily ropes as well as their guy-rope. On November 22 they even were drifting from the roadstead. The Persian soldiers almost lost them two anchors, which they fortunately were able to prevent. They therefore ended their letter by asking for their own crews.[184]

Hatem Khan arrived at Kong on December 7, 1741. Ebrahim Sahid paid him a visit and gave him a summary of the bad treatment the Dutch had given. Hatem Khan was very angry about this and said that if the Dutch had reason to complain in the future they should write to him immediately. He further told Sahid that Mozaffar `Ali Khan and Allahverdi Khan would go to Gamron and ask for the loan of de Ridderkerk for a voyage to Sind.[185]

The VOC council at Gamron replied on December 1, 1741 that if the two captains would be able to return to Gamron by subterfuge to do so without running any danger from the Persians on board. The council was afraid that these would become desperate and cause harm to the Dutch crew and the ships. It was also wondering whether there would not be any opposition from the Persians if the original Dutch crews would arrive, reason why the council believed that only through subterfuge the two ships might be able to return. The council therefore ordered both captains to consult one another and to report what possible loss the Company might suffer. For if the council would agree to act then it had to do everthing to save the ships and its crew. It therefore asked for information about the distribution of the number of Persians and Dutch crew for each ship.[186] Captain Zion wrote on December 9 that if their crews would have been in Kong they would have been able to depart already several times. It would be very easy and without danger to bring the crews to the ship with the sloop that was at Gamron. The number of Persian on board fluctuated, due to the constant coming and going of soldiers. Meanwhile, Hatem Khan had told them that they would be allowed to depart on

183. VOC 2584, Zion and Deeldekaas (Kong) to Koenad (21/11/1741), f. 2712-17; VOC 2584, Ibrahim Sahid (Congo) to Coenad (21/11/1741), f. 2242-44.

184. VOC 2584, Zion and Deeldekaas (Kong) to Koenad (27/11/1741), f. 2718-20. The captains protested once again, but Mohammad Taqi Khan said that Hatem Khan was arriving shortly and his house was being readied. VOC 2584, Zion and Deeldekaas (Kong) to Koenad (27/11/1741), f. 2721-22.

185. VOC 2584, Ibrahim Sahid (Congo) to Coenad (12/12/1741), f. 2246-48.

186. VOC 2584, Secret letter Council Gamron to Zion and Deeldekaas (01/12/1741), f. 2664-67.

December 11, 1741.[187] Captain Deeldekaas followed up on this issue on December 11. He had discussed the matter with Zion and others and had concluded that if it were up to him he would not permit this operation. The Persian would resist the taking of the ships, which would be impossible without the loss of blood. It also would lead to a new conflict between the Company and Persia. He therefore had decided to stay unless the council ordered otherwise. Deeldekaas had his hopes fixed on Hatem Khan who had arrived on December 8 and who had intimated that they might depart on December 11, 1741. In view of that news it was in his view not necessary to send the crews to Kong. He finally reported that he had 48 Persian soldiers on board and 24 so-called sailors.[188] On December 12, 1741 the council informed the captains that they would send men in the sloop and other vessels to help them sail the ships. It instructed both captains to be on their guard and to make sure that they remained in charge of the ammunition by making use of keys and the manner of storage. Also, to make sure that nothing of that kind would be lying around on deck that might be used by the Persians as a means of defense before the men that would be sent to them had arrived. Three shots from the east-point [presumably of the ship] would be the signal that the relief force had attacked the Persians and it was only then that they had to take over the ships. On arrival of the relief force they would receive further orders what to do with the ships and what to do with the Persian on board.[189]

HATEM KHAN'S ARRIVAL DIFFUSES THE SITUATION

Meanwhile Hatem Khan sent a letter to Koenad in which he expressed his surprise at the news that the Dutch refused to carry on trade and had closed the gates of their factory. He advised them that if this were true it was harmful to the shah and their own masters, and the shah certainly would not be pleased about it. So would he be so kind and open the gates again and begin trading. Koenad replied that the reason for stopping the trading was Emamverdi Khan, who, through his obnoxious conduct and continuous demands for equipment, only had hurt trade. However, every sincere person and genuine merchant who was not out to make a profit out of another man's loss was still welcome in the Dutch factory.[190]

On November 25, 1741 Mozaffar `Ali Khan arrived in Kong; he wanted to take the Dutch ships to Gamron. The *daryabegi* refused this, however, for they had to wait for Hatem Khan's arrival. After that the ships would be handed over to the Dutch captains, although Mozaffar `Ali Khan claimed that he had Hatem Khan's permission already for taking the ship.[191]

Hatem Khan had received Koenad's letter with complaints when he was at Jahangeri-yeh? (Gerongherieh) and wrote to tell Koenad that he was very angry about Emamverdi Khan's

187. VOC 2584, Zion to Koenad (09/12/1741), f. 2726-27.

188. VOC 2584, Deeldekaas to Koenad (11/12/1741), f. 2728-29.

189. VOC 2584, Secret letter Council Gamron to Zion and Deeldekaas (20/12/1741), f. 2669-70.

190. VOC 2584, Koenad to Hatem Khan (17/11/1741), f. 2316.

191. Mohammad Taqi Khan who had received Koenad's reply on 16 Ramazan (25/11/1741) wrote him not to worry so much about the ships; he had written him several times that he would wait till Hatem Khan arrived at Kong. He had information that the latter was at Simoncon [?] and was expected to arrive on 20 Ramazan (29/11/1741) at Kong. VOC 2584, Mohammad Taqi Khan to Koenad (received 06/12/1741), f. 2147.

behavior and said that in future the Dutch only had to write to him if they had similar complaints. Emamverdi Khan had acted without the shah's orders who would have been very displeased about his behavior. If Koenad had written about this before his death he would have ordered his immediate execution. Because the shah had ordered him to go as fast as possible to Kong, Hatem Khan would send the ships to Gamron on his arrival. Hatem Khan arrived in Kong on December 7, 1741 and the dragoman reported the bad treatment the Dutch had been exposed to and he received the same assurances. The ships would be accompanied by Mozaffar ʿAli Khan and Allahverdi Beg, who would ask for the use of *de Ridderkerk* for a voyage to Thatta.[192] Koenad and the council were fed up by that time, as is also clear by their decision to send men to Kong to get their two ships back, and wrote to Hatem Khan that such offenses should not happen again, for if so it would be better for the Dutch to depart from Persia than to stay. He further informed Hatem Khan that he would no longer tolerate the offenses he had been exposed to in Gamron, while he also advised him not to listen to rumor mongering and to return the two ships forthwith.[193]

Hatem Beg's arrival and promise that the ships would return to Gamron on December 11, 1741 made the Dutch change their plans for a planned escape from Kong with their ships. The plan had been drawn up after a secret correspondence between Koenad and the captains, who would get their crews back and sail away to Gamron despite any Persian opposition. When the ships returned in Gamron on December 17, 1741 Mozaffar Khan handed Koenad a letter from Hatem Khan. In this letter Hatem Khan informed Koenad that Nader Shah had given orders that the Dutch had to keep two ships ready in the roadstead to take Mozaffar ʿAli Khan to Sind. He therefore had given orders to load the royal ships, which he had found on his arrival in Kong, with Mozaffar ʿAli Khan's suite and baggage. The remainder of the suite and baggage to be transported by Dutch ships Hatem Khan informed Koenad.[194]

Koenad again was put in a difficult position. It had been made clear to how that the ship's loan was at the direct orders of the shah himself, a gesture that could not just be ignored. There was also the fact that the Dutch crews refused to board the ships as long as there were Persian troops aboard who had served under Emamverdi Beg. Koenad had requested Mohammad Baqer, ʿAli Soltan, Allahverdi Khan and Mozaffar ʿAli Khan to do so, but the result was nil. Also, the batters were useless, because of the inexperience of the Persian sailors aboard and which therefore had to be repaired. The Dutch crews refused to resume their work, because they feared that they again would suffer molestations, and that the alleged return of the ships was only a subterfuge to get them aboard again, for the Persians aboard could not sail the ship in the open sea. Koenad therefore proposed to Hatem Khan's representative, Allahverdi Khan, the new *beglerbegi* of Lar, to put only the two-master at his disposal together with a hired local vessel. For it was impossible to use *de Ketel* and *de Ridderkerk* under the present circumstances. Allahverdi Khan refused, however, so a stalemate was reached. For the Dutch crews still refused to board the ships as long as there were Persian soldiers aboard, because they had observed that even in the roadstead of Gamron the Dutch still were exposed to an increasing level of offenses by the Persians. In view of their disobedience to any authority Koenad was unable to

---

192. VOC 2584, Hatem Khan to Koenad (received 06/12/1741), f. 2149-51.

193. VOC 2584, Koenad to Hatem Khan (07/12/1741), f. 2345; VOC 2584, Koenad to Batavia (22/01/1742), f. 2488-90.

194. VOC 2584, Hatem Khan to Koenad (received 17/12/1741), f. 2167-69.

comply with Hatem Khan's request.[195] Despite Hatem Khan's orders to the *na'eb* of Gamron, Mohammad Baqer, and the *shahbandar*, Mirza Hadi,[196] to treat the VOC peronnel politely and not to offer offense or molest them, the situation did not change.[197] The *na'eb* insisted on transporting 80 horses and 200 men with *de Ridderkerk* and the two-master Koenad replied that this was impossible since *de Ridderkerk* needed repairs badly. He moreover pointed out, that their handling of the situation made the Dutch crews even less inclined to board the ships. For, when he had sent Moslem sailors employed by the VOC to the ships to help the Persian crew, the VOC sailors were chased away by soldiers of 'Ali Soltan who brandished their swords and even fired at them. When the Dutch crews heard about this they almost mutinied. The soldiers also took a VOC boat from the beach without permission, while the Persian authorities such as Allahverdi Khan responded rather indifferently to complaints, and only promised that they would look into the matter. Koenad warned Hatem Khan that if this situation was allowed to persist and something untoward would happen or even blood would flow it would not be his fault. He therefore asked Hatem Khan to order the Persian crew to leave the ships.[198] Hatem Khan reacted rather surprised at Koenad's letter and his complaints, for he only asked a small service, which would only take 30 days. He pointed out that in case of refusal the shah's displeasure would be the VOC's lot, for he reminded Koenad, many kings would desire to be allowed to execute such an order. He therefore advised him to give passage to Mozaffar 'Ali Khan and deal severely with the Dutch sailors, who after all were but the lowest of servants.[199]

Koenad meanwhile had been able to persuade Allahverdi Khan to accept the loan of *de Ridderkerk* only and to allow *de Ketel* to return to Batavia. Although repairs were necessary to the ships, and despite the agreement, Allahverdi Khan had not yet handed over the ships to Koenad by the end of December 1741. Koenad informed Hatem Khan about these developments while he at the same time pointed out to the latter that sailors in Dutch society were not the lowest grade "at least thus it will not be considered by our masters, for we are all equal to them." It took some more days before the final obstacles had been taken away.[200]

---

195. VOC 2584, Koenad to Hatem Khan (22/12/1741), f. 2346-50.

196. In 1739 Mirza Hoseyn was *shahbandar*. VOC 2510 (05/10/1739), but he was succeeded by Hajji Mohammad and Sheikh Hadi as *ham-qalam*. VOC 2510, f. 1458. In 1740, the deputy-governor (*na'eb*) was Mohammad Baqer Beg, *shahbandar* was Mirza Hoseyn and Sheikh Hadi was *ham-qalam*, while the qadi was Mullah Hasan. VOC 2511, Resolution Gamron (17/03/1740), f. 370, 376. Aqa Baqer (Aga Bakker) is also mentioned as *shahbandar* and *ham-qalam* of Gamron in 1740. VOC 2511 (16/03/1740), f. 1250; VOC 2584, f. 2131 (Sjeeg Haddie had been appointed *shahbandar* of Gamron and its districts in a letter dated Jomadi I/July 1741 from Mohammad Taqi Khan *mostowfi al-mamalek* to Koenad). In 1746 the *shahbandar* was Hajji Mohammad 'Ali. VOC 2705 (31/07/1746), f. 64.

197. VOC 2584, Tallega from Hatem Khan to the *na'eb* and *shahbandar* of Gamron (Shavval 1154/ December 1741), f. 2159-60 ("it is your duty to show friendship, to increase trade and the shah's profits. If, however, the Dutch servants had caused trouble then you have not acted well, because you have to see to it that order reigns.")

198. VOC 2584, Koenad to Hatem Khan (22/12/1741, f. 2251-54. The majority of the crew of *de Ridderkerk* was punished for abandoning ship. The council did not believe their claim that there were too many Persians on board and that their treatment was bad. It considered their objection too exaggerated (see Resolution Gamron of 06/12/1741). VOC 2584, Koenad to Batavia (22/01/1742), f. 2504-15 with further details and a list of the names of the ringleaders).

199. VOC 2584, Hatem Khan to Koenad (received 25/12/1741), f. 2171-73.

200. VOC 2584, Koenad to Hatem Khan (30/12/1741), f. 2358-59.

After much insistence from Koenad, Allahverdi Khan ordered Fath ʿAli Beg, the commander of the Persians aboard *de Ridderkerk* to send part of his men to vessels which would be hired at Qeshm.[201] After this order had been complied with *de Ridderkerk* raised anchor on January 5, 1742 under command of Jan Zion, the stalwart mate of *de Ketel*, who had been rewarded with this promotion for his attitude during the mutiny of October 1741. However, before he could sail away he had to deal with a new outbreak of unrest among the crew. They demanded that the leaders of the mutiny, who were kept in Gamron for transportation to Batavia be returned to their own ship. Zion replied that he would stand no nonsense from them, and that if they did not want to sail under these conditions they had better leave his ship. He warned them, however, that this time, they would not get off so easy as the first time and would be severely punished. This helped and assisted by the Persian soldiers the anchor was raised and the voyage to Sind via Qeshm to fetch water, firewood and ballast was begun.[202] Because of the continuous demands for the use of ships, loans, presents, and equipment and being invariably forced to take all kinds of offense the VOC staff was getting fed up. In January 1742 the council asked the governor-general for his approval "to have the Persian taste for once the saber" in case of a future case of unacceptable injustice. The resentment that the VOC council felt was not only because of the lack of appreciation by the Persian authorities for the services rendered, but also because the English enjoyed more respect (rather than trade), because they spent more money than the Dutch on Persian officials. This they could easily do, because they sold their ships to the shah at a profit of 200% of the real market value.[203]

---

201. VOC 2584, Allahverdi Khan (at the request of Koenad) to Fath ʿAli Beg (Faat Ali Beeq) aboard *de Ketel* (05/01/1742), f. 2173-79 (there are too many people on board; Dutch have reason to complain; it is your mistake and responsibility; when vessels from Qeshm arrived transfer them, so that there will be no problem when there is a storm); VOC 3584, Reply (no date), f. 2189-81 (Crew has my respect; I'll talk to the captain what has to be done; I do not want them to be dissatisfied).

202. VOC 2584, Zion to Koenad (07/10/1742), f. 2732-34; VOC 2584, Instruction for captain of *de Ridderkerk* (05/01/1742), f. 2416-18 from which it is clear that Mozaffar Khan went separately to Sind in the *Fatti Sangi*. Also, the captain was instructed to use his own pilots and do his own sounding, while further details were given concerning the location of Diwel-Sind.). The ship *de Ridderkerk* sank near Karachi in early 1742, for details see VOC 2593, Clement to Batavia (31/10/1742), f. 1744-50. The damage suffered was 7,000 *tuman*s or Dfl. 297,500 and an indemnification request was sent to Nader Shah. Ibid., f. 1799-vs. For a lower estimate see VOC 2680, van der Welle to Batavia (10/08/1745), f. 56.

203. VOC 2584, Koenad to Batavia (22/01/1742), f. 2491-92, 2501. The Dutch also tried to blacken the reputation of the most offensive Persian officials by sending information on their doings to their Isfahan office, which had to acquaint the various authorities with that in the hope that this would result in their downfall. VOC 2584, Koenad to Batavia (22/01/1742), f. 2491; VOC 2584, Koenad to Aalmis(18/11/1741), f. 2542-43 (asks Aalmis whether he can do something to ruin Mohammad Baqer Beg, *na'eb* of Gamron, ʿAli Soltan the governor of Dashtestan, Nagha Gosjaal, a Banyan and his clerk (*molla*), Mirza Zahed Ahmad, an inexperienced rascal, Seyfollah Beg (Sevoela Beq) and Mohammad Taqi Khan *daryabegi* and in particular the first mentioned person. If yes, he was allowed to give presents proportional to the result. He was instructed to make sure that the result would be tranquility not moroseness. He also wanted a royal order that nobody was allowed to ask for ships without showing a specific royal order to that effect and that all officials were ordered to leave the Dutch in peace and not to demand the use of their supply vessel and their porters). To that end Koenad also wrote a letter to Nader to inform him about Emamverdi Khan's actions. VOC 2584, Koenad to Welie Nhamet now Sjahinsjah (18/11/1741), f. 2559-2607. The anger of the council at Gamron became even more when months later rumors circulated in Batavia that the so-called 'ship loans' was only a subterfuge to carry on private trade. The council suggested that the governor-general interrogate the crews of the ships concerned and if true then to punish the felons, if not true then to punish the rumor-mongers. VOC 2593, Clement to Batavia (31/10/1742), f. 1594-95.

MIRZA TAQI KHAN INCREASED AUTHORITY

In December 1741 (Shavval 1154) Mohammad Taqi Khan informed Koenad that Nader Shah had appointed him as *beglerbegi* and *saheb-e ekhtiyar* of Fars, the Garmsirat, Lar, all ports and islands, Jolfar, Bahrain, Kich-Makran, Kuhgilu, Aberquh, Nouwnat (?), Rudbar, Jiroft, etc. He intended soon to come to Gamron (he was at Tchaharloe [?] on 30 Ramazan) and asked Koenad to have the two ships ready for which Hatem Khan was supposed to have given him money. Mohammad Taqi Khan wanted to buy another two ships for the royal fleet, for which he promised Koenad a royal decree. In an earlier letter from Chirroen [?] he had written Koenad that he had heard about the bad treatment the Dutch had received from Emamverdi Khan. He therefore had written to him to explain himself, for he wanted to punish him. His death, however, had intervened; the shah certainly would have had him killed.[204]

He was as good as his word, for on April 21, 1742, the Dutch received three royal decrees from Nader Shah in which he thanked them for the services rendered to the Crown which he would recompense in time and ordered Mohammad Taqi Khan and Kalb ʿAli Khan, the newly appointed *sardar*, to treat the Dutch as good friends. Nader Shah at the same time asked the Dutch to sell him three ships against cash payment, while in another decree he invited the Dutch to send somebody to him if they had something to request, and he finally once again thanked them for services given to him. Both Mohammad Taqi Khan and Kalb ʿAli Khan separately also had informed the Dutch that they had been ordered to maintain friendly relations with them.

Meanwhile the Dutch were having trouble with the *shahbandar*, Mirza Hadi, who from the very beginning of his appointment had been troublesome. He, in March 1742, refused the customary New Year's present and wanted at least 60 *tuman*s, or else he promised to make so many difficulties for the Dutch that it would cost them 600 *tuman*s. Clement, the new Dutch director, wrote to Mohammad Taqi Khan to complain about this behavior which could hardly be qualified as friendly as Nader Shah had ordered. On April 23, 1742 Mohammad Taqi Khan replied that he would punish the *shahbandar* on his arrival in Gamron. When his brother, Abu'l-Hasan Khan arrived on April 23, 1742 in Gamron Clement reminded him of promise, but as he had expected he received many other promises but no action. Abu'l-Hasan Khan promised to have the *shahbandar* bastinadoed and asked Clement to select his own choice of *shahbandar* from three persons whom he mentioned. Clement, however, replied that he would be satisfied when Abu'l-Hasan Khan would do as he had promised, to which he said that he would do so. He also agreed that it was forbidden to take money from the VOC personnel, and that he therefore would pay the 50 *tuman*s that had been taken from them out of his own pocket, but this also proved to be a false promise. When Mohammad Taqi Khan himself came he also made similar promises, but on his departure he only reprimanded the *shahbandar* in the presence of Clement, although he had promised to dismiss him. Mohammad Taqi Khan again asked for the loan of the VOC sloop in the roadstead. Clement told him that he had not a proper crew, which was on *de Ridderkerk* doing royal service. To sail it with an undermanned crew was too great a risk, which he did not dare run. Mohammad Taqi Khan, however, replied that he would take the responsibility and would see to it that Arab sailors were

---

204. VOC 2584, Mohammad Taqi Khan *beglerbegi* (from Tchaharloe) to Koenad (15/01/1742 received), f. 2188-89; VOC 2584, Mohammad Taqi Khan (from Chirroen) to Koenad (received 15/01/1742), f. 2182-85.

sent to man the sloop. Out of fear that refusal would lead to a huge demand for money as in 1738 Clement gave in and so on May 1, 1742 manned by 12 Arab sailors the sloop sailed to Kong to bring grain and returned safely on May 10. Mohammad Taqi Khan did not forget to thank Clement for this service.

Meanwhile Kalb ʿAli Khan had scored a victory over the Hulas at Qassab (Gasaeb). He also asked for the delivery of several goods for which he promised to pay, but Clement replied that he did not sell them for the Dutch had bad experience with these promised payments. On June 2, 1742 both Kalb ʿAli Khan and Mohammad Taqi Khan arrived in Gamron with an army of about 4,000 men. Because of this victory Nader Shah had granted these daredevils 1,000 *tuman*s. Mohammad Taqi immediately asked the merchants at Gamron for a loan of 400 *tuman*s for one month as he had only 600 *tuman*s and he had to pay them immediately when the royal messenger arrived. As a result, the money was collected with the stick of which there was no lack.[205]

DINNER DISCUSSION BETWEEN CLEMENT AND MOHAMMAD TAQI KHAN

On June 5, Mohammad Taqi Khan invited Clement to dinner. During their conversation Mohammad Taqi Khan raised several issues, *inter alia*, a treaty between Persia and the Netherlands against the Turks and the sale of ships to Persia. Nader Shah knew that the Europeans had suffered defeat at the hands of the Turks and had lost many cities. Nader wanted to defeat the Turks and return the conquered towns to the Europeans and then together destroy the Turkish Empire. Clement replied that this issue was a complicated one. There was war ongoing in Europe; the Dutch and the Roman Emperor [of Austria/Germany] were not allies. The latter had been defeated by the Turks through treachery, but the two parties had made peace and many towns had been returned. As to a treaty to jointly fight the Turks Clement could not offer an opinion. The Netherlands were too far away from Turkey to wage war. At sea he believed the Dutch could win as they had 10 times more ships, reason why there there was peace and a good understanding between the Dutch and the Turks. Mohammad Taqi Khan then asked Clement whether he should advise the shah against sending an ambassador, to which the latter replied in the negative, because he did not know the intentions of the States-General. Mohammad Taqi Khan then asked whether such an ambassador might travel to Batavia on a Dutch ship. Clement said that if the shah wanted a treaty against the Turks the ambassador should go to Holland, for war in Europe was no business of the VOC. Mohammad Taqi Khan then asked how the ambassador might travel overland to the Netherlands. Clement told him that he could go via Russia and then take voyage with one of the many Dutch ships that were always to be found at St. Petersburg. Mohammad Taqi Khan then made the point that if Nader Shah did not want the Czar to know about this how then should the ambassador travel. Clement suggested that he might travel via Iskanderun, Aleppo or Smyrna. To Mohammad Taqi Khan's question how long these various journeys might last Clement answered that via Smyrna it would take 4 to 5 months and via Batavia to the Netherlands 16 months, which moreover was a dangerous journey. Mohammad Taqi Khan smiled and said that he understood that Clement was trying to make the prospect of sending an ambassador unattractive. Clement

---

205. VOC 2593, Clement to Batavia (31/10/1742), f. 1667vs-68r ('destroyed the Hulas near Sahaer"), 1796vs.

reacted that this was most certainly not the case; he wanted the shah to send an ambassador to the States-General and conclude a favorable agreement, because then trade might become better than it was right then. Mohammad Taqi Khan then in Clement's presence dictated a letter a letter for Nader Shah to his confidential clerk and said that he would inform Clement about the eventual result. He further asked whether Clement had any requests to make as the messenger would leave to court in the next three days. Clement then said that he wanted to make a claim for the indemnification of *de Ridderkerk*. After the offenses given by Emamverdi Khan, the disrespect offered by the local officials, the many services rendered by the Dutch at high cost and the low little return in trade the VOC would certainly depart from Persia if such indemnification would not be given. Mohammad Taqi Khan told Clement that he would support such a request, but he then would have to sell the shah two or three ships. Clement said he could not do that as his superiors had already written on that issue. Mohammad Taqi Khan then said: "why does the EIC sell me ships and the VOC, which is more powerful, refuses to do so; they must be afraid that they will not get their money." After some banter, Mohammad Taqi Khan said that he understood that Clement could not sell him ships, but he could at least positively support such a request. Clement replied that indeed he could and would do so, and added that the indemnification would certainly help in this matter. Mohammad Taqi Khan said that the governor-general should not be worried about payment for he would take of that shortly. Clement thanked him for that positive attitude and then reminded him of the Minab debt, which was still unpaid as the *kalantar* and tax collector of Minab had totally disregarded the royal orders. Mohammad Taqi Khan promised that he would see to it that it two months' time, when the date harvest began, a tax collector would be sent to collect the money, by force if need be. When Mohammad Taqi Khan asked whether Clement had another request the latter reminded him of the 17,000 *tuman*s owed by the royal court since August 1722. Mohammad Taqi Khan replied that this debt would be paid as soon as the VOC delivers one ship per year 1,000 *tuman*s would be paid off each time of that debt.[206]

Despite the very friendly meeting the Dutch had not given Mohammad Taqi Khan a present, although everybody else, including the English had already done so. After having waited for the present Mohammad Taqi Khan became angry and asked for two of the 12 ordered anchors. Clement replied that first money had to be paid for the goods that had been delivered in 1741, which he had promised to do. Mohammad Taqi Khan reacted that if Clement refused to deliver the other goods he would not pay for them and make other claims, which he had promised not to make. He added that if the ship of the royal fleet would suffer damage due to their lack of anchors the Dutch would have to pay. Mohammad Taqi Khan made it quite clear that he had raised these problems, because the Dutch had not given him presents as was customary and had not therefore shown him proper respect, which he had not expected from them. When Clement pointed out that his brother had recently received a considerable present he said that this had been from the governor-general. When Clement explained that all presents were from the governor-general or the Company rather, Mohammad Taqi Khan replied that in that case he would have asked his present already one year earlier. Clement seeing that he would get nowhere gave in to prevent more serious demands for money, stating

---

206. VOC 2593, Note concerning the discussion with Mohammad Taqi Khan *beglerbegi* (05/06/1742), f. 1853-1859vs.

that it was also for Kalb 'Ali Khan. His face having been saved Mohammad Taqi Khan showed himself very friendly again to the Dutch and sent Clement a present to show his satisfaction.[207]

NEW MASQAT CAMPAIGN

On June 18, 1742 Mohammad Taqi Khan, his brother, and Kalb 'Ali Khan left Gamron accompanied by the Imam of Masqat. The rebel Zeydi had expelled the latter from Masqat, where the forts and fleet were still loyal to him. Supported by the Persians he hoped to recover his country. To make the expedition a success a lot of preparations were made. Complete and half-complete gun carriages (Portuguese ones taken from them by the Persians in 1621) were melted and turned into six or eight lbs. cannons, while also many 16 and 24 lbs. balls were manufactured. Mohammad Taqi Khan's army had several metal pound cannons ready on gun-carriages. His army consisted of 6,000 to 8,000 cavalry and prospects for success looked good, since the rebels Bu'l-'Arab and Zeydie did not see eye to eye. Bu'l-'Arab had control over the interior and lived at Nizva (Nouswha), while Zeydie controlled the ports and their hinterland. There were daily skirmishes between the warring parties, alternating 'victories.' The English director Widwell had offered Mohammad Taqi Khan bombs, grenades and iron balls of 24 lbs. (which were being brought per the *Britannia* from Bombay), but Mohammad Taqi Khan declined the offer saying that he had enough of his own already. In October 1742 Abu'l-Hasan Khan returned blind and very ill from Phargonet [?] and went to Shiraz. On October 24 the shah's keeper of the wardrobe, Mir Zeyd Ahmad (Mier Seyd Agmed) and Mirza Mohammad 'Ali arrived at Gamron. According to rumors, they had received 70,000 *tuman*s (Dfl. 297,500) from Nader Shah to trade with throughout his entire kingdom and to bring all their purchases to Kalat. The oppression and violence suffered by the merchants on account of these two was indescribable, for they fixed prices to their own liking. The Dutch and English were not spared either. "We also had to taste the poisonous stick of the skunk of trade" when the "scourge of the Banader [ports]" Mohammad Taqi Khan and Kalb 'Ali Khan returned to Gamron on October 15. He handed the Dutch and English Companies on October 17 a list of goods, which he wanted. The Dutch charged him 1741 prices increased by the percentage of the depreciation of the Persian currency. Mohammad Taqi Khan did not like this and so Clement told him that however much he regretted it he had to do that, out of fear of the governor-general. Mohammad Taqi Khan replied that he feared Nader Shah like Clement feared the governor-general, though he assumed that Clement did not want to compare the two. Clement, however, replied that in business matters there was no special deal for the shah; for once he started to make exceptions trade would suffer. This would mean that the shah would suffer, for a country without a thriving trade cannot flourish. Therefore to make trade and the kingdom flourish it was only normal to treat the king just like his lowest subject in matters of trade. If Mohammad Taqi Khan wanted to change this policy, Clement warned, it would not be worthwhile for the VOC to stay any longer in Persia and had better abandon its factories there.[208]

However, Mohammad Taqi Khan was not someone easily impressed or persuaded. He threatened that if the prices were not lowered that he would make so much trouble for the VOC that it would cost them ten times more. Fearing for enforced delivery of 'treaty goods' and loans of ships Clement finally gave in. His only satisfaction was that the English lost

---

207. VOC 2593, Clement to Batavia (31/10/1742), f. 1803-05.

208. VOC 2593, Clement to Batavia (31/10/1742), f. 1806-12.

almost five times more on this 'deal' than the Dutch. Nevertheless, he offered as his opinion that it was no longer possible to stay in Persia in view of the fact that violence had become the norm, while there was no hope for improvement in this situation. His bitter comments were also induced by the presence of many generals and their troops in Gamron at that time. Their presence caused food, firewood, and water to become very expensive and almost unobtainable from which especially the local population suffered, whose misery was indescribable. Even the Dutch had trouble getting firewood and water, because the vessels, which they used to fetch them, were 'taken over' by the soldiers as soon as they beached. Clement, therefore, hoped that the assembled army soon would leave. Apart from those for the Masqat campaign there were 4,000 men commanded by seven governors (dukes), viz. Mohammad Taqi Khan, Dhu'l-Feqr Khan (Sulphagar Chan), Behbud Khan (Beboed Chan), Shah Qoli Khan, Mohammad Taqi Khan Masjeddie [?], Allahverdi Khan, Hatem Khan and Mohammad Sharif Khan (Mhamed Serie Chan) of Kerman were also expected. Dhu'l-Feqr Khan, Behbud Khan and Allahverdi Khan had to punish rebellious Baluch in Kich-Makran. The rest of the troops and generals were going to Masqat and troops and horses were shipped that way on daily basis. The Imam of Masqat was with these troops and was closely watched. Apart from Mohammad Taqi Khan and Kalb 'Ali Khan the other generals were Mohammad Taqi Khan Mesjeddie [?], and Allahverdi Khan. In addition to presents, for which these generals were constantly asking, Mohammad Taqi Khan also asked for new supplies for 12 ships in reply to Clement's request for payment for the previous delivery of which only 25 percent had been paid thus far. In that same month new orders arrived from Nader Shah for Mohammad Taqi Khan in which he was instructed to prepare as many ships as were needed for the transport of 20,000 soldiers and 2,000 horses together with six months' of supply. It was unknown for which purpose Nader Shah had given these orders, while it was totally unclear to Clement how the shah would ever get that many ships together.[209]

Because of the Masqat campaign many officials passed through Gamron and bothered the Companies with their demands for presents and the like. Clement had died on October 1, 1743 and the next day the Council appointed the deputy merchant De Poorter as *pro tem* director, because the available candidates of the merchant rank for various reasons did not want to take the job.[210]

On October 7, 1743 the new *sardar* of the Garmsirat, Mohammad Hoseyn Khan, arrived in Gamron and asked for the loan of the ship *de Valk* to transport himself and his servants to Jolfar. After having declined to the request, because the ship was filled with brimstone the *sardar* made it clear that he did not mind as long as the ship moved. In view of this attitude and his influence and kinship with Nader Shah de Poorter gave in and on October 9 the *sardar* sailed to Jolfar.[211]

---

209. VOC 2593, Clement to Batavia (31/10/1742), f. 1812vs-16.

210. VOC 2680, van der Welle to Batavia (10/08/1745), f. 170.

211. VOC 2680, Resolution Gamron (08/10/1743), unfoliated (also invoice of this trip); Ibid, Resolution Gamron (11/11/1743), unfoliated; VOC 2680, van der Welle to Batavia (10/08/1745), f. 37. Mirza Ja`far was the *soltan* of Jolfar at that time. VOC 2860, f. 199.

MOHAMMAD TAQI KHAN SHIRAZI'S REBELLION

On November 14, 1743, the Dutch heard rumors that Mohammad Taqi Khan had rebelled. The *sardar* Hoseyn Khan had presented him with orders from Nader Shah to pay into the treasury the costs for the Masqat campaign. Because he could not pay Mohammad Taqi Khan asked for a respite, but the *sardar* threatened him with severe punishment if he did not pay immediately. Because this was impossible and unacceptable to stomach, Mohammad Taqi Khan decided to kill the *sardar* and his suite after the latter's troops had sworn allegiance to him. Kalb ʿAli Khan was arrested and nobody was allowed to go to Persia. Apart from the rumors the Dutch also received indications that these rumors were true from the behavior of Abu'l-Hasan Khan, Mohammad Taqi Khan's brother, who was governor of Gamron. He not only had given orders to strengthen the fortresses on the islands and to bring supplies into Gamron from all parts, but he also imprisoned a royal *chapar* sent by Mohammad Hoseyn Khan from Sohar. He also had arrested another *chapar*. Mohammad Hoseyn Khan had learnt about Mohammad Taqi Khan's rebellion soon after his arrival in Jolfar and was said to have decamped from there with Shah Qoli Khan and had left to Kong.[212]

The Dutch informed Isfahan and Nader about these events; they also laid in new and large stores of water and firewood, and told their brokers to move their persons and goods into the factory. To avoid friction with the governor they tried to keep friendly relations. Therefore, they gave him, after repeated requests, ropes for the royal fleet (Dfl. 3343:10) and asked for the issuance of the silk decree. To their surprise, the Dutch indeed received the decree in December 1743, which, according to their Persian clerk, was the real thing. The governor received an expensive present for his trouble (Dfl. 3458:8), but this had only whetted his lust, for the fox then showed his real face and demanded 60,000 lbs. of iron on credit. He refused to accept the Dutch excuses, and threatened violent action, so that they deemed it safer to give him half what he had asked for. His *na'eb*, Aqa Baqer (Aga Bakker), gave an IOU.[213]

Mohammad Taqi Khan who arrived with the royal fleet on December 1, 1743 in Gamron on learning this sent his son Mirza Reza with the *Rahmaniyeh* with some other vessels to Jolfar to bring Allahverdi Khan and his troops to Gamron. He further sent Mohammad Baqer Lari, the *na'eb* of Gamron, with 600 men to Kong to arrest Mohammad Hoseyn Khan. On arrival in Jolfar, Reza Khan arrested Allahverdi Khan and the chief equerry and had them imprisoned in Hormuz. There they were taken together with Kalb ʿAli Khan into a boat by Mohammad Baqer Lari who strangled them and threw them into the sea.[214]

Shortly thereafter they again were bothered with a request for assistance, this time for the loan of their ship *de Horssen*, which was laden and ready to sail for Batavia. The reason for

---

212. VOC 2680, Van der Welle to Batavia (10/08/1745), f. 38-39; Ibid., Resolution Gamron (14/11/1743), unfoliated; Dutch text of the letter to Nader Shah detailing these events. VOC 2680, Resolution Gamron (20/01/1744), unfoliated.

213. VOC 2680, Van der Welle to Batavia (10/08/1745), f. 39-42; the silk decree was confirmed and sealed later on December 5, 1743 by Mohammad Taqi Khan. For the text, and his letter to the shah on the matter see VOC 2680, Resolution Gamron (09/12/1743), unfoliated.

214. VOC 2680, Resolution Gamron (12/12/1743), unfoliated. He had his son Mirza Reza (Miersa Resa), his deputy Mirza ʿAla al-Din (Miersa Aleddien), and his macebearer Ahmad Beg (Agmed Beek) with him. For the text of the letter to Nader Shah detailing these events see VOC 2680, Resolution Gamron (20/01/1744), unfoliated.

this request was that on December 22, 1743 Mozaffar `Ali Khan had arrived in the roadstead of Gamron with eight ships from Sind. He had sent his nephew `Abdol-Ghaffar Beg ashore to prepare lodgings for himself, who was arrested with the men accompanying him. A kinsman of Sheikh Madhkur of Bushehr, Aqa Sabir (?), a captain under Sheikh Gholam `Ali, deserted his ship to warn Mozaffar `Ali Khan about the rebellion and to advise him not to go ashore. It was then that the *na'eb* came to ask for Dutch naval assistance, for Mohammad Taqi Khan only had three ships and two grabs against Mozaffar `Ali Khan's seven vessels, while his biggest ship, the *Rahmaniyeh* was still at Jolfar. De Poorter refused, for the Dutch were not in Persia to wage war but to carry on trade, while he also had no authority to engage in any military action. The *na'eb* then sent for the VOC dragoman and on behalf of Mohammad Taqi Khan he threatened to send 600 men to the Dutch factory as soon as the *Rahmaniyeh* would have returned and then would obliterate the Dutch factory. The Dutch at that time had only 32 men ashore while the ships in the roadstead were not well armed. De Poorter therefore decided to close the gate of the factory, for the *na'eb* had said that all Dutchmen found outside the factory would be arrested. The council also decided on December 23, 1743 to remain neutral and to refuse any further requests from Mohammad Taqi Khan. The ships were ordered to remain neutral if the two Persian squadrons would attack one another.[215]

In the night of December 23-24, 1743 Mozaffar `Ali Khan used a stratagem and was able to take two ships and two *grabs* of the royal fleet. The other ship and one *grab* fled. Mohammad Taqi Khan therefore urgently asked the Dutch on December 27, 1743 for the loan of *de Horssen* to attack the royal fleet under Qeshm and to transport 50 of his soldiers to Suzeh (Sosa), on the [south coast of the] island, where Mozaffar `Ali Khan had gone forced by lack of water. He was able to send his men there who killed the landing party and ordered all the islands not to supply Mozaffar `Ali Khan with water, who then left in the direction of Bushehr. In reply to the Dutch refusal to lend *de Horssen* Mohammad Taqi Khan again promised to destroy the Dutch ships and factory on the return of the *Rahmaniyeh* and to kill all Dutchmen. De Poorter therefore decided to keep a sharp watch in the factory and to detain the two ships in the roadstead to support him in case of an attack. The VOC dragoman who went to see the *na'eb* reported that Mohammad Baqer Lari had said that the destruction of the Dutch factory would be very easy for Mohammad Taqi Khan, for he had already half of his 4,000 seasoned troops ashore. It was about that time that Kalb `Ali Khan, who had been imprisoned in Mohammad Baqer Beg's house, had been killed by his goaler and some *yuzbashi*s. After this deed his assassins fell out over the distribution of the former *sardar*'s possessions as a result of which one of the *yuzbashi*s was killed. The *sardar*'s servants were still imprisoned in the citadel, while the rumor was circulated that Kalb `Ali Khan had fled. To countervail any action from Mohammad Taqi Khan de Poorter sent a present to Mir Mehr-e `Ali, *kalantar* of Tezerg-Ahmadi who had always been a friend ("a white raven here") of the Dutch and acted as a kind of source of information on internal affairs. They hoped that in case of need they might call upon him, since the Dutch considered his loyal friendship to the VOC as something extraordinary for a Persian.[216]

---

215. VOC 2680, Van der Welle to Batavia (10/08/1745), f. 39-45; VOC 2680, Resolution Gamron (23/12/1743), unfoliated; for the text of the letter to Nader Shah detailing these events see VOC 2680, Resolution Gamron (20/01/1744), unfoliated.

216. VOC 2680, Van der Welle to Batavia (10/08/1745), f. 44-46; for the text of the letter to Nader Shah detailing these events see VOC 2680, Resolution Gamron (20/01/1744), unfoliated. In the letter,

On Saturday, January 18 (Dhu'l-Hijja) 1744 Mohammad Taqi Khan left Gamron accompanied by about 6,000 men and as his chief men, his brother Mirza Abu'l-Hasan Khan, his son Mirza Reza and Mohammad Taqi Khan Masjeddie [?] towards Shiraz. At that time it became known that the *sardar* Mohammad Hoseyn Khan had arrived in Shiraz and had arrested Mirza Esma`il, Mohammad Taqi Khan's brother. On his departure, Mohammad Taqi Khan appointed Mohammad Baqer Beg Lari as his *na'eb* and gave him a costly robe of honor, a golden water pipe and some troops. Mohammad Baqer Beg Lari behaved very oppressively towards the population and the Europeans. Trade came to a total standstill as a result of his activities, which led to the total ruin of the population of Gamron, Minab, `Essin and Faziyan (?). Even the peasants were unable to sow their land in peace due to his marauding activities, for he was ravaging town and countryside. He forced the shopkeepers to strengthen the walls of Gamron, while from others he took whatever he could without paying. Supplies were hard to obtain for the local population, but if they wanted to leave Gamron he allowed them to go; however, on their return the *rahdar*s took whatever supplies they had collected from them and in lieu of payment the poor people were beaten. The roads were strictly watched and letters were opened to check their contents. The Dutch therefore send their letters by sea via Bushehr to Isfahan to inform Nader Shah about this state of affairs. Furthermore, Mohammad Baqer Beg Lari had appointed two of his kinsman as castellan of Qeshm and Hormuz and had all his stolen goods taken there.[217]

His Lari troops, the only one he really could rely on, were partly already there and he himself intended to follow them later. With the rest of his troops he oppressed the population of whom very few had remained due to lack of food, so that, by April 1744, only a few reed huts and some poor Banyans were left; the town had become a ghost town. The Dutch and the English remained in their factories for Mohammad Baqer Beg Lari had given orders to molest all Europeans and their servants.[218] He himself had a special bodyguard of 32 black slaves. The Dutch had allowed most Banyan, Moslem and Armenian merchants to seek refuge in their factory. On March 6, 1744 `Abdol-Ghaffar Beg (the royal mace bearer) escaped from his prison and arrived in dervish clothes at 5.30 in the morning at the VOC gate. Mohammad Baqer Beg had extorted 100 *tuman*s from him and wanted more after which he intended to kill him. The *shahbandar*, Mirza Hadi, who also had been imprisoned, also sought refuge with the Dutch. Soon after `Abdol-Ghaffar's escape 25 Khorasani soldiers fled towards the Dutch factory which events made Mohammad Baqer Beg fearful of the future. After having collected his booty he intended to withdraw to Qeshm and seek security behind the walls of its citadel.[219]

Meanwhile, a letter from Nader Shah, written in Hamadan, arrived on April 4, 1744 brought by two couriers (*chapar*s) asking the Dutch to prevent any rebel to flee by sea. He had already sent troops to that end and the Dutch were ordered to look after the royal fleet and

---

the Dutch drew the shah's attention to the friendly attitude of the EIC towards the rebel, whom they had received friendly in their factory.

217. VOC 2680, Van der Welle to Batavia (10/08/1745), f. 47-48, 50; for the text of the letter to Nader Shah detailing these events see VOC 2680, Resolution Gamron (20/01/1744), unfoliated.

218. For the text of the letter to Nader Shah detailing these events see VOC 2680, Resolution Gamron (20/01/1744), unfoliated.

219. VOC 2680, Van der Welle to Batavia (10/08/1745), f. 49-50; VOC 2680, Resolution Gamron (22/03/1744), unfoliated.

the goods, which Mohammad Taqi Khan had left behind. The two *chapars* (Mhamed Beek Afsjaar and Hassan Alie Beek) had gone to Mir Mehr-e `Ali in Ahmadi (36 German miles east of Gamron), who passed it on to the Dutch. He informed the Dutch that he had sent Ebrahim Beg, a *yuzbashi* of the royal slaves (*gholam*s) to Mohammad Taqi with orders to report to *sardar* Mohammad Hoseyn Khan. However, his reply to the shah left no doubt about his godless intentions. The shah wrote that troops were coming from Kuhgilu, Khorasan and other parts, under the command of Allahverdi Beg, *na'eb* of the chief macebearer, to support the *sardar* and to defeat and capture the rebel. Nader Shah also wrote that he would forgive Mohammad Taqi Khan if he would show regret, though he expected that the latter would flee by sea. He therefore also had many troops in preparation to be sent to Jolfar and Masqat.[220] The *sardar*, Mohammad Hoseyn Khan, also sent a letter to the Dutch, in which he gave them "full powers over Gamron and Minab, including the toll revenues and whatever else needs to be done both at sea and on land." He further informed the Dutch that the three royal ships in the roads were still in the rebels' hands. He had ordered the governor of Kerman, Mohammad Salem Khan (Mhamed Salem Chan), as well as Mir Mehr-e `Ali Ahmadi in Reijsjaverdie [?] to mobilize their troops and march on Gamron. They had to arrest the *na'eb* of Gamron, Mohammad Baqer Beg, and Mirza Hadi the *shahbandar*, who always had been Mohammad Taqi Khan's right-hand man, their followers as well as to confiscate all their possessions, including those belonging to the rebel, his brother and son and to take the three royal ships that were still in the hands of the rebels and were lying in the roadstead of Gamron.[221]

The Dutch were suspicious of the origin of the royal letter after careful examination of its seal, and they believed that it had been written by the *sardar* himself in order to test the Dutch. The courier was interrogated who told them that the *sardar* had given him oral instructions that if the Dutch did not think the scheme advisable to take the letter to the English. Since the letter did not mention any of this, de Poorter contacted his English colleague. They both agreed that a joint non-committal answer had to be given, although separate letters had to be sent too. The VOC and the EIC jointly sealed the letter.[222]

On March 22, 1744 Mohammad Baqer Beg withdrew his demand for a contribution from the population after pressure from the Dutch, although he needed it, he claimed, for his old age. To boost his own morale the *na'eb* had the cannons of the citadel a few times fired and also the kettledrums beaten claiming that a *chapar* had brought news of Mohammad Taqi Khan's victory.[223]

Mir Mehr-e `Ali had added a note to the royal *raqam* in which he asked for Dutch support. De Poorter replied to his questions that if Mir Mehr-e `Ali had enough men he had best attack from the side of Suru (Zuru), from Neyband and from the side of the cemetery

---

220. VOC 2680, Resolution Gamron (09/04/1744), unfoliated. The decree was dated Moharram 1157/ March 1744.

221. VOC 2680, Resolution Gamron (09/04/1744), unfoliated. The letter was written on 20 Dhu'l-Hijja 1156/February 23, 1744 [should be 02/04/1744; the later date maybe is the date of reception] and brought by Godja Ouwas, an EIC servant.

222. VOC 2680, Van der Welle to Batavia (10/08/1745), f. 48-49; VOC 2680, Resolution Gamron (03/03/1744), unfoliated (Dutch text of the letter and decree).

223. Letter de Poorter to Nader Shah dated April 19, 1744. VOC 2680, after Resolution Gamron (14/04/1744), unfoliated; VOC 2680, van der Welle to Batavia (10/08/1745), f. 50.

before day-break in the morning. He had to go immediately to Mohammad Baqer Beg's house and to surround it. At the same time he had to inform de Poorter about it, so that he could put the factory in state of defense. He further advised Mir Mehr-e `Ali not to allow himself to be enticed by sweet words of the *na'eb*, but to attack him immediately and put him in prison. If the *na'eb* would flee to the citadel he had to inform de Poorter immediately who then would bombard the citadel. Finally, he wrote not to let anybody know of his plans and to send his letters to de Poorter's gardener in the hamlet D'aamheij [?].[224]

After this letter and urged by the two *chapar*s Mir Mehr-e `Ali came with about 500 foot soldiers under the cannons of the VOC factory at 2 o'clock at midnight on April 7, 1744. He at once asked whether he could count on artillery support for both the citadel and the house of the *na'eb*, so that the rebels would loose heart. He added that on pain of death he was not allowed to undertake anything without the help of the Dutch and that Nader Shah would recompense the VOC. He not only promised golden mountains, but `Abdol-Ghaffar Beg and Mirza Hadi, even kissed the hands of the Poorter. In views of the pros and cons the council decided to support Mir Mehr-e `Ali and promised artillery support when he would attack. The Dutch would bombard the three royal ships, the citadel and the house of the *na'eb*. After the agreement the soldiers supported by all arms-bearing inhabitants and VOC servants left the Dutch factory to attack the *na'eb*, whose positions were already under Dutch cannon fire. Without returning the fire the snake fled, two of the ships were a total loss and the sailors surrendered. The others also surrendered without a fight, though some fled. Mohammad Baqer Beg surrendered his person to de Poorter with his sword around his neck and asked for his intervention with the shah. When the English, who were bursting from envy, heard this they sent their dragoman and Bombay soldiers to the two *chapar*s to ask the Dutch to stop firing, in which case they would deliver the *na'eb* to them, whom they claimed to have already in their hands. However, the English broke their promise and took the *na'eb* to their factory and refused to deliver him. The Dutch considered this a dirty trick and so thought everybody else.[225]

The *chapar*s promised to inform the shah about the services which the Dutch had rendered to his cause. They also took with them two Dutch requests to the shah as well as to four ministers when they left on April 19, 1744. In his letter to the shah, de Poorter wrote of past events, as described above, as well as that Gamron was only a village where people lived in huts made of palm leaves. Of the Banyans few had remained so that trade was totally non-existent.[226] The *sardar* had sent two tax collectors (`Abd `Ali Beg (Abdalie beecq) and Budaq Beg (Boedacq beecq) appointed by Nader Shah to make an inventory of the rebels' possessions. These also returned 20,647 lbs. of iron of the 30,000 supplied to Mohammad Taqi Khan, while for the remainder they received an assignation on the revenue of Minab at 3 *mahmudi*s per 6 lbs. With regard to the Dutch claims for the loss of *de Ridderkerk* and other claims they were less fortunate, for Nader Shah did not reply to their requests bearing on these issues.[227]

---

224. VOC 2680, Resolution Gamron (09/04/1744), unfoliated. Letter de Poorter to Mir Mehr-e `Ali dated April 7, 1744; VOC 2680, van der Welle to Batavia (10/08/1745), f. 51.

225. VOC 2680, Van der Welle to Batavia (10/08/1745), f. 51-53, the cost of the gunpowder and balls were charged to the shah; VOC 2680, Resolution Gamron (09/04/1744), unfoliated.

226. For the texts see VOC 2680, after Resolution Gamron (14/04/1744), unfoliated.

227. VOC 2680, Van der Welle to Batavia (10/08/1745), f. 54-57. The value of the goods on board the ship was Dfl. 210,803:10 2/3, while also Dfl. 1,004:8:5 1/3 had been advanced to the Persian

That the shah was very pleased with the Dutch was not only clear from the fact that Mohammad Hoseyn Khan the *sardar* on his visit to Gamron paid his first visit to the Dutch, despite English attempt to have him first, but also from Nader's letter which was received on July 21, 1744. He thanked the Dutch for their support and informed them that the rebels would be killed and their wives and children sold into slavery. He had given full powers to that end to the *sardar* Mohammad Hoseyn Khan, Allahverdi Khan, and Mohammad Hasan Beg (Khan), who had to consult, however, Mozaffar ʿAli Khan in all matters. Mohammad Soltan had been appointed as governor of Gamron, and Mirza Qasem as *shahbandar*. Mirza Hadi would get a good appointment as recompense for his services. This was further confirmed by his decree received on July 27, 1744, which stated that the Dutch would get a separate silk decree granting them the full and unhindered trade in that commodity. Nader, however, asked the Dutch to send him an authorized and high-ranking person to negotiate a new silk contract. Since there was nobody who qualified, the council decided to send a polite but non-committal reply and to continue to try and get a silk contract in more indirect ways. It therefore sent Jacob Jan Sahid, the dragoman, to the governor of Lar, Mohammad Soltan (Mhamed Zulthoen), whom the shah had suggested they should contact if they had requests. This did not lead to anything, because of the death of Mozaffar ʿAli Khan, who had been appointed by the shah as the main contact person for the silk contract, so that venue also had been closed. The council informed Batavia that unless an ambassador was sent, who was authorized to spend a lot of money, there was no chance that the VOC would get a new silk contract. However, because of the unsettled nature of the government any contract would not have any permanence.[228] At that time, the new director van der Welle, who had just arrived from Batavia and had taken over command on July 24, 1744, presided over the council. Schoonderwoerd had been appointed as his second.[229]

In view of Nader Shah's attitude towards the Dutch, the council's reaction to the presents given by Aalmis, the VOC representative in Isfahan was understandable. Aalmis had given considerable presents to Qalij Khan and *sardar* Hatem Khan after these had threatened to tell the shah that the Dutch had supported Mohammad Taqi Khan. The council therefore decided to send a two-man committee to Isfahan to stop the illegal activities by Aalmis, on September 7, 1744. The committee withdrew the VOC staff from Isfahan leaving only assistant Buffkens and dragoman Sahid in charge of the office as a skeleton staff to maintain the Dutch right of occupation. A similar decision was taken with regard to Kerman and both offices were ordered not to give any presents anymore.[230]

---

government. VOC 2680, after Resolution Gamron (22/07/1744), unfoliated.

228. VOC 2680, Van der Welle to Batavia (10/08/1745), f. 58-68 plus presents given to whom. David Sahid had been sent to court to discuss that matter and had submitted his report on 31/08/1743. But because the report had been in French, and not all council members knew that language, it had been translated by two council members, so that it was only ready on 22/03/1744. VOC 2680, Resolution Gamron (21/07/1744), unfoliated. The first *raqam* was dated Safar 1157/March-April 1744 and had 10 seals affixed to it. VOC 2680, Resolution Gamron (22/07/1744), unfoliated. The silk related *raqam* was dated 18 Rabiʿ al-Avval 1151/May 1, 1744 and had 12 seals affixed to it. The new governor, Mohammad Soltan, had as *mostowfi* Mirza Hoseyn, and as *nazer* Mirza Qasem. VOC 2680, Resolution Gamron (30/09/1744), unfoliated.

229. VOC 2680, Resolutions Gamron (24/07/1744) and (25/07/1744), unfoliated.

230. VOC 2680, Van der Welle to Batavia (10/08/1745), f. 114-41; VOC 2680, Resolutions Gamron (20/08/1744), (09/09/1744), and (03/10/1744), unfoliated. Qalij Khan (Galieds Chan) was governor

END OF REBELLION BROUGHT NO IMPROVEMENT

On November 8, 1744 the *sardar*, Mohammad Hoseyn Khan, arrived in Gamron with 12,000 men, both foot and horse. He was joined by Mozaffar `Ali Khan with his fleet on January 5, 1745. This led to the usual presents and visits. They were later joined by Qalij Khan and other commanders in March 1745, who all went to Masqat.[231]

On September 30, 1745 Nader's reply was received in which he referred the Dutch for further discussion to Mozaffar `Ali Khan. The Dutch had helped him with ships' supplies at the end of 1745, and given him and his favorites presents to promote a friendly relationship. However, it was all in vain, for Mozaffar `Ali Khan died on February 13, 1746. In view of this development and the expected high cost of a mission the council advised Batavia to let things be the more so since trade prospects were miserable.[232] Merchants were exposed to heavy taxation and extortion due to the unruliness that prevailed in the country.[233]

But it was not only the merchants who were preyed upon by Nader. The population in general had become totally emaciated because of his greed and bloodlust, so that it had been forced to take up the sword against him out of desperation and hope of liberation. In 1746, Fath `Ali Khan, with about 6,000 men, rebelled in the Kerman area, because Nader had demanded 10,000 *tuman*s from him. In reaction Fath `Ali Khan started to plunder everything he could lay his hands on and did not even spare caravans. The population therefore asked Nader for help against Fath `Ali Khan, who sent Shahrokh Mirza at the head of an army of 10,000-12,000 men to quell the rebellion. Meanwhile, it was also uncertain whether Nader had concluded peace with Turkey. It was rumored in June 1746 that a Turkish ambassador was approaching Qazvin and that the dignitaries were preparing themselves for the official reception.[234]

In mid-1746, van der Welle reported that he did not know whether Nader wanted war or peace. It was reported that a Turkish envoy was en route to discuss peace. The governor of Isfahan and the courtiers, including Hasan `Ali Khan, the *mo`ayyer bashi*, had gone to Tehran (Theroen) to welcome him. Also, Shahrokh Mirza, Nader's grandson, was back in Isfahan. However, the information received was often of a changing nature and the entire country was topsy-turvy.[235]

In December 1746 it was said that Nader himself would come to Isfahan to quell Fath `Ali Khan's rebellion, while he also intended to inspect the Garmsirat. However, instead of Nader himself, Qalij Khan came to Gamron on December 24, 1746 with close to 4,000 men. The purpose of his visit was unknown at that time, although it was suspected that he would go

---

of Isfahan at that time; when he became governor of the lower lands (Garmsirat) and admiral, he was succeeded by Assur Khan (Assour Chan). VOC 2860, van der Welle to Batavia (10/08/1745), f. 125; VOC 2705, van der Welle to Batavia (31/07/1746), f. 101-03.

231. VOC 2680, Resolutions Gamron (25/11/1744); (05/01/1745); (26/01/1745); and (26/03/1745), unfoliated.

232. VOC 2680, van der Welle to Batavia (10/08/1745), f. 59-61, 64-8.

233. VOC 2705, van der Welle to Batavia (31/07/1746), f. 35, 46, 55, 58; Ibid., idem to idem (28/02/1747), f. 538.

234. VOC 2705, van der Welle to Batavia (31/07/1746), f. 59-62.

235. VOC 2705, van der Welle to Batavia (31/07/1746), f. 59-61.

to `Oman to subdue the Arabs.[236] This suspicion proved to be true. Although the Dutch did not report on the results of this `Oman campaign these cannot have been very successful. For on April 13, 1747 some 40 *tranki*s with about 4,000 men arrived in Gamron coming from `Oman. These troops had rebelled and were commanded by Mir Mehr `Ali. His commander, Qalij Khan, followed him with 3,000 men on April 27, 1747. The governor of Gamron, Fazlollah Soltan, opposed their landing. During the night a fierce battle took place, which turned into a sack of the town followed by pillage and arson. The population was killed to get their possessions. Those who were left fled to the Arab side of the Persian Gulf. The Dutch were afraid that the rebelling troops would also attack their factory and therefore they kept a special watch. They also took gunpowder from one of their ships to have sufficient firing power. Peace returned to the town when on June 8, 1747 Qalij Khan left Gamron. On October 15, 1747 a shot from the cannon on the citadel announced the news of the death of the tyrant Nader Shah.[237]

[To learn how the situation in Gamron in particular, and in the Persian Gulf in general developed see Willem Floor, *The Persian Gulf. The Rise of the Gulf Arabs. The Politics of Trade on the Persian Litoral 1747-1792* (Washington DC: Mage, 2007)]

---

236. VOC 2705, van der Welle to Batavia (28/02/1747), f. 538-39. Qalij Khan (Galieds Chan) was governor of the lower lands (Garmsirat), admiral and *sardar*. His first advisor was Mohammad Soltan (Mhamet Sulthoen) and his deputy (*na'eb*) was Mirza Baqer (Miersa Bager). VOC 2705, f. 725. Governor of Gamron was Mohammad Soltan (Mhamet Sulthoen). VOC 2705, f. 270.

237. VOC 2724, f. 9, 13-14.

CHAPTER THREE

THE SITUATION AS SEEN FROM KERMAN

END OF AFGHAN RULE IS NO IMPROVEMENT

From Armenian sources in Kerman it was learnt that the Abdali Afghans were threatening that town during the summer of 1730. The *beglerbegi* of Kerman, Taleb Khan, was on his guard. His government was becoming more tolerable, so much so that the populace wanted to keep him in his function [f. 95]. Mir Mehr-e `Ali reported on September 7, 1730, that Kerman was in effect besieged by the Abdalis, who were led by Dhu'l-Feqar Khan. The latter defeated Taleb Khan who had been forced to withdraw into the town with the remainder of his troops, according to Armenian sources received by the Dutch on September 21, 1730 in Gamron. He had been dismissed and in his place Nader had appointed Emamverdi Khan. The latter arrived in Kerman in the beginning of October of 1730. He extorted a lot of money from the populace and his manner of administration was in general oppressive. Many leading merchants and citizens therefore left to Isfahan [f. 134]. De Cleen had written to Kerman to find out what the reaction of the local authorities would be, if the Dutch would resume the wool trade there. On November 23, 1730 de Cleen received a letter from Emamverdi Khan in which he confirmed his friendship for the Dutch and replied that if they would send staff to Kerman to resume the wool trade he promised them his assistance. He wanted to cast three big cannons, and therefore asked for three cannon casters. He had sent this request a few days earlier to the English but had received no reply.[1] With the same messenger came a letter from Mirza Mohammad, the *kalantar* of Kerman, who was very pleased with the Dutch intention to start the wool trade in Kerman again. He promised to second one of his own men to ensure that wool could be collected.[2]

During his short stay Emamverdi Khan had collected already 3,000 *tuman*s. On December 2, 1730, it was reported that Emamverdi Khan publicly had declared himself for Nader and against the shah [f. 163]. In February 1731, Nader ordered Emamverdi Khan to proceed to Herat to teach the Abdalis a lesson [f. 210]. On November 5, 1731, it was reported that

---

1. VOC 2253, Imoem Werdie Chan to de Cleen (23/11/1730 received), f. 567-68.

2. VOC 2253, Calanthaar of Kerman, Miersa Mamed to de Cleen (23/11/1730 received), f. 569-70.

Nader had killed Taleb Khan, the former governor of Kerman, and that in his place Moham-mad Taqi had been appointed. He was said to have been ordered to march with 5,000 men to the Garmsirat to destroy Sheikh Ahmad Madani [f. 987].[3]

PROBLEMS OF THE SHAWL WEAVERS

On July 25, 1731, the new *beglerbegi* of Kerman, Mohammad Taqi Khan (Mhamed Takie Chan) arrived, followed by a *vakil*, appointed by Nader, named Khan Khadar Qoli Beg (?) (Chan Cha-daar Coelie Beecq), who also had authority in financial matters. At that time Nader was still be-sieging Herat and Farah and almost daily couriers (*chapar*s) arrived in Kerman from those parts. The shawl weavers received orders to reserve all ready-made shawls and those under production for Nader's account.[4] This caused a rise in price; shawls that normally cost 20 *mahmudi*s were priced at 60 *mahmudi*s. The order also caused a dearth of wool, which was hardly to be obtained anymore. In fact all goods and monies that were brought to Kerman were reserved by force for Nader, and its costs were assigned to the city's revenues.

ONLY NADER'S, NOT THE SHAH'S ORDERS ARE VALID

Kerman province like Yazd, Khorasan and Mazandaran were under the direct rule of Nader, where even the shah had no authority, for the royal decrees were only obeyed and respected when Nader had confirmed them. The latter also had declared null and void any royal decree, which he had granted during his stay in Isfahan in 1730. At their wool factor's suggestion, the Dutch therefore asked Nader to renew and confirm all their privileges.[5] Nader promised to instruct the governor of Kerman to assist the Dutch wool factor in the execution of his task. This was neces-sary, because in September 1732 about 500 people complained to the *beglerbegi* that due to the purchase and export of wool by the Europeans they had no work anymore and their families were without bread. Moreover, they could not implement Nader's orders to weave shawls and other fabrics. Not only did the Dutch and the English Companies buy a lot of wool, but they also em-ployed all the men and women who cleaned and carded the wool, whom they paid double wages. This caused hardship to the merchants and weavers. The *beglerbegi* summoned the representatives of the Dutch and English Companies and angrily asked them why they acted so insolently and ruined the populace by monopolizing the wool trade. The representatives replied that they had been engaged in the wool trade for decades that it had become a normal part of life in Kerman, for which they, moreover, had a royal decree allowing them to do so. The *beglerbegi* reacted by say-ing that the royal decrees had no value anymore; they had better stop buying wool, else he would know how to deal with them. The representatives discussed the matter together and decided to give the *beglerbegi* separately a present, which had the desired effect.[6]

---

3. The folio numbers between brackets on this page refer to VOC 2254, Gamronsch Dagregister (22/04/1730-31/04/1731), f. 95, 134, 163, 210; VOC 2254, Gamronsch Dagregister (01/05/1732-30/06/1732), f. 987; Emamverdi Khan requested three artisans to cast big cannons. VOC 2253 (received 23/11/1730), f. 567.

4. On all matters concerning the fabric known as *shal* or shawl see Willem Floor, *The Persian Textile Industry in historical perspective 1500-1925* (Paris: L'Harmattan, 1999), pp. 296-354.

5. VOC 2254, Auwannees to de Cleen (23/11/1731), f. 1201-03.

6. VOC 2322, Auwannees to de Cleen (30/09/1732), f. 437 vs- 438 vs.

NEW IMPOSTS AND CONTINUED PROBLEMS OF SHAWL WEAVERS

Despite their exemption from imposts and the like the VOC wool factor also had to contribute to the general tax demanded from the populace. Both Companies had to pay 50 *tuman*s. The English paid right away; but Hovannes protested. The EIC wool buyer Cordeux then gave presents to the authorities and induced them to billet 50 soldiers in Hovannes's house, who threatened him and wanted to give him the bastinado. He fled and appealed to the *beglerbegi*. Hovannes was ordered to pay, but was promised to get his money back by December 1732. Although not without difficulties, the money was repaid by the governor, but by charging the Zoroastrians for this amount.[7]

The problems of the shawl weavers still had not been solved. In June/July 1733, these again complained to the *beglerbegi* on a daily basis, viz. that they had almost been ruined. The *beglerbegi* who had already received a present from the English was kind enough to draw Hovannes attention to both facts. He was also helpful in turning a deaf ear to these complaints for which attitude Hovannes felt that he could not neglect to show his appreciation, the more so since it had been inferred that the *beglerbegi* might withhold his favor from the Dutch.[8] In September 1733, messengers arrived from Nader (Thamas Chan) with orders that the population of Kerman had to contribute 13,000 *tuman*s to pay his troops. The Dutch and English also had to contribute each 1,000 *tuman*s. Auwannees protested; the governor agreed to wait and see what the result would be of Nader's violent deeds after which he would act accordingly.[9]

On January 22, 1734, Qalij Pondi Khan, son of Sadat Khan (Geleeds Pondie Chan, son of Sadaet Chan) attacked the Kerman area with 6,000 men and pillaged, burnt and killed in the city's immediate surroundings. Hovannes was forced to retire into the citadel. Although he did not report it, later the Baluch probably left towards Gamron.[10] At the end of February 1734, Mohammad Taqi Khan was dismissed as *beglerbegi* and summoned to come to Shiraz. He was replaced by Esma`il Khan.[11] In April 1734, the population of Kerman was ordered to pay again a new impost, which led to a rise in the value of the silver `*abbasi*s *vis à vis* the copper *paisa*.[12] In June 1734, a *chapar* arrived in Kerman sent by Nader to his *vakil* in Kerman, Mirza Reza, to collect within two days a sum of 1,000 *tuman*s in silver money and to send it right away to Farah. Both Companies, despite their protest, also had to pay; 150 *tuman*s (EIC) and 80 *tuman*s (VOC) for which they received an IOU.[13] Apart from the money troubles, people were also troubled by the pressing of their riding and pack animals by Nader's soldiers. The high price of silver in Kerman had the effect that merchants from Isfahan, Khorasan and

---

7. VOC 2322, Auwannees to de Cleen (30/09/1732), f. 440r-vs; VOC 2322, Auwannees to de Cleen (09/11/1732), f. 446r-vs; Auwannees to de Cleen (21/12/1732), f. 47 vs.

8. VOC 2322, Auwannees to de Cleen (30/07/1733), f. 466-67.

9. VOC 2322 II, Auwannees to de Cleen (07/10/1733), f. 269.

10. VOC 2323, Auwannees to de Cleen (02/02/1734), f. 824.

11. VOC 2323, Auwannees to de Cleen (28/03/1734), f. 826.

12. VOC 2323, Auwannees to de Cleen (01/05/1734), f. 836.

13. VOC 2323, Auwannees to de Cleen (15/06/1734), f. 843.

elsewhere took their silver to Kerman, so that in August the price had dropped from 4.5 to 4 *mahmudi*s copper money per silver `abbasi*.[14]

On Monday March 21, 1735, the Dutch decided to appoint a Dutchman in charge of the Kerman office to buy wool there. When the new wool factor, Clement, arrived in Kerman the governor, Esma`il Khan, was in Seistan. His deputy Mohammad Qoli Beg wrote to Koenad, the VOC director in Gamron, that he would support the Dutch wool trade. The government of Kerman at that time was discharged not only by the *na'eb*, but also by two other officials, viz. Mostafa Beg and Mirza Asiyab [?] (Asjaeb). Nader's *vakil* or agent, Mirza Reza, however, was the center around which all matters turned. Because of this administrative arrangement it was not clear who was in charge of and responsible for what, which greatly confused the population. They were sent from one to the other without getting any results, which gave rise to many complaints. The Dutch remarked that the town officials were rather reasonable towards them.[15]

In June 1735, the inhabitants of Kerman were once again faced with yet another extraordinary impost. They had to pay 7,000 *tuman*s, half of which was for Tahmasp Qoli Khan in Herat and the other half was for Esma`il Khan in Seistan. Because cash was scarce the peasants were forced to sell their wool at the low price of 12.5 *mahmudi*s, a drop of about 25% as compared with mid-May. What was even worse was that in Sirjan, the plague had struck towards the end of May and was slowly making its way towards Kerman. Already 30 people had died. On May 25, the town officials made public that all sincere and believing Moslems should go to the mosques to pray and give alms to make the plague go away.[16] By July the plague was over. In the period prior to that day, some 50 to 60 people had died every day, but this was mainly ascribed to the heat, so there may not have been a plague at all, Clement concluded. Although the big merchants refused to sell wool at 12.5 *mahmudi*s and still believed that last year's prices might be realized the Dutch and the English concluded an oral agreement stipulating that the price of wool offered in small quantities would only be 11 *mahmudi*s copper money. Moreover, the wool price would not be increased without each other's consent.[17]

NADER'S VICTORIES MEAN MORE TAXES

On July 3, 1735 a messenger arrived from Nader bringing news of his victory against the Turks at Qars. He demanded that 200 men be sent to him, which led people to conclude that the victory apparently was not that big. To commemorate this happy event the population of Kerman and dependencies had to pay 2,100 *tuman*s, of which 100 *tuman* was for the messenger. On top of that, the town had to be illuminated during three days to celebrate the victory.[18] Isfahan had to pay 7,000 *tuman*s, Shiraz 4,000 *tuman*s and Gamron or Fars 3,000 *tuman*s. The money did not have to be paid right away, but had to be ready two months before New Year (*Nowruz*). The *saheb-*

---

14. VOC 2323, Auwannees to de Cleen (28/08/1734), f. 842; VOC 2323, Auwannees to de Cleen (28/08/1734) 853.

15. VOC 2416, Clement to Koenad (19/05/1735), f. 1875-77.

16. VOC 2426, Clement to Koenad (08/06/1735), f. 1896-1902.

17. VOC 2426, Clement to Koenad (22/07/1735), f. 2100-01.

18. VOC 2537, Auwannees to Koenad (22/07/1735), f. 911; VOC 2426, Clement to Koenad (22/07/1735), f. 2108.

e ekhtiyar or governor, Mirza Reza, was ordered to bring the money to Nader at the stipulated time. Mirza Reza had arrived on June 25 in Kerman and ordered on July 2 all merchants to sign a bond stating that if they were found to be exporting copper money out of Kerman that all their property would be forfeited, because this had been forbidden publicly on June 30. He also had ordered that the EIC representative sign the bond. The Dutch did not need do so, he said, for the VOC had 3,000 *tuman*s outstanding under the merchants and therefore could not be expected not to export goods to Gamron. Clement expected that this order would be revoked, because else trade would come to a total standstill. The EIC representative meanwhile was doing his best to be exempted from signing the bond.[19]

The agreement between the English and the Dutch had the desired result; their refusal to buy wool, unless against lower prices, resulted in prices varying from 13 to 15.5 *mahmudi*s. On August 1, 1735 again a messenger arrived, making public yet another victory of Nader. Again the town was illuminated for three days. This time there was a real reason to celebrate for Nader bestowed the victory money, which he again had demanded as a boon to the people. However, he demanded 200 men from Kerman and 300 from Seistan which were taken to him by the *kutval* (castellan) of Kerman, `Ali Beg.[20]

On September 16, 1735 a messenger arrived with the news that Nader had taken Ganjeh as a result of which the town was Illuminated for three days. Nader had also given orders that the *kalantar* Mirza Reza, the qadi, all mullahs, and the *kadkhoda*s of the town and from Boluk-e Eqta` had to keep themselves ready to come and join him when he would give the word. In total 100 persons had to prepare themselves. Similar orders had been given to the same class of people in other towns such as Isfahan (300 persons) and Shiraz (200 persons). It was not known why that order had been given, but all agreed that it had to be something of importance.[21]

VOC-EIC SQUABBLES

The rumor that the governor of Kerman would be replaced by one of Mirza Mohammad Taqi's servants was not confirmed. In fact, it was negated by the arrival of two messengers from Mohammad Taqi on September 28, 1735 with 82 camels loaded with silver money for the *sardar*s Tamasp Qoli Khan and Esma`il Khan. They also had a letter for Mirza Mohammad Reza, governor of Kerman and its districts, which did not make any mention of this. The Dutch in Kerman were very satisfied about the town officials in October 1735. For Mirza Mohammad Reza, the *saheb-ekhtiyar*, had praised the Dutch and had strongly criticized the English. Koenad had sent him a letter announcing the appointment of Clement and requested his assistance for Dutch trade activities. The English he said had sent no letter, but had silently fled from Kerman, thereby showing the lack of proper respect for the government officials in Kerman. The governor would inform Nader about this behavior, he promised. Other important officials, such as Tavakkol Beg, a confidante of Nader, also gave the Dutch a statement in which he declared that the VOC was a very respectable Company. On October 5, Mirza Reza even publicly paid a visit to the Dutch

---

19. VOC 2416, Clement to Koenad (22/07/1735), f. 2109-10.

20. VOC 2417, Clement to Koenad (26/08/1735), f. 3072; VOC 2417, Clement to Koenad (18/08/1735), f. 3080, 3084.

21. VOC 2417, Clement to Koenad (21/09/1735), f. 3093-94.

house accompanied by the *Sheikh al-Eslam*, Tavakkol Beg, Mirza Yusof, the *kalantar*, Mirza Reza's vizier, Mirza Qasem and various leading citizens. They had lunch at the Dutch house, which was the talk of the week in Kerman, for never before had a *Sheikh al-Eslam* paid a visit to a Christian, let alone had eaten there, which according to Clement was very good for the Dutch reputation. The EIC dragoman, who was still in Kerman, was hopping mad about this honor shown to the Dutch and tried by all possible means to induce Mirza Reza to bring a visit to the English house as well. He, moreover, was telling slander about the Dutch to Mirza Reza, which information was all passed on to Clement by Ebrahim Beg, *darugheh* of Kerman and confidante of Mirza Reza.[22]

NADER'S CORONATIONS MEANS MORE TAXES

The *saheb-e ekhtiyar* Mirza Mohammad Reza left Kerman on November 26, 1735 accompanied by all those who had been summoned to Qazvin. Esma`il Khan followed them two days later. Before he left, during his one and half day stay, he appointed Mohammad Qoli Beg as his *na'eb* at the intercession of Tavakkol Beg. Mohammad Qoli Beg had begged for this function on his knees, for Esma`il Khan had intended to give the post to his uncle Mansur Beg.[23]

Van Loon replaced Clement on March 3, 1736. Shortly thereafter, Kerman was again faced with new exactions from the brand-new king, Nader Shah. Nader had ordered to make him 5,000 grey hats of all kinds of cloth, which had to be embroidered all around and in front with the following texts: 1,000 hats with the text: *Ya Allah*, 1,000 with *Ya Rahman*, 1,000 with *Ya Rahim*, 1,000 with *Ya Karim* and 1,000 with *Ya Sobhan*. These were for Nader's lifeguard. By the end of April 1736 already about 4,000 had been sent to him that had led to a great scarcity of pack animals, which had been pressed into service by the town officials for this transport. The order for the hats had been brought to Kerman on February 14, 1736 which already at that time had caused problems for the Dutch with the transportation of their wool to Gamron. On April 1, 1736 a new order arrived in Kerman, viz. 5,000 pairs of boots had to be supplied for the cavalry. The muleteers as a result of the earlier and the later order had taken to the hills where they had hidden their animals, and whatever trouble the town officials took the animals could not be found. Nader also had appointed new town officials. Mirza Mohammad Reza was appointed as vizier of Isfahan and so did not come back, in his place a certain `Ali Beg was appointed; as vizier, Mirza Abu Taleb, former *divan-begi* of Shah Ahmad Khan, was appointed.

PREPARATIONS FOR THE QANDAHAR CAMPAIGN

On April 15, 1736 three ambassadors from Nader passed through Kerman; two of whom were sent to the Afghan leader Hoseyn Khan. They were Ashraf Soltan and Mirath Khan (Mheeraes Chan), both were Abdalis. Their *mehmandar* was Mir Mohammad Hoseyn. Further Mohammad Reza Beg Lacq was sent to a leader of the Baluch, `Abdollah Khan, to the side of Kabul, in the

---

22. VOC 2417, Clement to Koenad (15/10/1735), f. 3104-08. The fact that on October 21, 1735 Clement lent 50 silver *tumans* to Mirza Mohammad Reza (Miersa Mhamed Resa) may have had something to do with this friendly visit. Mirza Mohammad Reza was 'lending' and extorting money from everybody whom he could lay his hands on. By the end of December Clement had received already 36 *tumans* back. VOC 2417, Clement to Koenad (31/12/1735), f. 3141.

23. VOC 2417, Clement to Koenad (31/12/1735), f. 3137.

Moghul empire, situated in province Halroem Ragsoen [?] and Kalat. His mission was secret, but it was said that he brought orders to the Baluch to stock supplies and recruit many thousands to support Nader when he would attack Qandahar and to close the Moghul border to prevent an invasion from that side. The ambassadors to Hoseyn Khan were said to demand his surrender, that he send his children to Nader and ask forgiveness in which case he would have nothing to fear, for Nader would appoint him as governor of Qandahar. If not, disgrace would be his fate and Nader would come to punish and take him. The Dutch had doubts whether the Afghan leader would accept it, for he had 40,000 warriors and supplies for one year at his disposal. Nader apparently also did not believe it, for he ordered Tavakkol Beg per decree to stock 900,000 *mann* of wheat and barley, and later ordered 30,000 *mann* of gun-powder and 60,000 *mann* of lead to be collected in south-west Iran, for Nader wanted to proceed to Qandahar via Kerman.[24]

Tavakkol Beg sent the orders to the vizier of Kerman, Mirza Hoseyn, who immediately started to carry them out. This caused scarcity of bread, which was hardly available anymore. Later the order was alleviated somewhat, for the *na'eb* had made it known on April 22, 1736 (fearing a revolt) that everyone who had grain, could give it to the bakers at prices fixed by themselves, and bread could be sold at prices which were considered reasonable. This served to restore the supply of bread again to a normal situation without fixed prices. The result was that reasonable barley bread could be bought; however, no wheat bread was available in the bazaars. On April 27, 1736 a messenger from Nader arrived in Kerman with orders for the authorities. Nader repealed the order for grain to be taken from the community and also granted it 25% of the ordinary taxes, for he was not going to Qandahar. Hoseyn Khan had sent him the golden jewel studded key of Qandahar with the request to send a castellan with troops, and that he subdued himself obediently and would pay an annual contribution, for he knew that Mahmud Khan and Ashraf Khan had not gained anything with their rebellions. They had lost their lives, while their women and children were in slavery. The population of Kerman was very pleased that Nader would not come to Kerman. The three ambassadors left on April 28.[25]

Cockill, the EIC director, had arrived in Kerman on May 1, 1736 in a litter for he was ill. He did not pay visits to the authorities, which offended them. He therefore gave them presents, so the Dutch also were forced to do the same. Presents were given to Esma`il Khan, *beglerbegi*, the vizier Mirza Abu Taleb, the *vakil* `Ali Beg (Alier beecq) and the *kalantar* Mirza Yusef. Attempts were also made to send some hundreds of men to Nader. Their recruitment was done very secretively, but it was unknown for which purpose. It was said that Nader would march via Kerman to Qandahar after all. A certain Mirza Taqi (Miersa Tackie) came from Nader to Kerman to build caravanserais between Kerman and Qandahar every six miles; these he had to make into fortresses to serve as refuge for Nader's army. Nader also demanded all grain harvested that year, which caused much famine and misery. There was no food such as bread, wheat, barley, nuts, raisins, dates, etc. with the exception of meat, which was available in plenty in the bazaar.[26]

---

24. VOC 2417, Clement/van Loon to Koenad (24/04/1736 + appendix 29/04/1736), f. 3148-76.

25. VOC 2417, Clement/van Loon to Koenad (24/04/1736 + appendix 29/04/1736), f. 3176-88.

26. Count Cherubini died on May 25, 1736. Cockill asked leave to depart to pay him his last respects, which was granted, so he came off easily. VOC 2417, Clement/van Loon to Koenad (296/05/1736), f. 3191-3202.

Because the authorities pressed animals into service, pack animals hardly were available. They were used for transport of supplies to Seistan and Taraet [?]. Nader was said to come to Kerman in two months' time. Even caravans en route were stopped, like a Dutch one at Dastiyab (Destiaab) and Dowlatabad. Van Loon complained to the *beglerbegi* Mirza Taqi, who arrived in Kerman on July 3, 1736 and was a good friend of the VOC. He promised an order, which took time, for the English gave him presents and wanted a similar order. On August 17 van Loon had lunch with him to get the *ta'liqeh*. The English dragoman arrived with a letter, but the governor did not even read it, and had him wait for one hour and then said that it was all right. Two merchants came to Kerman at that time, 'Ali Mohammad, sister's son of Mostowfi Beg, and Hadi 'Ali Qoli. The first one was sent by Ebrahim Khan, brother of Nader, with 1,500 silver *tuman*s to buy wool in Kerman, but only the red kind and to send it to Gilan. They were exempted from *rahdari* and other imposts. There was also a group of four merchants who, out of fear that the VOC and EIC would try to prevent them from trading, had not yet bought wool and were only waiting for the result of the new developments viz. would the two new merchants be successful in obtaining wool. In that case, the Dutch expected them to buy wool as well, which would be disadvantageous for the VOC. Cockill feared this too; he even came to the Dutch on August 15, 1736 to deliberate how to prevent this. As a result, they threatened all leading wool merchants that, if they sold wool to other merchants, the Dutch and English would not buy the rest of their wool. The wool merchants therefore did not sell any wool to the others. The *vakil* 'Ali Beg (Alier Beeck) and the vizier Mirza Abu Taleb acted as *na'eb* in Kerman. They were well inclined to the VOC, for the Dutch got a *ta'liqeh* on August 19, but not the English, whatever they tried. On August 20 Esma'il Khan left with Mirza Taqi to Seistan to establish caravanserais with supplies and fresh water wells in every *manzel* or halting station.[27]

On September 16, 1736 a *chapar* from Mostafa Khan arrived, son of Hajji Geda 'Ali Khan (Hadje Gadalie Chan), former *beglerbegi* of Kerman, who, per rescript (*raqam*), informed the vizier and the *vakil* that they had been dismissed and had to move out of their house, for he had been appointed in their place. Kerman was without authorities for a time, until he arrived. On September 21 a *chapar* arrived in Kerman with information that Nader would come after one month in Kerman. Also that he had a *raqam* for the ex-*vakil* and vizier to recall the 300 diggers who had been sent to Isfahan on September 16 and to keep them in Kerman until Nader's arrival there. On September 20, 1736 2,000 *tuman*s silver were taken to Seistan. Also, by use of force, 200 pairs of carpets, 3,000 surcoats (cabayen; *qaba*), 3,000 caps, undercoats [also called *cabayen*], shawls, stockings, trousers, green shoes, boots, etc. were taken from the inhabitants as well as 4,000 cover blankets, fodder sacks, iron, nails, etc. for his cavalry. The poor artisans had to work almost gratis and were not allowed one minute of rest but were forced by bastinado and beatings to work. On the arrival of Esma'il Khan in Seistan the Afghans retired to Qandahar. Mohammad Reza Beg ambassador to the chief of the Baluch 'Abdollah Khan in Kalat returned on September 25. He visited the Dutch on September 28 and told them in secret that he could not believe that Nader would come to Kerman, or if he did, that he would be able to take Qandahar. For in that case not only Hoseyn Khan but also the Baluch would resist.[28]

---

27. VOC 2417, van Loon to Koenad (29/08/1736), f. 3211-26.

28. VOC 2417, Van Loon/Martijn to Koenad (23/09/1736), f. 3231-45. Emmanuel Martijn replaced

On October 14, 1736 a rumor was circulated that Nader had died against the Bakhti-yaris. The news caused consternation. It was said that Esma`il Khan had secret orders to con-tinue the preparations as if nothing had happened, and to make haste with the collection of the *soyursat* or extraordinary demand for supplies. Although it was said that Nader would not come the preparations to welcome him were continued. Daily messengers arrived in Kerman with conflicting information. The policy of the authorities was aimed at creating confusion, for they had to consider the Afghans (40,000 men) the Baluch (30,000 men) and the Moghuls (100,000-150,000 men) who were on the border at Kabul to await the result of Nader's ac-tions. Rebellions meanwhile increased as well as the level of extortion of the population. On October 13 news was received that the Baluch had rebelled at Ravar on the border of Kerman province. On October 14 ambassador Mohammad Reza Beg Lacq had returned from there. He went back with 500 selected men to subdue them.[29]

On November 14, 1736 Esma`il Khan and Mirza Taqi left for Seistan again to inspect the roads and the supply stores. On November 14 letters for the new *saheb-ekhtiyar*, Mostafa Khan, arrived informing him that Nader would leave Isfahan on November 20. The extortion in Kerman continued in such a way that the poor inhabitants and merchants were to be pitied. They were beaten severely and tax collectors stayed in their houses till the money had been obtained. The Banyans and merchants paid 1,500 *tuman*s silver money and gave it to Mostafa Khan.[30] The extortion of money still continued, the VOC and EIC also had to pay. From each Company 50 *tuman*s was demanded. From the English it was taken by force. The VOC was exempted because van Loon was ill and had to leave. It was also said at that time that Mirza Taqi would go as ambassador to Hindustan via Qandahar to claim 300,000 *tuman*s from the Mughal, or else Nader would come and get it.[31]

NADER PASSES THROUGH ON HIS WAY TO QANDAHAR

After the arrival of Nader's troops nobody dared to leave the town out of fear of being pillaged. On December 12, 1736 the troops had arrived and on December 22 Nader himself. On December 31 he went to Qandahar. All nobles and inhabitants, as well as the Dutch and English represen-tatives welcomed Nader. The Europeans greeted him and Nader ordered his mace-bearer to ask who they were. The English gave presents so the Dutch were also forced to follow suit. Nader ordered samples of wool. Mirza Taqi said that Nader wanted to send the samples to Gilan and Turkey to see which ones was the best kind to sell there. If it proved to be a feasible enterprise

---

van Loon as of September 17, 1736 the day he arrived in Kerman. The latter had been negligent and the council at Gamron had decided to send Clement to investigate why van Loon had sent no reports at all since Clement's departure and to return with him to Gamron. VOC 2416 Resolution Gamron (03/09/1736), f. 1286-87. On his return to Gamron van Loon was downgraded from the rank of book-keeper to that of assistant, meaning that in stead of Dfl 30/month he would only earn Dfl. 20/month. VOC 2417, Resolution Gamron (08/01/1737), f. 3699.

29. VOC 2417, Martijn to Koenad (19/10/1736), f. 3240-64.

30. VOC 2417, Martijn to Koenad (11/11/1736), f. 3273; VOC 2417, Martijn to Koenad (17/11/1736), f. 3276-77.

31. VOC 2417, Martijn to Koenad (19/10/1736), f. 3975-79. The text mistakenly mentions Clement, who had already left because of the extortion, for under such conditions Koenad considered it to be better that there were no Europeans in Kerman.

Nader intended to give some merchants money to buy wool in Kerman and sell it for him. The Dutch representative pointed out that for the VOC this was serious matter. The VOC only had come to Kerman for the wool trade and the merchants and thousands of other people lived from that trade. The merchants who came each year would then also stay away which would ruin the economy of Kerman. He pointed out that Nader could of course do what he liked, but the town and people would be ruined. Mirza Taqi promised to talk to Nader and to make him abandon this plan. Later Mirza Taqi told Hovannes that after lengthy talks Nader agreed to desist from his plan. Nader had an army of 80,000 consisting of soldiers, servants, stable boys etc. and 900 sutlers. Nader had lent the latter group 80,000 *tuman*s at 40% rate of interest. Nader held court outside town in the house of Esma`il Khan; his baggage remained outside the town being stored in tents.[32]

Nader was stopped at the Helmand River, for the Afghans contained the passages and fords with cannons and the river had a strong current. The people of Kerman continued to be very much troubled for an assignation of 6,000 *tuman*s of goods was issued on them, while 4,000 pack animals also had to be supplied. Khan Jan and Pir Mohammad Khan were expected in Kerman to go with Abu'l-Hasan to Bam. Therefore orders were given to keep 600 men ready, as well as 200 oxen to transport the cannons to Seistan. Camels also were pressed, so that for a long time no caravan was expected to come to Kerman.[33] Khan Jan and his troops arrived on March 3, 1737 and stayed for five days, during which time they caused much damage. On March 9, he left with Pir Mohammad and Abu'l-Hasan Khan, the latter only as far as Bam. He returned on March 18. It rained for 10 days in March, so that many houses were destroyed and the town really had become one big ruin.[34]

One group of his soldiers stayed in the suburb of the Zoroastrians, the remainder outside the city. The troops were well clothed, but committed all kinds of untoward actions, which were indescribable. They burnt all doors and windows. The city was plundered, and ruined in such a manner as had never happened in man's history the Dutch remarked. Nader deemed the present from the Zoroastrians too insignificant and he ordered that they had to pay 200 *tuman*s or they had all to become Moslem. He appointed a tax collector who beat the money out them. Some were so sorely pressed that they sold everything, even their wife and children in order to remain Zoroastrian. Esma`il Khan, the former *beglerbegi* of Kerman, was given the bastinado and Abu'l-Hasan Khan was appointed in his place. The provost general, the vizier Mirza Abu Taleb was strangled and his property confiscated. Mirza Hoseyn (Miersa Hassim) was again appointed as vizier. The *saheb-ekhtiyar*, Mostafa Khan, was also dismissed and his function given to Abu'l-Hasan Khan. After Nader's departure the new governor asked the Dutch and English each for a loan of 500 *tuman*s. Hovannes claimed that he did not have that much money. But when the English gave 100 *tuman*s in order to be rid of a worse treatment he also gave 90 *tuman*s, the more so since the governor promised repayment after 20 days when the tax collectors would have returned from the villages. The governor also borrowed money from the merchants and the inhabitants of Kerman while his tax collectors beat money out of the poor people so that many sold their house, property, and children to feed the greed of

---

32. VOC 2417, Auwannees to Koenad (13/02/1737), f. 4140-49.

33. VOC 2417, Auwannees to Koenad (27/02/1737), f. 4165-66.

34. VOC 2417, Auwannees to Koenad (19/03/1737), f. 4169.

the officials. The city did not look like it had been before and its ruin became worse every day. Trade had come at a standstill, for there was no money and no caravans arrived. Pir Mohammad Khan had remained in Kerman to wait for Khan Jan to jointly march against the Baluch.[35]

From Qandahar information was received that after Nader had taken some villages an Afghan chief, Musa Dangi (Moessa Doengie), with 300 families had subjected himself and had offered to supply the army for one month at his expense, Nader had given him a robe of honor in exchange for the offer and his help in indicating a ford across the river Helmand. After that Nader's army crossed and had enclosed the citadel of Qandahar. Hoseyn Khan refused to surrender because he had sufficient supplies for all his needs. Nader therefore ordered to build a town and a fortress opposite the Qandahar citadel. The surrounding countryside he ordered to be sown with grains so that its produce might be used as food for his army.[36] On April 18, 1737 a *chapar* from Nader's army arrived in Kerman who told that as yet no battle had taken place with Hoseyn Khan and that the army was busy building the town and fortress. There only had been scrimmages during the night, which resulted in deaths on both sides. The *chapar* had orders for Abu'l-Hasan Khan to send Nader 10,000 *mann* of powder and 15,000 *mann* of lead which order he immediately carried out.[37]

NEWS FROM INDIA

The officials were as greedy as the tax collectors in Kerman and took whatever they could lay their hands on. A new *beglerbegi*, Mohammad Sharif Khan, arrived on December 21, 1738 in Kerman. Nader was said to have taken Peshawar at that time, while the news about the defeat and death of Ebrahim Khan and many of his soldiers against the Lezgis also was known in Kerman. Nader immediately appointed a new governor, Amir Aslan Khan (Amier Aslan Chan), who went to Tabriz to raise a new army and march against the Lezgis. On February 17, 1739 a *chapar* arrived with news on the advance of some Uzbek troops towards Herat and Mashhad who had been expelled by Reza Qoli Mirza, who had been appointed viceroy of the whole country. Balkh was still in Persian hands. Nader appointed Abu'l-Hasan Khan as the viceroy's chancellor, and ordered the viceroy only to stay two months per year in Isfahan. After *Nowruz*, he had to travel through Persia and both of them separately had to report on their findings to the shah after his return from India. The governor of Kerman was ordered by Nader to supply Mohammad Taqi Khan who was in Mashhad with 1,000 soldiers and one year of supplies. Mohammad Taqi Khan, who had joined Nader at Peshawar, not only had been reinstated as *beglerbegi* of Fars, but also had been made a *sardar* and was shown great kindness and affection by Nader, who issued a decree ordering all governors to obey Mirza Taqi Khan. When the governor of Kerman learnt this he sent the *kalantar* to Mohammad Taqi Khan to ask him to travel via Kerman. In short, Mohammad Taqi Khan stood in higher esteem with Nader Shah than ever before.[38]

The year 1739 was a difficult one for Kerman, since the mortality among the sheep and goats was estimated to be as high as 90% due to pest. Nevertheless orders from the viceroy

---

35. VOC 2417, Auwannees to Koenad (13/02/1737), f. 4150-53.

36. VOC 2368, Auwannees to Koenad (07/04/1737), f. 3806.

37. VOC 2368, Auwannees to Koenad (19/04/1737), f. 3806 vs.

38. VOC 2477, Auwannees to Koenad (19/02/1739), f. 795-800.

were received in early May to make him 3,000 woolen caps which led to even higher prices. Life consequently was very expensive in the town, which was aggravated by the actions of the *kalantar*. A few leading citizens complained about him to the viceroy who sent Mehr Beg (Mheera Beek) to investigate. Nevertheless the *kalantar* continued with his actions and made life even worse for the inhabitants than before. The merchants moreover were beginning to leave Kerman because the *beglerbegi* started to levy the taxes again. The inhabitants who had decreased in number and were very poor nevertheless were forced to pay the full quota and their lot grew worse every day.[39]

On July 3, 1739 an envoy from the viceroy arrived in Kerman with two *raqam*s from Nader; he also brought the rumor that Shah Tahmasp had been murdered.[40] A new affliction was the arrival of three officials coming from Nader's army at Lahore, viz. Mohammad Qoli Khan, appointed governor of Bahrain, a royal *vakil* also destined for Bahrain and a vizier for that island. The governor had a *raqam* for the *beglerbegi* of Kerman ordering him to hand over 270 *tuman*s and 500 men from the Kerman forces. He also had to give 500 *tuman*s and 500 men to Mohammad Taqi Khan and then to proceed to Bahrain. But this was a slight burden compared with the orders given by the viceroy who had demanded that Kerman send 722,000 *mann* of grain to Mohammad Taqi Khan in Gamron, and that the cost of the grain as well of its transportation had to be borne by the population of Kerman.[41]

Later the letters do not mention this matter anymore, but the *beglerbegi* Mohammad Sharif Khan together with the *kalantar* Mirza Yusef oppressed the people of Kerman so much (whether in connection with the grain order is not reported) that the emaciated and ruined people complained to the viceroy. The latter dismissed both officials and appointed Mozaffar Khan Nishapuri, his former *nazer*, as *beglerbegi* and Mohammad Qoli Beg Afshar as *na'eb* of Kerman and Hajji Mir Borhan (Bouhtoen) as *kalantar*. He also sent two envoys, who had orders to restitute the money which the two accused had taken unlawfully from the inhabitants. These two envoys arrived on September 12, 1739.[42]

THE FRENCH COME TO KERMAN AND NEW DEMANDS FROM NADER

M. Beaumont, the chief of the French EIC, has received permission from Mohammad Taqi Khan to trade in wool in Kerman and open an agency there. He even was allowed to build a house. The Dutch did not like this because it would drive up the price of wool and make it more difficult to get it. Mozaffar Khan tried to make Kerman flourish again and the reports only say good things about him. The viceroy also had given Mozaffar Khan orders to make him 500 matchlocks, so that the governor asked the Dutch in Gamron for 12,000 lbs. of iron rods (2,000 *mann* or 20 donkey loads) to make matchlocks, because he could not get it in Kerman.[43]

---

39. VOC 2520, Auwannees to Koenad (21/05/1739), f. 1318-24. The vizier of Kerman was Mirza Hoseyn. VOC 2510 (30/05/1739), f. 1227.

40. VOC 2510, Auwannees to Koenad (08/07/1739), f. 1332.

41. VOC 2510, Auwannees to Koenad (18/08/1739), f. 1340-42.

42. VOC 2510, Auwannees to Koenad (15/09/1739), f. 1346. For this reading of the *kalantar*'s name see Ahmad `Ali Khan Vaziri Kermani, *Tarikh-e Kerman (Salariyeh)* ed. Ebrahim Bastani-Parizi (Tehran, 1352/1973), p. 541.

43. VOC 2510, Koenad to Batavia (25/12/1739), f. 129-30; VOC 2510, Mozaffar Khan to Koanad

On November 1, 1739 a *chapar* from Nader arrived in Kerman with orders for the *beglerbegi* to send him 30,000 woolen waistbands, 5,000 capes, 20,000 *cabasjalls* [probably *qaba*s or overcoats made of coarse shawl], 5,000 caps of cloth, 10,000 shirts and trousers, and 5,000 woolen caps. The viceroy to combat the scarcity of money had new copper *paisa*s struck the value of which he put at 3 *methqal*s, although the new coin was 1 *methqal* less in weight than the old ones.[44] In December 1739 new orders arrived from Nader to send him 20,000 shawls to be used as overcoat (cabayen; *qaba*) and 5,000 woolen caps, which caused a rise in the prices of wool. On December 6, 1739 a *chapar* arrived reporting that Nader was at Kabul at that time and would go to Sind to punish Miya Nasir, ruler of Sind.[45] When the *kalantar* returned from Gamron on December 30, 1739 he and the *beglerbegi* sent for Hovannes and the EIC representative, because Nader had ordered overcoats, which were unobtainable in Kerman and they would send a *chapar* to both Companies' representatives. On January 5, 1740 a *chapar* from Kabul arrived, bringing orders from Nader to collect that year's wool clip and to convert it into 30,000 woolen caps. The *chapar* had the required amount of money for that purpose which he distributed among the population.

On January 19, 1740 Hajji 'Ali Mardan Khan passed through Kerman on his way to Kuhgilu of which he had been made *beglerbegi*. He told Hovannes that Nader had sent all his heavy artillery towards Herat with the intention to attack Miya Nasir, the ruler of Sind. Moreover, the viceroy had issued orders to the *beglerbegi* of Kerman to come with all his officials to Teheran to celebrate New Year there. What the real purpose of it all was nobody knew.[46]

On February 1, 1740 Mozaffar Khan sent for Hovannes and said that he wanted to borrow 200 *tuman*s from him. When he refused Hovannes was forced to do so. The governor then left to Teheran giving Hovannes an assignation on his vizier, Mohammad Zaman Beg, who gave an IOU in return. Mozaffar Khan, who left on February 19, 1740 to Tehran was accompanied by Mirza Hasjoen [?] the vizier, the *mostowfi*, and 12 *kadkhoda*s. The officials and people of Kerman also lodged a complaint with the viceroy about the tiranny of the former *beglerbegi* Mohammad Sharif Khan. The viceroy in reply sent tax collectors who took the *beglerbegi*, the *kalantar* Hajji Mir Borhan and 20 *kadkhoda*s to the shah to be punished. The *kalantar* appointed his brother Mirza Hoseyn as his *na'eb* and left on February 21 with his group. Meanwhile, Nader had departed for Sind, but not before sending an ambassador to Turkey (Sardar Khan; Serdaar Chan) and Russia (Hajji Mejdi Khan [Hadje Metje Chan]).[47]

VOC ABANDONS KERMAN — LAST LOCAL NEWS ITEMS

Because the VOC directors did not want Kerman wool anymore, which only yielded losses (too expensive, bad quality) the council in Gamron decided on February 26, 1740 that Auwannees had to return to settle his account with the Company and that the office in Kerman would be

---

(29/10/1739 received), f. 1265-67; VOC 2510, Receipt for 2,000 *mann* of iron (05/11/1739), f. 1397; VOC 2510 (received 29/10/1739), f. 2510.

44. VOC 2510, Auwannees to Koenad (19/11/1739), f. 1356-57.

45. VOC 2511, Auwannees to Koenad (14/12/1739), f. 1334-35.

46. VOC 2511, Auwannees to Koenad (22/01/1740), f. 1341-42.

47. VOC 2511, Auwannees to Koenad (20/02/1740), f. 1349-51.

closed.[48] Auwannees did not leave for another year, and therefore, we still have some information from Kerman. But his troubles were not over. Auwannees was in trouble with the *kalantar* Hajji Borhan (Hadje Boeroen) who claimed that he had given 1,600 *tuman*s in safe-keeping, in which claim he was supported by 'Abdol-Ghaffar Beg (Abdul Gaffar beecq), the nephew of Mozaffar 'Ali Khan (Mhozaffar Alie Chan) the admiral who died in May. He claimed that Auwannes had kept 200 *tuman*s and 40 chintzes in safe-keeping. Nader replied to both requests that he left the issue to the Dutch to resolve, after having heard both parties.[49]

On May 28, 1740 Mozaffar Khan returned to Kerman *chapar*wise having with him in manacles Nader's representative, named Mirza Hassjoen [?] and two *mostoufi*s to take 1,600 *tuman*s from him in accordance with the royal orders. He then had to take these three people and all dignitaries of Kerman to Herat to see Nader. The former *beglerbegi* Mohammad Sharif Khan and the *kalantar* Mir Borhan (Boeroen) had their nose cut off at Nader's orders as soon as they had arrived at court. The former then was appointed macebearer and the *kalantar* received a robe of honor and 200 *tuman*s. The viceroy also went *chapar*-wise to Herat to see his father, who had given orders to translate the Bible into Persian. He moreover also had ordered to gather all the clergy and to have them discuss with one another the points of their religion. Nader on the basis of their arguments intended to choose the best of the religions to which he wanted to be converted.[50] On July 19, 1740 Hovannes learnt from a *chapar* coming from court that Nader had selected by lot a culprit from among the group of Kerman dignitaries whom he ordered to be strangled. Hovannes believed him to be the vizier Mirza Hassoen [?]. The remainder of the group with Mozaffar Khan was ordered to follow Nader's army to Orgenj.[51]

A *chapar* sent by Mohammad Taqi Khan told Auwannees in secret that his master, when he had arrived at court, was told by the shah that he had to leave. Nader was angry with him, because so many complaints had been submitted to him about his behavior. After five days Nader was satisfied with the explanation offered by Mohammad Taqi Khan and he was shown much honor again. However, Mohammad Taqi Khan requested to be dismissed as *beglerbegi* and to be allowed to remain at court. Nader asked him several times to stay on, but he asked to be excused and then finally he was dismissed. There was as yet no successor, though the shah's *nazer*, Emamverdi Khan, was a strong candidate. Meanwhile, an Uzbek ambassador had come with costly presents to subjugate himself. Nader was not satisfied, for if the Uzbeks were sincere they would have sent him 15,000 men and the royal treasury. If this was not delivered he would come himself to get it. He had already marched from Herat for five days into that direction and would attack Bokhara and Orgenj if he were not given satisfaction.[52]

Emamverdi Khan was indeed appointed. Mir 'Ali Khan (Meer Alie Chan) was dismissed and he was replaced as *beglerbegi* by Mohammad Taq Khan Majidi [?] (Mhamet Tachie Chan Masidie), who had been *beglerbegi* of Kerman in the past, and then had been general of the Imam Reza shrine at Mashhad. Mohammad Baqer Beg had to continue as *na'eb* of Gamron, while Mohammad Khan Beg (Mhamed Chan beecq), son of Shah Nazar Khan (Sjanazer

---

48. VOC 2511, Resolution Gamron (26/02/1740), f. 287.

49. VOC 2705, van der Welle to Batvia (31/07/1746), f. 62-63.

50. VOC 2511, Auwannees to Koenad (16/06/1740), f. 1354-56.

51. VOC 2511, Auwannees to Koenad (19/07/1740), f. 1368.

52. VOC 2511, Auwannees to Koenad (26/06/1740), f. 1361-62.

Chan), became governor of Lar. He had been chief carpet spreader (Scharas basje of opperste veger; *farrash-bashi*). Hatem Beg became *beglerbegi* of Shiraz, and `Ali Beg Soltan (Alie beecq sultoen) governor of Shustar. Emamverdi Khan would like to have been granted Mohammad Taqi Khan's full authority over all other governors. The new governor of Lar passed through Kerman, as did Emamverdi Khan en route to their posts. The former said that the latter had orders to raise a large army in Fars in two months to attack Masqat. Mohammad Taqi Khan, though without function, was held in great esteem by the shah. The latter was said to have marched his army to from Herat to Qara Tepeh (Hare theppe) and to march two weeks later to Orgenj. The Kerman notables were forced to accompany the shah, and one of them, who had been selected by lot, Nader had strangled.[53] Emamverdi Khan, who was ill, and the *daryabegi* arrived at Kerman on July 28, 1740. The latter had to go to Shiraz to raise 1,500 men and march to Bushehr. The royal fleet had to go to Laft for reparations.[54]

[To learn how the situation in Kerman further developed see Floor, *Textile Industry*, chapter five]

---

53. VOC 2511, Godja Auwannees Ghiroen to Koenad (19/07/1741), f. 1363-68.

54. VOC 2546, Auwannees to Koenad (31/11/1740), f. 1836-38.

CHAPTER FOUR

THE REVOLT OF SHEIKH AHMAD MADANI IN LARESTAN
AND THE GARMSIRAT (1730-1733)

The revolt of the Sunni Arabs of Larestan and the Garmsirat in the early 1730s has been analyzed by Arunova and Aubin.[1] Both authors concluded that this revolt led by Sheikh Ahmad Madani, who later co-operated with Mohammad Khan Baluch, was the expression of social discontent and not just another outbreak of sedition by a local, rebellious robber-baron and war-lord. Arunova came to this conclusion, because the Shi`ite population of Kerman had joined the revolt of the Sunnis of Larestan and the Garmsirat. Aubin, for the same reason, although he adduces the support of the Shi`ite population of Lar for his argument, also argued this point. Both authors used mainly Iranian sources for their study. Arunova in addition used Russian archival sources, while Aubin made use of some reports in the French archives. The latter suggested that more information on this subject would be available in Dutch and British sources, which is indeed the case. The information used here is from the Dutch archives and makes Arunova's and Aubin's conclusion on the Sunni revolt less acceptable that it has been until now.

The first time Sheikh Ahmad Madani is mentioned in Dutch sources is in June 1725 when Ra'is Abu'l-Hasan, captain of the troops from Sulgari (a village in Larestan) fought with a certain "Ahmed Mhadanie, an Afghan," whom he defeated.[2] This fight formed part of the revolt of the Larestan area against the Afghan invaders, which was led by two Safavid generals, viz. Mohammad Vali Khan Shamlu and Sayyed Ahmad Khan. The Afghans, who held Lar, but not its citadel, since the first part of 1724 and Bandar `Abbas since November 3, 1725, were supported by a motley force consisting of Baluch, Dargazini tribesmen and of the local Sunni population of Larestan. At the orders of Mohammad Vali Khan Shamlu, *beglerbegi* of Kerman, a local Baluch chief, Mir Mehr-e `Ali, *kalantar* of Tezerg-Ahmadi, moved from his township on 9 May 1725 to liberate Lar. He took Safidban and killed the Afghans who held

---

1. M. R. Arunova and K. Z. Ashrafiyan, *Gosudarst'vo Nadir Shaha Afshara* (Moscow, 1958), pp. 153-58; Jean Aubin, "Les Sunnites du Larestan et la chute des Safavides," *Revue des Etudes Islamiques* 33 (1965), pp. 151-71 (in particular p. 167f).

2. VOC 2038, Miersa Mhamed Naiem to 'tLam, received 13 June 1725, f. 280.

it; next he took Mhasai Ghoen (?) where he was opposed by the local population. After a fight and a short siege the population surrendered. It is also the first time that Evaz (Ahvas, Evas) is mentioned as a Sunni village; here the Afghans under the Afghan governor of Lar, Khodadad Khan, regrouped after their defeat.[3]

Towards the end of 1725 the Afghans had retaken Lar, although it took them until 31 May 1726 to effect the surrender of the citadel. Bandar ʿAbbas was only retaken on 22 December 1727 by Zabardast Khan, who dislodged Sayyed Ahmad Khan. The Afghans continued to hold Bandar ʿAbbas until 9 January 1730, when Baru Khan, its Afghan governor fled to Lar, which the Afghans did not hold much longer either.[4]

During the 1726-1730 period the Afghans certainly were not the absolute masters of Larestan or the Garmsirat. In fact, they were only obeyed in those places where they had a strong garrison or when they sent an army to subjugate a certain township or village. In October 1729 Neda Khan, the Afghan governor of Lar, was unable to destroy Sulgari, because he lacked the proper artillery. He was also opposed at the village of Gheyst (?). For his logistical and military support Neda Khan relied on the local Sunni Arab petty rulers. He himself mentioned the support by the *sheikh al-shoyukh* Saned, son of Rama, while in January 1730, and probably much earlier (see above), he had joined forces with Sheikh Ahmad Madani in the latter's stronghold of Morbagh. He also mentioned a certain Sheikh Mohammad Majid (sjeeg Mamed Madjed), who was supposed to have taken over the function of Baru Khan at Bandar ʿAbbas.[5]

However, the Afghans and the Sunni Arabs were not the only ones to infest the area. On 29 April 1730 the Dutch received information that Baluch marauders had pillaged the area near Minab and were coming towards Bandar ʿAbbas, as a result of which many fugitives poured into that town. At the same time Sheikh Jabbara[6] was making the area around the islands of Larek and Qeshm insecure through his constant attacks. The soltan (deputy-governor) of Bandar ʿAbbas, Mir Mehr-e ʿAli, sent some men to Qeshm on 7 May 1730 who returned after one week without having been able to seize Sheikh Jabbara, whom they had engaged twice. On 21 June 1730 the sheikh was again reported to be near Basidu (township on Qeshm) with a great many vessels intending to attack British interests. The English therefore sent the *Britannia Galley* to Qeshm, but found no sign of the pirate's presence.[7] However, of greater

---

3. VOC 2038, Agmet Chan to 'tLam, received 30 June 1725, f. 292-95; Mier Mheer Alie to 'tLam, received 13 June 1725, f. 281-84. On the events during the Afghan occupation see Floor, *Afghan Occupation*.

4. On the events see Floor, *Afghan Occupation*.

5. VOC 3168, Nedda Chan to de Cleen, from Morbaaq on the Arab side (sic!), received 5 February 1730, f. 488-89; Ibid., Nedda Chan to de Cleen, received 23 October 1729, f. 463-64. In this last letter Neda Khan asked the Dutch for 100 balls of 1.25 *man-e Tabriz* (7.5 lbs.) as well as good gunners, who had to be sent to Saned, son of Rama, who would take care of further transportation. The English Gombroon Diary also states that Sheikh Ahmad Madani agreed to help the Afghans cross the Persian Gulf, for example, Ashraf Shah's brother, nephew and company, see Gombroon Diary 13/24 June 1730 as quoted by L. Lockhart, *Nadir Shah, a critical study based mainly upon contemporary sources* (London, 1928), p. 44.

6. Sheikh Jabbara, chief of the Hula Arabs of Bandar Taheri.

7. VOC 2254, Gamronsch Dagregister (Gamron Diary), f. 12 (29 April 1730), f. 23 (7 May 1730), f. 70 (21 June 1730); end March 1730 letters from Mir Mehr-e ʿAli and other reported that about 12,000

impact on the security of the area were the activities by Sheikh Ahmad Madani, the leader of the Sunnis in Larestan.

On 1 May 1730 it was reported in Bandar `Abbas that Sheikh Ahmad Madani had made common cause with groups of Afghans and Baluch to subjugate the Garmsirat at the orders of the fugitive Afghan leader Shah Ashraf. Sheikh Ahmad Madani had extended his power in such a way that he was collecting the royal revenues by force in the area between Lar and Shiraz. He also attacked Lar itself and the vizier (governor) of that town urgently appealed for help from Mir Mehr-e `Ali. He wrote that if he would not get help within three days he would be forced to surrender the citadel of Lar to Sheikh Ahmad Madani, who had a force of 6,000 men, amongst whom were many Afghans. Mir Mehr-e `Ali informed the Dutch on 14 May 1730 that he had received orders from Tahmasp Qoli Khan (the later Nader Shah) to come to the relief of Hajji Ghani Beg in Lar. However, it was too late, for on 21 May 1730 news was received in Bandar `Abbas that Sheikh Ahmad Madani had taken the citadel of Lar. He was said to have gone from there to Congistan (Bandar-e Kong?) and to have massacred its population, and that he soon would come to Bandar `Abbas itself. This news was followed by information that 2,000 men, who had been sent to the relief of Lar, had been routed by Sheikh Ahmad Madani's forces.

Apparently, to induce him to join forces with the Safavid party, Tahmasp Qoli Khan (Nader) confirmed Sheikh Jabbara as governor of Bahrain, who then was said to have sent troops to Lar to help to defeat Sheikh Ahmad Madani. On 7 June 1730 it appeared that Sheikh Ahmad Madani was moving towards Bandar `Abbas and was at three days' journey's distance. Mir Heydar, Mir Mehr-e `Ali's son, fled that same night with some men from Bandar `Abbas to his ancestral stronghold of Tezerg-Ahmadi and it was said that his father was soon to follow. The *shahbandar* (customs-master), Mirza Mohammad, had two vessels ready for his flight on the beach, while many families were actually leaving town already. Sheikh Ahmad Madani's force was said to number 500 men only, which number was later even reduced to 100 men, who on 8 June 1730 were at six hours' distance from Bandar `Abbas. However, on 11 June 1730 they turned back and probably pillaged a caravan that on 17 July 1730 was reported to have been seized at three days' journey from Bandar `Abbas. They later were still in the area preying on travelers.[8]

On 18 October 1730 it was reported that Sheikh Ahmad Madani on receiving the news that Mohammad `Ali Khan, *beglerbegi* of Shiraz,[9] was about to move against him had taken to his heels and had disarmed and sent away all Afghans who were in his service.

Baluchis were said to be near Minab and advised the Dutch to be on their guard. Mir Mehr-e `Ali also asked for supplies such as gunpowder, lead, dates, and barley. On 5 April 1730 the Dutch decided to give him these supplies. See (also for a specification of these supplies), Ibid., 6 May 1730, f. 129.

8. VOC 2254, Gamronsch Dagregister, ff. 12, 27-29, 47, 49, 51-53, 57, 78.

9. Mohammad `Ali Khan b. Aslan Khan, *tupchi-bashi* during the siege of Isfahan. He fled with Tahmasp Mirza from the besieged city in the night of 7/8 June 1722. On 11 June 1730 he returned to Isfahan and it became known that he had been appointed *beglerbegi* of Fars with the same jurisdiction as Lotf `Ali Khan Daghestani in 1717, see VOC 2253, Schorer to de Cleen, Spahan, 1 July 170, f. 900-01. In 1732 he was sent as ambassador to India, where he died on his way back in Thatta, see Riazul Islam, *Indo-Persian Relations* (Tehran, 1970), p. 141.

However, in view of subsequent events this piece of information seems quite unlikely and untrue.[10] Sheikh Jabbara was also on the move at that time and was angaged by Mir Mehr-e `Ali near Kalatu (Callatoe) on 17 November 1730. Mir Mehr-e `Ali claimed that he had defeated Sheikh Ahmad Madani's forces, which partly consisted of Afghans. However, this force was still around Ghamir a few days later.[11]

Meanwhile, Mohammad `Ali Khan indeed was moving against Sheikh Ahmad Madani. To that end he had appointed a new governor of Bandar `Abbas, Mohsen Khan, who arrived there on 18 November 1730.[12] He persistently urged the Dutch to patrol the sea with their ships to stop Sheikh Ahmad Madani's men from escaping the ring which Mohammad `Ali Khan had laid around them. Because Mohsen Khan did not leave off asking for the sea patrols the Dutch decided to send the sloop *de Maria Laurentia* out to sea for appearance's sake. On 27 December 1730 the sloop left Bandar `Abbas and returned on 3 February 1731 without having to report anything on the enemy's movements.[13]

On 29 January 1731 a messenger from Mohammad `Ali Khan arrived in Bandar `Abbas with the news that he had defeated Sheikh Ahmad Madani and that the latter had sued for peace. He had refused, for he wanted to destroy these rascals once and for all. He apparently was not successful in doing so, for Mohammad `Ali Khan ordered Mohsen Khan to destroy Ahmad Madani at Morbagh. Mohsen Khan asked the Dutch for 3,000 lbs. of gunpowder, which they refused, although he repeated his request the next day as well as the days thereafter, but he invariably received the same negative reply. Although he was ill, Mohsen Khan left Bandar `Abbas with his force on 22 February 1731 via Khezr and `Essin, which hamlet he only left on 1 March 1731.[14]

Later the Dutch learnt that Sheikh Ahmad Madani, assisted by Sheikh Jabbara, who apparently had changed sides once again, had been defeated by Mohammad `Ali Khan and had been forced to withdraw into the citadel of Anak (?), which the *beglerbegi* had surrounded with his troops.[15] Sheikh Ahmad Madani had offered peace and 8,000 *tuman*s for the *beglerbegi*

---

10. VOC 2254, Gamronsch Dagregister, f. 136.

11. VOC 2254, Gamronsch Dagregister, f. 145, 155.

12. VOC 2253, de Cleen to Batavia, 15 May 1731, f. 136, 138, which states that Mohsen Khan had orders to collect troops from Bandar `Abbas and the islands and to use these to attack Sheikh Ahmad Madani at Morbagh; see also Ibid., Resolutie Gamron, 17 January 1731, f. 388.

13. VOC 2254, Gamronsch Dagregister, f. 153, 176, 178, 207. On 5 January 1731 de Cleen wrote to Mohammad `Ali Khan "to-day 27 Jomadi al-Thani it is ten days ago that I have sent ships to patrol [the sea] against Sheikh Ahmad." VOC 2253, f. 615. One of the reasons for the Dutch to patrol the coast was the willingness of the *shahbandar* to repay a debt of 5,000 *tuman*s, which had been assigned on the customs revenues of Bandar `Abbas, if he would be enabled to force Sheikh Rashid b. Sa`id of Basidu to settle his account of the customs administration. The *shahbandar* therefore asked the Dutch to ferry troops across to Qeshm, which were commanded by his son-in-law, who would enforce the settlement of Sheikh Rashid's account, if need be. However, this project did not materialize, because the *shahbandar* was suddenly replaced. VOC 2253, de Cleen to Batavia, 15 May 1731, f. 72-74.

14. VOC 2254, Gamronsch Dagregister, f. 203, 212-16, 218, 222. Mohsen Khan appointed the new *shahbandar* as his deputy or *na'eb* in his absence. Ibid., f. 218 reports that a messenger arrived in Bandar `Abbas on 28 February 1731 with information that Mohammad `Ali Khan had been defeated by Sheikh Ahmad Madani and was surrounded by him.

15. VOC 2254, Gamronsch Dagregister, f. 225 (21 march 1731); on 14 April 1731 (Ibid., f. 231) it was rumored that Mohammad Khan Baluch intended to come from Kerman to Bandar `Abbas with his troops

personally, but he had refused. Meanwhile, Mohsen Khan had died en route in early April.[16] Later that month news was received that Sheikh Ahmad Madani had been able to escape and was being pursued by Mohammad ʿAli Khan's forces. On 29 April 1731 totally unexpected it was made public in Bandar ʿAbbas that peace had been concluded between Mohammad ʿAli Khan and Sheikh Ahmad Madani, who would pay 5,000 *tuman*s to Shah Tahmasp II and 300 *tuman*s to Mohammad ʿAli Khan. However, this news was soon thereafter contradicted by information received on 3 May 1731 that Sheikh Ahmad Madani had defeated Mohammad ʿAli Khan, who, with the loss of 4,000 men, was running back to Shiraz.[17]

According to a VOC messenger, who had passed through the fighting area on his run from Bandar ʿAbbas to Isfahan, Mohammad ʿAli Khan had been contained by Sheikh Ahmad Madani at one day's journey above Lar, so that his troops suffered from lack of food. He did not dare to cut through the enemy lines to reach the supply train from Shiraz and Darab. Sheikh Ahmad Madani had offered him 9,000 *tuman*s and all his arms, if Mohammad ʿAli Khan would not percecute them anymore, which offer the latter declined to accept. He demanded 9,000 *tuman*s for Tahmasp II, 6,000 *tuman*s for himself, all of Sheikh Ahmad Madani's arms and 30 young virgins. Sheikh Ahmad Madani refused, however, saying that he would resist until he would be destroyed or be forced to pay what Mohammad ʿAli Khan had so unreasonably demanded. Whether this report is true is difficult to tell, but it certainly must have had some truth, for Mohammad ʿAli Khan's reputation had suffered considerably. The steward (*nazer*) of the royal assayer (*moʿayyer-bashi*) told the Dutch in Isfahan that the *beglerbegi* of Fars only spent his time whoring and drinking and did nothing to suppress the rebels.[18]

On 2 June 1731 it was rumored that Sheikh Ahmad Madani had complained to Shah Tahmasp II about Mohammad ʿAli Khan's behavior and had requested to recall him. For he and his people were loyal subjects of the Shah and wanted to remain so. The governor of Lar, Hajji ʿAli Qoli Khan, was reported to have concluded a peace agreement with Sheikh Ahmad Madani on the condition that the Sunnis would pay their customary taxes and be responsible for that which would be stolen between Lar and their dwelling places. However, this seems unlikely in view of Sheikh Hazin's statement that only the Shiʿis paid taxes and that the Sunnis remained scot-free.[19]

Moreover, on 27 September 1731 it was already rumored that some of Sheikh Ahmad Madani's men were on the road again to undertake some mischief.[20] This news was confirmed by a letter from Lar to the *shahbandar* of Bandar ʿAbbas on 9 October 1731 stating that the Arabs of Morbagh, supported by Afghans, had come near the town with the purpose to rob and pillage the area. The population had panicked and many had packed up their possessions

---

to suppress Sheikh Ahmad Madani's revolt.

16. VOC 2254, Gamronsch Dagregister, f. 230 (9 April 1731).

17. VOC 2254, Gamronsch Dagregister, f. 238, 242.

18. VOC 2255, van Leijpsigh to de Cleen, Spahan, 20 April 1731, f. 2304-22. Mohammad ʿAli Khan was back in Isfahan on 5 July 1731 with 2,000 men with orders to march to Hamadan to watch Ottoman movements. VOC 2322, van Leijpsigh to de Cleen, Spahan, 26 July 1732, f. 288.

19. VOC 2254, Gamronsch Dagregister, f. 932; Sheikh Ali Hazin, *The Life of Sheikh Ali Hazin*, translated by F. C. Belfour (London, 1830), p. 228.

20. VOC 2254, Gamronsch Dagregister, f. 968.

and had taken refuge in the citadel. Hajji Qoli Khan, the governor of Lar, was preparing himself to oppose this threat the same letter reported.[21] The governor, however, left Lar and went to Bandar `Abbas where he arrived on 23 October 1731. Two days earlier a letter from an Armenian had reported Shah Tahmasp II's defeat against the Ottomans and that the Arabs of Morbagh with the Afghans were on the move pillaging the country as far as Shiraz.[22] On 28 October 1731, the presence of the Afghans in `Essin was reported, who numbered only 50 men, according to a fugitive. Most of the inhabitants of Bandar `Abbas prepared themselves to flee at moment's notice, while it was said that the officials, the governor included, were at their wit's end. The Dutch sent for soldiers from their ship *de Schoonauw* to strengthen the garrison of the Dutch factory.[23]

Some hajjis who arrived in Bandar `Abbas on 31 October 1731 reported that Sheikh Ahmad Madani had taken Lar and had laid siege to its citadel assisted by Sheikh Jabbara and Sheikh Rashid of Basidu. It was said that 5,000 troops had been sent by Tahmasp Qoli Khan (Nader) from Kerman to destroy Sheikh Ahmad Madani, but this was not confirmed. Early November 1731 it was learnt that Ahmad Beg, the brother of Baru Khan, with 500 men had pillaged a caravan coming from Shiraz.[24] Later it was reported that the *beglerbegi* of Shiraz was coming with a powerful army to crush Sheikh Ahmad Madani and the Afghans which he harbored.[25] But among the population of the Garmsisrat it was believed that Mohammad `Ali Khan had been totally defeated by the Ottomans together with Shah Tahmasp II and that the country was without an effective government. In Lar it was rumored that the Sunnis, the Safidbanis, the Afghans and the Arabs would try to proclaim Sheikh Ahmad Madani as king. In fact, the hajjis who had come to Bandar `Abbas in October 1731 had referred to Sheikh Ahmad Madani as Shah Ahmad![26]

The latter effectively controlled the roads between Lar and Bandar `Abbas and another caravan had fallen into his hands when a dispute had arisen between his men and the people of the caravan. To show his good intentions Sheikh Ahmad wrote to the Dutch informing them that he had ordered Passelaar Esma`il Safidbani in Khormut to return the goods to the owners and allow the caravan to depart.[27]

---

21. VOC 2254, Gamronsch Dagregister, f. 978.

22. VOC 2254, Gamronsch Dagregister, f. 980-81; on Shah Tahmasp's defeat see Lockhart, *Nadir*, p. 55f.

23. VOC 2254, Gamronsch Dagregister, f. 983-84.

24. VOC 2254, Gamronsch Dagregister, f. 985, 987, 1001.

25. VOC 2254, Gamronsch Dagregister, f. 1003. Mohammad `Ali Khan had left Isfahan for Shiraz on 17 October 1731. VOC 2255, van Leijpsigh to de Cleen, Spahan, 3 November 1731, f. 1842

26. VOC 2254, de Cleen to Batavia, Gamron, 19 July 1732, f. 517; VOC 2254, Gamronsch Dagregister, f. 985, 1012-13; VOC 2254, Relaas VOC loper Golum Alie, Gamron, 9 November 1731, f. 1188-90.

27. VOC 2254, Gamronsch Dagregister, f. 1001, 1031-32; VOC 2254, Ismael Sefiedboenie to Sahid (VOC dragoman in Bandar `Abbas), received 29 November 1731, f. 1190-92 reports that his son had taken the VOC property from the Afghans, who had stolen it at Banaru. The term Passelaar may be refers to the function of road-guard or tax-collector, for *pasalari* was a kind of tax levied in the Garmsirat. It is also possible that it refers to the title of *sepahsalar*, or chief commander, which would fit the alleged royal aspirations of Sheikh Ahmad Madani.

On 24 December 1731 some 300 Afghans on horse and 500 on foot were said to have arrived at Ghamir at three days' journey from Bandar `Abbas. Already in the evening of the next day it was rumored that the Afghans had invaded the town to sack it. The result of this rumor was total panic, while the real cause of the rumor had only been caused by the accidental burning of a hut west of the town. The only ones who benefited from the panic were the thieves.[28]

One month later Bandar `Abbas again was in consternation when on 22 January 1732 a group of 150 fleeing Afghans passed the town into the direction of `Essin. They robbed everything they could lay their hands on and killed and wounded a lot of people outside the Isfahan gate. The next day a smaller group of 25 Afghans followed the main force.[29]

Finally, the rumors about the coming of an army to suppress Sheikh Ahmad Madani were confirmed when Hajji `Ali Qoli Khan informed the Dutch that messengers (chapars) from Mohammad `Ali Khan and Mohammad Baluch Khan,[30] beglerbegi of Kerman had arrived in Jevem, stating that on 17 January 1732 (14 Rajab 1144) they had arrived at Fasa and intended to go to Masahendjoen (?).[31] Later both beglerbegis informed the Dutch about their progress. By the end of January 1732 they had taken Mezahedjom (?), but part of the enemy had been able to escape into the mountains. They pursued them and had been able to contain them. Their most important leaders (kakhoda) came with their swords around their neck to plea for mercy. This was granted to them and they were given into the safe-keeping of the kalantar of Jahrom. The village of Mesahendjoen was totally razed so that nothing remained. Their army then proceeded to punish the other Sunnis and it arrived on 4 February 1732 (7 Sha`ban 1144) in Khormut and Safidban. The population was treated in the same as was the village, which was totally destroyed. Because there still were many enemies who had escaped Mohammad `Ali Khan asked the Dutch to patrol the sea and seize all fleeing Sunnis.[32]

Somewhat earlier Mohammad `Ali Khan had asked the Dutch to seize Sheikh Rashid's ships or to destroy them, because he was causing considerable damage to passing vessels and merchants.[33] May be as a result of these developments Sheikh Rashid, according to the shahbandar of Bandar `Abbas, had offered to subject himself and come with his men to Bandar `Abbas to protect the town. The shahbandar, Mirza Mohammad, asked the Dutch to prevent Sheikh Rashid to flee from Basidu. He himself had sent a kinsman of his, Seyfollah Beg, to Basidu to persuade Sheikh Rashid to remain there. However, the shahbandar would appreciate

---

28. VOC 2254, Gamronsch Dagregister, f. 1022-23.

29. VOC 2254, Gamronsch Dagregister, f. 1030-31.

30. Mohammad Baluch Khan had left Isfahan to destroy the Sunni Arabs on 16 December 1731. VOC 2255, van Leijpsigh to de Cleen, Spahan, 28 december 1731, f. 1881; see also VOC 2254, Gamronsch Dagregister, f. 1038 (8 February 1732).

31. VOC 2254, Hajealie Coelie Chan from Jahiem to de Cleen, received 21 January 1732, f. 1213-15; he also asked the Dutch to give some gunpowder to Amir Heydar (Ammier Heyder).

32. VOC 2254, Mhamed Alie Chan and Mhamed Boloeds Chan to de Cleen, received 13 February 1732, f. 1225-27.

33. VOC 2254, Mhamed Alie Chan to de Cleen, received 4 February 1732, f. 1220-24; Sheikh Rashid is called the son of Sahid (Ibid., f. 1222).

it if the Dutch would patrol the shipping routes and seize Sheikh Rashid, if he did not do so.[34] The Dutch decided to comply with this request, because they hoped that it would help them in collecting their claim on the customs revenues of Bandar ʿAbbas. They therefore sent two ships to contain Qeshm Island and wrote Sheikh Rashid that he need not worry about his position and should stay in Basidu.[35] Sheikh Rashid apparently had no great trust in the outcome of the events in the Garmsirat, for it was reported that he was preparing his flight to Masqat. On 1 April 1732 it was learnt that 500 houses had been burnt down in Basidu and that Sheikh Rashid had demanded 500 *tuman*s from the population to rebuild them.[36]

Sheikh Rashid replied to the Dutch that he had no bad intentions and only wanted to support the Shah and that he would rely on the *shahbandar* for guidance.[37] However, one month later he wrote to the Dutch that he wondered whether he really could safely remain in Basidu. For in early April 1732 Mir Heydar with some Ahmadi soldiers had plundered, pillaged and destroyed the villages of Pol-e Khamir, Dizhgan (Diesgoen) and Jasiekad. All cattle had been stolen as well as a great amount of other property. Moreover, Mir Heydar had taken 140 men, women and children to Bandar ʿAbbas claiming that they were enemies. Sheikh Rashid asked the Dutch to see to it that these poor people, who were all subjects of the Shah, would be indemnified. If this would not happen he saw no other way out than that everybody would flee from the area.[38]

On 3 March 1732 it was reported that Mohammad Khan Baluch was on Sheikh Ahmad Madani's heels, who had withdrawn into the mountains where he was being pursued by some troops.[39] At about the same time, Sheikh Belal of Makran was infesting the area around Minab with a force of 800 men. He had plundered the whole area and had collected an enormous number of cows, camels, sheep, and goats. Sheikh Ahmad Madani was slowly being contained.[40] To close the circle around him even more Mohammad ʿAli Khan reiterated his earlier request to the Dutch to patrol the shipping lanes and look out for fleeing enemies, for he had them contained at a place five German miles from the sea. He therefore asked the Dutch specifically to guard the coast near Bandar Taheri (Bhender Taher) and Morbagh (Morbaag) to make their professed affection for the Shah more tangible. Despite his apparently hopeless position Sheikh Ahmad Madani was able to conclude a peace agreement with Mohammad Khan Baluch on the condition that he paid 1,000 *tuman*s, 500 oxen and camels, and 200 donkeys. This news was confirmed on 31 April 1732 in a letter from Mohammad ʿAli Khan. After a long siege and having suffered many casualties the enemy had been forced to come out of the citadel with their swords hanging around their neck to demand pardon. Sheikh Ahmad Madani had been able to convince the *beglerbegi*s to leave him and his commanders alive, although Mohammad ʿAli Khan took some important hostages with him amongst whom some Afghan

---

34. VOC 2254, Miersa Mhamed to de Cleen, received 27 February 1732, f. 1270-73.

35. VOC 2254, Resolutie Gamron, 27 February 1732, f. 647-66.

36. VOC 2254, Gamronsch Dagregister, f. 1050.

37. VOC 2254, Sjeeg Rasjet to de Cleen, received 15 April 1732, f. 1274.

38. VOC 2254, Sjeeg Rasjet to de Cleen, received 15 April 1732, f. 1278-81; VOC 2254, Gamronsch Dagregister, f. 1054. Dizhgan or Dizhgun is close to Khamir. Jasiekad I have not been able to identify.

39. VOC 2254, Gamronsch Dagregister, f. 1045.

40. VOC 2254, Gamronsch Dagregister, f. 1044, 1048.

and Dargazini commanders. He even allowed some of them to visit their families before taking them to Shiraz. Sheikh Ahmad Madani also had given his assurances as to the security and peace in the area. Mohammad `Ali Khan then had returned to Shiraz on 26 April 1732 (20 Shawwal 1144). The population of Bandar `Abbas cursed Mohammad `Ali Khan for allowing himself to be deceived for a second time by Sheikh Ahmad Madani. Especially the merchants were totally disgusted and decided to reduce their trading activities.[41]

On 2 May 1732 it was said that the real reason for peace had not been the alleged straights in which Sheikh Ahmad Madani had been, but the fact that Shah Tahmasp II as well as Tahmasp Qoli Khan had summoned Mohammad `Ali Khan to court. The cost of fielding the army against Sheikh Ahmad Madani, moreover, had cost the royal treasury 16,000 *tuman*s so far.[42]

The peace was not a lasting one, for on 13 August 1732 it was publicly discussed in Bandar `Abbas that Sheikh Ahmad Madani with 30,000 men intended to attack Basidu. This rumor caused most wealthy merchants to move from there to Bandar `Abbas. One month later more merchants left Basidu at the advice of Sheikh Rashid himself.[43] On 17 November 1732 it was rumored that Mohammad Khan Baluch, Amir Khan and a certain Khalil Khan had joined their 8,000 men strong force with that of Sheikh Ahmad Madani and that they were on the move in the area. This information may be true for at that time Mohammad Khan Baluch had left Isfahan with an army of about 12,000 men to destroy Sheikh Ahmad Madani.[44] For unknown reasons, however, he laid siege to Jahrom, a town that always had been a staunch supporter of the Safavid cause. This siege may have been the reason why people thought that Mohammad Khan Baluch had made common cause with Sheikh Ahmad Madani. The reasons

---

41. VOC 2254, Gamronsch Dagregister, f. 1056-64. The Dutch were taken by surprise and they later would point out to both Shah Tahmasp II and Tahmasp Qoli Khan (Nader) that Mohammad `Ali Khan had urged them to patrol the seas, which they had done. After two months he suddenly had concluded peace and so the Dutch had lost another two and a half months due to the fact that the sailing monsoon had passed. Their total cost for the maintenance of the crews and the two ships amounted to 635 *tuman*s and 29 mahmudis. VOC 2322, de Cleen to Thamas Sjah, 3 October 1732, f. 478-84 vs and de Cleen to Thamas Coelie Chan, 3 October 1732, f. 485-89 vs. VOC 2254, Mohammad `Ali Khan to de Cleen, received 1 April 1732, f. 1243-46. That the situation had not been normalized is also clear from VOC 2254, Mhamed Alie Chan to de Cleen, received 18 May 1732, f. 1252-53 in which he asked the Dutch to prevent Sheikh Ahmad Madani's sister, who had contacted ship owners to ferry her and her goods across the Gulf, from fleeing and taking her goods with her.

42. VOC 2254, Gamronsch Dagregister, f. 1065. The recall of the troops probably had been caused by the planned campaign against Baghdad and the coming 'dynastic' troubles leading to the dethronement of Tahmasp II on 1 October 1732. See on these events Lockhart, *Nadir*, pp. 55-64. Mohammad `Ali Khan arrived in Isfahan on 30 June 1732 to join Tahmasp II's army that was going to Baghdad. Mohammad Khan Baluch was also reported to be in Isfahan at that time. VOC 2322, van Leijpsigh to de Cleen, Spahan, 26 July 1732, f. 288.

43. VOC 2269, Gamronsch Dagregister, f. 6604.

44. Mohammad Khan Baluch returned from the royal court to Isfahan on 12 September 1732 (VOC 2254, f. 763). After Tahmasp II's dethronement he was one of the many new governors whom Tahmasp Khan (Nader) appointed. Mohammad Khan Baluch became governor of Kuhgilu and was charged to punish the Hulas and other Arabs, or in general the Sunnis. He left Isfahan with about 12,000 troops in early October 1732. VOC 2322, van Leijpsigh to de Cleen, Spahan, 20 October 1732, f. 337. Mehdi Khan Astarabadi, *Jahangosha-ye Naderi* ed. Sayyed `Abdollah Anvar (Tehran, 1341/1962), p. 189 also states that Mohammad Khan Baluch, governor of Kuhgilu and Amir Khan (Qereqlu) had been charged to punish the Arabs. Khalil Khan is unknown to me. VOC 2269, Gamronsch Dagregister, f. 6604.

for the siege, as I have said, are unknown. According to the *Jahangosha-ye Naderi* a dispute had arisen between Amir Khan Qereqlu, deputy-governor of Fars, and Ghani Khan, governor of Jahrom.[45] This dispute may have been occasioned by the dethronement of Tahmasp II, for Ghani Khan had defended his town against the enemies of the Safavid cause since 1722. In addition, the rough and oppressive treatment by the new governors appointed by Tahmasp Khan (Nader) after Tahmasp II's dethronement[46] may have contributed to resist Mohammad Khan Baluch. The more so, if the rumor that he was in league with Sheikh Ahmad Madani was true. Especially the behavior of Mohammad Vali Khan, the new governor of Lar, may have triggered this decision. At the end of September 1732 Mohammad Vali Khan had arrived in Lar and from the very beginning had treated the notables (*a'yan*) and people of Lar in an oppressive way. The *kalantar* of Lar, Mirza Baqer, became the focus of the enmity between the governor and the local population, which finally led the *kalantar* to kill the governor and some of his men in December 1732 or in January 1733.[47] Aubin rightly diagnosed this revolt as an expression of social protest; however, such protests were by no means uncommon in Iranian history both before and after this event. I disagree with Aubin where he sees links between the Lar revolt and that of Sheikh Ahmad Madani, for there were not any. Mohammad Khan Baluch immediately left with part of his army to Lar, leaving the remainder to continue the siege of Jahrom. When he arrived in Lar he used no force against the population, but came to an understanding with the leading citizens. The latter, however, felt insecure about the co-habitation with Mohammad Khan Baluch and with a great number of their fellow-citizens they left Lar after a short while and withdrew to the surrounding villages.[48]

In January 1733 Sheikh Ahmad Madani informed the Dutch of the fact that after the dethronement of Tahmasp II the people of Jahrom down to the Garmsirat jointly had charged him with the management of their interests. He had accepted to do so on the condition that the people's leaders swore an oath of allegiance to support him in his endeavors to force the enemy to repent, which, he observed, held especially for Mir Mehr-e 'Ali, the deputy-governor of Bandar 'Abbas. Because he had heard that considerable property belonging to 'Ali Mardan Khan had arrived from India in Bandar 'Abbas he asked the Dutch to seize these goods and

---

45. Astarabadi, *Jahangosha*, p. 201.

46. VOC 2322, van Leijpsigh to de Cleen, Spahan, 12 September 1732, f. 291 vs.

47. VOC 2322, van Leijpsigh to de Cleen, Spahan, 12 September 1732, f. 292; Hazin, *Life*, pp, 98-103. VOC 2232, de Cleen to van Leijpsigh, Gamron, 5 October 1732, with appendix of 13 october 1732, f. 121 states that "the Chan appointed for Lar and Gamron is still in Lar; Mohammad Vali Khan also informed the Dutch about his appointment.

48. Hazin, *Life*, pp. 100-03. There is no evidence that Mirza Baqer, the *kalantar* of Lar, appealed to the Sunni population of Larestan for help, and this also seems unlikely in view of past and subsequent events in the area. The version given by Mohammad Rasul Karamati, *Tarikh-e delgosha-ye Evaz* (Tehran, 1333/1954), pp. 29-30 lacks conviction, since he states that the Sunnis and Mirza Baqer united their forces after fights between Shi`is and Sunnis in Evaz, which had been incited by Mohammad Vali Khan. Mirza Baqer's statement (Astarabadi, *Jahangosha*, p. 201), also seems unlikely, for why were Mirza Baqer of Lar and Ghani Khan killed by the punitive expedition and Sheikh Ahmad Madani left unpunished? Mohammad Vali Khan's murder must have taken place in December 1732, for de Cleen writes to van Leijpsigh in Isfahan on 9 February 1733 (VOC 2322, f. 229) that Mohammad Khan Baluch was believed to be in league with the Sunnis and to have joined forces with them. He had been in Lar with a force of 1,000 men, but he left the city already in February 1732, although de Cleen did not know where Mohammad Khan Baluch had gone. De Cleen also mentioned that the roads as far as Shiraz were made unsafe by the Sunnis.

keep them until the time that the rightful Shah was back on the throne. He also asked the Dutch to continue their support for the Shah and of those activities that would lead to the downfall and destruction of his enemies. Meanwhile Sheikh Ahmad Madani had collected a force of Arabs and Sunnis to take reprisal against a group of robbers who had attacked and robbed a group of herders. With that force he was moving into the direction of Shiraz, Lar, and Jahrom.[49]

The Dutch replied to Sheikh Ahmad Madani's letter on 27 February 1733 that they as his sincere friends had not expected to be treated as they were by his men. A group of his men had come to `Essin, Tasin and other places and had committed all kinds of violent acts and had even attacked caravans, while robbing and killing innocent defenseless people. As a result of these activities trade in Bandar `Abbas had been ruined, which hardly could be called a gesture of friendship or a sign of his desire to restore peace and trade.[50] The events referred to had taken place on 13 February 1733, when crowds of peasants had fled into Bandar `Abbas with all their belongings down to their huts made of date tree branches to seek refuge under the walls of the Dutch factory. They had fled out of fear for Afghans who were at `Essin. Their leader, Mohammad Safidbani, wrote a letter to Mir Mehr-e `Ali that he had come to Bandar `Abbas to guard and keep the town for Shah Tahmasp II and he swore on Imam `Ali's head that his men had strict orders not to molest anybody on pain of corporal punishment. The people of Bandar `Abbas had no trust whatsoever in their intentions and declined the honor of their protection. On 16 March 1733 another group of robbers, 300 men strong, came close to Bandar `Abbas to take whatever they could lay their hands on. The poor people did not have time to save all their property and thus lost a great number of cattle.[51]

On 17 March 1733 (29 Ramazan 1145) a group of Sheikh Ahmad Madani's troops had come near and in Bandar `Abbas. They behaved in such a way that the population suffered much and trade came to a standstill. They even stole a herd of cattle outside Bandar `Abbas that belonged to VOC servants, to wit:

90 heads of sheep	at 10 *mahmudis* per head	900 *mahmudis*
310 head of rams	at 10 *mahmudis* per head	3,100 *mahmudis*
7 head of cows	at 80 *mahmudis* per head	400 *mahmudis*
4 head of donkeys	at 100 *mahmudis* per head	400 *mahmudis*
Total		4,900 *mahmudis*

Sheikh Ahmad Madani's troops had also taken three herders with them, one of whom was able to escape. The Dutch asked Sheikh Ahmad Madani to return the herders and their stolen property in cash or kind. They assumed that the incident had happened without Sheikh Ahmad Madani's

49. VOC 3222, Sjeeg Achmed Madenni to de Cleen, received 25 February 1733 per *tranki* from Kong, f. 452-53. Although this letter appears to bear out Astarabadi's and Karamati's statements it is interesting to observe that Sheikh Ahmad Madani did not mention that any Shi`is had joined his troops. He only stated that the chiefs of Larestan had united forces with him, but he only marched with a force consisting of Arabs and Sunnis. The Safavid supporter Mir Mehr-e `Ali was denounced by him! The Dutch did not believe Sheikh Ahmad Madani and commented that he only pretended his love for the Safavids to further his own ends, see VOC 2322, de Cleen to Batavia, Gamron, 30 September 1733, f. 134.

50. VOC 2322, de Cleen to Sjeeg Aghmed Madennie, Gamron, 27 February 1733, f. 520vs-21 vs.

51. VOC 2269, Gamronsch Dagregister (extract), f. 6605-verso.

knowledge and undoubtedly the whole affair had already given rise to his displeasure. Neverthe-less, they also informed him that if their request was not complied with he could be sure that the Dutch did not lack the means to get back their property.[52]

Sheikh Ahmad Madani's reply was received via Basidu on 7 April 1733. He wrote that the cursed and evil race of Dargazinis had been responsible for the misdeeds. He therefore intended to march on 3 April 1733 (10 Shawwal 1145) to Jahangiriyeh (Jehoengierie) to punish them and take revenge on them for what they had done. He would punish them in such a way that they would loose all inclination to repeat their misdeed. After he would have punished them he would release the two herders and return the VOC property, "for God knows that I want to live in peace with you."[53] Sheikh Ahmad Madani apparently was unperturbed by the news that Mohammad Khan Baluch and Amir Khan had arrived with their army at that time near Evaz and intended to attack him.[54] From a later letter by Sheikh Ahmad Madani we know that he had left Morbagh and had marched to Bagh and Evaz to ostensibly punish the Afghans and Dargazinis for their misdeeds committed at Bandar 'Abbas. His purpose had been, he stressed, to restore law and order. However, when he had arrived at Evaz he had been attacked by troops led by Mohammad Khan Baluch and Amir Khan. He had put up a fierce resistance as a result of which both parties had decided to conclude peace. Both Khans had charged a certain Caardest Chan with the administration of Bandar-e Kong and Basidu and had instructed him to to see to it that Kong had to flourish again as in former times. He therefore had to invite old and new merchants to help restore the old mercantile port. Since Mohammad Khan Baluch had asked Sheikh Madani to assist Caardest Khan he had given the latter his confidante, Mohammad Ahmad, as his advisor. Sheikh Ahmad Madani asked the Dutch to assist Caardest Chan, if he would ask them for the loan of ships or other services, for the welfare of Kong was in everybody's interest.[55]

Sheikh Ahmad Madani's letter was accompanied by one from Caardest Chan himself who informed the Dutch that he had learnt that Sheikh Rashid intended to withdraw his own property as well as that of others from Kong and move it to other places. He therefore asked the Dutch to send a ship to Kong to prevent this and to patrol with smaller vessels near Basidu. Although he had been given full powers he preferred to consult the Dutch about these matters

---

52. VOC 2322, de Cleen to Sjeeg Aghmed Madenni, Gamron, 17 march 1733, f. 522-23.

53. VOC 2322, Sjeeg Aghmed Madenni to de Cleen, received per tranki from Basidu (Basidoor) on 7 April 1733, f. 455-56.

54. VOC 2322, Mhamed Chan Boloeds to de Cleen, received per messenger on 8 June 1733, f. 460-vs in which he announced his appointment as governor (hertog) of Lar and Bandar 'Abbas by Tamas Chan (Nader). For de Cleen's reply (27 June 1733), see Ibid., f. 529-vs. VOC 2269, Gamronsch Dagregister (extract), f. 6606 (4 April 1733). According to Astarabadi, Jahangosha, p. 207, Mohammad Khan Baluch, governor of Kuhgilu, Shushstar and Dezful together with Amir Khan Beg, deputy-governor of Fars, had been ordered to recruit new troops after Nowruz 1145 (March 1733) and to rejoin Tahmasp Khan two months later.

55. VOC 2232, Sjeeg Achmed Madenni to de Cleen, received 21 June 1733, f. 462 vs-463 vs. Caardest Chan and Mohammad Ahmad are unknown to me. In view of what Astarabadi, Jahangosha said about Mohammad Khan Baluch's mission and the subsequent events one may wonder whether he really fought with Sheikh Ahmad Madani.

and wanted to know whether he should make Basidu or Kong flourishing again, or should he remove the population from Basidu to Kong?[56]

The Dutch replied to both letters on 22 June 1733. To Sheikh Ahmad Madani they replied that they did not want to give their opinion about the matters that he had raised. To Caardest Chan they wrote that their own work had priority over all other business, so that they had no time to spend on other people's affairs, especially on affairs that did not concern them at all.[57]

On 5 September 1733 it was reported that Sheikh Ahmad Madani was recruiting troops with the intention to come to Bandar `Abbas. At the end of the same month groups of Afghans and Baluch were pillaging Minab; they then moved to Rudun and surrounding villages, which area was also pillaged. The poor peasants with their families flooded into Bandar `Abbas on 12 October 1733 to seek refuge under the walls of the Dutch factory. The Afghans, under a chief named `Alam Khan, came as close as `Essin and had enslaved a great number of people.[58]

Meanwhile, Caardest Chan and Sheikh Ahmad Madani had made preparations to take Basidu. On 11 and 12 October Caardest Chan landed on Qeshm Island and overran the island with his force after having defeated Sheikh Rashid. The latter and all leading citizens were taken prisoner; houses were burnt, pillaged and many people were killed. Many merchants who had gone to Basidu to seek refuge before the approaching Baluch marauders lost all their property. They had been forced to pay 6,000 *tuman*s and Sheikh Rashid 2,000 *tuman*s. The Baluch meanwhile had been plundering Band `Ali and Bandar `Abbas was in total consternation. On 17 October 1733 some Baluch even entered the town, but were beaten off at the English factory. A force of 5,000 men coming from `Essin, which approached the town, was repulsed by the cannons of the citadel and of the Dutch and English factories. On 22 October 1733 the town panicked again when about 10 Baluch entered Bandar `Abbas. Although there were 3,000 to 4,000 fugitives these robbers seized 26 people behind the Dutch factory without meeting any opposition from them. At that time it was also reported that the Baluch were infesting the area near Lar.[59]

Sheikh Ahmad Madani informed the Dutch and English Companies on 20 November 1733 that Basidu was his. In his clemency he had charged Sheikh Rashid, whom he had taken with him, with the control over the customs of Basidu with orders to induce the population and merchants there of his good intentions. He asked the Europeans to encourage all merchants and others who were his subjects to go to Basidu and to continue their trade and other activities as before. He assured them that they would not be exposed to extortion and troubles. Sheikh Rashid would separately contact the European Companies to discuss further matters.[60]

The English contacted the Dutch about this letter. De Cleen and Cockill, the directors of both factories, held an informal meeting on the beach from 22.00 to 23.00 hours on 21 No-

---

56. VOC 2232, Chaardest Chan to de Cleen, received 21 June 1733, f. 461 vs-462.

57. VOC 2322, f. 528-29.

58. VOC 2269, Gamronsch Dagregister (extract), f. 6606.

59. VOC 2269, Gamronsch Dagregister (extract), f. 6606-vs.

60. VOC 2232 (second part), f. 277-78.

vember 1733. Cockill told that his representative in Basidu had informed him that Caardest Chan was about to come with armed troops to Bandar `Abbas on 22 November 1733 and had advised the Europeans not to interfere with his operation. Both directors agreed that they should act jointly and protect the town, the *shahbandar* and the merchants. They therefore sent a joint reply to Sheikh Ahmad Madani telling him not to come to Bandar `Abbas, to continue his support for the Safavid cause and to be assured of their friendship. They also sent a letter to Caardest Chan telling him not to come to Bandar `Abbas for the time being in view of the fact that they were waiting for Sheikh Ahmad Madani's reply to their letter. If, however, he would persist in his intention to invade the town the European Companies would act in accordance with what would be required at that time.[61]

Sheikh Ahmad Madani replied that he hoped that they were still good friends, for he still considered himself to be one. He repeated that they could assure all merchants of his sincere intentions. Since they had heard nothing from Sheikh Rashid he would inform them about his plans when he arrived in Lar.[62] This letter was followed by another one in which Sheikh Ahmad Madani informed the European Companies of the fact that Mohammad Khan Baluch had sent messengers (*chapar*) from Shiraz to conclude friendship and unity. He therefore intended to meet him and to leave Morbagh on 19 December 1733 (10 Rajab 1146) with his army consisting of Afghans, Dargazinis, Arabs and of *my own nation*.[63]

In November 1733 the Dutch had learnt about Mohammad Khan Baluch's revolt, which Sheikh Ahmad Madani implicitly referred to. Mohammad Khan Baluch had hurried back to Baghdad in June 1733. He was just in time to be put in charge of the 4,000 horse and 12,000 foot that Tahmasp Khan (Nader) had left behind to continue the siege of Baghdad, while he himself went out to meet Topal Osman Pasha.[64] When he suffered a devastating defeat on 17 July 1733 Mohammad Khan Baluch fled with the 4,000 horsemen to Shushtar leaving the 12,000 infantrymen to be butchered by Ahmad Pasha.[65] He was able to secure Shushtar's support for his rebellion and then moved on to Kuhgilu, which was reported to have rebelled as well, according to news received in Isfahan on 6 October 1733. At that time nobody had any idea of Mohammad Khan Baluch's intentions for the same report mentioned that the latter

---

61. VOC 2232 (second part), f. 280 (Madani), f. 281 (Caardest Chan); Ibid. Resolutie Gamron, 21 November 1733, f. 282-90. De Cleen wrote to Batavia (VOC 2269, 20 November 1733, f. 6533 vs) that although he feared that Sheikh Ahmad Madani would attack Bandar `Abbas he believed that he could cope with that situation, since he had four ships on the roadstead with 300 men crew and in the factory he had a staff of 167 men (including the military). If need be he could have taken the fort on Qeshm island. He stated that in his view it would be necessary to occupy the islands on the coast of near Bandar `Abbas to force the Iranian government to repay its debt to the VOC, which amounted to Dfl. 1,876,736:11:- at that time.

62. VOC 2323, received 8 December 1733, f. 405-06.

63. VOC 2323, received 8 December 1733, f. 403-04.

64. VOC 2322, de Cleen to Batavia, Gamron, 30 September with appendix of 30 November 1733, f. 44 vs.

65. VOC 2322, Hey to de Cleen. Basra, 19 August 1733, f. 427-28. According to VOC 2269, Extract Spahans Dagregister, f. 6609 vs (5 August 1733) 15,000 men had been left behind by Nader commanded by Chan Jan, Mhamed Chan, Mhamed Resa Chan, and Mhamed Rahiem Chan who all perished there.

had been expelled from Kuhgilu.[66] It was only a fortnight later that the news of Mohammad Khan Baluch's rebellion became public in Isfahan. It was said that he had made common cause with Sheikh Ahmad Madani, that he had amassed a capital of 40,000 *tumans* for his revolt, and that Sheikh Belal of Makran had raised an army of 12,000 to jointly march with him to Shiraz. All Afghans, Baluch, Hazaras, and Dargazinis in Isfahan were arrested, apparently to be killed or to prevent them from joining Mohammad Khan Baluch it was believed. Later, on 23 October 1733, they were set free again, but the *kadkhodas* had to stand security in case they deserted and left the city.[67] Although in the beginning also reports were received that Mohammad Khan Baluch was in fact recruiting troops to reinforce Tahmasp Khan's (Nader) forces[68] the main news item in Isfahan for the remainder of 1733 was the (often unreliable and conflicting) news about Mohammad Khan Baluch's rebellion. On 29 October 1733 it was said that he had joined forces with Sheikh Jabbara and Sheikh Ahmad Madani and had already minted coins in Shah Tahmasp II's name.[69] The next day part of his 20,000 men strong force was already reported to be at 20 German miles from Isfahan to collect supplies. Mohammad Khan Baluch was also said to have written to the *sardar* Tahmasp Qoli Beg Jalayer, governor of Isfahan, that if he would not come and meet him on the battle field he would come and pay him a visit in the city.[70] The *sardar* meanwhile was recruiting troops, mainly untried peasants who did not even dare to fire a match-lock. On 2 November 1733 it was rumored that the Lurs also had joined Mohammad Khan Baluch's rebellion, who one day later was believed to be either in Shushtar or in Kazerun. He was calling people to join his banner and gird their swords to defend Shah Tahmasp II and the religion of Morteza ʿAli against the proud and ungrateful Tahmasp Khan (Nader).[71]

A great many rumors were circulating during the last few months of 1733 in Isfahan, but it was impossible to verify their veracity the Dutch observed. At the same time there was also uncertainty about the fate of Tahmasp Khan (Nader); was he dead or not, where was he, had he really defeated Topal Osman Pasha as had been made public on 29 November 1733, or was it a strategm to mislead Mohammad Khan Baluch and those hesitating which side to choose?[72] Furthermore, there was the fact that rumors abounded the restoration of Shah Tahmasp II and that he even had gathered his own troops about him in Mazandaran. The fact also that troops, which had been sent by *sardar* Tahmasp Beg Jalayer to seek out the advance troops of Mohammad Khan Baluch, either were disarmed by the Lurs, were defeated, or sometimes

---

66. VOC 2323, Spahans Dagregister, f. 887.

67. VOC 2323, Spahans Dagregister, f. 892 (19 October 1733), f. 896 (23 october 1733).

68. VOC 2323, Spahans Dagregister, f. 893.

69. VOC 2323, Spahans Dagregister, f. 919 (9 December 1733).

70. VOC 2323, Spahans Dagregister, f. 923-24.

71. VOC 2323, Spahans Dagregister, f. 907 (14 November 1733). According to Hazin, *Life*, p. 240 "Mohammed Khan Baloch, commander-in-chief in Fars having disagreed with Tahmasb Coli Khan, had, through fear of his life, wrested his head from the rein of obedience and set up a profession of servitude and fealty to Shah Tahmasb. As the people were afflicted with tyranny and were naturally attached to the exalted Safavean family, and as he boasted of his devotion to that house, they inclined to his party, and he had an immense army."

72. VOC 2323, Spahans Dagregister, f. 908-09.

even defected, increased uncertainty.[73] Finally, the behavior by the *sardar* himself was puzzling. He had arrived in Isfahan on 22 October 1733 and had begun extorting much money from the people of Isfahan, both in the city and in its dependencies. Supplies were stocked in the citadel, which moreover was repaired and reinforced, while he also recruited new troops.[74] On 14 November 1733 the *sardar* made public that all inhabitants had to sell their arms to his soldiers or hand them over to his servants on pain of death and confiscation of one's property.[75] This and other measures were considered to be sign of his fear that the population of Isfahan might revolt, or when he would leave the city towards Shiraz that they would close the gates against him and declare themselves for Mohammad Khan Baluch.[76] The fact also that he was going to leave Isfahan a few times with his army, but each time put this off until a later date reinforced such a supposition. The Dutch in Isfahan, however, recorded in their Diary that the *sardar* need not have such fear, because:

> The Isfahanis are smarter than women and great cowards, who are only capable
> of swallowing their pilav [rice] and to dress themselves up to please their whoring
> women.

The information about Mohammad Khan Baluch was not very reliable either. He sent letters to the *sardar* daring him to come out of the city and meet him on the battle field, but despite the recurrent rumors he was not at Aberquh, or even at six days' journey from Isfahan, or had sent troops to Kerman and Yazd to take these cities. The most repeated rumor was that he was at Shiraz, which was considered the most likely place for him to be.[77] Mohammad Khan Baluch probably took Shiraz at the end of November 1733 after having first defeated troops commanded loyal to Tahmasp Khan (Nader) and commanded by Mohammad Qasem at Behbahan. He then had marched on to Shiraz where a battle took place against troops led by Nazar Qoli (Nezer Coelie) just outside the city in which he was victorious. Many supporters of Tahmasp Khan were killed by him and only the leading Khorasani commanders were left unharmed and were imprisoned in a fortress. However, 100 Khorasanis who had fled into the citadel lost their nose and ears and were sent by him to Isfahan, where they arrived on 14 December 1733.[78]

According to Mohammad Khan Baluch himself, he was supported by the people of Kermanshah, the Feylis, those of Lurestan, the Bakhtiyaris, and the people of Shushtar, Arabistan, Kuhgilu and Shiraz.[79] Another source roughly provides the same kind of information

---

73. VOC 2323, Spahans Dagregister, f. 894, 899, 901.

74. He ordered all Khorasanis in Isfahan of whatever trade to report to him and join his army as soldiers. He also ordered the city officials to report to him each day at sun-set on pain of the bastinado. VOC 2323, Spahans Dagregister, f. 902-03.

75. VOC 2323, Spahans Dagregister, f. 907.

76. VOC 2323, Spahans Dagregister, f. 913, 915.

77. VOC 2323, Spahans Dagregister, f. 901 (29 October 1733), f. 903 (3 November 1733), f. 920 (7 December 1733).

78. VOC 2323, Spahans Dagregister, f. 911 (24 November 1733), f. 923 (10 December 1733), f. 925 (14 December 1733).

79. VOC 2323, Mhamed Chan Boloeds to de Cleen (from Shiraz), received 27 January 1734, f. 819-20.

about his supporters.[80] It is interesting that Mohammad Khan Baluch does not mention any support of the Baluch, although it was said that he commanded 80,000 of them,[81] and rumors at that time indicated that the Baluch who marched on Kerman and infested the Garmsirat would also join his cause. However, this was pure speculation, for the Baluch were just on their annual marauding tour of south-eastern Iran, while the people of Yazd, e.g., had sent 500 matchlock-men to the support of the *sardar* in Isfahan; the Kermanis took refuge into the citadel out of fear for their alleged liberators.[82] It is difficult to ascertain the extent of the support for Mohammad Khan Baluch. The fact that he claimed that other rebellious sections of the population such as the Lurs and the Bakhtiyaris had joined his cause did not mean that they really had done so. From subsequent events one get's the impression that Mohammad Khan Baluch received very little, if any, support from that side.[83] The only real support he had were his own troops and those of Kuhgilu. Even the support of the Sunni Arabs was not total, while it is questionable whether the population of the Garmsirat in toto joined his cause as has been asserted by various sources. It would appear that from the very beginning he had trouble with his Arab supporters, who even temporarily left him when he took measures against their pillaging of the population of Shiraz.[84]

On 1 January 1734, a decree (*raqam*) from Tahmasp Khan (Nader) was made public in Isfahan in which he announced that he had concluded a peace treaty with the Ottomans and that he had left Baghdad on 23 December 1733 to punish the rebel Mohammad Khan Baluch. Ironically the same decree ordered the governor of Isfahan not to use violence against the population of Isfahan. The next day the *sardar* marched with 8,000 men towards Shiraz.[85]

Tahmasp Khan marched via Shushtar, where he massacred the population, and Kuhgilu to Shiraz where he arrived on 4 February 1734 (27 Sha`ban 1146).[86] Apart from the punishment dealt to those of Shushtar, one of his generals, Qasem Khan, was sent to suppress the rebellion of the Ka`b Arabs under their chief Farajollah. An army of 5,000 men were sent to destroy them and their settlement of Qobban (Gabban). In accordance with the peace treaty concluded with Ahmad Pasha the Iranian commander asked the governor (*motasallem*) of Basra to withhold any protection from those Ka`b Arabs, who would flee to Basra and to

The Feylis were Lurs and I do not know why they were mentioned separately from other Lurs.

80. VOC 2269, Auwannees (Hovannes) to de Cleen. Kerman, received 23 December 1733, f. 6616 (Hov'annes was the VOC wool-buying agent in Kerman).

81. Mohammad Kazem, *Nameh-ye `Alamara-ye Naderi* ed. N. D. Miklukho-Maklaj 3 vols. (Moscow, 1960), vol. 1, p. 566 (f. 272 b).

82. VOC 2323, Spahans Dagregister, f. 916 (2 December 1733), f. 920 (7 December 1733), f. 963 (13 February 1734).

83. VOC 2322, van Leijpsigh to de Cleen. Spahan, 20 November 1732, f. 311, for example, reports that towards the end of 1732 Tahmasp Khan (Nader) had his hands fully occupied with the Arabs (of Hoveyzeh) and the Bakhtiyaris at Shushtar, who were said to cooperate with each other. Other groups such as the Lurs and the Baluch also were resisting central authority rule prior to the Mohammad Khan Baluch rebellion, and thus one may speak of parallelism of interests rather than of a united common front.

84. VOC 2323, Spahans Dagregister, f. 925 (14 December 1733).

85. VOC 2323, Spahans Dagregister, f. 936-37.

86. VOC 2323, Mahmoed Chan Amirie Sulthoen of Lar to de Cleen, received 13 February 1734, f. 822. According to Astarabadi, *Jahangosha*, p. 211, Tahmasp Khan arrived on 26 Shah`ban 1146 at Shiraz.

supply him with five galleys with their crews, which had to be well-supplied with military supplies and provisions. On 26 January 1734 Khalifeh Efendi was sent with the five required galleys and sailed to Haffar where the Iranian troops were said to be. On 31 January 1734 the *motasallem* sent the provisions consisting of grains and butter. A new request for provisions and fodder from Qobban reached the *motasellem* on 7 February 1734, who already three days later sent five well-stocked galleys to Qobban, where the Banu Ka`b and other Arabs were said to be under siege in their fort.[87]

At the beginning of Janaury 1734 there was some conflicting information about the fate of Mohammad Khan Baluch. He was said to have defeated the *sardar*, or to have been defeated himself, while on 27 January 1734 it was reported that he had marched with 12,000 men to Shushtar.[88] On one thing the information in Dutch sources agree, however, viz., that Mohammad Khan Baluch had fled without having given battle, although his troops had been formed into battle-array. This news was both recorded in Isfahan and Basra.[89] The Isfahan of-fice also records a rumor that battle had been given at a place at three days' journey from Shiraz and that Mohammad Khan Baluch had lost 10,000 soldiers and had fled with the other rebel leaders.[90] On 19 February 1734 a decree from Tahmasp Khan (Nader) was made opublic in Isfahan in which he announced that the rebel Mohammad Khan Baluch had fled, that he did not know where he had gone, and that he had arrived in Shiraz.[91] That city felt his wrath and many who were suspected to have supported the rebellion were killed. The province of Fars, moreover, was punished by having to pay 100,000 *tumans*, of which Shiraz had to pay 14,000 *tumans*. *Sardar* Tahmasp Beg Jalayer was sent in pursuit of Mohammad Khan Baluch with 5,000 men, who was believed to have fled to Lar.[92]

The information that no battle had taken place is also indirectly confirmed by a letter from the *sardar*, who does not mention such an event, but only that he had arrived in Shi-raz to destroy Mohammad Khan Baluch, who had escaped, together with the sultan of Lar, Mahmud Khan Amiriyeh, and 13,000 men (the latter had joined him later). The *sardar* took Lar, captured Yahya Khan, the deputy of Mohammad Khan Baluch, and killed him. Moham-mad Khan Baluch fled to Evaz and then to Morbagh, where he was said to received the sup-port of 12,000 to 15,000 Sunnis.[93] On 22 March 1734 information was received in Isfahan

---

87. VOC 2323, Extract Dagregister Bassoura, f. 202-44. For the vicissitudes of the Banu Ka`b see Willem Floor, "The rise and fall of the Banu Ka`b. A borderer state in southern Khuzestan," *IRAN* XLIV (2006), pp.277-315.

88. VOC 2323, Spahans Dagregister, f. 955-56.

89. VOC 2323, Spahans Dagregister, f. 958 (1 February 1734); Ibid., Extract Dagregister Bassoura, f. 2043 (5 February 1734).

90. VOC 2323, Spahans Dagregister, f. 959 (4 February 1734).

91. VOC 2323, Spahans Dagregister, f. 961. It is of interest to note that Tahmasp Khan did not mention that a battle had taken place between him and Mohammad Khan Baluch in which he had been victorious. This reinforces the conclusion that indeed no battle had taken place, for Tahmasp Khan always publicized his victories in great detail in his decrees.

92. VOC 2323, Spahans Dagregister, f. 962, 964. VOC 2356, Hey to Batavia. Gamron, 9 November 1734, f. 38 reports that the inhabitants of the Garmsirat had been ordered by *Sardar* Tahmasp Qoli Beg to pay 4,000 *tumans* or Dfl. 170,000. The VOC broker and other VOC servants were ordered to pay 300 *tumans* to this contribution against which Hey protested to Tahmasp Khan.

93. VOC 2323, Spahans Dagregister, f. 969 (27 February 1734). At that time Tahmasp Khan also

that the *sardar* had been defeated by Mohammad Khan Baluch and Sheikh Ahmad Madani. The governor of Isfahan, therefore, was ordered to prepare 60,000 strong hair sacks, each of 1.5 cubit (*gaz*) length and to send these within one month to Shiraz. The sacks, after having been filled with sand, had to be used to storm the enemy's defenses.[94] Both the *sardar* and the soltan of Lar asked the Dutch and the English (at the orders of Tahmasp Khan) to patrol the Persian Gulf with their ships from Masqat to the Sea of Abyssinia to seize all rebels, whether they were Shi'is, Sunnis, or Baluch.[95] Since the latter had been addressed to both Companies they deliberated about this request and decided to give a joint reply with the purpose to delay matters, which by then would have been resolved by themselves. The Companies congratulated *sardar* Tahmasp Beg with his victory. With regard to his request for ships they relied that they would be willing to assist him, but the distance between Masqat and Abyssinia was about 300 German miles dotted with about 100 ports and towns. The European ships, moreover, were too heavy and drawing too much water to prevent lighter *tranki*s to seek refuge in those ports, because of banks and shoals or night landings. He had to realize that traveling by sea was more difficult than by land. If Tahmasp Beg would indicate exactly where the fugitives were or whereto they would flee it would be easier for them to assist him. They finally assured him that it was not that they were unwilling to help, but that it was just not feasible.[96]

Because Tahmasp Beg did not reply to this letter both Companies wrote him on 22 February 1734 stating that they still had not received his answer. At the same time, they informed him of the fact that in the area around Bandar 'Abbas the whole countryside was in consternation because of marauding Baluch near Minab. They, therefore, had been forced to fetch cannons from their ships to defend themselves and the poor miserable population.[97]

Both the Dutch and English believed that after this letter Tahmasp Beg would not reiterate his earlier request and leave the matter be, the more so since rumors had it that the campaign was going favorable for him. However, on 29 March 1734 both Companies, separately this time, received the same latter sent from Harm with the request to send ships to Bandar-e Charak (Bhender Sjarak) whither Sheikh Ahmad Madani, Mohammad Khan Baluch, their Afghans, and other rascals had fled. The Companies were ordered to patrol the sea-lanes and keep these closed.[98]

---

believed that Sheikh Ahmad Madani was the governor of Lar, for according to a Dutch report he demanded that he deliver Mohammad Khan Baluch in chains to him, see VOC 2476, f. 922. Soon after the fall of Lar new officials were appointed. Apart from the sultan of Lar, Mahmud Khan Amiriyeh, there was Miersa Takkie wackiel of Lar (VOC 2323, f. 830, his letter to de Cleen was received on 3 April 1734) and Agha Mahmoed Messie, Coetwaal of Lar, who wrote to de Cleen (Ibid., f. 827-28, received on 29 March 1734) that near Dors (?) VOC messengers had been waylaid by robbing Sunnis.

94. VOC 2323, Spahans Dagregister, f. 983 (22 March 1734). This news item leds credence to Karamati's account (*Tarikh*, p. 39) that according to local tradition Evaz was heavily defended.

95. VOC 2323, Thamas Beecq to Dutch and English East Indies Companies, received 13 February 1734; Ibid., de Cleen to Batavia. Gamron, 22 September 1734, f. 192.

96. VOC 2323, Resolutie Gamron, Tuesday, 18 May 1734, f. 509-10; Ibid., de Cleen & Cockill to Tahmasp Beg. Gamron, 14 February 1734, f. 513-15.

97. VOC 2323, de Cleen & Cockill to Tahmasp Beg. Gamron. 22 February 1734, f. 517-18.

98. VOC 2323, f. 518-20; Ibid., Tahmasp Beg to de Cleen, received 29 March 1734, f. 828-29. On the route taken by Tahmasp Beg see Aubin, "Les Sunnites," p. 168.

The Companies again delayed reacting to this letter, for although they were convinced that a victory for Sheikh Ahmad Madani would lead to the total ruin of Bandar `Abbas they did not expect much peace and quiet either from Tahmasp Beg's victory. They, therefore, preferred to wait until they had further information on the result of the campaign. This information was received on 11 April 1734 from a fleeing Afghan, who reported that Sheikh Ahmad Madani had been defeated and that he and his troops were fleeing in all directions. Both Companies again had an informal meeting and decided that same night to send each one a ship. The VOC sent *de Segbroek* and the EIC the *Britannia Galley*; these would sail the following day to stay behind Qeshm to watch out for figitives. After that date the news of the victory was confirmed by other reports. The victory was so devastating that the sultan, Mir Mehr-e `Ali and the *shahbandar*, Mirza Esma`il, said that there was need anymore for the European ships to patrol the sea lanes. Both directors discussed the new situation and de Cleen decided to recall the Dutch ship.[99]

At that time, both ships were behind Qeshm and learnt on 12 May 1734 that the enemy was hiding near Qeysh, so they set course for that island. However, the Dutch ship received orders to return to Bandar `Abbas where it arrived on 14 May. According to its captain, the enemy was on the island of Qeysh where they were contained. Among them were said to be Mostafa (Menstoffa), the brother of Sheikh Ahmad Madani.[100] In view of this information the Dutch decided to send *de Segbroek* back to the island, because if the English would not recall their ship the enemy surely would be caught. Mohammad Latif Khan, who had arrived in Bandar `Abbas on 14 May 1734, was informed of this decision. He had a letter from Tahmasp Beg, written in Kemeshk (Commiscq) in which he stated that Mohammad Latif Khan was governor of Dashtestan, Kazerun, and Zoelunad (?) and supervisor of all sea-ports charged with the preparation of a few ships and vessels to destroy the rebels. Tahmasp Beg did not doubt that both Companies would assist him in the purchase of these ships and all that was required to assist him in being successful.[101]

In the night of 18 May 1734, after refreshing its supplies, *de Segbroek* sailed away and on 22 May met the English gally the *Prince of Wales* near Basidu. They both sailed to Qeysh where they arrived on 25 May 1734. The *Britanania Galley* and Sheikh Rashid with two ships and five other vessels still contained the island. The captain of the *Britannia Galley* told his colleagues that he had tried to induce the rebels to board his ship. He had promised them free passage to Basra. This would have worked, he maintained, if Sheikh Rashid's men had not given the plan away. This had led to a fight in which the English had suffered two casualties and five wounded. The European captains decided to act united, although it soon became clear

---

99. VOC 2323, f. 521-25.

100. Although Karamati, *Tarikh* does not mention this brother a fact is that this and other family members of Sheikh Ahmad Madani had escaped, for Tahmasp Beg later told van Leijpsigh in Isfahan that although Sheikh Ahmad Madani was dead this did not mean that he intended to leave his family alone, who had fled and gotten away. VOC 2357, van Leijpsigh to de Cleen. Spahan, 5 November 1734, f. 1115.

101. VOC 2323, f. 521-25; Ibid., Thomas becq from Commiscq to de Cleen via Mhamed Lettief Chan, f. 531-32. This is the second time that the central government tried to organize the nucleus of a fleet. On this matter see Willem Floor, "The Iranian Navy during the Eighteenth Century," *Iranian Studies* 20 (1987), pp. 31-53 or Willem Floor, *The Persian Gulf. The Rise of the Gulf Arabs. The Politics of trade on the northern Persian littoral 1730-1792* (Washington DC: Mage Publishers, 2007), chapter two.

that the two English captains did not, or at least, tried not to inform their Dutch colleague, Captain Hageman, about all that was going on. For on 30 May 1734, Sheikh Jabbara had taken up position west of Qeysh and had invited the English captains to come and see him. They had not informed the Dutch about it, but the latter learnt about it, whereupon the Dutch captain demanded that a Dutchman also would go to Sheikh Jabbara. The latter only informed him that he was waiting for orders from Tahmasp Beg, which the Dutch did not believe. On 2 June 1734 Sheikh Rashid informed the Europeans that a *tranki* with 100 Afghans would try to run the blockade that night. Due to heavy patrolling the enemy gave up its plan and drew the *tranki* ashore. The next day at the request of Sheikhs Jabbara and Rashid the European ships bombarded the redoubts and *tranki*s on the beach, which showed that if they had to make a landing a pathway could be cleared. On 4 June 1734, a letter from Mohammad Latif Khan arrived in which he ordered both sheikhs Jabbara and Rashid to obey the orders of the European captains. His emissary, with their permission, went ashore on Qeysh to see whether the rebels were still on it. He returned on 8 June and reported not have seen any rebels except for three old men and an old woman, whom he had transferred to Sheikh Jabbara. He told the captains that they might as well return to Bandar `Abbas, to which the captains reacted, "did he have written orders to that effect?" The emissary asserted that Captain Louis (Lewis?) had these orders. Captain Hageman then asked whether together they should try to get hold of Sheikh Rashid's ships as had been ordered. The English captains replied that these were their orders, but again they were not clear whether these included participation by the Dutch.

On 1 June 1734 Mohammad Latif Khan had informed both Companies that he had learnt that the crews of the Arab ships and vessels at Qeysh intended to flee. He therefore asked the Companies to instruct their captains to see to it that these ships with their crew would return with them to Bandar `Abbas after the end of the operation at Qeysh. Captain Hageman was instructed to comply with this request and to act jointly with the English captains, who would receive the same orders from Waters, the EIC director.

On 10 June 1734, the Dutch had taken position behind Sheikh Rashid's ships. Captain Louis's mate came aboard and informed Hageman that Louis had arrested Sheikh Rashid after he had invited him for a cup of coffee on his ship. Hageman was furious and asked whether they had not formally agreed to discuss, plan and act jointly? He told the English that henceforth he would treat them the same way as they had done to him, i.e., he would inform them after the fact. At the same time Hageman seized Sheikh Rashid's other ship and sailed away and arrived that night at Kong. The English tried to induce Hageman to hand over the ship to them, but he told them no. On 12 June the English informed Hageman that they wanted to give Sheikh Rashid to possibility to visit Basidu for two days. They further suggested he allow the Arab crew of the seized second ship to go ashore as well, for Tahmasp Beg only wanted Sheikh Rashid and the ships they asserted. Hageman reacted saying it would be better if they executed their orders rather than pleasing Sheikh Rashid. Hageman ordered Sheikh Rashid to instruct the captains (*kadkhodas*) to bring the ship to the Dutch roadstead and the *grab* to the English one and to have the crews stay aboard. He also ordered the ships to be searched as a result of which money and ammunition was found. Near Basidu Hageman ordered to take the lifeboat from the ship, which was returned after they had passed Basidu. On 14 June 1734 they met Mohammad Latif Khan on the *Robert Galley* in the company of another two-master. The next day Sheikh Rashid and his two ships were handed over to Mohammad Latif Khan and the whole fleet was ordered to return to Basidu. On 22 June Mohammad Latif Khan sent his own vessels to Charak, for the European ships the sea was too wild to sail through the canal. On 23 June *de Segbroek* returned to Bandar ʿAbbas, where it arrived on 25 June ar 22.00 hours. Meanwhile, it had been relieved by *de Castor & Pollux*, which had arrived at Basidu on 22 June and which had been promised to be sent back within a few days. Because of the behavior of the English captains the Dutch decided to cancel their agreement with the English for joint planning and action and only show them outward friendship.[102]

Meanwhile, Tashmap Beg had written a letter to the Companies, which was received on 3 June 1734 in which he stated that he had Mohammad Khan Baluch and all his men in his power. Sheikh Ahmad Madani had already been captured by him, so that for the time being there was no need to buy ships anymore.[103] A letter that arrived on 7 June 1734, however, still discussed the condition of the purchase of ships. It ordered the Companies to send ships as soon as possible to Kong to take in soldiers to destroy the enemy. A the same time, Tahmasp Beg thanked the Companies for the ships lent for the Qeysh operation, about the result of which he had as yet no information. On 23 June another of Tahmasp Beg's letters arrived in which he thanked the Dutch for having put their ships at his disposal.[104]

Sheikh Rashid was taken to Tahmasp Beg Jalayer on 13 July 1734. The Dutch learnt that he and Sheikh Jabbara had to pay a fine of 10,000 *tumans*.[105] Mohammad Khan Baluch was taken to Isfahan together with his wife's brother and Delaver Beg, the last Afghan deputy-governor of Shiraz.

> They have been thrown in prison in the governor's house. Mhamet Boloeds had hidden his face for the rabble, because they welcomed him with offensive and mocking words and gestures. The sardaar has captured sjeeg Achmed Madennie and the other rebels; he wants 60,000 tomans from them which takes time, reason why the sardaar did not hesitate to send these three.
>
> 17 June. In the morning a tent was pitched for the mahjaar basje (*moʿayyer-bashi*) in front of the gate of the alie kapie (ʿAli Qapu Palace). He appeared there and had Mhamet Chan and the two other brought before him. He mockingly invited Mhamet Chan to come and take a seat with him in the tent. However, the other replied that there was no time for that and that he had better execute the orders which he had received. The other, thereupon, gave orders to take out the eyes of that Boloeds with a pointed knife, and to behead the other two. Mhamed Chan also asked that favor, but this was refused. However, he suffered the pain like a man without making any movement to the great amazement of the spectators. Afterwards the blind

---

102.   VOC 2323, Report by Captain Hageman. Gamron, 4 July 1734, f. 461-580.

103.   VOC 2323, Tahmasp Beg to de Cleen, f. 839. On the events leading to their capture see Hazin, *Life*, pp. 249-50, 265f. It is quite unlikely that Mohammad Khan Baluch was captured on Qeysh as is clear from the report by Captain Hageman. Already on 27 April it was reported from Basra that Sheikh Ahmad Madani had been captured and that Mohammad Khan Baluch had fled again. VOC 2323, Extract Dagregister Bassoura, f. 2051.

104.   VOC 2323, Tahmasp Beg to de Cleen, f. 843-44.

105.   VOC 2323, Hey to Batavia. Gamron, 22 September 1734, f. 207.

man was taken to the mahjaar bashe's house, while a surgeon was ordered to heal his wounds.[106]

Sheikh Ahmad Madani was killed as well, whether in the Garmsirat or at Tahmasp Khan's (Nader) court is not known. The rebels' followers were transported to Khorasan in accordance with Nader's usual forced resettlement policy. The VOC wool factor in Kerman reported on 30 September 1734 that so far 6,000 Arab and Sunni families had been transported to Khorasan.[107]

Both Sheikhs Rashid and Jabbara emerged unscathed from their ordeal. Mohammad Taqi, the deputy governor of Siraz, farmed out the customs of Bandar `Abbas to both Sheikhs for the sum of 20,500 *tuman*s for a period of two and a half years. However, Tahmasp Khan (Nader) did not agree with this decision and by October 1734 he had reappointed Mirza Esma`il Zamindavari, who had been on the point of leaving Bandar `Abbas.[108] Tahmasp Khan, who had been clearly wrongly informed, also wrote a letter to both European Companies on 23 May 1734 (6 Safar 1148) in which he expressed his surprise at the fact that the Europeans had taken Sheikh Rashid prisoner and had taken him to Bandar `Abbas, while he had given orders to capture Sheikh Ahmad Madani. The Europeans were ordered to send Sheikh Rashid immediately to Tahmasp Beg Jalayer and also to send him a letter explaining how this event could have taken place.[109] The Dutch replied on 16 October 1734 and informed Tahmasp Khan about the real course of events, stressing that it had been the English who had seized and imprisoned Sheikh Rashid.[110] The Dutch supported their explanatory letter by a letter from Sheikh Rashid himself,[111] and from Mirza Esma`il, the re-instated *shahbandar*.[112] A similar letter was sent to Mirza Taqi Shirazi and to Mirza Mohammad, the royal treasurer.[113] Neither the Dutch nor the English heard about the matter anymore, and thus ended the aftermath of Sheikh Ahmad Madani's rebellion.

Discussion: In view of the course of events described above it is difficult to accept the exceptional nature of Sheikh Ahmad Madani's revolt as Aubin and Arunova/Ashrafiyan have submitted. There is no evidence (in fact only evidence to the contrary) of any possible collaboration of Mohammad Khan Baluch's forces and the Shi`ite population of Kerman. The

---

106. VOC 2323, Spahans Dagregister, f. 2024-25 (16-17 June 1734); Ibid., de Cleen, Hey to Batavia. Gamron, 22 September 1734, f. 212 states that after Mohammad Khan's eyes had been taken out he was left to die.

107. VOC 2323, Hovannes to de Cleen. Kerman, 30 August, 1734, f. 853 and VOC 2356, Idem to idem. Kerman, 30 September 1734, f. 143-44; VOC 2323, Spahans Dagregister, f. 999 (1 May 1734) reports that the Afghan Ghani Khan (Ganni Chan) had arrived in Isfahan with 5,000 troops and many male and female slaves. An Arab Sheikh in Kuhgilu province, moreover, had to pay 3,000 *tuman*s and to give his son and family as hostages.

108. VOC 2356, Hey to Batavia. Gamron, 9 November 1734, f. 35-37.

109. VOC 2356, Tahmasp Khan, *vakil al-dowleh* to de Cleen, received 21 September 1734, f. 131-33.

110. VOC 2356, Hey to Tahmasp Khan. Gamron, 16 October 1734, f. 121-26.

111. VIOC 2356, Sheikh Rashid to Tahmasp Khan. Gamron 16 October 1734, f. 119-20.

112. VOC 2356, Hey to former *shahbandar* Mirza Esma`il with regards to Sheikh Rashid and his reply written on Hey's letter, dated 9 October 1734, dispatched to Tahmasp Khan on 16 October 1734, f. 115-18.

113. VOC 2356, f. 127-30.

evidence for a collusion between Sheikh Ahmad Madani and the Shi`ite population of Lar-estan and the Garmsirat is not strong. Apart from partisan statements by Mirza Mehdi Asta-rabadi and the unlikely reason for such collusion by Karamati there is no real evidence. Hazin, an eye-witness of the events that are the pivot for the case of a Sunni-Shi`a collusion makes no mention of it, in fact his account makes it highly unlikely. There seems to be some grounds to assume that there has been a short-lived 'marriage de raison' between Sheikh Ahmad Madani and Hajji Ghani Khan of Jahrom. However, this is incompatible with the fact that Mohammad Khan Baluch killed Hajji Ghani Khan and Mirza Baqer, the *kalantar* of Lar, but concluded an agreement with Sheikh Ahmad Madani. He even went so far as to give him an advisory role in the administration of the Garmsirat. The fact also that Sheikh Ahmad Madani, despite his claims that he supported the Safavid cause, continued to terrorize the countryside and finally made peace with his professed enemies makes it highly unlikely that the beginning of 1733 saw a change of the normal situation. This normal situation was that Sheikh Ahmad Madani preyed on his Shi`ite neighbors as he had done since 1724.

If we, moreover, take a look at the two rebel leaders we see in fact two old comrades in arms. Mohammad Khan Baluch had come to Iran as one of Mahmud Khan's commanders in 1722 and had helped to destroy the Safavid state. He had assisted in the siege of Isfahan and had shared in its spoils. He was a trusted commander of both Mahmud Khan and Ashraf Khan. Under the latter he became *beglerbegi* or governor-general of Fars (1727-28) and later ambassador to the Ottoman court. It is therefore quite likely that previous contacts had existed between these two upholders of the Afghan occupation. After the restoration of the Safavid dynasty Sheikh Ahmad Madani continued to enjoy relative peace and independence, and, very important, he paid no taxes. Mohammad Khan Baluch enjoyed both the favor of Tahmasp II and the latter's chief general, Tahmasp Khan (Nader). He had been sent by both (in 1731 and 1732) to subdue the rebellious Sheikh Ahmad Madani, but each time he failed to do so and came to an understanding with him. The reason for Mohammad Khan Baluch's rebellion is not known; it has been mentioned that Tahmasp Khan suspected him of plotting and he had therefore sent for him. The coincidence of Mohammad Khan Baluch's defeat at Baghdad in 1733 as well as Tahmasp Khan's, whose career semed to have reached its end, may have trig-gered him to go it alone. Neither his love for the Safavid dynasty nor that of the suffering of the population can have been the moving force of his rebellion in view of his bloody career. Sheikh Ahmad Madani came to his assistance, probably for old times' sake, but more likely to secure his own quasi-independent position. The support for Mohammad Khan Baluch was neither large nor general, in fact there was very little of it. One can therefore conclude that the special geographical (mountainous, not easy accessible conditions of Larestan, combined with the special position of the Sunnis in that area were the deciding factors for the rebellion. The Shi`ite population which had not remained scot-free and in fact had borne the brunt of both Afghan and Afsharid oppression had more cause to rebel than any other group, but did not do so. The conclusion, therefore, is that Sheikh Ahmad Madani's rebellion had definite and clear-cut social causes, but these had nothing to do with the interests and welfare of the Shi`ite population.

CHAPTER FIVE

DUTCH TRADE IN AFSHARID PERSIA (1730-1753)

INTRODUCTION

For 98 years, from the first establishment of a trading post in Bandar 'Abbas in 1623, trade results in Persia had been good for the Dutch. But all that changed with the fall of the Safavid dynasty in 1722.[1] The following eight years were a disaster, not only for Persia, but also for the Dutch and others trading with Persia. Due to Afghan misrule the country was ruined and long-distance trade came to a halt. The Dutch lost a considerable amount of money when they lent 17,000 *tuman*s to Shah Soltan Hoseyn on August 30, 1722, only a few days before Isfahan fell and the shah was deposed. Their loss became even more significant when his Afghan successor, Mahmud Khan Ghalzai (r. 1722-25) extorted 20,000 *tuman*s from the Dutch office in Isfahan.[2] If one adds to that the losses incurred in connection with the Hormuz affair in 1729 and the higher overhead due to the need to keep a military force in Bandar 'Abbas the loss was substantial. The only significant trade that the Dutch still carried on inside Persia took place in Kerman until 1725. The only profits that still were made, however meager, was through the VOC trading station in Basra. The Dutch held out because they hoped for improvement of the political and economic conditions, and for payment of the money owed to and stolen from them. They were slow to adapt to the changing circumstances, possibly because of the private interests of the VOC staff.[3] The Dutch were, of course, not the only ones to lose substantial amounts of money. Most, if not all Persian merchants (Moslem, Armenian and other) and private persons had experienced the same loss, sometimes were tortured or killed for their money. The English and other Europeans present in Persia at that time also lost property.

When, in 1729, Ashraf Shah Ghalzai (r. 1725-29), the Afghan usurper of Safavid rule, was ousted from his throne at Isfahan and Shah Tahmasp II's general (Tahmaspqoli Khan, the later Nader Shah) and his troops re-established Safavid rule over Persia, the Europeans,

---

1. Floor (2000); Ibid., (1988); Ibid (1996).

2. Floor (2000), pp. 169, 178, 180f.

3. Floor (1998); Ibid, (1999b).

including the Dutch, were very optimistic about trade prospects. They hoped that Persia would once again become a thriving economy, which once again could play an important role within the inter-Asiatic trading network. They expected the eight years of high financial losses, fear, anxiety and little or no trade would be transformed into years of expanding trade, good relations with the shah, and above all into rising profits. For the Dutch this was particularly important, because their previous losses had been so substantial. At the end of Afghan rule, the VOC claim on the Persian government amounted to Dfl. 1,871,736:11, which was an enormous sum in those days.[4] Tahmasp II intimated that he would pay this debt, once the economy and his revenues were growing again.[5]

Despite this initial optimism, engendered by Tahmasp II's friendly attitude towards the Europeans, and especially the Dutch, trade prospects remained poor. Not only was Persia again embroiled in a war with Ottoman Turkey in the West and in pacification of the Afghans in the East, but there was also government interference with trade in general, and with trade privileges of the Europeans in particular. After Tahmasp II's return from his disastrous campaign against the Ottomans in 1731 the Armenians were forced to give him 1,330, the Banyans 785 and the Isfahanis 8,000 *tuman*s. Money became very scarce in Isfahan, which was inimical to trade. The more so, because the shah had given orders that silver and copper money had to be accepted without any distinction between them. This made trade impossible, but the Dutch expected this order to be revoked shortly.[6]

This situation of depressed trade due to military operations, shortage of cash, and government interference with the market, became structural after Tahmasp II had been deposed and Tahmaspqoli Khan, his chief general (later Nader Shah), became the regent for the deposed shah's infant son 'Abbas III on September 2, 1732. Persian merchants complained to the Dutch that their prices were too high, making it impossible for the Persians to sustain their business.[7] On the occasion of New Year (*Nowruz*) in 1733, three leading merchants, Mirza Shokrollah (Miersa Suckerla), Hajji Amin (Hadje Amien) and Hajji Safi (Hadje Seffie), came to VOC factory in Isfahan. They reminisced with the VOC agent, Mattheus van Leypsigh, and recalled the good old days, prior to 1722. In those days, when Hajji 'Abdol-Vahhab (Hadje Abdoel Wahaab) was chief merchant, they would send their agents each year to Bandar 'Abbas to buy goods from the Dutch. Now they were afraid to do so because of the grasping hands of Tahmasp Khan Jalayer (Thamas Chan, governor of Isfahan at that time). The situation was so bad that nobody would pay anything for a house in Isfahan. Many wanted to abandon their house and leave, but they were prevented from doing so, and feared being informed upon. 'Abdol-Vahhab had died a few months earlier. His son, Hajji Amin, was said to still have ample funds. The sons of the late chief merchant Hajji 'Abdol Reza, Hajji Safi and Hajji Qasem, also had funds to start trading.[8] These and others were wary to invest in trade due to the

---

4. VOC 2269, de Cleen to Batavia (30/11/1733), f. 6534 vs. (the major components were the loan made to Shah Soltan Hoseyn in 1722 and the money extorted by Hoseyn Khan Ghalzai).

5. VOC 2255, van Leypsigh to de Cleen (1/28/1731), f. 2222-24; Ibid. (23/9/1730), f. 2194-97.

6. VOC 2255 (30/5/1732), f. 1991-92; Ibid., (3/11/1731 + appendix 2/12/1731), f. 1807-08.

7. VOC 2254 19/7/1732. f. 424.

8. VOC 2322, (22/3/1733), f. 344, 348vs, 394 vs-395r. According to VOC 2322, f. 350 (22/3/1733), the VOC broker in Isfahan had to borrow money from Moslem lenders at 2-3%/month.

unhealthy attention the regent, the future Nader Shah, paid to wealth accumulated by others. This interest was not restricted to Persian merchants only, for Nader sought money and advantage wherever he might get it. Even the mighty Dutch East Indies Company, did not escape.

Trade conditions did not improve. In Bandar ʿAbbas the little trade that was still carried on was due to the presence of the Dutch and the English.[9] The situation worsened when Nader (Tahmaspqoli Khan) ordered Hajji Zeyn al-ʿAbedin (Hadje Seijnel Abadien), the chief merchant (*malek al-tojjar*), to supply him with whatever he needed. Tahmasp II had appointed this merchant. On 25 November 1730, he paid a visit to the VOC factory in Isfahan to inform its chief that Tahmasp II had appointed him as deputy-*shahbandar* (deputy customs master) and chief merchant. It was his task to buy the best of all merchandise landed in Bandar ʿAbbas and other ports and to distribute the remainder among the other merchants. He would depart shortly for Bandar ʿAbbas and asked van Leypsigh for a letter of recommendation to the VOC director there.[10] He does not seem to have thrown his weight around at that time, as he did later in 1733. At that time, as a result of new instructions, Zeyn al-ʿAbedin, tried to impose himself on the other merchants and interfere with their trade. The Dutch therefore in September 1734 finally lodged a formal complaint against Zeyn al-ʿAbedin, who had convened all merchants, brokers, and caravan leaders (*caffiladaars*) and had obtained an undertaking from them that they would not buy any goods from the VOC warehouses in Isfahan or from Bandar ʿAbbas without his permission. "This constrains trade and causes much damage to the country. No merchant will dare to come here [Bandar ʿAbbas] once this becomes known. Those in the city who live from trade will be severely hit. The hajji wants to buy all the best goods and leave the rest for the others. I have talked to the *shahbandar* about this and shown him the royal decree granting the VOC free trade." The letter ended by asking for Nader's intervention to put a stop to this activity.[11]

Nader reacted positively to the Dutch request by dismissing Zeyn al-ʿAbedin as chief merchant, but this did not mean that there were no more problems. In 1734, the merchants could only hope that the deteriorated trade situation would improve. The country was in shambles, money was scarce, and trade only occurred in small lots.[12] In addition to the ongoing war with Ottoman Turkey, the rebellion by Mohammad Khan Baluch and Sheikh Ahmad Madani in 1734 added to the population's misery.[13] There was an outbreak of plague in Kerman province in 1735, because of which many died.[14] Furthermore, the numerous irregular and increasing fiscal contributions that were demanded from the population exhausted the country. This was not good for trade, of course, and was the major reason why the Dutch caravans did not come, as van Leypsigh explained to the authorities in Isfahan. Trade was

---

9. VOC 2322, de Cleen to Batavia (30/9/1733 + appendix 30/11/1739), f. 151.

10. VOC 2255, van Leypsigh to de Cleen (28/1/1731), f. 2278-9; see also VOC 2255 (3/11/1731), f. 1858 in which he informed de Cleen that after the hot season he would come to Bandar ʿAbbas, which did not happen.

11. VOC 2356, Hey to Thamas Coelie Chan and Miersa Takkie, (28/9/1734), f. 108.

12. VOC 2416 (4/2/1734), f.1841.

13. Floor (1983).

14. VOC 2416, Clement to Koenad (8/6/1735), f. 1901.

dead in that city, and if prices were offered for goods at all they were very low.[15] Nader Shah had added to the desolation by forcing large groups of Armenians to migrate to other parts of Persia. They were supposed to come to villages around Isfahan. By July 1736, they had only gone as far as Chamen Sawa (Saveh?) where they were ordered to stay. They suffered much. Nader also seemed to have sent some to Khorasan. Many died like animals; they only received one *mann-e shah* (5.9 kg) of dry bread per day en one donkey to transport their possessions.[16] Various government officials were trying to extort money from Armenian merchants, while Nader (Thamas Chan) had issued a decree in early 1736 by means of which he claimed the inheritance of those Banyans who had died without an heir. He later revoked that decree, probably after having received a financial inducement to do so.[17]

A new crisis arose in early March 1736, when van Leypsigh was preparing a caravan for departure to Bandar `Abbas. Road guards (*rahdars*) came to tell him that in the future the Dutch also had to pay imposts such as *rahdari, gushi, mohrdari* and *malek al-tojjari*, or else their goods would remain at the *rahdar* station. Van Leypsigh went to see the deputy governor of Isfahan, Fazel `Ali Beg, to protest. The latter explained to him that the reason was that Nader, who had just been hailed as the new king, had ordered that everybody, without any exception, had to pay *rahdari*. Nader had abolished the farming of the *rahdari* system, and even the governors had to pay these imposts. The road guards had to pay a certain amount per year to Nader and they had to make sure that they collected that amount. They even had levied *rahdari* on tobacco that had been sent as a present for Nader himself. Fazel `Ali Beg also said that the text of the Dutch trade privileges did not mention the exemption of *rahdari* explicitly, and therefore the Dutch also had to pay. Van Leypsigh reported that the EIC had paid *rahdari* up to then, but in secret. He therefore paid, but the *rahdars* did not give him a receipt, because they did not do so with anybody.[18]

The Dutch protested against this new imposition to Mohammad Taqi Shirazi, Nader's main counselor, who promised them new decrees, which would exempt them from payment of *rahdari* and other imposts. He reminded the Dutch that, at their request, he had dismissed the chief merchant Zeyn al-`Abedin in 1734. As a result trading conditions had improved, because merchants had been reassured that they could trade without interference. The Dutch acknowledged this, but informed Mirza Taqi that the reason trade was still in such a deplorable state was that the merchants had been ruined. Money was scarce, and as a result trade was almost dead. The merchants found it hard to even recover their fixed costs. Mirza Taqi assured the Dutch that in the future they would be exempt from *rahdari*. He also gave assurances to the Banyans and ordered his son and brother to restore to them goods that had been taken from them.[19]

---

15. VOC 2416 (30/8/1735), f.2195; cloves e.g. 135 *mahmudi*s per *mann-e shah*. VOC 2416, 1/9/1735, f. 2251.

16. VOC 2416, van Leypsigh to Gamron (23/7/36), f. 2508. On this deportation of Armenians see *The Chronicle of Abraham of Crete*. Annotated and translated by George A. Bournoutian (Costa Mesa, 1999), pp. 48-49.

17. VOC 2416 (8/3/1736), f. 2373, 2376.

18. VOC 2416, 8/3/1736, f. 2339-48; on *rahdari* see Emerson and Floor (1987), pp. 318-27; on the other taxes see Floor (1999a), index.

19. VOC 2416 (23/3/1736), f. 2424-26, 2431.

Despite Mirza Taqi's assurances the *rahdari* situation remained still unclear. The road guards took two *mahmudis* from VOC messengers at every station and the Dutch still contested payment. Finally, the Dutch received a new decree (*raqam*), which exempted them from payment of road and other duties (*rahdari va gheyrow*).[20] Van Leypsigh told the authorities that if the Dutch did not receive the decree they would be forced to leave Persia over the *rahdari* issue. He said they would be better off in Basra, for there were no problems there. They had to understand that a merchant sought profit where he could find it, and in Persia there was not much trade right then. Van Leypsigh further reported that some courtiers had said, "The Europeans only bring bark of trees, rags and fruits; who needs them?"[21] Despite the new decree the road guards still refused to let Dutch messengers pass without payment. Van Leypsigh wrote to the chief of the road guards or *rahdar-bashi*, Mohammad ʿAli Beg.[22] This put a stop to the demand for payments temporarily, but the road guards still caused occasional problems.[23] Also, presents still had to be given. For example, in the fall of 1740 the Dutch gave presents en route to Isfahan to: the *kalantar* at Khormut, the road guards at Lar, the *kalantar* at Biriz, Aqa Mohsen, the *zabet* of the *qeysariyah* of Shiraz, the road guards and qadi at Maʾin, the road guards at Yazdekhvast, and the road guards at Mayar and Orchini.[24]

Moreover, paying the road guards was only one of the problems that the Dutch had to deal with in 1737. The cost of traveling was another, for it was very expensive. Prices for animals, food and fodder were double what they had been before. Also, sometimes the travelers needed to take food and fodder with them for as many as for four halting places.[25] Trade over the Caspian had become unsafe due to piracy by Russians and Cossacks.[26] A cameleer contracted by the VOC in Kerman in December 1737 to transport goods to Bandar ʿAbbas undertook to bring these in 45 days to Bandar ʿAbbas at 315 *mahmudis* or Dfl. 133:17 per *mann*, exclusive of *galaty* of 1 *mahmudi* or Dfl. 0:8:8.[27] For comparison, freight cost from Kerman to Bandar ʿAbbas in 1718 had amounted to 14 *mahmudis* per *carga* exclusive of *galaty* of 1 *mahmudi*.[28] Assuming that the *mann* used in 1737 was the *mann-e shah*, of which there are 36 per *carga*, this means that freight cost were about 250% higher in 1737 as compared with 1718. If a *mann-e Tabriz* had been used, of which there are 72 per *carga*, the rise in cost would have been 500%.

---

20. VOC 2416, van Leypsigh to Koenad 17/7/36, f. 2459-62, 2471-73, 2478.

21. VOC 2417 (26/12/1736) f. 3919, 3931. This was an old ploy that Persian officials regularly used in their discussions with the Dutch. See, e.g., Floor (1987), p. 22.

22. VOC 2416 (23/7/1736) f. 2505.

23. See e.g. VOC 2583 (6/11/1741), f. 1416. The Dutch not only gave a normal note, but also copy of the royal edict (*raqam*) to avoid delays to the road guards.

24. VOC 2546 (Resolution Gamron 4/10/1740, f. 371; VOC 2584, (resolution Gamron 21/10/1741), f. 2434 (*zabet*). For a discussion of this trade route and its various stations see Floor (1999c).

25. VOC 2448 (3/8/1737), f. 1367. Barley in Isfahan rose from 2 *mahmudi*s to 5 and straw from 2/5 to *mahmudi* in 1743. VOC 2680, f. 199.

26. VOC 2448 (3/8/1737), f. 1375.

27. VOC 2448 (29/12/37) f. 1464.

28. VOC 1928, Auwannes to Gamron (25/7/1718). The term *galaty* probably is *khalʿati* meaning present or gift. One *carga* or load is a term to refer to one camel load, in this case two bales of raw silk of each about 240 lbs. or a total of 480 lbs. or 216 kg.

Because trade continued to be very disappointing in Bandar `Abbas, while Dutch trade in Basra was suffering from extortion by the local authorities, the VOC council in Bandar `Abbas in May 1737 decided to accept the invitation by the Persian government to start trading in Bushehr on a trial basis. They calculated in addition that if the situation in Basra worsened trade might be continued with Basra from Bushehr.[29] At that time, no merchants came to Bandar `Abbas, because the presence of the expeditionary force for the conquest of Masqat scared them off.[30] The military preparations also impeded Dutch efforts to get payment of the debt to the VOC (17,000 *tumans* from the shah + 600 *tumans* from the district of Minab). For they had made no progress, Mohammad Taqi gave the excuse that he was too busy to deal with their demand, but on June 6, 1737 he gave Carel Koenad (the VOC director in Persia (1736-41) a decree ordering the authorities in Minab to pay the Dutch.[31]

Despite the new decree the debt was not paid. There were a variety of other troubles that year. A very strong rainstorm combined with an earthquake in January 1738 caused much damage and many houses in Bandar `Abbas were swept away; and that the roads to Shiraz had become impassable.[32] On top of that, the Dutch were told on 8/1/1738 that their privileges had been confirmed, only for them to be revoked on 20/1/1738, which was very disconcerting. They were declared to be valid again in March 1738.[33] Trade in Bushehr, where the Dutch had opened a trading station in 1737, was not much better. In fact, it was dead, because of presence of an army commander. In trade all deals were quoted in white money, but at 50% discount,i.e., 100 *mahmudis* equaled 150 *mahmudis*, indicating a scarcity of good money.[34]

There was no money in Isfahan either, and sale of goods took place with bills at five months to be paid in three installments. The Banyans had drawn bills from all over, even from India to pay Nader Shah and his officials. As a consequence, trade was dead in Isfahan.[35] This was also due to the fact that Isfahan by that time was a deserted and desolate city. In 1736, a census had been done of all inhabited houses in Isfahan and it was found that there were 8,000, compared with 90,000 in Shah Soltan Hoseyn's reign and 40,000 even during Ashraf Khan Ghalzai's reign when, in 1727, he was demolishing many houses to build walls around his new inner city.[36] This demonstrated the ruin of the town, which was empty of people and, according to the Dutch, "this violent government cannot change that."[37] But the situation was

---

29. VOC 2448 (resolution Gamron 26/5/1737), f. 373, f. 482-99.

30. VOC 2448 (resolution Gamron 13/6/1737), f. 402.

31. VOC 2448 (resolution Gamron 8/8/1737), f. 613, 615. Contains details about the history of the debt of the royal court. The first request was made in mid-1735 to which a reply came on 13/3/1736 and on 8/8/1736 (see also 26/6/1736 Isfahan letter). VOC 2448 (resolution Gamron 5/10/1737), f. 685-92 (decree Nader regarding the repayment of 100 *tumans* per year of the Minab debt); VOC 2477 (1/4/1739), f. 263-64.

32. VOC 2448 (resolution Gamron 20/1/1738), f. 906-07.

33. VOC 2448 (resolution Gamron 20/1/1738), f. 921-2 (later reinstated VOC 2448 (resolution Gamron 3/3/1738), f. 1993-94).

34. VOC 2448 (18/2/1738), f. 2411; VOC 2448 (21/4/1738) f. 2429.

35. VOC 2448 (31/8/37), 1387-89.

36. On this new inner city see Floor (1998), p. 250. For a picture of the remains of its walls see Shafaqi, Sirus. *Joghrafiya-ye Esfahan* (Isfahan, 1353/1974), photograph 18.

37. VOC 2416, van Leipsigh to Koenad (17/7/1736), f. 2500. Hanway, vol. 1, p. 230 reported that that

not only desperate in Isfahan. For example, plague broke out in Qom where 6,000 people died in October 1737. As a result the town was empty, because the population had fled, and the plague also broke out at Golpeygan.[38] Many merchants left for Basra where they were well received. The head (*kadkhoda*) of the Armenian community asked Mohammad Taqi Shirazi to be more reasonable with the collection of taxes, for then the merchants would return. If he would reduce his levy to 7-8% like before, if things went as expected he then could re-impose the 10% rate later.[39]

The commercial situation in the emaciated city of Isfahan was so moribund by the end of 1737 that even the arrival of the suite of the Ottoman ambassador failed to revive trade. Normally, an embassy was a trade caravan in disguise and provided a boost to the turnover of trade. However, there was hardly any interest in fabrics. Some of them (*spreijen* or coverlets, *salempouris* and *sjeklassen*, both a kind of chintz) only could be sold with loss. For kerchiefs (*neusdoeken*) nothing was offered at all. Van Leypsigh therefore wanted to hang one entire piece in a chintz shop in the bazaar to attract attention for its alternative use as headwear. Spices still sold, but only in small quantities. Moreover, the road guards continued to be difficult. They wanted to see the royal decree (*raqam*) each time, and not just a simple note stating that the Dutch were exempt from paying road duties. But the situation in Isfahan was not as alarming as elsewhere in the country. At the end of December 1737, van Leypsigh reported that according to the latest information 9,000 people had died in Qom, and as many as 17,000 in Tabriz, and near that city 250 people died each day. Most of the northern parts of the country were devastated.[40] In 1738, the Bandar `Abbas area had been struck by a plague of locusts, so that in 1739 there were few dates or packing materials to be had.[41] In April 1739, the road between Shiraz and Bandar `Abbas was occupied by a tribal group referred to as Loulouwie, whose marauding forced the messengers to make a detour via Yazd.[42] Koenad wrote in mid-1739: "some time heaven will come to the assistance of this ruined country and these pitiful people."[43] At the end of 1739 there was no human being, animal, or vessel at Bandar `Abbas or the other side of the Gulf that had not been pressed into the royal service.[44] It was no wonder that trade was all but dead.

To encourage trustworthy merchants to pay with cash and to have their agents in exchange for this to receive the goods in Bandar `Abbas, van Leypsigh had spoken with four Banyan merchants who had listed 14 commodities that they were interested in buying (sugar, pepper, cloves, nutmegs, cinnamon, chintzes, *chaim channis* [chintz variety], cassas, sappan wood, muslins [*mallemollen*], small coverlets [*spreijen*], large *longi*s, and *sjoukouriassen*). They

---

Isfahan in the 1740s only had 5,000 inhabited houses and that Qazvin had only 1100 inhabited houses as compared with 12,000 before 1720.

38. VOC 2448 (26/10/1737), f. 1433; Ibid (4/11/1737), f. 1445.

39. VOC 2448 (4/11/1737) f. 1439-40.

40. VOC 2448 (29/12/1737), f. 1456-58, 1471-2, 1483-84.

41. VOC 2477 (resolution Gamron 3/3/1739), f. 167.

42. VOC 2477, van Leijpsigh to Gamron (12/4/1739), f. 496. I have been unable to identify this tribal group.

43. VOC 2510, f. 1432.

44. VOC 2510 (25/12/1739), f. 121.

wanted to buy them at last year's prices, or if times were quiet, at the current year's prices for an amount of 1,500 *tumans*, which would be paid in Isfahan after six months with 1,200 *tumans*. This was very disadvantageous for the VOC, for such a transaction would yield an estimated loss of 25%. This was due to the high "rate of exchange" when sending money from Isfahan to Bandar ʿAbbas, which amounted to 22%. The rate from Bandar ʿAbbas to Isfahan was from 12 to 15%. Van Leypsigh told them that in that case there was no deal. He did not allow them to send letters with the VOC messengers so that they could not inform their *vakils* or agents to delay things in Bandar ʿAbbas to their own advantage. Mockingly he wrote, "Under these conditions we might have been able to sell goods with a value of 5,000 *tumans*."[45] In Bandar ʿAbbas the *shahbandar* kept a sharp watch on all trade, including by the Dutch. In December 1739, Aqa Hoseyn (Aga Hossein), the *shahbandar*, accused one of the VOC staff of smuggling spices. After an investigation by Koenad the culprit was identified, demoted and put under arrest.[46] The little trade that still took place was on the basis of 6-9 months' credit, but even then no payment followed.[47] Money was so difficult to get that van Leijpsigh had to ask the Bandar ʿAbbas office to send him some, because even at an interest of 2.5% per month he could not get it in Isfahan.[48]

GOVERNMENT INTERFERENCE WITH TRADE

Government frustration about the shortage of money also found its expression in its unpredictable interference with the market. After having first appointed a chief merchant who also had to take care of the royal commercial interests, Nader had dismissed him after a vigorous complaint by the Dutch. Then in August 1736, Nader Shah appointed a number of merchants to buy supplies for his army. But again, he dismissed them in April 1737, because he did not trust them and wanted to have his money in the treasury.[49] He also had made a similar commercial trial with the trade in *kork* or Kerman goat hair in 1736, but this attempt was not followed through either. In fact, more disturbing were Nader Shah's direct claims on goat hair, through his demand for woolen clothing and other textiles, which caused a drop in the marketable supply of goat hair and was one of the reasons why the Dutch abandoned the goat hair trade in 1739.[50]

Up to 1739 Nader Shah mostly left foreign trade to its own devices. But when he went to conquer India and entrusted the rule over Persia to its eldest son, the latter immediately appointed royal merchants to take over the control over the long-distance trade, i.e., the trade in luxury goods such as European imports and the silk trade. In 1739, the British merchant Spilman reported:

---

45. VOC 2477 (29/4/1739), f. 437-39.

46. VOC 2511 (resolution Gamron 27/12/1739), f. 215-33; see also Ibid., (resolution Gamron 26/1/1740, f. 242-54.

47. VOC 2510 (30/6/1739), f. 630. People used the rosary or *tasbih* to calculate the days of their installments to repay; VOC 2357, Koenad to Batavia (24/8/1735), f, 270

48. VOC 2510 (18/8/1739), f. 652. Interest rate in May 1738 had been 2.5%/month VOC 2476 van Leypsigh to Gamron (18/5/1738), f. 880.

49. VOC 2448 (14/4/1737), f. 1314.

50. Floor (1999b), pp. 367, 369. Goat hair, usually mixed with other wool, was locally used to weave all kinds of textiles, including shawls. The Dutch used it to make hats. Floor (2000b), p. 171.

Hitherto the Trade from Astracan to Persia had been free and open, and foreign Merchants importing Goods into Persia might carry them to what Market they pleased; but this Year all Goods that arrived at Rashd were obliged to be sold there, and that the Shach would not permit any one to buy them except his own Marchants; for altho' they may keep the Good by them if they do not like the Price the Shach's Merchants offer; yet they could not carry them to any other Market, or sell them to any other. Also that the Shach had engross'd all the Raw Silk to himself, so that those who would buy Silk must buy it of his Merchants, and not of the Persian Boors as formerly.[51]

Thus, in 1739, Nader Shah's son instituted a foreign trade monopoly through his chief merchant, who was his treasurer at the same time. He was the sole buyer and seller of all European imports. This merchant had received a loan of one million rubles or 100,000 *tuman*s, but he had to pay 30% interest and had to pay back the loan in a short number of years. He also had the silk monopoly and therefore appointed a royal merchant (*kupecheen* [sic; *kupets*]) in each town at the beginning of 1739. When a Russian ship arrived in Gilan with a cargo of Dutch cloth and indigo it did not unload its goods because the vice-regal merchants wanted to fix the price of indigo at 140 *mahmudi*s (normal price 200) and cloth at 32 *mahmudi*s (normal price 40) and demanded in addition a 5% customs duty. The Russians refused to accept these terms.[52] The vice-regal merchants were quick to enforce the fixed prices on those merchants who had landed their cloth in Gilan and wanted to buy silk. The next step was that the governor's officials then forced the merchants to sell these goods to them at a lower price so that they might satisfy Nader Shah's demands for money.[53] On 14/8/1739 a courier (*chapar*) from the viceroy arrived in Isfahan with instructions to the governor to 'lend' him money to buy cloth, sugar, spices and fine fabrics. Money was taken from the merchants, and the warehouses of the Banyan merchants were broken open and part of their goods were taken out of there at prices fixed by the governor.[54] This was a time-honored practice that rulers and/or governors occasionally had imposed on the business community. It was known as *tarh* or forced sale.[55]

The government's interference did not stop at the wholesale level. Shopkeepers in Northern Persia had to buy European products from the shah's warehouses. Royal merchants bought goods in 1739 at 3% abatement, which suggests that even Nader Shah did not want to distress the Armenian merchants too much. The trading rules seem to have been softened somewhat after Nader's return from India. The British merchant John Elton was told that all his goods would be bought by the royal merchant who would pay for it as much as any other merchant. Alternatively he was allowed to go to Mashhad and negotiate with the shah. In

---

51. Spilman (1742), p. 7. Hanway (1753), vol. 1, p. 20 literally produces the same text, with the exception that instead of the shah he wrote the "Shah's son." Du Cerceau (1748), vol. 2, p. 107 reports that the shah's merchant in 1739 only wanted to sell silk at a price that was 20% higher than the market price.

52. VOC 2510 (18/8/1739), f. 673-74

53. VOC 2511, Aalmis to Koenad (12/121739), f. 857.

54. VOC 2510 (18/8/1739), f. 678-79.

55. On this practice see Floor (2000b), p. 52f.

1745, Nader Shah ordered 100,000 crowns to be used in trade by his merchant, Hajji Safi, the customs collector of Rasht. Half of that amount had to be spent on silk and Persian manufactures. These goods had to be exported to Russia and sold or to be forwarded to Europe for sale. Hajji Safi bought 200 bales of silk and took these with him to Astrakhan. He said he would make 60% profit, which Hanway believed would not enamor him to Nader Shah. For apart from the fact that Nader needed more money, he was not ignorant of the profit rates in trade.[56]

It would seem that this foreign trade monopoly remained restricted to Northern Persia and the trade with Russia. An attempt was made to impose the same monopoly in the south failed, or rather was not enforced. In early 1740, the viceroy's merchants sent silver fabrics to be distributed over the ports of Bushehr, Delam, and Rig and they also wanted to force it on the VOC through the same system of *tarh* or forced sale.[57] Since the end of February 1739, there had hardly been any trade in Bandar `Abbas. The merchants were afraid of extortion by the officials. The Dutch reported that it had never happened before that the merchants were forced to only buy the best-selling goods and even then they had to risk whether they could sell them at a reasonable profit.[58] Also, trade caravans had to pass through the ruined lower lands where hardly any food supplies were to be obtained because the officials took all these.[59] The Dutch, therefore, protested against these proceedings. Mohammad Taqi Shirazi issued an order in December 1739 that nobody was allowed to bother the VOC broker in Bushehr or to impose a price on his goods, for this was contrary to commercial custom.[60] No further attempt was made to impose state control over foreign trade in the south, although the VOC and EIC suffered from other impositions such as loans of ships, equipment and money.[61]

The return of Nader Shah from India and the fall from power of Reza Qoli Mirza had a short-lived beneficial impact on trade. Rather than demanding long-term credit, in 1740, merchants in Isfahan were willing to pay half with cash, half on credit, while respecting the mercantile custom to allow 0.5 – 1 *mahmudi* price reduction for some goods. Aalmis, van Leypsigh's successor in Isfahan observed, "God be praised merchants can now sit peaceful in their shops, while until recently when Reza Qoli Mirza was still vice-roy they had all (from high to low) been miserably treated."[62] This did not mean that Nader Shah lost interest in milking trading activities in a concerted fashion. In June 1741, he appointed Aqa Mohammad (Aga Mhamed) as chief merchant (*malek al-tojjar*) of the entire country, and the Dutch commented that he "has to fix the prices of all goods that are produced in Persia as well are imported from abroad". Like his brother `Ali Akbar (Alie Ekker) he would visit Isfahan to inspect all merchandise, after which he intended to pay a visit to the Persian Gulf ports. The poor merchants feared that they would be skinned just as in the days of the viceroy when his merchants scoured the

56. Spilman (1742), pp. 20, 26, 29-30, 32, 44; Hanway (1753), vol. 1, pp. 25-26, 29.

57. VOC 2511, Schoonderwoerd to Koenad (5/4/1740), f.1102.

58. VOC 2477, Koenad to Batavia (12/5/1739), f. 48.

59. VOC 2511 (resolution Gamron 22/7/1740, f. 627. This situation was not typical for the Isfahan-Bandar `Abbas route only. Hanway, vol. 1, pp. 239, 260 as well as Russian diplomats report the same situation in Northern and Western Persia, see Arunova and Ashrafiyan (1958), p. 234-35.

60. VOC 2510 (1 Ramazan 1152/December 1/12/1739), f. 1280; see also Ibid., f. 1276.

61. Floor (1987), pp. 31-53.

62. VOC 2546, Aalmis to Gamron (18/8/40), f. 1098, 1209.

land to fleece everybody.[63] Hanway related that between the time that van Mierop traded in a flourishing Mashhad, and his own visit in 1744, the town had become totally ruined and trade was depressed.[64] Trade results in Bandar ʿAbbas were also discouraging. Koenad wrote that profits might have been higher if he had had more sugar, cloves and nutmegs, which had been in high demand by the merchants. Also, the extortions by the officials, from which nobody was exempted, increased, as did the trouble created by marching troops.[65]

As Mohammad Taqi Khan had promised, the 60 Banyans under VOC protection were exempted from all duties and imposts and even the deputy governor (*naʾeb*) of Bandar ʿAbbas was not allowed to even levy one *dinar* from them. The relevant order (*taʿliqah*) from Hatem Khan (Hattem Chan), governor-general (*beglerbegi*) of Fars was received on 20/3/1741.[66] Nevertheless, they continued to be interfered with; Emamverdi's courier (*chapar*) harassed Choshaal (?), the chief of the Banyans, who was broker of both the EIC and VOC. The courier had been sent to get pearls and when he was told that there were none he wanted to give the Banyans the bastinado. The *naʾeb* had to be called and the Dutch asked Emamverdi Khan to stop this nonsense, because the Banyans were trustworthy people, leaving aside the matter of the offense given to the VOC.[67] The Europeans Companies were not the only ones to employ Banyans to promote their commercial interests. Mohammad Taqi Shirazi, one of the most important politicians in Persia and probably the one person whom Nader trusted, had a commercial agent (*vakil*) in Bandar ʿAbbas to look after his interests. His name was Gesjaal ketgoda Moltani, or Gesjaal (?), chief (*kadkhoda*) of the Moltani Banyans, and he probably was the same as the Choshal mentioned above.[68] The major non-European merchants in Bandar ʿAbbas were from Hyderabad (Heidrabadies) in what is now Pakistan and Banyans, who all belonged to the caste of the *Bangasalies* and *Derwellies*. It was for these reasons that Mohammad Taqi Shirazi may have made a positive gesture toward the Banyan community.[69] If self-interested officials such as Mohammad Taqi Shirazi oppressed them too much he might, of course, eventually hurt his own commercial interests.[70]

Despite the fact that the royal factors stayed in the north, trade was and remained very depressed in the south, for merchants were exposed to extortion and high taxes, and therefore did not dare to come to Bandar ʿAbbas. Also, the shah's lust for war prevented normal trade.

63. VOC 2583 (18/7/1741), f. 1335-36.

64. Hanway (1753), vol. 1, p. 256 ("plainly shews how rapid a progress Nadir Shah made in the ruin of Persia, even of his favourite city.")

65. VOC 2583, Koenad to Batavia (31/12/1741), f. 38-43. Wherever Nader's troops passed through an area they totally pillaged all villages. See, for example, Hanway (1753), vol. 1, pp. 236, 239, 259-60, 391.

66. VOC 2546, f. 1795-96; in a marginal note Mohammad Taqi Shirazi's order exempting a different number of Banyans, including six male children. Ibid, f. 1796-97.

67. VOC 2546, (21/11/1740), f. 1904-08.

68. VOC 2417 (26/12/1736), f. 3912.

69. VOC 2323 (3/8/34), f. 847; VOC 2510 (25/12/1739), f. 956. For the role and presence of Indian merchants and craftsmen in Persia see Floor (2000b), pp. 22-25.

70. VOC 2510, Koenad to Batavia (25/12/1739), f. 956.

The VOC brokers (*dallals*) were oppressed by Mohammad Taqi Khan and could not pay.[71] There was also interference by Sheikh Madhkur (Sjeeg Maskoer) with Dutch trade in Bushehr and Koenad therefore asked the Persian admiral (*daryabegi*) based at Bushehr to order him to desist.[72] The Dutch looked at opportunities to develop the pearl trade, but that was not an alternative either. There was no-one they could trust with such large amounts of money. Also, Nader had just decided to strongly develop the pearl fisheries and had ordered his officials in Bahrain and Bushehr to do so – to which end already 300 vessels had already been prepared.[73] Auwannees, the VOC's Armenian wool buyer based in Kerman, had already reported in October 1740 that Nader Shah allegedly had ordered the building of a castle near the site where pearl fishing took place and that this trade had to be declared his monopoly.[74]

Even the closure of the English East India Company's office in Isfahan did not encourage Dutch trade in 1740.[75] The only positive development for the VOC was that in 1740 it seemed as if the Minab debt finally would be paid. Scarcity of money was still a major problem, for when the Dutch wanted to collect their money from the officials in Minab they (the *kadkhodas*, *kalantar* and *kotval*) told the Banyan Paboe Kalamtjent (?) that he had to wait. Then they told him that they could pay only in kind, such as in cows, wet dates, dried dates etc. for there was no cash.[76] This offer was accepted, but the pretexts and excuses continued. Also, the bales of dates weighed 12 instead of the usual 16 *mann*. The tax collector (*mohassel*) did not want to fix the price, stating that it was none of his business.[77] The Dutch did not get much, despite the fact that the officials were fleecing the local population in such a way that most of them absented themselves during the day and only returned home at night. Because they were poor and the dates were not ripe yet they could not pay. The VOC Banyan sent his chief servant (*shater-bashi*) to ask the tax collector (*mohassel*), who had been sent for that purpose to the governor (*shahryar*) of Minab, why as yet no money had been collected. The tax collector replied that he could not get it, because there was nobody in town. "Tell me where to find a person and immediately I will collect money." The Banyan told him that he had received a list with the names of all debtors and that he had to do his job. The dates that served as partial payment of the debt had to be fetched by vessel to be taken to Bandar `Abbas, for which a *tallega* (sic; *ta`liqeh* or official order) from the *na'eb* was required to avoid unnecessary trouble.[78]

---

71. VOC 2705 (31/7/1746), f. 35, 47, 55.

72. VOC 2546 (12/10/1740), f. 1883-85.

73. VOC 2705 (31/7/1746), f. 58-59.

74. VOC 2546 (13/11/1740 received), f. 1838. This probably refers to the Naderiyeh castle at Rishar, see Floor (1979), p. 170. However, this castle already existed under that name in 1737.

75. According to the Russian agent in Isfahan, Nader's government oppressed the merchants to such an extent that he took all their money so that they could not pay their debts and went bankrupt. Arunova and Ashrafiyan (1958), p. 246.

76. VOC 2546 (29/8/1740), f. 1819.

77. VOC 2546 (received 26/10/1740), f. 1822-23.

78. VOC 2546, (23/11/1740), f. 1827-29; for details regarding the payment see VOC 2546, f. 1824-27; see also f. 1830-31 (tallega of Emamverdi Khan to the *na'eb* of Gamron to collect the debt) and f. 1834-35 (total amount collected in Minab (Minaaw) and list of expenses between 15/8/40-31/12/40).

In the following years there was hardly any trade due to continuing oppression, the military operations, the rebellion of half of Nader's navy,[79] and the worsening economic situation in the country in general.[80] The forced orders to supply Nader's army caused much dismay among the trades people and craftsmen in Isfahan in 1740, according to Kalushkin, the Russian agent in Isfahan. Lerch, German physician in Russian service, wrote that in 1745 in Rasht there were 15 caravanserais for merchants, which were all almost empty. He only saw one caravan moving from Tabriz to Rasht. In Darband, a caravanserai with 150 shops had just been built at the orders Nader. They were all empty and no merchant was in sight. Lerch noted that wherever he went merchants were exposed to oppression. Nader even had heavily fined Russian merchants in Shamakhi, Tabriz, Ardabil and Isfahan. The merchants in Rasht did not have the money and the visiting Russian embassy lend them the money. Golitsyn, the ambassador, also ordered all Russian merchants to depart Persia for Astrakhan. Only those who had to wind up business stayed. Armenian merchants also departed for Astrakhan. Russian diplomats noted that trade in Persia was dead because the merchants were bankrupt; many therefore left Persia.[81] In early 1747, the Dutch reported that trade was still depressed, and no merchants came to Bandar ʿAbbas.[82] This, of course, was understandable in view of Mirza Taqi Shirazi's rebellion (in 1743-44), the Masqat war, and the marching of troops along the roads. Everybody was relieved when a gunshot finally announced that Nader Shah was dead.[83]

COMPOSITION OF VOC IMPORTS

IMPORTS

Persia's principal imports were luxury goods, mainly agricultural products and a few manufactured items. Very few goods were imported for productive uses. I will discuss only the principal Dutch imports and mention other products where appropriate. Some commodities that were imported and/or exported by other merchants, but not by the Dutch, are therefore not discussed here.

The Dutch imported the following goods: spices (mace, cloves, nutmegs, and cinnamon), pepper, powdered and candy sugar, metals (tin, lead, iron, steel zinc), fabrics, wood, gumlac and some other products such as coffee, curcuma (white turmeric or *curcuma zeodoria*),[84] camphor,[85] and benzoïn (an aromatic resin or *styrax bezoin*)[86] in very small quantities. From

---

79. See Floor (1987).

80. For the rise in prices in Tabriz, for example, as well as other misery see Arunova and Ashrafiyan (1958), p. 248f.

81. Arunova and Ashrafiyan (1958), p. 247; Lerch (1769), pp. 378, 402, 432.

82. VOC 2705 (28/2/1747), f. 538-39. For the same situation in Northern Persia see Hanway (1753), vol. 1, pp. 233-34, 356, 377, 387; Arunova and Ashrafiyan (1958), pp. 247-48; Cook (1770), vol. 2, p. 292.

83. Floor (1989), p. 47.

84. VOC 2843 (1752-53), f. 27 (980 lbs. of Java curcuma)

85. VOC 2804 (1750-51), f. 10-11 (502 lbs.); VOC 2804 (1750-51), f. 10-11 (1000 lbs. of benzoin); VOC 2863 (1753-54), f. 44-45 (524 lbs. of camphor)

86. VOC 2748 (1745-46), f. 106-07 (623 lbs. of benzoin). VOC 2843 (1752-53), f. 27 (3366 lbs. of bezoin); VOC 2863 (1753-54), f. 44-45 (3352 lbs. of benzoin).

Tables 1 and 3 it is clear that the bulk of Dutch sales were in spices, pepper, and sugar (crystal and candied). Their dominant position in spices is understandable since they had a quasi-monopoly of these products. Their pepper position also was strong. There was competition from other producers (India) in pepper, but not enough to really threaten the VOC position. There were many sugar producers and the EIC and Asian competitors imported Indian sugar.[87] The Dutch only imported Java sugar, which was of great economic importance to Batavia.

Table 5.1: How much the VOC sold per year by commodity during 1730-1752 (in lbs)

Year/Item	Cloves	Nutmegs	Cinnamon	Sugar	Candy	Pepper	Zinc	Tin	Iron	Steel	Sappan-wood	Gumlac	Lead
1730-31	3462	11959	1040	456128	81279	188194	–	–	15810	–	28818	–	–
1731-32	748	12967	8691	98393	91366	6000	–	38198	–	–	26648	–	–
1732-33	11450	18001	2289	161914	33431	38743	–	–	–	–	19413	–	–
1733-34	24895	6869	7868	41781	6656	98271	–	–	14281	–	36493	–	–
1734-35	19510	16140	10028	331686	120696	133105	4916	36135	–	–	–	–	–
1735-36	–	–	–	–	–	–	–	–	–	–	–	–	–
1736-37	14834	5819	5396	129434	39530	69133		19825	3021		31635	7955	–
1737-38	10054	7676	9431	149259	171835	108807	10194	–	21191	–	–	–	–
1738-39	8496	3797	5722	189713	69146	16763	–	–	5954	15	–	–	–
1739-40	16670	229	9143	373227	62540	85653	183	–	16983	49	–	–	–
1740-41	4118	–	3456	89622	682	156454		8912	15937	–	40890	–	–
1741-42	12157	5905	2711	–	2183	41759			89229	–	–	1428	–
1742-43	6537	376	3960	–	–	292903		130	18096	180	–		–
1743-44	1079	1179	783	9878	14286	61242	1241	–	1111	–	–		–
1744-45	918	949	1460	116097	39477	104112			11093	–	58860	1200	–
1745-46	2947	1536	101	125551	34896	116229	–	80	33918	–	14740	229	–
1746-47	996	1131	641	9874	674	25804	–	967	58501	–	–	–	–
1747-48	1986	573	630	–	–	18338	–	10089	108488	750	–	–	–
1748-49	4558	6147	2002	134244	41857	95395	–	18647	–	2493	–	6847	–
1749-50	4848	3824	2590	125244	–	384	257	11103	56567	–	–	–	–
1750-51	3209	2960	–	–	–	74607	–	–	57624	–	–	–	–
1751-52	–	–	–	–	–	–	–	–	–	–	–	–	–
1752-53	4246	6096	1302	113427	6882	–	–	14162	48064	195		980	15798
1753-54	4800	2612	1716	173433	64468	–	–	55295	11113	105	–	–	14793

Source: VOC 2255 (1730-31; 1731-32), f. 2069, 2071; VOC 2322 (1731-32; 1732-33), f. 82-83, 86-87; VOC 2356 (1733-34), f. 25-26; VOC 2416 (1734-35); VOC 2448 (1736-37), 1663vs-64; VOC 2546 (1740-41), f. 62-63; VOC 2593 (1741-42), f. 1666; VOC 2680 (1742-43; 1743-44; 1744-45), f. 70-71, 74-75, 78-79; VOC 2748 (1745-46; 1746-47; 1747-48), f. 106-07, 112-13, 120-21; VOC 2766 (1748-49), f. 46-47; VOC 2787 (1749-50), f. 32; VOC 2804 (1750-51), f. 10-11; VOC 2843 (1752-53), f. 27; VOC 2863 (1753-54), f. 44-45.

What is noteworthy is the considerable drop in the level of VOC imports compared with the years prior to the fall of the Safavids in 1722. Overall imports dropped by about 80% and this probably also held true for other goods not mentioned here. Although the Dutch were not the only merchants trading in Persia, VOC imports dominated foreign trade, especially trade in the commodities mentioned here.

---

87. In 1733-34 rice was imported. VOC 2356 (1733-34), f. 25-26 (90,084 lbs).

Table 5.2: Decline in imports between 1710 and 1740 (in lbs)

Product/Year	Ca. 1710	1740 (average figures for a number of years)
Sugar, powdered	800,000	<100,000
Sugar, candy	250,000	<100,000
Cinnamon	20,000	1,000
Cloves	25,000	3,000
Nutmegs	15,000	5,000
Pepper	250,000	<100,000
Copper	25,000	0

Cinnamon imports averaged 20,000 lbs./year and dropped to the 1,000 lbs/year level. Cloves imports averaged 25,000 lbs/year and fell to below 3,000 lbs/year. Nutmegs imports had been around 15,000 lbs/year and dropped to below 5,000 lbs/year level. Pepper imports hovered around 250,000 lbs/year and dropped to 100,000 lbs/year.[88] Sugar imports experienced the same sharp decline, from 800,000 lbs/year to less than 100,000 lbs/year in the case of powder sugar and 250,000 lbs/year to less than 100,000 lbs/year in the case of candy sugar.[89] The import of the various metals was erratic, which is surprising given the almost continuous state of war Persia was in you would have expected large, may be even growing, imports of metals needed to feed the war machine. This implies that domestic production of these metals must have increased, although there are no reports confirming this, or that imports by others had expanded. The latter is highly unlikely, not only had the Dutch dominated the import of these commodities, but they did not mention either that their competitors were undercutting their position. The most important aspect was that prior to 1722 the VOC imported some 25,000 lbs/year of copper and now it exported it in larger quantities from Persia![90] Nothing much is known about the other imports other than that they were minor and erratic as well. Coffee, which had been a major import item,[91] now hardly exceeded 1,000 lbs/year, and was only imported intermittently.[92] It is of interest to note here that Persians preferred Ceylon coffee to Java coffee.[93] Imports of cottons had also dropped significantly.[94] Trade in broadcloth was difficult as it had been throughout the Safavid period and the reasons for this had not changed. There was continued competition from Aleppo, where English and French merchants offered broadcloth against low prices, while the Russians brought it via Astrakhan to Gilan. The VOC was badly located in the south, and also suffered from the fact that the broadcloth did not come directly from the Netherlands, but via Batavia, which took

---

88. Floor (200b), pp. 135-39.

89. Floor (200b), p. 133.

90. On the mining of metals in Safavid Persia see Floor (2000b), pp. 305-06; on copper imports see Ibid., p. 146. In 1733-34, the VOC still imported 9,887 lbs. of Japanese copper. VOC 2356 (1733-34), f. 25-26.

91. Floor (2000b), pp. 142-43.

92. VOC 2748 (1745-46), f. 106-07 (548 lbs./Ceylon coffee), (1747-48), f. 120-21 (800 lbs./ Ceylon coffee); VOC 2843 (1752-53), f. 27 (750 lbs./ Java coffee); VOC 2863 (1753-54), f. 44-45 (1250 lbs./ Java coffee).

93. VOC 2511, Koenad to Batavia (31/7/1740), f. 60.

94. See Floor (2000b), p.150-56.

too long. The English and French timed it better. The Persian merchants therefore had Qazvin as an alternative market for broadcloth.[95] The import pattern was as it had been in the late Safavid period and thus holds no surprises. The main point of interest with regards to these as well as the other imports is their reduced level, reflecting the dire straits the country was in.

Table 5.3: How much the VOC sold per commodity per year (in Dutch guilders)

Item/Year	Cloves	Nutmegs	Cinnamon	Sugar	Candy	Pepper	Zinc	Tin	Iron	Steel	Sappan-wood	Gumlac	Lead
1730-31	17322	40793	3125	56135	29951	51968	–	–	2594	–	2369	–	–
1731-32	47062	55243	3200	35594	12770	2125	–	29319	–	–	2831	–	–
1732-33	69077	73546	8219	45875	14800	16465	–	–	–	–	2406	–	–
1733-34	104691	24839	19954	7998	2183	32250	–	–	2343	–	3493	–	–
1734-35	82045	46247	25434	63498	39610	43683	2559	19093	–	–	–	–	–
1735-36	–	–	–	–	–	–	–	–	–	–	–	–	–
1736-37	62381	16673	13686	24174	10594	27415	–	11657	454	–	3893	2492	–
1737-38	–	–	–	–	–	–	–	–	–	–	–	–	–
1738-39	–	–	–	–	–	–	–	–	–	–	–	–	–
1739-40	–	–	–	–	–	–	–	–	–	–	–	–	–
1740-41	21022	–	10713	21691	239	80639	–	7499	2976	–	6881	3251	–
1741-42	33189	17735	7281	–	672	17999	–	–	14389	3:11	–	586	–
1742-43	33521	15883	11867	–	–	126296	–	126	2918	57	–	–	–
1743-44	4553	3384	1984	–	–	22281	491	–	1512	–	–	–	–
1744-45	3673	2749	3505	20688	10259	37878	–	--	1510		6992	415	–
1745-46	11793	4450	243	24859	10364	53201	–	39	1617	–	2188	79	–
1746-47	4229	3210	1509	2507	307	9745	–	477	9623	–	–	–	–
1747-48	9937	1660	1513	–	–	7648	–	6438	18795	278	–	–	–
1748-49	22943	17911	4834	29483	16632	38353	–	9007	–	932	–	2893	–
1749-50	–	–	–	–	–	–	–	–	–	–	–	–	–
1750-51	17882	9181	–	–	–	28757	–	–	12065	–	–	–	–
1751-52	–	–	–	–	–	–	–	–	–	–	–	–	–
1752-53	22732	18165	3468	26513	3217	–	–	7944	183	63	–	504	3323
1753-54	24235	7326	3901	36486	21097	–	–	27142	2494	34	–	–	3101

Source: VOC 2255 (1730-31; 1731-32), f. 2069, 2071; VOC 2322 (1731-32; 1732-33), f. 82-83, 86-87; VOC 2356 (1733-34), f. 25-26; VOC 2416 (1734-35); VOC 2448 (1736-37), 1663vs-64; VOC 2546 (1740-41), f. 62-63; VOC 2593 (1741-42), f. 1666; VOC 2680 (1742-43; 1743-44; 1744-45), f. 70-71, 74-75, 78-79; VOC 2748 (1745-46; 1746-47; 1747-48), f. 106-07, 112-13, 120-21; VOC 2766 (1748-49), f. 46-47; VOC 2787 (1749-50), f. 32; VOC 2804 (1750-51), f. 10-11; VOC 2843 (1752-53), f. 27; VOC 2863 (1753-54), f. 44-45.

EXPORTS

The few Persian exports were mainly agricultural raw materials, food products, some minerals, and very few manufactured goods. As in the case of VOC imports the export pattern had remained the same, albeit at a sharply reduced level. There were two changes: there was no more silk export, and rather than importing copper this commodity as had been previously the case it was

---

95. VOC 2511, Koenad to Batavia (31/7/1740), f. 52, 65. In general see Floor (2000b), pp. 156-59.

now exported. In fact, the main Dutch export commodity was bullion and old copper. The major Dutch export commodity during the 17th century had been raw silk, but the last export of raw silk had taken place in 1714. After the expulsion of the Afghans in 1730 the Dutch intermittently had expressed an interest in raw silk, but nothing came of it.[96]

The second most important export commodity was Kerman goat hair. The Dutch had been involved in this trade since 1658, but stopped trading in this product in 1740, after excessive government interference. Dutch trade in goat hair was only resumed in 1750.[97]

Table 5.4: Exported quantities of goat hair (kork) 1721-1763

Decade	VOC (lbs.)	EIC (lbs.)
1721-1730	104,870 lbs.	?
1731-1740	259,660 lbs	379,009 lbs.
1741-1750	1,098 lbs	111,699 lbs.
1751-1760	69,675 lbs	297,243 lbs.
1760-1763	4,300 lbs	40,625 lbs.

Sources: Floor, *Textile Industry*, p. 381, table 8; Matthee, Rudi, "The East India Company Trade in Kerman Wool, 1658-1730," in *Etudes Safavides* ed. Jean Calmard (Paris/Tehran, 1993), pp. 367-69.

Other products that were exported by the Dutch included wine, fruits, rosewater, gum, nuts, asafetida, madder, dates, skins, sulfur, wheat, red oxide, rock salt and the occasional *lapis tutia*,[98] *aureum pigmentum*,[99] *pruimellen*,[100] dates, almonds, galls, gum. These types of exports were in very small quantities and showed an erratic and intermittent pattern. There usually were dried fruits among the exports, but in small quantities. Rosewater and wine also were included, but also in small quantities, as were some velvets or carpets. Most of these exports were for Ceylon, Malabar or Coromandel. Once in a while, three or four horses for Ceylon were exported. The red earth and the sulfur were destined for Coromandel and Malabar, and the wheat was for Batavia.

---

96. Floor (1988), pp. 2-5; Ibid., (1996), 323-68; Ibid., (200b), pp. 172-77. I will discuss the matter of Dutch interest in silk during the Afsharid period in a separate study.

97. For details see Floor (1999 b), pp. 369-70.

98. Zinc ore, from the Latin *lapis* or stone and from the Persian *tutiya*, calamine [ZnCO3], which became the English tutty, zinc oxide. The Persian word *tutiya* is derived from a word that means smoke. It refers to the fact that zinc oxide is evolved as white smoke when zinc ores are heated with charcoal. According to Teixeira, *tutiya* was only produced in Kerman province. "It is made by kneading up the earth of the mountains with pure water, and covering therwith certain clay moulds. Next they bake these in furnaces like a potter's, draw them out when well baked, and strip them. What is stripped off is the tutia, which is afterwards carried in boxes to Harmuz, for sale." Teixera, Pedro. *The Travels*. tr. William F. Sinclair, Hakluyt Society (London 1902 [1991]), p. 218 and notes 2 and 3 for more details.

99. Orpiment is a rare mineral that usually forms with realgar. In fact the two minerals are almost always together. Crystals of orpiment are extremely rare as it usually forms masses and crusts. The yellow color is special to orpiment and can be confused only with a few other minerals. The word orpiment is derived from the Latin *auripigmentum*, or golden pigment. Its use as a dye or pigment is limited due to its instability.

100. This term refers to one of the many varieties of prunes (*alu*).

Wheat had occasionally been exported by the VOC prior to 1721, but in the 1730s there was a sustained demand for it from Batavia. The available quantities were erratic, as a function of the climatic, market and political conditions in Persia. In 1737-78, for example, wheat was very difficult to obtain because the Persian authorities commandeered much of it to feed the Masqat expeditionary force.[101] There also was the problem of quality, to which Persian exports paid no heed, for the Omanis bought wheat without looking at quality, whether there was barley mixed with it or not. Therefore, you could never buy wheat in pure unadulterated form.[102] Wheat was also difficult to get in early 1740, due to the lack of rain. Schoonderwoerd, the VOC chief at Bushehr, reported in February 1740, "Life is difficult here, for there is hardly enough for man and animals. In Kuhgilu the situation is better. There you pay Ms. 12 per *mann* of 108 lb., but it is impossible to get it cleaner than mixed with 1/6 or 1/8 [parts] of barley."[103] Grain remained scarce in Bushehr, and the Dutch only were able to buy 30 loads (*lasten*) by September 1740. The Persian authorities asked Schoonderwoerd not to buy any more so that the poor might get their bread, which he complied with.[104]

Table 5.5: Export of wheat in selected years (in lbs.)

Product/Year	1736	1739	1741	1742	1746
Wheat	43,115	89,964	61,897	80,819	3,000

Wheat was not the only commodity that caused supply problems. The same held for madder (*runas*), which was almost impossible to obtain in 1740. The Banyans at Shamakhi could not induce anyone to go to Darband and get it out of fear to be killed by the Lezgis.[105] As shown in Table 6, the average annual volume of madder export was about 10.000 lbs.

Table 5.6: Export of madder in selected years (in lbs.)

Product/Year	1732	1737	1739	1740	1741	1745	1746
Madder	30,000		10,000	10,000	22,000	5,000	10,000

The Dutch had not exported much asafetida (*katirah*) prior to 1730, but due to the lack of other exportable commodities they made an effort to find agricultural products that might yield reasonable profits. Asafetida, for which there was a demand in India, therefore figured for a while among VOC exports.

---

101. See e.g. VOC 2448 (Journal Bushehr October 1737), f. 1530.

102. VOC 2448 (23/11/1737), f. 1510 (The Omanis bought it at a price of 7.5-8 *mahmudi*s).

103. VOC 2511, f. 1400-01.

104. VOC 2546(18/9/1740), f. 1335. A *last* when used for grain was equal to 30 hectoliter; in case of a ship's load it was two tons. For wheat the *mann-e hashemi* was used equal to 105 lbs. VOC 2448 (24/8/1737), f. 1504. For other products the *mann-e qapan* equal to 7.5 lbs. was used. VOC 2416 (10/12/1736), f. 173.

105. VOC 2546, Aalmis to Gamron (15/1/1741), f. 1245.

Table 5.7: Export of asafetida in selected years (in lbs)

Product/Year	1737	1739	1740	1745	1746
Asafetida	10,000	10,000	10,058	10,000	10,000

Sometimes rather large quantities of sulfur and red earth were exported, mainly to Coromandel and Malabar. Apart from the limited demand for this commodity it also served as ballast for the departing ships.[106]

Table 5.8: Export of sulfur and red earth in selected years (in lbs.)

Product/Year	1740	1741	1745	1746	1747
Sulfur	25,000	-	397,566	244,394	25,876
Red earth	-	3,000	-	13,000	300,000

Rosewater (*golab*) had been a regular export item in the Safavid period, and thus limited quantities of the product continued to be exported during the Afsharid period as well.[107]

Table 5.9: Export of rosewater in selected years (in cases)

Product/Year	1732	1735	1739	1740
Rosewater	50	100	84	84

The most important export commodity was specie. This included a variety of currencies: Spanish reals, old and new silver Persian `abbasis, Indian gold rupees or *mohurs*, Surat rupees, Turkish *zolotas* and piasters, Persian copper *paysas*, European gold ducats and silver reals, Dutch *leeuwendaalders*, ducatons, imperial thalers, Persian *naderis* and *vali ne`matis* as well as copper ware and copper cakes. Some of the gold and silver came in melted form in bars (gold ducats) or plates (silver `abbasis).

BALANCE OF PAYMENTS

Persia continued to suffer from the fact that apart from silk and some minor products it had no commodities for export. Silk production in the Caucasus had suffered significantly as a result of the devastating military campaigns against the Ottomans and the Lezgis in Armenia, Georgia and Shirvan. Likewise, silk production in the Caspian provinces had decreased as a result of war and the plague. Other exportable goods could not compensate for the shortfall in the availability of silk. The production of Kerman goat hair always fell short of demand by the VOC and EIC, while its value was lower than that of silk.[108] Other export products, as has been discussed above, were mainly drugs and dried fruits, which were minor items both in volume and value. The combined

---

106. Floor (2000b), p. 177-78.

107. See for details Floor (2000b), pp. 165-66. One case contained 54.5 liters of rose water.

108. See for details Floor (1999a), chapter five; Ibid (2000b), pp. 171-72, 176.

export value of these commodities was not sufficient to pay for the high value luxury commodities that Persia continued to import, though at a much reduced level. Consequently, Persia had a deficit on its current account with South-Asia as in the previous centuries. The traditional positive current account with Ottoman Empire may not have existed anymore. If it did, it would have been greatly reduced by the state of war that existed between Afsharid Persia and Ottoman Turkey (1732-1736 and 1744-46) and the impact of Nader Shah's "economic policy", which either discouraged or banned trade with the Ottoman Empire. Fortunately, the trade balance with Russia, which always had been positive for Persia, had grown in size. This was because a significant share of the goods that normally would have been exported to the Levant (in particular raw silk) now was exported via Russia.[109]

Persia having no gold or silver mines (apart from one silver mine near Kerman that was worked for some time, but proved to be unprofitable)[110] could only get specie through import or conquest. The conquest of India only had a temporary effect, partly because most of the booty was hoarded and the remainder was spent on military expenditures. The other so-called conquests only resulted in net-losses to the Persian economy due to the damage done to both the newly taken, and only temporarily held, territory and Persia's own productive capacity. You would expect that the military expenditures would have had at least some positive impact on economic production. This does not seem to have been the case. The orders for military equipment to a certain extent may have used underutilized production capacity, which would have resulted in growth. Likewise, the payment of Nader's large army of more than 200,000 soldiers also must have had some growth impact on the economy. After all, the soldiers were also consumers. However, the general insecurity, the tyrannical behavior of the officials, the low government payments for the goods it bought, the high cost of living for the craftsmen and the crushing weight of the high fiscal burden resulted not only in eliminating the potential growth impact of these expenditures but by actually reducing economic growth. In addition, the army's operations seem to have had a negative impact on the productive capacity far beyond the area of the immediate military theatre. The soldiers extracted often more than the locally available surplus, sometimes at artificially lower than market prices and sometimes by just taking without paying for it. Consequently, agricultural productive capacity suffered due to a significantly reduced population as we all due the incessant demand for pack animals because of their high mortality rate during army operations.[111]

To stop the outflow of specie, and thus reduce the deficit on the current account, the government tried to ban the export of specie. Shah Tahmasp II and Nader Shah both prohibited the export of coin from the kingdom, but only with temporary results, as these regulations could be, without difficulty, evaded indirectly, or even directly, by bribing the authorities. It was evident that only by developing the export trade, or by reducing imports, the overwhelming balance against Persia could be rectified. Another way to deal with the problem was to 'correct' the weight and alloy of the coinage to make it less attractive for export. I that case the government collected the old silver and copper money and coined new currency of less weight and alloy.

---

109. See on these issues Floor (2000b), pp. 227-28, 237-40 and Floor and Clawson (2000a)

110. VOC 2416 (4/2/1734), f. 1953-54; VOC 2323, Auwannes to de Cleen (28/8/1734 rec.), f. 853.

111. Hanway (1753), vol. 2, p. 26; Arunova and Ashrafiyan (1958), chapter 6; Cook (1770), vol. 2, pp. 315-16, 323, 328-31, 400.

The scarcity of specie, even of copper money, began to be felt immediately after the defeat and expulsion of the Afghans at the end of 1729. As a result, the shah issued a decree in October 1732 stipulating that the export of ducats was only allowed on payment of a duty of 5% to be paid in so-called white, or good silver, money. The ducats had to be declared and exported in bags, which were inspected and then sealed by the agents of the master of the mint (mo`ayyer-bashi). In 1733, the Dutch observed that for export purposes the loss was less on copper money than on silver `abbasis or golden ducats.[112] Copper prices continued to rise, due to the general scarcity of money. Many traders were forced to have recourse to barter, which was also practiced by the EIC.[113] In early 1734, Nader (Thamas Chan) ordered new copper coins of 5 methqals to be minted, which had to be accepted as paysas.[114]

When Nader (Tahmasp Khan) declared himself shah in March 1736 he began making changes in the country's monetary policy. In mid-1736 he had decreed that the double paysa copper coin henceforth would be worth only a single one. In Isfahan, in December 1736 this paysa decree was revoked, so that the previous double paysa was again current as a single one, but it was forbidden to export this coin. Each Banyan and banker (sarraf) was permitted to keep not more than the value of 50 mahmudis in his shop or house on pain of a fine of 12 tumans.[115] Payments therefore were realized by money drafts. This was not without problems. For example, a draft was drawn by the VOC Isfahan office on its Bandar `Abbas office in December 1736 to an amount of 350 tumans in white money at 25%, with a current rate of exchange of Ms 43750 or Dfl. 18593:15:- on condition that the amount would be paid at Bandar `Abbas after 45 days. This was very disadvantageous for the Dutch, for white money was hardly to be found there. Trade was carried on by barter or was paid with paysas, old pieces or copper zolotas (sjalottes) and the like. If the draft had been paid in black money it would have yielded a loss of 50%, not 25%, or more with Ms 65625 black or white 535 tumans equivalent to Dfl. 22312:10:0.[116] In March 1737, no distinction was made anymore between copper or silver money in Kerman, because both were equally scarce.[117] In Isfahan, in June 1737, Nader Shah once again decreed that the double paysa henceforth was worth only one paysa, and the road guards were ordered to see to it that no copper was exported.[118] The little silver that still was to be had at Bushehr was sold in small lots at a premium (at 15-16 mahmudis) or was exported to Basra, where higher prices were obtained.[119]

On March 7, 1738 a decree was issued stating that Nader Shah had decided to strike new `abbasis of 1 dang or 1/6 methqal less weight. Before this date the `abbasis had been 7 dangs or 1 1/6 methqal. Nadir Shah also had ordered to strike coins of 9 dangs or 1.5 methqal, which would be passed off as if they were 3 mahmudis, of which some had already been coined

---

112. VOC 2322, f. 78-97.

113. VOC 2416, f. 209-10.

114. VOC 2416, (3/6/1735), f. 1953

115. VOC 2417, van Leypsigh to Gamron (26/12/1736), f. 3940-41.

116. VOC 2417, (Resolution Gamron 19/1/1737, f.3717.

117. VOC 2417 (19/3/1737), f. 4170.

118. VOC 2448 (11/6/1737), f. 1346

119. VOC 2448 (23/11/1737), f. 1511.

by the end of March 1738. Further, it was decreed that the ducat of pure gold weight, whose weight had been 18 *mahmudi*s new money was as of then 1 *paysa*. Those persons having `abbasi*s of 7 *dang*s could only spend then as if they were 6 *dang*s. If they would bring them into the Mint to have them coined they would have to pay *seignorage* (minting fee), but they would receive the difference in value, or about 1.5 *paysa*. This decree was published all over Persia.[120] Despite the fact that now even long-distance trade was carried on with copper money or copperware, "one counts here never with black [=copper], but always with white [=silver] money at 50% agio for white money, so that 100 *mahmudi*s in reality is 150 *mahmudi*s copper money"[121] Because of this measure, `abbasi*s and *paysa*s disappeared from circulation and rose in value, as did copper ware and copper cakes.[122] New copperware was preferred to old, while copper pots obtained less (16 *mahmudi*s) than plates and vessels (22 *mahmudi*s) in Isfahan.[123] Smart traders even tinned old copper, to give it a new shine, and circulated it as the real new stuff at a price of 14-15 *mahmudi*s. *Paysa*s, which were more amply available at Bushehr, were preferred to copperware, but obtained a premium of 40%.[124]

The Dutch, who were allowed to export specie, nevertheless found it difficult to obtain cash, because as soon as the governor learnt that they were collecting small amounts of gold or silver he would interfere. Gold ducats could be had in small lots of 20 pieces at 18 silver *mahmudi*s per piece. However, if one wanted to buy 100-200 pieces the price rose by 4-5 *paysa*s. If you wanted say 12,000, that number would have to be forced out of the hands of the treasurer. Besides, one would have to pay more, so that the price exclusive of transport costs, would be 19 silver *mahmudi*s, thus yielding a loss of 1 *mahmudi* compared with the current price at Bandar `Abbas. Van Leypsigh, the Dutch agent in Isfahan, wrote that to get 5.000 *tuman*s in `abbasi*s of seven *dang* or 1 1/6 *methqal* he would have to pay in new coin and with an agio of 7%. The Luri namad, for which 5 to 6 *tuman*s was paid, obtained an agio of 3% for a small number. If one wanted say, 500 *tuman*s, the agio would rise to 5% in silver coin. In one year one might collect at most 2,000 *tuman*s from the city and the surrounding villages while the administrative overhead would be 12%, because one had to appoint a special person for doing that. Gold coins of fine alloy cost 23 silver *mahmudi*s, of lesser alloy 22 silver *mahmudi*s. But these would have to "forced" out of the hands of the Mint master, who, moreover, would demand 0.5 *mahmudi* more. The best silver is Ms. 1 9/10 and Ms. 1 4/5 per *methqal*. It still was not permitted to transport copper coins without permission from the governor. Double *paysa*s still had to be accepted as single ones, as a result *paysa*s had become very scarce. Van Leypsigh, therefore, considered it best for the VOC to trade in copperware, which cost, exclusive of cost, 16 *mahmudi*s and copper plates, 22 *mahmudi*s. The merchants sold these at 12.5 *mahmudi*s, but according to the VOC broker one might not collect more than 1000 *tuman*s in one year.[125]

---

120. VOC 2448, van Leypsigh to Gamron (7/3/1738), f. 2352-53.

121. VOC 2448, Schoonderwoerd to Gamron (21/4/1738), f. 2429; VOC 2448 (18/2/1738), f. 2415.

122. VOC 2448, Koenad to Batavia, 30/4/1738, f. 1804-05, 1836, 1874; [1886] new ducat.

123. VOC 2476 (21/8/1738), f. 898.

124. VOC 2476 (14/6/1738), f. 1043-44.

125. VOC 2476, van Leypsigh to Koenad, (21/8/1738), f. 899-900.

Though Batavia had instructed its Bandar `Abbas office to get as much refined copper as it might, it had little success in doing so. The reason was that export of all specie, in particular of black *paysa*s, was forbidden. Further, that these *paysa*s were very much in demand by other merchants, so much so, that they accepted for 100 *tuman*s even 1,000 *tuman*s copperware or cakes. Everybody took what he could get, and accepted copper the way it was being offered in the market. But the Dutch did not buy any old copperware, because it was mostly burnt through, so that there was no profit in it.[126] A further problem was that refining old copper was impossible in, for example, Bushehr, because firewood was very expensive viz. 4-5 *mahmudi*s per *mann-e hashemi*.[127] Copper had become the monetary basis of all trade by that time. There was little gold and silver to be had, and often there was none.[128]

In February 1740, Nader Shah published a decree, which stated that henceforth the new trade coin would be the silver piece of five *mahmudi*s or one *naderi*. It was forbidden to use the terms `abbasi, tuman, etc.[129] From this decree it is clear that Nader Shah was engaged in a monetary experiment aimed at pegging the Persian currency to that of India.[130] But there were many more Indian (Thatta, Delhi and Agra) rupees in circulation than *naderi*s.[131] Although prices fluctuated, copper money (*paysa*s) and copperware remained expensive and scarce. So much so, that in 1742, the Dutch report that "old copperware and paysa coins have totally disappeared, so that we are sometimes in trouble when the ships have to depart, because we have to change the rupees into the said Persian [copper] coin."[132] The cash scarcity caused also other problems that impeded normal financial operations. Merchants, to avoid sending cash, made use of drafts to facilitate trade. This became more difficult due to the change in the copper – silver ratio. For example, in Bandar `Abbas the agio on drafts was 25%, while in Isfahan it was as high as 50-75% for silver *mahmudi*s in 1742. This meant that a holder of a draft of 100 silver *mahmudi*s would receive in Bandar `Abbas at 25% agio the sum of 132,5 copper *mahmudi*s, while in Isfahan he would get 150-175 copper *mahmudi*s. This made it 15% more profitable for merchants to transport copper from Isfahan to Bandar `Abbas than to send a draft. To resolve this problem Nader Shah gave orders that the value of the silver and copper *mahmudi* would be the same, and that the charging of agio was forbidden.[133]

---

126. VOC 2510, Marginal note to "Eis 1739" (Batavia, 15/10/1738), f. 1448; VOC 2511, f. 1400.

127. VOC 2476 (12/1/39), f, 1100-01, 1104 (At that time silver had become very rare, and at Bushehr it was unobtainable even with an agio of 40%.)

128. VOC 2477 (14/5/39), f. 80.

129. VOC 2546. Order by Nader Shah (Welie Nemad; Vali Ne`mat) concerning the coinage received on 15/9/1740 f. 1841-42. The EIC records also report the proclamation that silver coinage (Abassees, Mamoodees and Nadirees) be called in and replaced with rupees – "being of the same Value with those he [i.e. Nader] stamped in India...which, if the exchange continues to fall here, ... must have a very good effect on the Trade carried into this country..." India Office, Gombroon Diary, G/29, 5 February 1740 (i.e. 16 February, New Style). I thank Michael Axworthy for this EIC reference.

130. See on this issue my forthcoming book written in collaboration with Patrick Clawson and Rudi Matthee, *The Financial History of Iran, 1500-1925*.

131. VOC 2593, f. 1623.

132. VOC 2593, Clement to Batavia (31/10/1742), f. 1623 vs.

133. VOC 2593 Clement to Batavia (31/10/1742), f. 1623-28.

The currency situation remained in a confused state throughout the 18th century, especially after 1750. Although there had been a major influx of booty into Persia after the conquest of India in 1739 much of that had been hoarded by both Nader Shah himself as well as his commanders. In fact, Nader Shah gathered all the gold and silver that he could lay his hands on and transferred it to his treasury in the Kalat-e Naderi. As a consequence, the specie, which had to be exported to make up for the deficit on the trade balance was composed of a great variety of coins and metals (see Table 10). Over time precious metals, including Persian struck coins, became scarce, and copper (both coins and metal) came to dominate the composition of the specie that was exported.

Table 5.10: Dutch export of specie from Persia (1732-1747)

Item/Year	1732	1733	1734	1735	1736	1739	1740	1741	1742	1743	1744	1745	1746	1747
Spanish Reals	9000		3148	645 342	103	1025	84 1870		8089				4.000	
Gold Rupees	856		26			40	50	233	322			100	225 80	
Gold Ducats	21.000	7014	100 637 9500	5070	1175	300	1066 1500 moor	1006 1150 3600 Moors	2270 2600 moors			900	420 M 800	
Ducats Melted	4934	750	402	1023 ducaton		1785 1991 1806	636							
Imperial Thalers				97	84									
Silver `Abbasi	13758 724	8.500		2256			3919*		1582*				300*	
Zelottas	20886	13.450		37819	64115	12533 17900	1716	28000	12650				7000	
Zelotas Light			17.000											
Zelotas Heavy			3419											
Lion Dollars			929		10		625							
Wellie Mehmeds							82000	40000					49200 2800 doubles	
Persian Rupees							500	1500	13500				5000	
Reals Silver		684				1094 192 398	323	700 555*						
Rupees Silver			100											2823
Piasters					14095	5600 9500	2751	15000	10.000				8917	520 29.000

Item/Year	1732	1733	1734	1735	1736	1739	1740	1741	1742	1743	1744	1745	1746	1747
Naderis Silver								4584	110672			20835		
Rupees Surat												4600		
Paisas Copper	6.5	81880	53.280 107280	140382	67950	30500 20.000 9988	9860							
Old Copperware					60622 lb	21729 35970 40466	7702						60509	62501 Dfl. 36173
Copper Cakes						700 lb	6000	33700						10493
Unrefined Copper								25200				23068		

Source: VOC 2323 (22/9/1734), f. 248; VOC 2357 (24/8/1735), f. 442-45; VOC 2416 (10/12/1736), f. 448-49; VOC 2417 (4/4/1737), f. 3666; VOC 2476 (25/2/1739), f. 138-40; VOC 2477 (14/5/1739), f. 164-65; VOC 2510 (25/12/1739), f. 173; VOC 2511 (31/7/1740), f. 208-09; VOC 2511 (31/7/1740), f. 210; VOC 2546 (15/4/1741), f. 150-53; VOC 2593 (22/1/1742), f.172; VOC 2705 (31/7/1746), f. 147-48; VOC 2680 (10/8/1745), f. 191-92; VOC 2705 (28/2/1747), f.555.

* The *zolota*, originally a Polish coin, was greatly used by the Ottomans after 1690. It was 2/3 of the weight of the *gurush*, later only 3/4. It is also referred to as *isolott* and *sjalotte*.

In 1747, some 29,000 piasters with a value of Dfl. 52,200 were exported as well as Dfl. 36,173 in old copper ware.[134] In 1748, the Dutch exported various coins (ducats, Surat rupees, reals, *zolota*s, piasters) to a value of Dfl. 58,359 in addition to Dfl. 39,647 in old copper.[135]

VOC PROFIT OR LOSS?

I have left open the question whether the VOC operation in Persia was still a profitable undertaking. The decline in the level of VOC sales in Afsharid Persia was also reflected in the decline of the gross profits of its Persian directorate as compared with the preceding and following period. Table 11 shows that the Afsharid period was a commercial low point for the VOC. It was so bad that even during the Afghan occupation the VOC had been able to realize more profits. It is true that the profits during the Afghan period mostly came from trade at Basra, but the VOC also traded with Basra during the Afsharid period.

Table 5.11: Gross average annual profits of the VOC's Persian Directorate (1700-1754)

Years	Amount (in Dutch Guilders)
1700-1709	402,859
1710-1719	363,728
1720-1729	185,856

134. VOC 2724, f. 24.

135. VOC 2724 (25/3/1748), f. 217; VOC 2748 (10/10/1748) f. 240. From Basra Dfl. 124,120 in gold was exported to Coromandel. VOC 2748 (10/10/1748), f. 261.

Years	Amount (in Dutch Guilders)
1730-1739	72,587
1740-1749	73,912
1750-1754	137,131

Source: VOC 2762, chapter 15

From tables 12 and 13 it would seem that the VOC had nothing to worry about, for annual profit rates were mostly around 150%. But annual turnover was much reduced and with the VOC's high overheads it was questionable whether it was worthwhile to maintain the operation, even if profits were still made. These profit rates were inflated, because they were gross figures. If corrected for loss on the export of specie, the loss due to too high book rates for Persian currency, the government debt to the VOC and loss of interest thereon, as well as the cost of the various loans of money, services and ships to the Persian government, trade results were negative. Fortunately, Schoonderwoerd, the chief of the Bushehr factory wrote a position paper on the subject when, in 1748, he assumed the responsibility of VOC operations in Persia. I have not much to add to his analysis, which is appended to this study. I would only state that things were even worse than Schoonderwoerd presented, because he did not include in his analysis the cost elements I referred to above. He was, of course, fully aware of those costs. However, the purpose of his report was to show that even leaving aside these externalities, as economists would call them, the Persia operation was a losing business. From his clear-cut analysis, based on hard commercial data, it is clear that the VOC should have abandoned the Persia trade rather than continue it. This was also Schoonderwoerd's proposal, which was not accepted. What did the VOC do?

In 1747 the XVII[136] decided to separate the Bandar `Abbas and Basra office. The latter would be supervised directly from Batavia, and Bushehr would be under the Basra office. The governor-general considered this a long overdue decision to reduce the cost of the profitless Bandar `Abbas directorate. It would only be continued on a modest scale, commensurate with the little trade that still was there. Batavia had already instructed Bandar `Abbas to abolish the Isfahan office on 23/10/1743, which had been confirmed by the decision of the council of Bandar `Abbas on 20/8/1744. But Batavia was angry at the fact the Bandar `Abbas had decided on 7/9/1744 to disregard its earlier decision and send two agents to Isfahan. This had cost a substantial amount of money and had not led to the abolishment, but only to the transformation of the Isfahan office. The excuses adduced to justify its continuation were considered to be subterfuges. Batavia finally had approved that Buffkens and the dragoman Sahid with one clerk would stay in Isfahan, at their own expense. In 1747 Batavia had decided that even this arrangement was not acceptable anymore and that it had to be abolished as well. Only Sahed could be kept on to facilitate correspondence, and the cost should not exceed Dfl. 1,000 per year.[137] The XVII approved of the decision taken by Batavia; they had been surprised by the

---

136. The council of managing directors of the VOC numbered seventeen persons, and therefore was referred to as the Seventeen (*de Zeventien*) or the Seventeen Gentlemen (*Heeren Zeventien*).

137. VOC 1001 (15/5/1747), f. 319-23.

increasing losses, which were so high "that it had not happened in a century." If soon no better results were shown they would take measures that the staff would not like.[138]

Table 5.12: How much profit was made per commodity during 1730-1753 (in %)

Item/Year	Cloves	Nutmegs	Cinnamon	Sugar	Candy	Pepper	Zinc	Tin	Iron	Steel	Sappanwood	Gumlac
1730-31	1406	9344	744	21	80	71	–	–	49		302	
1731-32	1782	3991	1060	179	133	128	–	95	–		420	
1732-33	1714	4802	1031	206	178	187	–	–	–	–	423	–
1733-34	1164	3238	712	106	106	138	–	–	69	–	306	–
1734-35	1164	3196	712	114	106	140	24	62	80			
1735-36	1164	3315	712	121	68	177	24		57			
1736-37	1164	3302	712	135	68	177	–	76	57		389	93
1737-38	1420	3196	871	131	68	259	74	–	57	–	–	–
1738-39	1425	3195	732	117	68	223	–	–	57	50		
1739-40	1168	4124	731	182	80	225	–	–	80	53		
1740-41	1168	3160	730	–	90	210	–	–	62			15
1741-42	1201	3561	773	–	91	215	–	–	65	66		
1742-43	1367	4124	652	–	–	217	–	–	42			
1743-44	1452	4356	696	94	65	235	–	–	59			
1744-45	1384	4397	655	114	91	235	–	–	57		488	65
1745-46	1424	4219	681	132	107	234	–	-80	57	–	636	73
1746-47	1498	4057	724	169	250	211	–	123	83			
1747-48	1780	4156	840	–	–	240	–	137	93	102	–	–
1748-49	1792	4179	745	135	198	288	–	138	83			
1749-50	1134	1290	–	–	–	200	–	–	178			
1750-51	1266	1416	–	–	–	157	–	–	145	–	–	–

Source: VOC 2255 (1730-31; 1731-32), f. 2069, 2071; VOC 2322 (1731-32; 1732-33), f. 82-83, 86-87; VOC 2356 (1733-34), f. 25-26; VOC 2416 (1734-35); VOC 2448 (1736-37), 1663vs-64; VOC 2546 (1740-41), f. 62-63; VOC 2593 (1741-42), f. 1666; VOC 2680 (1742-43; 1743-44; 1744-45), f. 70-71, 74-75, 78-79; VOC 2748 (1745-46; 1746-47; 1747-48), f. 106-07, 112-13, 120-21; VOC 2766 (1748-49), f. 46-47; VOC 2787 (1749-50), f. 32; VOC 2804 (1750-51), f. 10-11; VOC 2843 (1752-53), f. 27; VOC 2863 (1753-54), f. 44-45.

In 1747, Batavia also had decided to keep the royal Persian debt off the books, and record it as a loss. These costs included the cost of keeping the citadel of Bandar ʿAbbas in 1729 and the destruction of the Portuguese fortress there, the debt owed as a result of the money extorted from Lispensier in 1721 in Kerman and from the wool buyers in 1716 and the money borrowed from Macare in 1712 in Isfahan (Dfl. 618,229). There was in addition the money extorted in 1722 (Dfl. 722,500) of which the shah had repaid Dfl. 302,215:19:8 in 1732, so that still Dfl. 103,523:8 was owed on this item. The same applied to Schorer's debt and the loss incurred at Lar in 1722.[139]

---

138. VOC 331, XVII to Batavia (10/9/1746), unfoliated.

139. VOC 1001, Batavia to Gamron (20/5/1747), f. 462-63, 473; (see resolution 6/12/1746). On the

Table 5.13: Profits per commodity group during 1730-1754 (in %)

Item/Year	Spices	Bulk Goods	Piece Goods	Woolens	Total
1730-31	2407	–	–	–	59
1731-32	1581	74	22	–	129
1732-33	2366	–	95	–	245
1733-34	1201	113	16	31	167
1734-35	1294	108	17	26	134
1735-36	–	–	–	–	–
1736-37	1203	128	20	14	161
1737-38	1659	166	40	–	294
1738-39	1785	151	49	–	179
1739-40	1103	204	41	–	224
1740-41	1225	225	33	–	139
1741-42	1346	111	12	–	105
1742-43	1347	201	21	–	155
1743-44	1503	169	31	–	102
1744-45	1186	170	33	–	159
1745-46	1716	171	39	–	152
1746-47	1607	135	33	43	162
1747-48	1653	123	45	86	140
1748-49	1974	166	48	61	137
1749-50	1068	191	51	–	143
1750-51	1310	148	59	–	187
1751-52	–	–	–	–	–
1752-53	1211	135	31	27	160
1753-54	1099	100	42	20	117

Source: VOC 2255 (1730-31; 1731-32), f. 2069, 2071; VOC 2322 (1731-32; 1732-33), f. 82-83, 86-87; VOC 2356 (1733-34), f. 25-26; VOC 2416 (1734-35); VOC 2448 (1736-37), 1663vs-64; VOC 2546 (1740-41), f. 62-63; VOC 2593 (1741-42), f. 1666; VOC 2680 (1742-43; 1743-44; 1744-45), f. 70-71, 74-75, 78-79; VOC 2748 (1745-46; 1746-47; 1747-48), f. 106-07, 112-13, 120-21; VOC 2766 (1748-49), f. 46-47; VOC 2787 (1749-50), f. 32; VOC 2804 (1750-51), f. 10-11; VOC 2843 (1752-53), f. 27; VOC 2863 (1753-54), f. 44-45.

Because there was no discernible change the XVII were exasperated; not only because of the disappointing trade results. They considered the letters written by the council at Bandar `Abbas to be incomprehensible. The XVII therefore gave up reading them and awaited Batavia's overall assessment to get an understanding what was going on in the Persian directorate. It apparently did not matter who was in charge there and the XVII instructed Batavia to make sure that the staff produced better commercial results. If admonitions and reprimands did not help they would

events concerning Macaré, Lispensier, Schorer and the occurrences at Kerman in 1716, Lar in 1722 and Bandar `Abbas in 1730 (the so-called 'Portuguese' citadel) see Floor (1988), pp. 11-45; Ibid., (1998a), pp. 71-80, 235-64, and Ibid., (1988b), pp. 125-26.

be forced to use stronger means. The XVII approved of the activities undertaken to obtain a silk contract, but did not understand why the price of silk was so high. Through the overland route silk was transported in large quantities; apparently merchants found it profitable to do so.[140] Trade results remained disappointing, which the XVII ascribed to the lack of drive and attention by the staff, "if not worse." The VOC could not possibly continue on the same footing to trade in Persia and the XVII were close to abandoning the Persia trade because trade there was a disaster and debts were not paid. "It is certain that we never had more cause to do so than now", they wrote, but because Batavia had decided to split the Persian Directorate (Bandar ʿAbbas alone; Bushehr and Basra forming a new directorate) they would wait and see what results this would give. But if the results of the direct voyage of the ship *Huis ten Donk* were not positive "we absolutely desire to depart from there altogether," and the XVII left it to Batavia whether trade would be continued in the factories other than Bandar ʿAbbas.[141]

In 1750, the XVII decided to continue with the Bandar ʿAbbas factory despite the fact that Batavia had written that for the next 10 years no good trade result might be expected, because Batavia had also argued that it was important, at lower cost, to maintain the free un-hindered sea route in the Gulf; and therefore they put off a final decision to a later date.[142] On June 24, 1747 Batavia had decided, in view of the general dissolution of trade in Persia without hope for a speedy revival, to maintain only one merchant or junior-merchant as director, 3-4 assistants and one surgeon at Bandar ʿAbbas.[143]

CONCLUSION

International trade with Persia resumed after 1730, although at a much lower level than that of the pre-1720 period. The population of Persia had been plundered and had suffered war and famine. Consequently, the productive base of the country needed time and the right socio-economic and political parameters to recuperate. This did not happen, due to the belligerent policy pursued by Nader Shah who won most of his battles against his neighbors, but none of his wars and in the process crippled the remaining productive capacity of the economy. Trade suffered because of the reduced purchasing power of the decreasing and overtaxed population, the higher overheads for trade due to payment of 'protection money', other demands made on traders, and deprecia-tion of the coinage.[144] As a result, trade results were the worst since the VOC had started to trade with Persia in 1623. The VOC director in Bandar ʿAbbas proposed closure of operations in Persia, but the VOC directors believed that by cutting overhead that trade once again might be profitable after Nader Shah's death in 1747. There was indeed an upsurge in sales, but this was a temporary phenomenon that soon was deflated due to renewed fighting among Nader Shah's successors. Persia's population had been reduced significantly in size and moreover was exhausted and impoverished.[145] Karim Khan Zand, who emerged victoriously from the succession struggle

---

140. VOC 331, XVII to Batavia (14/9/1748), unfoliated.

141. VOC 331, XVII to Batavia (11/10/1749), unfoliated.

142. VOC 331, XVII to Batavia (18/9/1750), unfoliated.

143. VOC 779, Besogne (24/6/1747), f. 200; VOC 1003, Batavia to van der Welle (22/8/1749), f. 538-40; Floor (1989), pp. 47-48.

144. Floor (1983), "The Revolt"; Ibid., (1987); Ibid., (1367/1988)].

145. VOC 2710, f. 1480; Floor (1989) and Ibid, (1992).

was able to impose himself on most of Persia' territory. Trade prospects remained suppressed because the population had been decimated and financially weakened by the succession wars.[146] Despite the relative peaceful interlude of Karim Khan Zand's reign succession wars started again after his death in 1779 and were finally ended only in 1796 when the Qajar contender was able to defeat the last Zand pretender and take Mashad and Tiflis. A British traveler observed in 1790 that "Manufactures and trade are at present greatly decayed in Persia, the people having had no interval of peace to recover themselves since the death of Kerim Khan to the present period, but if a regular and permanent government were once again to be established, there is little doubt but they would flourish."[147] This is what finally happened, though it took some more years to do so.

---

146. Perry, pp. 246-71
147. Francklin (1790), p. 147.

APPENDIX

Source: VOC 2710, f. 1480-83

CONSIDERATION WITH REGARDS TO FREE TRADE AND COMMERCE IN THE PERSIAN GULF

by

Jacob Schoonderwoerd (15 June 1748)

Private persons should not be encouraged to trade here. It is also better for the VOC to keep for itself the private trade in spices, pepper, tin and the purchase of return cargos for Patria.

This I will demonstrate, on the basis of my 20 year experience here. The more so since there is no prospect for reconstruction in this once thriving kingdom, which situation will at least persist for another ten years. The population is totally impoverished and exhausted and has been reduced to one-fifth of its previous number if not less. If the VOC wants to continue to hold on to its trade turnover then there is nothing to do here for private merchants, for it will result only in loss if not total ruin [for them]. There is not much profit for the VOC either, for, as is clear from the case of the English, the goods remain lying unsold and thus remain idle losing interest. They therefore sell them cheaply (they cannot afford not to sell them) [at prices] often below the VOC fixed prices, which makes that the VOC will have to keep these goods. It is furthermore possible that trade traffic will become so substantial and the imports so voluminous that the sale [of goods] will not be possible due to too much supply. The increase in Dutch traffic will, however, be to the disadvantage of the English and others, but this will only last as long as profits can be made, in which the Dutch also will have to reduce [their voyages]. If there will be a trade revival again then the English (due to the proximity of Bombay) will get into the act immediately. However, the principal argument is that the VOC has made very little profit during 1730-1746, and that it would make much more profit by transferring its public trade to private [merchants] without running the risk of loss of interest on its investment. To wit:

I. The general profits of this directorate since 1730-31 till 1745-46, according to the net yields (the administrative profit is no real profit, while there certainly will have been losses on the exported bullion as well as on the profit/loss [balance] of the return cargos)[1]

The Overhead According to the Records	Dfl. 3134081:14:0
	2698112:04:0
More Gained than Spent in 16 Years of Each Year	Dfl. 27248:-
	453969:10:0

II. The profits of Gamron alone during that period were 2238843:05:0

The Overhead	2184226:14:0
Profit	54614:11:0

Or each year Dfl. 3413:04:0

From this [table] it is clear how small the profits were and that it was not worthwhile to continue to trade here with so much staff in the murderous climate. Moreover, if risk, interest on money, depreciation of the ships would be calculated precisely then it would become evident that [in fact] the VOC was losing money, because the imports at Gamron from Batavia and the Western comptoirs amounted to: Dfl. 734818:02:0

Following the custom of the private [merchants] if one has to make at least 20%, not counting risk, interest on capital, and depreciation of the ships this would them amount to:

Dfl.	734818:02:0
Deduct profit	435969:10:0
More lost than gained	Dfl. 298848:12:0

Although that which has been sent from Gamron during that period as mentioned above has yielded a surplus of 12% to 13% it will be clear after examination that this is only appearance, because the money [exported] from Basra only has resulted in some 40% loss in Bengal, and [bullion] represents a large share of the return cargos.

The profit on spices at Gamron amounted during that period were according to the net yields Dfl.1165571:09:10

Or on average per year Dfl. 72848:07:0

If an amount of Dfl. 20-25,000 as expenses is deducted, because here only seven Europeans would remain:

One director

One second and warehouse-master

One secretary and store-keeper

---

1. On these issues see Floor (1992), p. 444.

One or two clerks

One physician

One gunner, then it would be easy to keep this at Dfl.20,000:00:0

And the VOC would profit Dfl. 52848:07:0

Or more than was shown above 3414:03:0

Dfl. 49435:03:0

Apart from consulage and other profitable items, and all that without much risk, taking into account that private merchants would be obliged to transport the spices either paying freight or not, or else the VOC has to send a small ship here with spices every two years which also would take the return cargos, or with a Basra voyager if the VOC will continue to trade there. This could be a quite successful undertaking, in particular if such a ship would sail to Surat with freight, pearls and goods, which during this period of war between the French and the English may well yield 40-50,000 Rupees in freight. Otherwise this will attract private merchants. If the VOC continues to do business as usual then there will not be anything of interest in the Gulf for ordinary merchants, because strangers have more freedom than we, who are deprived of two important commodities, viz. tin and pepper.

The appendices are rough figures, but making them more precise will not change much in the analysis.[2]

Year	General Profits	General Expenses
1730-31	111272:19:8	188343:11:8
1731-32	169943:00:10	162251:09:12
1732-33	171297:05:08	142253:00:6
1733-34	221640:06:00	153160:08:11 1/5
1734-35	265298:14:0	137417:16:13
1735-36	188734:04:00	924625:19:0
1736-37	202729:12:08	210506:00:0
1737-38	214824:03:08	151124:18:15 2/3
1738-39	181177:09:00	173316:05:06 ½
1739-40	267378:00:04	216690:15:09
1740-41	251043:12:08	186733:01:04
1741-42	155159:12:08	239024:00:01
1742-43	297381:06:05	191272:17:04

2. The available data that offer a detailed list and cost of the cargos of departing VOC ships bear out Schoonderwoerd's opinion about the robustness of his figures. Those interested to consult these detailed, although incomplete, lists see VOC 2254 (19/7/1732), f. 643-45; VOC 2322 (30/9/1733), f. 137vs-138r; VOC 2323 (22/9/1734), f. 248; VOC 2356 (9/11/1734), f. 49-50; VOC 2537 (28/8/1735), f. 442-45; VOC 2416 (10/12/1736), f. 448-49; VOC 2417 (4/4/1737), f. 3666; VOC 2476 (25/2/1739), f. 138-40; VOC 2477 (14/5/1739), 164-65; VOC 2510 (25/12/1739), f. 173; VOC 2511 (31/7/1740), f. 208-10; VOC 2546 (15/4/1741), f. 15-53; VOC 2593 (22/1/1742), f. 172; VOC 2705 (31/7/1746), f. 147-48; VOC 2680 (10/8/1745), f. 191-92; VOC 2705 (28/2/1747), f. 555.

Year	General Profits	General Expenses
1743-44	110867:04:00	120973:18:00
1744-45	159345:18:00	151032:18;12
1745-46	165988:03:12	149385:03:00
Profits	3134081:14:03	2698112:04:6 11/30
Expenses	2698112:04:06 11/30	
More profit	435969:09:12 19/30	In 16 years

B.

Year	Gamron Profits	Gamron Expenses
1730-31	84410:4:8	161582:6:8
1731-32	165092:18:10	140826:0:8
1732-33	168087:3:0	113584:7:0
1733-34	182204:14:0	145637:10:3 1/5
1734-35	247400:8:0	118444:9:0
1735-36	152502:18:0	105561:17:8
1736-37	140412:9:8	148989:17:7
1737-38	158572:19:8	112811:14:14 2/3
1738-39	100180:5:8	132721:6:10
1739-40	175796:14;8	180178:12:14
1740-41	180564:7:8	145064:6:8
1741-42	101017:16:8	202187:3:9
1742-43	156247:3:13	156136:1:12
1743-44	38213:3:8	87235:6:8
1744-45	79937:9:8	122435:15:4
1745-46	83250:17:12	110829:18:0
Equipage goods	24949:2:0	
	2238841:5:11	2184226:14:1 13/15
Expenses	2184226:14:1 13/15	
More profit	54614:11:9 2/15	

C.

Year	Profits on Spices at Gamron According to the Net Yields
1730-31	58799:8
1731-32	109307:6:14
1732-33	123190:9:8
1733-34	138796:11:0
1734-35	143346:10:8
1735-36	56574:5:0

Year	Profits on Spices at Gamron According to the Net Yields
1736-37	86365:16:0
1737-38	82114:18:0
1738-39	56231:18:0
1739-40	85709:0:8
1740-41	53820:10:8
1741-42	72800:8:0
1742-43	56181:10:0
1743-44	9303:17:8
1744-45	17450:5:0
1745-46	15578:16:4
	1165571:9:10

D. Memorandum of all goods, which have been imported here between 1730-31 and 1745-46

Year	Name Ship	Imported From	Amount	Total Per Year
1730-31	Schoonhoven	Batavia	130074:2	
	Idem	Malabar	10225:9	
	De Faam	Surat	116:12	140466:3
1731-32	Prins van Wallis	Surat	116:12	
	Windhond	Batavia	137919:5:18	
	Idem	Malabar	15775:14:8	242118:19
1732-33	?	Surat	116:12	
	De Jacoba	Batavia	181251:8	
	Castor & Pollux	Idem	63665:19:8	
	Idem	Malabar	20599:8:0	265683:0
1733-34	Barbesteijn	Batavia	266030:14:8	
	Elsbroek	Idem	66388:4:0	
		Surat	201:19:8	332620:18
1734-35	Valkenesse	Batavia	262457:14:0	
	Noordwijkerhout	Same	39911:8:8	
	De Caroline	Surat	333:4:8	302702:7
1735-36	Stadwijk	Batavia	113925:14:8	
	Rittem	Same	31778:0:0	
	Same	Malabar	15836:5:8	161540:0
1736-37	D'Anthonia	Batavia	68626:1:0	
	T'Huijs te Foreest	Same	171990:4:8	240616:5:8
1737-38	D'Adriana	Batavia	100976:5:8	
	Opperdoes	Same	111161:14:8	
	Same	Malabar	41640:11:0	
	Same	Surat	478:2:8	254256:13:8

Year	Name Ship	Imported From	Amount	Total Per Year
1738-39	'tHof niet altijd Somer	Batavia	124052:8:0	
	Same	Ceylon	5810:12:0	
	Same	Malabar	1985:17:8	
	Binnewijsend	Batavia	53206:8:0	
	Same	Malabar	5327:7:8	190382:13:0
1739-40	Middenrak	Batavia	113984:14:0	
	Steenhoven	Same	22178:19	
	D'Valk	Same	4922:19	
		Surat	783:9:8	
	'tSlot Kroonenburg	Batavia	50066:18:8	391539:0
1740-41	D'Ketel	Batavia	287967:8	
	Same	Cochin	5644:8:8	
	Ridderkerk	Batavia	55130:9	348742:5:8
1741-42	D'Cornelia	Batavia	131864:5	
	Same	Cochin	2508:7:8	
	Duijff	Batavia	69569:16	203942:8:8
1742-43	NO DATA			
1743-44	Horssen	Batavia	233999:17	
	Same	Surat	453:8:8	
	D'Heer Arendskerke	Batavia	173212:13:8	
1744-45	Oosterhout	Batavia	91386:1:8	
	Same	Malabar	1187:2:8	
		Surat	77:13:8	92650:17:8
1745-46	Wildrijk	Patria		99163:4
			Total	3674090:13:8

E. Memorandum of the Exports from Gamron in the following years, to wit:

Year	Name Ship	Exported To	Amount	Total Per Year
1730-31	Borselen	Batavia	131714:11:8	
	Same	Bengal	66:00:8	131780:12
1731-32	D'Swillington	Surat	1046:10	
	Schoonauwen	Batavia	222835:8	
	Same	Bengal	2256:2	
	D'Hopvogel	Same	167410:7:8	
	Same	Ceylon	52360:17	
	Same	Coromandel	23802:1:8	
	Same	Cochin	907:10	470618:16

Year	Name Ship	Exported To	Amount	Total Per Year
1733-34	Prince van Wallis	Surat		418:0:8
1734-35	Elsbroek	Batavia	63277:18:8	
	D'Carolina	Surat	474:17	
	Valkenesse	Batavia	244305:2:8	
	Same	Bengal	56:19:8	
	Noordwijkerhout	Batavia	104806:2	
	Same	Ceylon	3461:17:8	
	Same	Coromandel	920:2:8	
	Same	Malabar	753:19	418056:18:8
1733-34	D'Jacoba	Batavia	203099:8	
	Same	Colombo	4909:10	
	Same	Coromandel	629:11:8	
	Same	Malabar	419:11	
	Windhond	Batavia	119362:1	
	Carbessijn	Batavia	250960:7:8	
	Castor & Pollux	Same	61733:5	
	Same	Ceylon	3217:9	
	Same	Coromandel	642:7:8	
	Same	Malabar	418:6	645391:16:8
1735-36	Caroline	Surat	560:13	
	Le Brigantijn	Malabar	590:15	
	De prince van Wallis	Surat	766:17	
	Jinny	Bengal	337:4:8	2255:9:8
1736-37	Stadwijk	Batavia	401787:1:2	
	Same	Ceylon	8250:9:2	
	Same	Coromandel	7926:19:10	
	Same	Malabar	1145:00:10	
	Caroline	Surat	30:11	
	De Faam	Same	513:2	
	Rittem	Batavia	126469:16:8	
	Same	Ceylon	7221:12:8	
	Same	Coromandel	19794:18:8	
	Same	Malabar	931:9	
	Lakererin ?	Coromandel	641:9:8	574612:9:8

Year	Name Ship	Exported To	Amount	Total Per Year
1737-38	'tHuijs te Foreest	Batavia	240906:14:8	
	Same	Ceylon	12723:17	
	Same	Coromandel	27663:9:8	
	Same	Malabar	690:13	
	Ladilegent	Surat	123:16:12	
	Opperdoes	Batavia	89137:1:14 13/15	
	Same	Ceylon	16680:15:8	
	Same	Coromandel	720:8:8	
	Same	Malabar	2061:16	
	Same	Bengal	73:19	
	The Expedition	Same	31:7	390813:18:10 13/15
1738-39	Adriana	Batavia	121348:3:0 1/5	
	Same	Ceylon	929:0:8	
	Same	Coromandel	8457:19:4	
	Same	Bengal	93:18:8	
	Same	Malabar	435:10:4	
	Anthonia	Batavia	65330:2:8	
	Same	Ceylon	1224:4	
	Same	Malabar	197:0	
	Same	Coromandel	19694:4:8	
	Precaution	Bengal	141:0:4	
	Robbert Galley	Surat	33:9:8	217902:12;4 1/5
1739-40	Binnewijsend	Batavia	146913:6:2	
	Same	Ceylon	2182:4	
	Same	Coromandel	2123:4	
	Same	Malabar	678:9	
	Robbert Galley	Surat	490:15:8	
	Steenhoven	Batavia	196275:1	
	Same	Ceylon	10049:19	
	Same	Coromandel	9639:18:8	
	Same	Malabar	565:2	
	'tHoff niet altijd Somer	Batavia	4528:7:8	
	Same	Ceylon	10049:19	
	Same	Coromandel	48615:0	
	Same	Malabar	3857:4:8	
	Robbert Galley	Bengal	728:9	430966:1:2

Year	Name Ship	Exported To	Amount	Total Per Year
1740-41	Le Diligent	Surat	93:18:8	
	Middenrak	Patria	103:7	
	Same	Batavia	141070:10:8	
	Same	Malabar	1130:14:8	
	'tSlot Kronenburg	Batavia	97526:17:8	
	Same	Ceylon	18139:7	
	Same	Coromandel	37051:4:8	295115:19
1741-42	D'Ketel	Batavia	326495:5:12	
	Same	Ceylon	8354:13	
	Same	Coromandel	7916:7	
	Same	Malabar	335:5:8	
	D'Salamander	Surat	164:18	
	Bomketch	Surat	406:10	
	Lancaster	Surat	638:17:8	
	Lyon Grab	Surat	887:3	345198:19:12
1742-43	Cornelia	Batavia	121121:17	
	Same	Ceylon	19086:19	
	Same	Coromandel	15526:6	
	Same	Malabar	1152:14	
	Faam	Surat	501:3	
	Duijff	Batavia	412549:18	
	Same	Ceylon	2291:0:8	
	Same	Coromandel	26954:18	
	Same	Malabar	2046:11:8	
	Augusta	Bengal	10:2:8	601241:9:8
1743-44	La Fortune	Surat	1046:6	
	Fenny	Bengal	90:18	1137:4
1744-45	Horssen	Batavia	99531:10	
	Same	Ceylon	7285:6	
	Same	Coromandel	59815:1	
	Same	Surat	2525:3	
	Same	Malabar	293:9:8	
	'sHeer Arendskerke	Batavia	111122:5:8	
	Same	Ceylon	8335:5:8	
	Same	Coromandel	30706:11:8	
	Same	Malabar	185:3	
	D'Janny Jagoon	Bengal	113:8	319913:3

Year	Name Ship	Exported To	Amount	Total Per Year
1745-46	Fatta Ramanie	Surat	344;17	
	Oosterhout	Batavia	59197:6:8	
	Same	Ceylon	12322:1:8	
	Same	Coromandel	52560:1:8	
	Same	Cochin	887:15	125311:19:8
			Total	4970735:9:12 18/25

SELECTED BIBLIOGRAPHY

1. ARCHIVES

National Archief (National Archives), The Hague, The Netherlands. Eerste afdeling (first section). Records of the Verenigde Oostindische Compagnie (VOC) (Dutch East Indies Company)

Overgekomen brieven en papieren (Letters and papers received).

Bataviasch uitgaande brievenboek (Batavia's outgoing letterbook).

Resoluties van de Heeren XVII (Resolutions of the XVII).

2. BOOKS AND ARTICLES

Arunova, M.R. & Ashrafiyan, K.Z. *Gosudarstvo Nadir Shaxa Afshara* (Moscow, 1958).

Axworthy, Michael. *The Sword of Persia: Nadir Shah, from Tribal Warior to Conquering Tyrant* (London, 2006).

Bournoutian, George A. tr., *The Chronicle of Abraham of Crete* (Costa Mesa, 1999)

———. *Abraham of Erevan, History of the Wars 1721-1738* (Costa Mesa, 1999).

Brosset, M. F. *Collection d'Historiens Arméniens.* 2 vols. in one (St. Petersbourg, 1875-76 [Amsterdam, 1979].

Cook, John. *Voyages and Travels through the Russian Empire, Tartary, and Part of the Kingdom of Persia* 2 vols. (Edinburgh, 1770 [Newtonville, 1997]).

Du Cerceau, *The Compleat History of Thamas.Kouli Khan, Late Sovereign of Persia in two parts* (London, [1748]).

Emerson, John and Floor, Willem. "Rahdars and their tolls in Safavid and Afsharid Iran." *JESHO* 30 (1987), pp. 318-27

Floor, Willem. "A Description of the Persian Gulf and its inhabitants in 1756," *Persica* 8 (1979), pp. 163-86.

———. "The Revolt of Shaikh Ahmad Madani in Laristan and the Garmsirat (1730-1733)," *Studia Iranica* 8 (1983), p. 63-93.

———. "The Iranian Navy during the Eighteenth Century," *Iranian Studies* 20 (1987), pp. 31-53.

———. *Commercial Conflict between Persia and the Netherlands 1712-1718*, University of Durham Occasional Paper Series no. 37 (1988).

———. *Hokumat-e Nader Shah* (Tehran: Tus, 1367/1988), translated by Abu'l-Qasem Serri

———. "The Decline of the Dutch East Indies Company in Bandar 'Abbas (1747-1759)", *Moyen Orient & Océan Indien* 6 (1989), pp. 45-80.

———. "The Dutch and Khark Island, 1753-1770, A Commercial Mishap," 24 (1992) *IJMES*, pp. 441-460.

———. "The Dutch and the Persian Silk Trade", in: Ch. Melville ed. *Safavid Persia* (London 1996), pp. 323-68.

———. *The Afghan Occupation of Persia, 1722-1730* (Paris 1998);

———. *The Fiscal History of Iran in the Safavid and Qajar Periods* (New York, 1999 a).

———. *The Persian Textile Industry, Its Products and Their Use 1500-1925* (Paris, 1999 a).

———. "The Bandar ` Abbas–Isfahan Route in the late Safavid Era (1617-1717)," *IRAN* XXXVII (1999 c), pp. 67-94.

———. and Patrick Clawson. "Safavid Persia's Search for Gold and Silver" *IJMES* 32 (2000 a), pp. 345-368.

———. *The Economy of Safavid Persia* (Wiesbaden: Reichert, 2000 b).

———. *Safavid Government Institutions* (Costa Mesa, 2001).

———. "The Secular Judicial System in Safavid Persia," *Studia Iranica* 29 (2000), pp. 9-60.

———. "The *sadr* or head of the Safavid religious administration, judiciary and endowments and other members of the religious institution," *ZDMG* 150 (2000), pp. 461-500.

———. "The khalifeh al-kholafa of the Safavid sufi order," *Zeitschrift der Deutschen Morgenländischen Gesellschaft* 153 (2003), pp. 51-86.

———. *The Persian Gulf: A Political and Economic History of Five Port Cities, 1500–1730* (Washington, DC, 2006)

———. *The Persian Gulf: The Rise and Fall of the Gulf Arabs, The Politics of Trade on the Persian Littoral, 1747–1792* (Washington, DC, 2007)

Francklin, William. *Observations made on a tour from Bengal to Persia, in the years 1786-7* (London, 1790).

Hanway, Jonas. *An historical account of thre British trade over the Caspian Sea.* 4 vols. in 3 (London 1753).

Lerch, Johann Jacob. "Nachricht von der zweiten Reise nach Persien ... von 1745 bis 1747", *Magazin für die neue Historie und Geographie an gelegt von D. Anton Friedriech Büsching*, vol. 10 (Halle 1776), pp. 367-476.

Lockhart, Laurence. *Nadir Shah* (Cambridge, 1938).

Nasiri, Mirza Naqi. *Alqab va Mavajeb-e Dowreh-ye Salatin-e Safaviyeh* ed. Yusof Rahimlu (Mashhad, 1371/1992) translated into English with commentary by Willem Floor as *Titles and Emoluments in Safavid Iran* (Washington DC, 2008),

Perry, John R. *Karim Khan Zand* (Chicago, 1979).

Ricks, Thomas M. *Politics and Trade in Southern Iran and the Gulf, 1745-1765* (Indiana University, unpublished dissertation 1974).

Sha`bani, Reza. *Hadith-e Nader Shahi* (Tehran, 2536/1977).

———. *Tarikh-e ejtema`i-ye Iran dar `ar-e Afshariyeh* (Tehran, 1359/1980)

Spilman, James. *A Journey through Russia into Persia by Two English Gentlemen who were there in the Year 1739* (London 1742).

Tehrani, Mohammad Shafi`. *Tarikh-e Nader Shah*. ed. Sha`bani, Reza (Tehran, 1349/1970)

INDEX